*A Publication of the Horace Mann-Lincoln
Institute of School Experimentation
Teachers College, Columbia University*

COOPERATIVE
PROCEDURES
IN
LEARNING *BY*

ALICE MIEL *PROFESSOR OF EDUCATION*

TEACHERS COLLEGE, COLUMBIA UNIVERSITY   *AND*

ASSOCIATES

GREENWOOD PRESS, PUBLISHERS
WESTPORT, CONNECTICUT

The Library of Congress has catalogued this publication as follows:

Library of Congress Cataloging in Publication Data

Miel, Alice, 1906–
   Cooperative procedures in learning.

   "A publication of the Horace Mann-Lincoln Institute
of School Experimentation, Teachers College, Columbia
University."
   1. Group work in education. 2. Teacher-student
relationships. 3. Curriculum planning. I. Title.
[LB1032.M54 1972]   371.3   77-168965
ISBN 0-8371-6238-6

Foreword

A GREAT DEAL of the literature that has to do with pupil-teacher planning or the use of cooperative procedures in learning is in the form of argument. And the argument is persuasive to most of us. The protagonists usually start by clarifying and elaborating certain principles of democracy or of learning and then proceed logically to the conclusion that cooperative classroom procedures must be used if these principles are accepted. The principles are almost always accepted verbally, but for various reasons the implied changes in classroom practices do not make their appearance.

One important reason for this disparity between professed belief and actual practice is that we have too few pictures in our minds of what cooperative learning procedures look like. This book by Alice Miel and her associates goes far toward supplying that lack. It includes scores of concrete, and often quite complete, descriptions of just what a group of experimentally minded teachers actually did as they tried to develop more skill in working cooperatively with their pupils. These teachers not only tried out methods that were new to them, but they looked carefully at the consequences and generalized from them. These generalizations are reported and one of their unique values is that they are based upon firsthand experience.

As is true of most of the publications of the Horace Mann–Lincoln Institute of School Experimentation, *Cooperative Procedures in Learning* represents the work of many people and emphasizes the experimental approach to curriculum improvement. The teachers whose activities are reported in the chapters that follow this foreword were committed to learning about pupil-teacher planning by experimenting with practices that gave promise of being more effective, studying the results of this experimentation, changing their procedures and convictions when the facts warranted such change, and then experimenting again. This is the method of science used by practitioners who want to improve their practices.

STEPHEN M. COREY
Executive Officer
Horace Mann–Lincoln
Institute of School Experimentation

Contents

PART TWO

*Trouble Points Met by Teachers in Using
Cooperative Procedures*

Tables and Charts

COOPERATIVE

PROCEDURES

IN

LEARNING

CHAPTER I

Introduction: The Story of a Cooperative Study

THIS BOOK reports the findings of some classroom teachers and other school people who have been working with the staff of the Horace Mann–Lincoln Institute of School Experimentation in an effort to learn more about cooperative procedures in our schools. The way these professional workers went about their study is an example of action research or cooperative experimentation. The group saw a problem needing attention; action to solve the problem just where it arose (in typical public schools) was planned cooperatively; together the experimenters looked at the consequences of what they had tried; this led to new views of the problem, more action, and more evaluation, with the researchers continuously identifying dependable principles and techniques.

The term "cooperative procedures" as used in this report includes group purposing–planning–acting–evaluating, which are interrelated and often concurrent activities. Throughout the following pages the terms "group process," "group work," and "cooperative work" are used synonymously with "cooperative procedures."

The Institute staff committee and the representatives of the co-operating schools began with three assumptions. The first was that the school is responsible for developing an understanding of the nature of cooperative procedures and for teaching the skills involved. An important aspect of maturing in a democracy is acquiring the attitudes and the ability necessary for effective cooperation in the solution of the increasingly complex problems facing modern man.

A second assumption was that learners should participate in determining the purposes toward which they will work. There is a growing body of evidence that individual as well as group purposes are better matured and developed in a group setting.

1

A third assumption was that knowledge is of little value unless it is related to action. Group procedures, if properly used, are an unusually effective means of building a bridge between knowledge and action.

Thus, cooperative procedures were seen as a set of skills to be learned and, at the same time, as a method of increasing the quality of all learning.

THE STUDY IS LAUNCHED

The interest of the Institute in a study of cooperative procedures in schools began at a conference held at Teachers College, December 12–15, 1944. One purpose of the conference was "to clarify . . . projects for study and make tentative decisions to carry them forward." Because of requests of the schools associated with the Institute, one of the work groups set up for the conference was devoted to "developing skill in planning." In this group, Bucks County, Pennsylvania, public schools were represented by Charles Boehm; the Horace Mann–Lincoln School of Teachers College, by Hildegard Hartig; Kansas City, Missouri, public schools, by Roscoe Shores; and Montgomery County, Maryland, public schools, by Etheleen Daniel and Fern Schneider. Consultants were Lennox Grey, Amy Hostler, Alice Miel, and Helen Storen.

This group prepared an outline in which some of the major aspects of cooperative planning were identified. On the basis of the principles and techniques suggested in this outline, associated schools were to set up experimental studies of cooperative procedures.

PURPOSE AND SCOPE OF
THE PRESENT STUDY

By common agreement the study was limited to consideration of various situations in which pupils participate in cooperative work. Cooperative procedures were to be treated primarily as a method of learning. At the time when the major part of the study was in progress, the school years 1945–46, 1946–47, and 1947–48, it was believed that cooperative procedures were a rather radical departure from usual classroom methods and that relatively few teachers and other adults were skilled in their use. Before exact studies could be made under public school conditions, it was necessary for a greater number of persons to obtain a larger measure of skill in using group processes. Consequently, the efforts of all in the study were directed toward definition of problems involved in cooperative work and toward discovery and testing of effective techniques and procedures, with the major purpose of helping educators, preservice and inservice, to increase their understanding and skill.

The study thus resolved itself into two aspects: (1) Discovering how to increase the ability of teachers and other professional educators to help pupils to learn cooperative procedures. (2) Learning the conditions under which pupils of various ages, levels of intelligence, and backgrounds of experience can have rewarding experiences with group work.

JOINT ENDEAVORS OF ASSOCIATED SCHOOLS

Two of the four associated schools represented at the exploratory meeting, Kansas City and Montgomery County, cooperated actively with the Institute in the study of cooperative procedures. They were later joined by representatives of the Battle Creek, Michigan, public schools. Other schools which have been involved to some degree are P. S. 44, a New York City junior high school, the public schools of Denver, Colorado, and of Springfield, Missouri, and the Horace Mann–Lincoln School of Teachers College. Aspects of the study were carried forward through a series of workshops involving Institute and associated schools' personnel during the summers of 1945 and 1946[1] and at a spring work conference in 1947.

WORK IN INDIVIDUAL CENTERS

Kansas City, Missouri

The most extensive study and experimentation went on in the individual centers. In Kansas City concerted work on cooperative planning began early in 1945 when about twenty-five persons were chosen from a larger group of volunteers to serve as a steering committee. The committee representative, Blanche Longshore, prepared a comprehensive report entitled *A Study Intended to Assist in Organizing and Developing Cooperative Planning in Kansas City.* This document was used extensively by the committee as a basis for their experimentation during the following years. Meetings of the committee were used largely as a laboratory situation for discussing and improving upon the cooperative techniques the members them-

---

[1] See *The Teacher's Role in Pupil-Teacher Planning* (New York: Bureau of Publications, Teachers College, Columbia University, 1947), 27 pp.

selves were using. In addition, each member carried out in his own situation a special project involving cooperative planning. Group members and the Institute consultants helped each individual to evaluate his project. They identified the general principles involved and suggested solutions to problems that arose. In this way support was lent to the individual experimenter.

Accounts of projects undertaken by individual members and analyzed by the steering committee as a whole after their first full year of work, as well as certain parts of the Longshore report, were published as a bulletin in June, 1946, by the school system, under the title *Cooperative Planning—The Key to Curriculum Development.* This document made it possible for the committee to share its experiences with others in the school system and elsewhere. Reports on committee projects also appeared from time to time in the local curriculum bulletin distributed to Kansas City teachers. During 1946–47 the Kansas City committee, with support from the school administration, cooperated with the Institute staff in the production of a film, *Learning Through Cooperative Planning.*[2] This film was another medium used for making the committee's learnings available to other teachers.

Montgomery County, Maryland

Guided by a bulletin on procedures for cooperative planning issued by the central office in 1943, teachers in Montgomery County had been working to increase the quality and quantity of pupil-teacher planning before the cooperative study with the Institute was started. Four schools in the county cooperated closely with the Institute consultants. These four centers undertook no joint activities but worked in their own buildings, experimenting and recording, evaluating, and experimenting some more.

Other Centers

Battle Creek, Michigan, public schools and P. S. 44, a New York City junior high school, entered the study in the fall of 1946. In Battle Creek a study group on cooperative planning, open to all interested teachers, met monthly. In these meetings experiences with pupil-teacher planning were exchanged and members discussed kinds of records to send to Institute headquarters.

[2] Distributed by the Bureau of Publications, Teachers College, Columbia University.

P. S. 44 also had a monthly study group made up of volunteers. Their concern was to learn how to improve democratic participation on the part of their students. The contribution of the Horace Mann–Lincoln School of Teachers College took the form of a film, *We Plan Together*, planned and produced by an eleventh grade core group with the help of their teachers and an Institute consultant. This film was released in the spring of 1947.[3]

Although Denver, Colorado, and Springfield, Missouri, were not "official" participants in the cooperative planning study, individual teachers continued to experiment with the process and some took part in the summer workshops.

Many of the teachers whose work is reported had tried cooperative procedures in their teaching before but wanted to know more about them. For some others a new way of working had to be learned but there was willingness to venture. The consultants too were learners; they began with a few hunches resulting from their experience, but they wanted to sharpen their understandings. A distinctive thing about the study was that not one of the participants was merely a teacher of others; all were in it together to learn as much as possible.

WORK OF THE INSTITUTE STAFF

Four staff members at different times worked as consultants on the study—Kenneth Benne, Alice Miel, Chandos Reid, and Alice Stewart—helping teacher groups to plan problems and to work on the ways of recording findings.[4] Most of the running records in the report which follows are those of the author's own observations, taken in longhand in classrooms; other sources of records are noted in the text. All analyses were made by the writer. In addition to editing *The Teacher's Role in Pupil-Teacher Planning* and helping to produce the films *Learning Through Cooperative Planning* and *We Plan Together*, Institute consultants prepared a bulletin to aid experimenting groups and individuals.[5]

In every center those cooperating in the study made it possible for

[3] Distributed by the Bureau of Publications, Teachers College, Columbia University.

[4] The way in which different Institute consultants worked is analyzed in a report by Marcella R. Lawler entitled *Work of the Consultant; Factors That Have Facilitated and Impeded His Work in Selected Elementary Schools of the Horace Mann–Lincoln Institute of School Experimentation,* unpublished Ed.D. project report, Teachers College, Columbia University, 1949.

[5] *Guide to Study and Experimentation in Cooperative Planning in Education* (New York: Bureau of Publications, Teachers College, Columbia University, 1947), 37 pp.

their experiences to be shared widely. They understood and assumed willingly the obligation to record and discuss findings as one of the responsibilities involved in cooperative research. They arranged opportunities for Institute consultants and other observers to make records in their classrooms and to discuss what all might learn from each instance of cooperative planning studied. They themselves kept records and wrote accounts of entire projects. They engaged in group discussion of problems and findings as the study progressed. At the close of the study they submitted to final interviews to sum up what they had learned. All of these forms of cooperation were for the purpose of sharing results with an audience of teachers and other educational workers whom they could not meet face to face. The influence of the study on their associates with whom they could have personal contact cannot be measured; nevertheless it must not be discounted.

THE BASIC DATA

The records of what went on, kept by people from the associated schools, teachers in the author's classes who had similar concerns, and members of the Institute staff, constitute the basic data on which this book is based. These records range from a single note that a certain activity was in progress to copies of records of plans developed with pupils and running records of discussion periods. All the records used have one decided asset—they furnish detail. They also have their limitations. First, there are many gaps which will become apparent as the reader progresses and which are summed up in the final chapter where needed studies are discussed. One important shortage is in records of group work at the secondary school level. The smaller number of examples from junior and senior high schools is partly accounted for by the fact that most teachers cooperating in the study were elementary teachers. This was true in all field centers except P. S. 44, New York City, itself a junior high school.

Another reason for the comparative lack of secondary school examples is a fact that can hardly be disputed, namely, that by and large throughout the country more opportunity is given to elementary school children to participate in group work than is made available to high school youth. One large factor in this situation is the greater amount of departmentalization in high schools which may tempt a teacher to feel that some other teacher is or ought to be assuming responsibility for teaching skills of cooperative work while he himself concentrates on the subject to be taught. Besides, when a teacher meets a class of students scheduled for a particular subject for a limited time each day, he may use lack of time to excuse failure to use cooperative procedures with students. Opportunities for cooperative work, where they do exist for youth, are likely to occur in the "fringe" activities of the school, in the school council and in clubs, for example. However, some high school teachers were able to report extensive use of cooperative procedures with students in classes, showing that some of the barriers commonly cited are not insurmountable when the teacher wants to find a way.

A second limitation of the records is that they usually give the impression that the group is absorbed in only one project at a time. As an example, take Miss Merlin, a fifth grade teacher whose work is referred to at more than one point in this report.[6] One thing Miss Merlin contributed was a detailed account of a newspaper project involving a great deal of cooperative planning. To this report she appended a list of other cooperative enterprises going on in her class at the same time.

Treasure Chest
1. Raising money for the books
2. Participating in selection of the books for the chest
3. Submitting designs for the outside of the wooden chest
4. Decorating the chest
5. Making scrapbooks
6. Purchasing other materials that will be included

Library Council
Memorial Day Program
Music Festival for Music Week
Choir and Chorus
Orchestra
Tournaments
    Marble (just finished)
    Baseball

In reading the details of the newspaper project, one might be quite unaware that so much else was going on in Miss Merlin's classroom. It will be well for the reader, as he is being told of the progress of one enterprise in a teacher's classroom, to keep in mind that the class and small groups and individuals within it very likely have many other irons in the fire at the same time.

A third limitation of the records is that they usually picture in detail only a fragment of an ongoing activity. There may be a running record of one planning session out of a whole series which a

---

[6] To allow freedom in analyzing and criticizing records frankly, in order that they may be of the most help to all, all names of teachers used in this volume are fictitious. Correct names and professional addresses of contributors to the report are listed in the Appendix.

given project entailed. It should be recognized too that the running records were taken in longhand usually by an observer who did not know the names of the children. Some of the give-and-take of the discussion was missed as a result, and it was not always possible to note in the record the facial expressions and manner of speaking that would make possible a more adequate interpretation of what went on. Also there was not an opportunity to show in the records who was contributing much and who was saying little. However, the consultant who personally took most of the records used in the report had a few opportunities to check her version against those taken for the same discussion session by a school principal and a teacher, both of whom knew the children and situation well. The consultant's record in each case was in accord with the others in general but contained more of the details of the various contributions. In analyzing the records, the consultant had the benefit of actually seeing most of the sessions reported, so that judgments as to human relations in the situation could be made with some confidence. Unfortunately, because of limitations of space, it has seldom been possible to give a running record of a complete planning session in its entirety in this book.

Diaries and accounts furnished by teachers usually describe events not witnessed by the consultant. They are necessarily less detailed than the running record when it comes to showing what was actually said and done by different members of a group during a given planning period. Too, these reports are subject to some bias, because all of us like to remember the things that went especially well.

As for the records of plans supposedly made by teachers and pupils together, it was not always possible to judge whether they were genuinely a product of group thinking unless one had witnessed their development.

Within these limitations this book is an attempt to paint as true a picture as possible of what really happened when teachers and pupils used various opportunities to plan together. It represents the final step, projected in the early days of the study, to prepare "a publication generously illustrated with experiences all kinds of teachers and pupils have had with cooperative planning, the outline and extent of content to be determined by the evidence accumulated." The body of the report is divided into two parts. The first deals with opportunities for cooperative work used by teachers and pupils in the study, and the second with trouble points encountered by teachers as they tried to learn the process along with their pupils. There is also a concluding chapter summarizing the teacher's role in cooperative procedures and the need for further studies.

The closing of the formal cooperative study of associated schools with Institute staff has not meant cessation of learning for any of the participants. There are always new things to learn about ways people can best work together. The responsibility of organized education to promote that learning for cooperative human relationships is a continuing obligation. It is hoped that this book may contribute to the human relations goal of education.

PART ONE

Opportunities for Cooperative Planning in Schools

How are we going to make our room attractive for our tea? What crops shall we plant in our plot in the school garden? What shall we make for the Christmas bazaar? How shall we organize for work on the terrace today? What resources do we have for studying our state? What scenes shall we have in our play? What program shall we have when incoming sophomores and their parents visit us this spring? What outdoor jobs will the different rooms do this spring? How can Ronnie get the most out of his trip to Florida for himself and for us? Each of these questions is a key to a dynamic opportunity to learn through cooperative procedures. Such opportunities abound in some schools; there is a curious lack of them in other schools.

If educators are to discharge their responsibility for helping children develop understandings and skills in the area of group process, they must find and utilize appropriate opportunities for educative experience with that process. If educators are to make use of the motivation that comes from group planning of learning experiences, they must seek the proper occasions for pupil participation in curriculum planning. In other words, cooperative procedures in education are both something to be taught and a method of teaching.

In this part of the report we examine some of the opportunities commonly used in schools to enable children and youth to learn through cooperative procedures; and we draw certain generalizations with regard to over-all favoring conditions for group work.

The outline for Part One emerged from an inspection of all the different kinds of records that had been gathered in the study. As these records were read and analyzed they seemed to group themselves into eight categories of planning activities:

1. Planning use of time
2. Planning for improving and caring for the classroom
3. Planning conduct in terms of people and situations
4. Planning studies
5. Planning products
6. Planning service projects
7. Planning to solve all-school problems
8. Evaluating as part of cooperative work

These types of opportunities that seem to have been widely used by teachers cooperating in the study have been made the basis for the eight chapters of Part One that follow.

CHAPTER II

Planning Use of Time

As teachers and supervisors become interested in giving pupils opportunities to learn cooperative procedures, they cast about for a likely beginning point—one that will not be too difficult for the adults to manage as they are gaining new skills of classroom leadership and that appears to be within the capabilities of the younger members of the group. Quite frequently, it seems, educators concerned with elementary schools decide that planning the daily schedule is just the opportunity they are searching for. In fact, there are school systems in which elementary teachers have been instructed that henceforth they are to plan the day with their children and that plans must be recorded on the chalkboard for the benefit of the class and of any supervisor who chances to visit.

Now it will readily be agreed that helping pupils to look upon time as a resource at their disposal and to learn to make wise use of their time in school is both an opportunity and a responsibility. However, planning the daily schedule is only one small part of the problem of time use. Furthermore, for reasons that are developed in later pages of this chapter, schedule-planning quite often represents the poorest beginning point for teachers and pupils wishing to explore the possibilities of cooperative approaches to teaching and learning. In the case of teachers and pupils in most secondary schools, the schedule is planned centrally, leaving no chance for one group to plan in this area.

It is the purpose of this chapter (1) to examine experiences of teachers and pupils with daily schedule-planning and (2) to investigate other possibilities for learning how to budget time.

EXPERIENCE WITH DAILY SCHEDULE-PLANNING

Pupil Manipulation Not Cooperative Planning

Someone had given Miss York an entirely wrong notion of the purposes of schedule-planning with children. She changed to the new procedure because she was told to do so, still believing that she and the children should come out with the same schedule they would have had if the teacher had made the plans by herself. The clever teacher, Miss York believed, could "get the children to choose the right things." For her, "cooperative" planning of the day was an elaborate guessing game for the children.

This is the way program-planning in Miss York's fifth grade class looked to another teacher, one with less experience, who had been asked to observe Miss York in order that she might learn how to plan with pupils.

> Miss York began by asking, "What did you see in the newspapers yesterday of nationwide importance?"
>
> Many answers were disregarded until someone said, "The coal strike." From this the teacher led a discussion about coal—where it comes from, how it's formed, etc.
>
> The next question: "What subject area would this come under for our study today?"
>
> Answer: "Social studies." (The class has been studying Pennsylvania in their geography books.)
>
> In relation to "coal," another subject area, as the teacher called it, was involved by the leading question, "What word can you think of that rhymes with coal?" "Goal" was suggested and accepted.
>
> Teacher: "Today we shall study the *oa* family and learn to pronounce and spell words of this family. What subject area will this come under?"
>
> After many wild guesses, some bright child finally gave forth with "language arts."
>
> So the planning period droned on for forty-five minutes. Nothing was written on the board as "they" planned. Orally every "subject area" was accounted for and time allotted for each. The manner of the children was at all times respectful, attentive, but reserved. The teacher tried to draw out every child to answer one of her many questions.
>
> It reminded me of the old catechism method of question-answer learning. I made up my mind then and there that if that was an example of good planning after thirteen years of experience, I'd rather have no class planning than a farce such as that.

One is forced to agree with the teacher observing that this planning period was a farce. One thinks of the Corka cartoon in which little "Mr. High I. Q." is standing before his class, concluding a speech with this remark: "And so I won't make any campaign promises. Everybody knows our class officers always do pretty much what the teacher wants anyhow."

Fortunately, few teachers are as misguided as Miss York.[1] The example serves to point up several things, however. First, it is important that the teacher have a clear understanding of purposes that may be accomplished by cooperative planning of a schedule; there must be a feeling in teacher and children that *we* made this program together, *we* have established some goals we really want to accomplish, *we* have learned that we cannot do everything, *we* must make some choices. Second, the example illustrates a danger to avoid, the temptation to put something over on children, to fool them into thinking they have shared in a plan when they actually have not. Third, the example demonstrates how very difficult it is to give children a chance to choose among alternatives when there are few choices open to them or when they do not know that there are other possibilities for use of their time. It is highly probable that Miss York herself was not aware of ways of spending time in school other than that of holding classes in each of the familiar subjects in turn.

Taking First Steps

When Miss MacKelvy introduced schedule-planning to a new third grade group, the children came out with general routine plans like the following:

A.M.	P.M.
Arithmetic	Spelling
Reading	Writing
Social Studies	Reading
Free Time	Free Time

This teacher, while realizing the shortcomings of such planning, saw two values upon which she could build in the future—the children had a general guide for the day's responsibilities, and they themselves had allotted time to carry out the responsibilities. In this case the teacher had not tried to trick the children into choosing subject areas which she had in mind. Rather, the children knew of nothing else to suggest. Their awareness that a day has a plan, and their confidence that they had made the plan they were following, were two steps in the direction of more mature planning.

A running record kept by Miss Durham while one of her first grade children was leading the group in planning activities for the day

[1] A similar, though less devious, example of program planning in another classroom in Miss York's school system is reproduced in *The Teacher's Role in Pupil-Teacher Planning* (New York: Bureau of Publications, Teachers College, Columbia University). In this pamphlet the teacher in question is named "Teacher A."

shows rather typical procedure for that grade level. A representative excerpt follows.

> JAMES K. We will share.
> BARBARA. We will play games.
> JAMES M. We will have poems.
> LESLIE. We will count.
> VINNIE. We will talk about Thanksgiving.
> DOUGLAS. We will write.
> WALTER. We will play games.
> TEACHER. Walter, Barbara said that. Can you think of something different?
> Walter shakes head for no.
> ANITA. We will read.
> TEACHER. There is something left out we do every day.
> MARTHA ANN. We will sing.

It is rather easy to see in this record that children are more or less recalling items usually appearing in their program. In fact, the teacher's remark that "there is something left out we do every day" would tend to lead the group in the direction of recalling previous plans. Thus, group planning in this case was limited to one phase only, that of gathering suggestions from the group. Steps not illustrated here are those of evaluating suggestions and of choosing among a number of ideas. It would have helped the group to have a sense of commitment to these "plans" had the teacher asked a question such as "Shall we try to do all these things today?"

Choice-Making in Kindergarten

Giving young children an opportunity to choose among alternatives with regard to the daily schedule is not a simple matter, as Miss Haynes discovered when she decided to experiment with planning a day with her kindergarten children. When the children had listed their choices, she found that no rest time was included. The teacher reports the way in which she handled the situation.

> I asked if I might make a suggestion and suggested rest (a most unpopular pastime). As my reason I added that with such a busy day we were going to be very tired. "But," said Arnold, "maybe we won't have time."
>
> I felt it was my responsibility as an adult member of the group to look after physical welfare.
>
> Then I questioned, "What shall we do first?" . . . Rest was put in third, at my suggestion.

Miss Haynes had at least three additional choices of action in this instance: (1) She could have taken no part in making the plan; (2) she could have offered her suggestion as any other group member, not expecting it to be accepted just because it was given by the status leader in the group; or (3) she could have stated limits within which the children might plan (for example, she could have said that rest was required). The first alternative is a denial of the teacher's role as a group member. This course would be especially inadvisable with young children. The second is perhaps what the teacher was trying to achieve in this instance, but she failed for several reasons. She ignored Arnold's suggestion and showed that this was a matter to be settled by superior adult wisdom; the group had not had experience in choosing among suggestions, and there is no evidence that this procedure was used with the group of suggestions as a whole.

The third choice would appear to be best in this instance. It is the function of the status leader to help the group define the limits of its authority. This setting of limits should be open and aboveboard and, if possible, done in advance to avoid the necessity of a veto. In other words, as a group starts to make a plan, members should be able to feel confident that plans made by the group will be followed if they stay within recognized limits.

Miss Haynes had greater problems before her, as a continuation of her record shows. After the teacher and children had had a thrilling time carrying out their first plan, watching a house-moving operation down the street, they returned to the school.

We were entering the kindergarten room when the phone rang and the secretary informed me that the movie "The Bus Man" had arrived. That cut into our plan for the day. What could we leave out?

I called the children over and told them the news and said that something would have to be left out of our plan. "Which shall it be?" Need I say the answer in unison was "Rest."

I do not know whether I was too autocratic in this or not, as I rationalized it in my mind later. "Why did I ask them if I weren't willing to take their decision?" But I reasoned that young children are not capable of making decisions regarding health and physical requirements. Was I wrong?

At least I explained that when one is four or five years old there are things he must do every day: eat, sleep, get dressed; and that rest in school is the same as sleeping. (I felt that if we were to leave it out it would lose its significance.) Inasmuch as there were songs on the plan, I suggested that we leave them out. This is probably what I should have done in the first place, but it was a significant learning for me.

Miss Haynes saw one other alternative to flat rejection of the children's proposal, namely, not giving the children a choice in the first place. If she had been interested in having them gain experience in choice-making, however, there were two other courses open to her. If the teacher and children had had a clear understanding that matters of "health and physical requirements" were to be left in the teacher's hands, Miss Haynes could have given the children the opportunity to rearrange their plans for the day without exposing herself to the necessity of overruling them. Or she could have abided by their decision for this one day without great damage.

At any rate, the teacher felt she had learned something from the experience, and it is unlikely that the children were damaged greatly from this one experience with the veto. If, however, in instance after instance throughout their school career they were to meet such refusal to let them test the consequences of their own ideas, they would have little chance to experience true choice-making and would almost certainly acquire a warped idea of cooperative planning.

Drawbacks in Schedule-Planning

Several teachers in the study found, after early trials of cooperative schedule-planning, that there were definite limitations to this procedure. Miss Knight, for example, tells why she eliminated schedule-planning as a daily routine with her second grade children.

> I have found that planning the day is a very discouraging experience. The difficulty I am sure is the children's and my lack of experience in this sort of thing. For the time being I have eliminated writing the plan with the children the first thing in the morning. I try to let them plan when they have an opportunity to make a choice.

An observer in a first grade classroom questioned the value of cooperative schedule-planning as he saw it carried on. When he entered, he saw a busy scene as children arrived at school and began to occupy themselves usefully.

> As I entered the teacher was encouraging some boys to clean things up. They were picking up loose blocks. As others came in they did various things. One started to work on a drawing. Another brought a book that he showed to several others. Two girls worked on a small loom, weaving a mat.

When, as the observer noted, "it was time to start," the teacher told the children to put away their unfinished things, remarking that they had so many things to do.

She gathered the children around her and asked, "What have we to do?" One child said, "String popcorn." The teacher wrote it on the board. Another said, "Play." "We do that every day. What do we do on Friday?" "Assembly," said several.

They listed several other things—singing, completion of block building, and so on.

The visitor made an astute observation in his record at this juncture, raising a point that has, no doubt, bothered many a teacher.

It is hard to judge the effectiveness of the morning planning period. It might be a more natural thing if everyone came at once. As it is, people are interrupted doing things to plan things to do. It would seem an advantage to have planning serve a real planning function instead of using it as an excuse to look at writing on the board—important as that is.

Even though, in the visitor's opinion, "part of the planning was real and served to focus the attention of the group on the day's activities," it is probable that this group planning period was poorly timed. When individuals appear to have adequate plans for themselves for a period of time, it indeed seems wiser not to "interrupt doing things to plan things to do." Necessary plans for the rest of the day could well be made at the end of a busy work-play period. In other words, planning for a day does not always have to come when the school day officially begins, nor does planning use of time necessarily have to be a group activity.

Improvements in Schedule-Planning

Miss Turk has furnished an account which shows the setting in which plans for the day are made in her first and second grade classroom.

Children come to school every morning eager to tell about the things which have happened to them since leaving school the day before, so each morning we talk about the interesting things that have happened. We end these discussions by making the most interesting events into a news bulletin for the day.

After our discussion period we make our plans for the day. These plans are usually very complete. The children tell me the different things which they wish to do for the day and I list them on the blackboard.

An example of plans made when the children were in the midst of a post-office unit shows quite a contrast with the routine plans which Miss MacKelvy reported. The plans read as if children had really had a hand in them and they reflect the "busyness" of a going concern:

Study reading	Make a list of words we will need
Make up a story about the postman	when we write the story about
Discuss: The postman and his duties	the postman
	Study spelling
Sell stamps	Draw, easel-paint or finger-paint
Discuss: Health of the postman	Play in the gym
Janice has a story ready to read about the postman	Read library books
	Work on numbers

Planning for the day did not end with making this list. The teacher goes on to say that "the children decided to talk about the postman and his duties first so the second grade could write a better story." After this discussion was held, led by Garrett, the children's choice, and recorded on the board by the teacher at the children's request, postal clerks were elected to work in the post office for the day. The second grade children named words they might need in writing their stories and then proceeded to write independently while the teacher worked with the first grade composing a group story.

Later after Janice had read her book, the teacher volunteered to read a poem she had found. And so the day went. Planning was alternated with carrying out plans; children made detailed plans for a block of time as they needed them; the teacher felt free to propose additions to the plan with the possible result that the children believed they had the same privilege.[2]

OTHER POSSIBILITIES FOR LEARNING TO BUDGET TIME

Planning for a Block of Time

Whether or not they invite children to participate in planning the day's schedule, many teachers feel it extremely important that children help plan in detail given time blocks in the program. Some teachers prefer to use that approach in initiating children into planning use of time. Miss Miller's approach may be used as an example. She uses the long work period provided daily for her kindergarten children as an opportunity for each of them to make a plan for use of that time. This planning is done at the begin-

---

[2] For an additional example of schedule-planning in which there was genuine choice-making, see Chapter XIV, page 406.

ning of the work period, with each possible activity, such as playing
with blocks or painting, taken up in turn. As soon as the children
interested in a particular activity have made their choice and the
teacher is assured they know how to go ahead, they are encouraged
to leave the planning group and proceed with the chosen activity.

One afternoon in Miss Miller's room four children showed what
their choice was by going at once to a block structure built by the
morning group and by starting to demolish it. The teacher casually
included them in the planning group by saying, "If you are going to
take that down, you'll have to take the blocks carefully. If we do
that, where do we start?" "At the top," was the ready answer.

"Do you want me to take this down?" one boy asked.

"That's up to you. If you are going to use the blocks for something
else, you'll have to decide."

Another boy said, "I like blocks but I don't like to choose them because they go bangity-bang."

"Oh, since when?" Miss Miller replied cheerfully. "When do they
go bangity-bang? When we're careless, isn't it?"

Soon the block group had reached the six Miss Miller had suggested, but she added a seventh who wanted to join, and then said,
"Now, that's all if you're not too disappointed. There are all these
chances left."

The whole affair proceeded so quickly and pleasantly that the
group remaining longer with the teacher did not become restless. If
too many wanted the same activity, the teacher helped them decide
who should have the opportunity that day. Children who found it
hard to make up their minds were not pressed to make a hurried
decision, for they were holding up no one else's progress.

Another kindergarten teacher, Miss Fallon, using a similar plan,
holds up before the children a chart illustrating various activities.
As a child names his choice, she thumbtacks a small card bearing his
name in a space at the right of the illustrated activity.

Planning for a similar period in Miss Daly's first grade is done
without a group meeting. Children go directly to a large chart entitled "Choose Your Work Here." Twelve activities are listed on this
chart, with an illustration of each one and a label underneath: paint,
work (on workbench), puzzles, finger-paint, blocks, look at books,
make books, draw, sew, clay, scissors and paste, work in bakery
(current opportunity for dramatic play). Children sign their names
under their chosen activity on a three-by-five-inch pad thumbtacked

there for that purpose. Miss Daly says the children use surprisingly good judgment about not overtaxing any one facility.

Miss Rezny shows in a diary entry dated September 11 how she began planning use of time *within* a schedule she had made.

> After the opening of school, I drew the children's attention to the day's schedule which was on the board and asked them if they would like to share in planning our day. This was completely new to them, as I knew it would be, for our school has not yet emerged from the rather confined area of mainly teacher-planned work. I think I used good judgment in choosing today because art comes first, and planning for this would put less strain on them and me, as it proved. They decided they would like to draw freely for a couple of periods "just to get their hands in" (their own expression). They asked me to play the "real" work, meaning arithmetic, spelling, etc.

Wisely, Miss Rezny did not urge her children to take too much responsibility for their time schedule at first. She knew that plans for reading and arithmetic could be made with the children later. By that time they might have changed their minds about what "real" school work was.

Miss Durham uses group planning to help her first graders busy themselves with worth-while activities while she is working with one reading group. When she asks, "What are some of the things you can do while I help one group read?" she gets such responses as these:

> VIOLET. Put my head down.
> BARBARA ANN. Study the words on the cards.
> DANIEL. Write my name.
> TIMOTHY. Read the charts.
> JAMES. Look at books.
> BETSY. Teach someone the words.
> JUDY. Learn the numbers on the calendar.
> JOHN. Play and build with the strips I brought to school today.

This is an example of helping children to make specific plans for using a given block of time. As the year goes along the teacher would doubtless help the children to increase the range of possibilities for independent work. Another line of improvement would be to follow through a little further on the children's suggestions. It is not clear from the record whether or not mere gathering of suggestions such as these from different children in turn gives each child a sufficient basis to make an individual plan for use of his time while the teacher is occupied with the rest of the class. It is important that plans be definite and clear to each individual who is to live by them. Sometimes, to make sure of this, it is necessary to clinch plans in some way, either orally or in writing. A simple question may accomplish this: "Does this list have a suggestion for everybody? Does anyone need help in making a plan for this time?" Each teacher will want to try out various ways of going beyond the gathering of a list of suggestions to building a commitment to a plan.

Although Miss MacKelvy saw some slight benefits from the routine program planning that her third grade children did in their early attempts at planning their time, she was not satisfied to let the matter rest there.[3] As she thought the matter over, she decided that such barren planning had certain weaknesses: it did not promote the children's thinking together, it did not develop imagination, it did not meet needs and interests of individuals, it gave the teacher little opportunity to know the children, and it did not take care of plans for worth-while experiences during free time. A first step she took with the children was to ask them to evaluate their experience with program planning. In this evaluation the children recognized three things: (1) Situations often arose requiring planning in advance of a day; (2) responsibilities for care of the room were not included; (3) some children never helped with the planning.

From September until Christmas vacation Miss MacKelvy worked with her group to develop more competence in planning. Still she found the children were not effectively carrying over their planning into the use of free time. This she began to work on in January.

Miss MacKelvy set the stage by placing materials about the room and then observed closely for a week what the children did during the free period each day. At the end of the week she suggested that they take time to discuss the things accomplished. The results were rather discouraging. No one had anything definite to show. A few had painted or drawn pictures which had been destroyed. The few excellent readers had spent all their time reading. Many had wandered aimlessly around the room, making chalk marks on the board or visiting. Many could not remember how they had used their time.

When the pupils were asked to evaluate this experience, some thought just being quiet and occupied was all that mattered. Some recognized the waste of time and criticized those children who disturbed others. Many admitted that they did not know what they could do and asked what they would be allowed to do.

[3] See page 15.

This was indeed a challenge for Miss MacKelvy, and we could wish for a detailed account of how she solved the problem. We do have her word for it that as the result of the evaluation and plans made for correcting the difficulties, the children had accomplished much by March. Children had begun to take advantage of materials and other resources around them and to be less dependent upon the teacher. Groups with common interests were forming to explore and discuss new findings, sharing them with the class in general discussion periods. Shy and retiring children were beginning to join groups and to make suggestions. The class, in general, was becoming eager for the free period to arrive.

Miss MacKelvy's experience drives home the fact that children do not come ready-made with ability to make good use of free time in school. They cannot be said to have come of age until they have acquired a certain amount of independence from adults in employing themselves usefully. This is an aspect of time use where there is need for individual responsibility within the large framework of group planning. Planning a *general* daily schedule with a group can hardly be expected to develop this individual ability of self-direction.[4]

Learning Long-Term Planning

Another improvement on time-planning is to move from planning for a day to planning for a week in advance. Apparently Miss Grossman, who had indicated in an early diary notation a problem of schedule-planning with her first grade children, found long-range planning to be a solution. Her diary entry in late October shows satisfaction with plans for the coming week.

> We talked about next week and planned our activities. We have much ahead of us. Our play will be given Wednesday. It would be nice to give a dress rehearsal for the kindergarten. Our pumpkin will have to be cut Monday. We must plan our party. We decided to make our own applesauce rather than have ice cream. The children are looking forward to next week.

Miss Lambert learned that when her fifth and sixth grade girls and boys planned their work for a week ahead, they could save time by listing their "standing appointments" once and for all and by working out only the changing parts of their program.[5]

[4] The reader is referred to pages 429–431 for a detailed account of how individuals were helped to plan for themselves.

[5] The way in which evaluation of a week's accomplishments in this class was combined with planning for the next week is illustrated on pages 239–245.

A running record from Mr. Kinder's fifth grade class offers a good chance to study the way in which a skilled teacher and group proceeded with their planning for the week ahead.[6] After some pleasant preliminaries on a Monday morning the teacher read off items in the plan made one week previous, stopping at various points to have children evaluate what had been accomplished. For example, he asked, "Are you satisfied with our work on the fairy scene of our play?" Two children in turn approved of spending more time on the scene, but a third had doubts. The teacher let the discussion move freely from child to child, at one point entering his opinion that "we probably will be able to go faster after we've put ourselves into these roles; but you have a good point, George, and it is something we'll have to consider."

This contribution prompted a class member to say, "Maybe we should see what other things we want to do and then decide how long to spend on this scene." Not the teacher but a pupil commented, "Yes, that's good."

After four additional items had been checked off as completed, it appeared that time for creative writing was needed. "Can't we finish our writing during our free time?" was one child's proposal. "Some of us need help with our writing. Maybe we'd better plan at least one time for conferences," was the opinion of another.

At this point the teacher clinched a decision by asking whether work on the fairy scene and time for creative writing should be included in the plan for the week. The record continues.

TEACHER. Now we had some other jobs under way. Will we want to plan some time for them this week? Some people were working on silhouettes for the mural. What about the party? Are the plans all complete for it? Let's get some of these items listed and then talk more about them.

Individuals made suggestions one at a time and the teacher wrote them on the board. There were few comments during this procedure. The list included:

The fairy scene of our play	Check on committees and evaluate them
Creative writing and conferences	Plan next steps for the mural
The mural silhouettes	Arithmetic
Complete party plans	Spelling

[6] For the complete record see *The Teacher's Role in Pupil-Teacher Planning* (New York: Bureau of Publications, Teachers College, Columbia University). In this pamphlet the teacher in question is named "Teacher D."

Lunchroom committee

Use of the microscope

Reading to increase speed

Library reading—for reports

on our mural

Visits to Miss ——'s room

Evaluate free activity periods

Report of the movie committee

Play

Dancing

Swimming

Rhythms

Centers

CHILD. That's too much to get done in this week.

TEACHER. What happens when you have so much to do in a short time?

CHILD. Just do what you can do and that's all.

TEACHER. How do you decide which things you will do?

CHILD. Some things are more important than others.

TEACHER. Of course, some of the items we have listed here are things you can do during your own free time, aren't they?

Individuals made suggestions as to those activities which they could take responsibility for doing during free time. The list included:

Working on silhouettes

Arithmetic

Spelling

These excerpts show a genuine planning situation. Here was a group with so many things under way that choices had to be made among them. Children were doing independent thinking; they were willing to express an honest difference of opinion, yet willing also to listen to other points of view and to change their minds when the line of argument was reasonable.

In Mr. Kinder's class, weekly planning was combined with planning for each day as the remainder of the foregoing record indicates. Other teachers also have found it desirable to give children experience with both short-term and long-term planning.

Miss Daly's plan for developing independence during the work period did not occur in a vacuum. Daily planning operated as part of long-range planning for the school year and for each week in turn. Of her experiences, Miss Daly writes:

I have found that long-range planning in the first grade is necessary to gain continuity for a whole program of work. We spent much time this year in discussion to determine children's interests. We walked through the neighborhood visiting children's homes as a group. We set up a study of the community as our over-all plan for the year. I recorded these plans in the form of a large chart, using pictures from magazines to illustrate various people "who help us." As each helper has been studied he has been checked off on the chart and the children and I have decided which one to take up next.

Miss Daly adds that a weekly plan is made every Monday morning.

Miss Baker in her long experience with group planning in the elementary school has learned that daily plans mean little unless set in a stream of ongoing enterprises that are absorbing to children, just as she has become convinced that daily plans must be reinforced by more detailed plans for particular periods in the day.

One day in April these plans were found in Miss Baker's second grade room, the first two on the chalkboard in the front of the room, the third on tagboard.

Plans for Today	Work Period Today
Make weather report	Work on the hall picture
Plan our work period	Make our cards and pictures for the sick boy
Read our stories	Work on our spring riddles for the boy
Study our spelling	Clean the window seat
Have some number work	Clean the art supplies closet
Play games outside	Make the drawing book for the sick boy
Have a work period	Rake around the kindergarten door
Sing with Miss Crane	Rake the terrace
	Make the wrappings for the presents

Jobs to Be Finished by Easter
Sketch the terrace
Rake the terrace
Transplant ferns
Work on the birthday box
Get soil for the seeds
Plant the seeds for our mothers
Make some new paintings
Clean the closet
Wash and wax shelves, window seats, and tables

Without seeing how these plans were developed with the children, one cannot state with assurance that they were the result of cooperative planning. There are legitimate ways and unethical ways of arriving at what may look like a *group* plan. However, observing Miss Baker's general ways of working with her group and noting the self-confidence and clear purpose of her children as they went about the jobs they had undertaken, one feels confident that the plans quoted were a genuine group product. One has greater doubt when he finds daily plans containing such items as these:

Spelling—Find a little word in a big word
English—Put garden words in alphabetical order
Arithmetic—Carrying

"Reading to Learn": How to reproduce words into models and pictures
Pen and ink practice on "found"

Or a monthly plan like this:

Read books to gather information about Thanksgiving
Make booklets about Thanksgiving
Try to keep a fourth-grade standard of art
Improve our vocabulary
Review our 2, 3, 4 tables
Begin our 5 tables
Begin to multiply and divide by 5
Add and subtract with dollars and cents
Finish reading "Snow Treasure"
Plan to make a mural about "Snow Treasure"
Work for neatness of all written papers
Improve our reading skills
Work with the use of capital letters

On the other hand, one has reason to believe that children are learning the realities of planning when in mid-October one sees posted in a room:

Things We Plan to Do (September)	Things We Plan to Do (October)
Paint the bookcases	Paint the bookcases
Paint the wall	Paint the chairs and table
Paint the chairs and table	Take a walk to see signs of autumn
Make a book of our stories	Bring rope
	Have races

Finding that unfinished projects like painting furniture had been carried over into the next plan and were either completed or being worked on gives the observer assurance that the plans had meaning for the children.

CONCLUSION

Many opportunities for planning time besides those illustrated in this chapter arise in the typical school. There is the period after a big enterprise, such as a play or making Christmas gifts, when it is time to gather together the loose ends and take account of unfinished business to be cared for in the days ahead. During the enterprise there is the problem of working out schedules that may not be typical, "for there is a deadline to meet and all schedules must be thrown off balance." There is the occasion when, for some reason or other, the regular teacher is to be away for a short or a long period. Children and teacher may plan together the use of the time when the group will be on its own or in the charge of another person. Time for small groups to meet and work, and time for them to report to the larger group, must also be planned.[7] Budgeting class time for these and other purposes is a highly appropriate opportunity for secondary school students, who have fewer opportunities to plan use of time in school.

Besides planning work periods and use of free time, there should be a clear plan for every block of time in the school day—play periods, art periods, lunch periods, language arts periods, and so on. Planning for a play period can well be done on a long-term seasonal basis as well as from day to day. Many routines in connection with various activities in the school day can be planned once and reviewed only occasionally as need arises. Not all planning of special periods need be done in the large group; often small groups can take responsibility in turn.[8]

Pupil planning of the use of time is undoubtedly a splendid educational opportunity. Teachers take one important step in this direction when they let pupils know there is a plan for their time in school. In this way pupils can begin to learn the value of having a plan. If there is to be no choice for group members, it seems better for the teacher to announce necessary plans rather than to go through the motions of "drawing" his own plans from the children.

The next stage in development may be to gather suggestions for the day's schedule. Group planning of the schedule may be improved if the teacher helps the group to go beyond the suggestion-gathering stage, at least securing a general commitment to the plans.

Teachers take a further step when they encourage children to make intelligent choices among alternative ways of using a given block of time. Part of intelligent choice-making depends upon knowing limits to group autonomy; part depends upon being aware of a number of possibilities.

Teachers help children still more when they widen the range of planning and give children opportunity to make short-term plans within cooperatively developed long-range plans.

[7] See Chapter XIV, pages 511–512, for an account of such planning.
[8] The use of small groups to save the time of the larger group is discussed in some detail in Chapter XIV.

CHAPTER III

Planning for Improvement and

Care of Physical Surroundings

WHETHER a school has fixed seats and dingy walls or modern furniture and bright colors, whether twenty to forty people share the same room for four or five hours a day or a different group moves into and out of a common classroom each hour of the day, every school offers opportunities for cooperative planning to improve and care for the classroom. Growing plants must be watered; cut flowers must be arranged and at the proper time discarded; bric-a-brac must be dusted; bulletin boards must be changed frequently; library and other collections of materials must be kept orderly and available for use; materials must be arranged for easy access. Besides all the routine housekeeping jobs that accumulate as standards of living rise, there are decisions to be made now and then with respect to seating, finding storage space, or bringing about some improvement in the appearance of the classroom. All of these opportunities may be used as occasions for learning to plan and carry out responsibilities.

This chapter reports ways in which teachers in elementary schools have turned opportunities for improving and caring for the classroom into educative experiences for children and suggests points to consider in providing such experiences. The shortage of examples at the secondary school level should not be taken as an indication that the same opportunities and needs do not exist. Many junior and senior high school classrooms would benefit from more attention to appearance and usability. The general fact that there seems to be less use of cooperative procedures in secondary schools and that few secondary teachers were involved in this study accounts partially for the lack of examples. Another factor at work is that high school teachers spending only forty-five minutes to an hour with a group of students must make some choices among possible opportunities for cooperative work with their pupils. To many, care of the classroom may seem to be of minor importance compared with other responsibilities which the students might assume. Actually, as will be shown in this chapter, teachers in the elementary school must make similar choices. Teachers at all levels, however, might well consider the advisability of giving at least minimum group attention to the physical environment for learning and of helping the pupils to discover the most efficient ways to handle these matters without taking too much time away from other more important concerns. There will be results not only in an improved appearance of the classroom but also in group morale. Things that happen in a place one helps to care for often take on added importance.

PLANNING FOR ROUTINE HOUSEKEEPING JOBS

A great many elementary classrooms have posted somewhere a list of "helpers" or "housekeepers." Many are the opportunities inherent in this simple device. Continuing responsibilities must be decided upon—watering plants, dusting, arranging books, caring for the bulletin board, and so on. The best ways of doing these jobs must be planned, such as how often to water plants and how much water to give them. People to do the jobs must be selected periodically, or a plan must be made for rotation. The way in which responsibility is or is not assumed by various individuals must be evaluated in order that the group may help its members learn to be dependable. These values are not realized automatically and may even be vitiated by the process of teacher appointment of helpers and periodic reminders by the teacher that jobs have been left undone. Time to plan and do and evaluate must be provided.

Determining Readiness for Responsibility

A teacher may easily make the mistake of assuming that children have an adequate background of experience for planning and undertaking responsibilities for housekeeping. Miss Grossman quite by accident learned one day that she had been overestimating the readiness of her first grade children to take on housekeeping jobs. She recorded in her diary in early fall:

Today we went on with our discussion of family life. We talked about helping Father and Mother. Only one or two children seemed to have an opportunity really to cooperate with Mother or Father at home. Salvatore said: "All my father does is lick me." Howard remarked: "My mother says to get out of her way and play."

"No wonder these children didn't understand what I meant by room helpers," Miss Grossman added. After she discovered this gap in the experience of some of her children, she wisely gave some time to building the necessary background for intelligent group planning for care of the classroom. "We are thinking now of ways we can help at home and in school," she wrote.

Shortening Routine Planning

Teachers of young children are justified in giving considerable time to choosing jobs for a week, for it is through this process that a job becomes important and the nature of it is understood by the child. However, teachers sometimes allow routine appointment of room helpers to occur week after week with little profit for the group. This is most likely to happen in cases where teachers have thought of few other opportunities for cooperative planning. In classrooms where there is much group business to transact, teachers and pupils have to learn short cuts to planning that still maintain the interest and concern of the entire group.

One such short cut is for the group to plan a way of rotating jobs. When this happens the major time investment is given to making the initial plan. An example is a scheme used in a high school shop for cleanup at the end of each class period. The plan, worked out by teacher and boys together, is reported by a high school counselor.

> A list of the jobs to be done is printed on a sheet and each boy rotates in the different jobs. One boy acts as superintendent each week and checks the sheet when each job has been done satisfactorily.

That the teacher rarely had to intervene is undoubtedly a result of the fact that a cooperative decision had been made.

In a second grade classroom children choose their successors as room helpers by selecting one of the group of nameplates tacked on a special bulletin board and tacking it in place after the name of the job in question. A group which sets out to do so can work out an effective plan for rotating work.

Evaluating Room Helpers

Time spent evaluating room helpers is usually a good investment in developing a feeling of responsibility toward work.

Miss Lambert has a "Helpers Club" in her fifth and sixth grade room. Each week the children evaluate the way in which they have fulfilled various responsibilities. An excerpt from a running record taken by an outside observer during one of the club meetings will illustrate the procedure used. Shirley, the president, is in charge.

BILL. I think I've improved on the blackboards that was mentioned.

SHIRLEY. Who'd like to say something on blackboards?

ANN. I've improved on dusting. The teacher didn't have to remind me so much.

JOE. I think Lester done good on the sink.

SALLY. I think Grace did better on the wastebaskets.

GEORGE. I disagree. Miss Lambert had to remind her.

HOWARD. I think Cathy did pretty good on the flowers.

TEACHER. What about the flowers?

MARY. She did pretty good at sprinkling the flowers. She put papers down first.

GRACE. I think the books on the shelf are a lot better, but lots of times they are not put back where they belong. Big and little ones are mixed.

ANN. Sometimes people don't help put them back the way they should.

TEACHER. What suggestion do you have?

ANN. Put them back right.

GRACE. But the helper should straighten them sometimes.

SHIRLEY. Betty, do you have anything to say?

BETTY. I think I could do a little better.

MARILYN. Joyce has done a good job in the lavatory.

MILDRED. I'll say so. The washbowls *shine*.

SHIRLEY. Joyce, anything to say for yourself?

JOYCE. I have tried my best.

TEACHER. You have succeeded, Joyce. What about athletics, Bruce?

BRUCE. I get kind of scared.

LESTER. That was the first time you were leader. I think you did well.

NEIL. I haven't done very well on the lights. Someone else does it.

SALLY. I think we should let Neil turn out the lights unless we think he is going to forget.

BILL. I think Richard did well on the maps when we used them. . . .

Several observations may be made from this record. First, it is apparent that friendly relationships among the children have been established. They are quick to praise one another but not afraid to give criticism where they believe it to be necessary. They are secure enough in the group to criticize themselves and to meet the criticism of others without defensiveness.

Second, good thinking is illustrated. Ann points out that sometimes the rest of the group do not cooperate with the helpers as they should. Sally believes the group should give a helper a chance to show whether or not he will carry out his particular responsibility.

Third, it is evident that group members rather than official leaders carry most of the responsibility for moving the discussion forward. The president determines whether someone has more to offer on a certain point. The teacher merely raises questions to cause further thinking and gives a word of praise.

Finally, the record gives some idea of the number of different responsibilities assumed by the children for their own comfort and convenience.

Meeting Reluctance to Assume Responsibility

It is not always easy to build desirable attitudes toward shared responsibility. An eighth grade girl who had always been considered a model of cooperation surprised her teacher one day by saying, "I'm tired of being teacher's helper." This may be an adolescent expressing a new-found independence of adults. It is possible, however, that rebellion on this particular point might not have occurred if the girl had had a different experience in being a helper. Perhaps she had not known a group situation like Miss Lambert's. Perhaps her history was one of a succession of teachers choosing helpers rather than one of group members accepting responsibilities.

Even a teacher with an excellent conception of shared responsibility may run into difficulty with older children who have not had opportunities to learn the discipline required. The problem is complicated for a person like Mrs. Tambling, whose art room is shared by pupils from early grades through the tenth. Her professional diary early in the school year is filled with her worries. She wishes the pupils would feel that the art room is theirs—theirs to enjoy and theirs to care for, but she finds that this feeling of responsibility is not built in a day or even in a month. In the middle of October she wrote:

Today I was put on the spot! We have very poor storage space in our room. Child after child lost work from previous lessons. The attitude was, "Somebody stole my drawing." "Somebody stepped all over my paper."

I took it to the class. They didn't want to stop to solve it. They don't like being made to think and can't see why the problem should be solved by them; my ideas are better. Of all of the group only three volunteered sensible solutions. Others raised their hands frantically and then suggested some Rube Goldberg contraption for a laugh, or suggested a fantastic punishment for anyone caught stealing a drawing. They and I know the drawings are lost, not stolen.

The idea of a student's art room isn't going over. They don't feel it's theirs and liberty is clearly license, not responsibility. I see them so little—two forty-minute periods a week—that there is no chance to build a real relationship or rapport.

What does a teacher do if a group refuses to take responsibility seriously? Three days after the foregoing entry, Mrs. Tambling reported what she tried.

Well, I've solved the problem of lost work, but I had to do it. Each child made an envelope of colored paper for his work. Only one child in each class is to collect or give them out. All work must be kept in these and any left around will be thrown out. The shelves for storage look better and the children seem relieved to have a definite assignment, although some considered it a nuisance to interrupt their other work.

Perhaps Mrs. Tambling was right to give her girls and boys a little definite direction as a relief from the large amount of uncharted freedom with which she had gratuitously presented them. She was too wise to give up at that point, however. She entered in her diary on the same day this credo: "I'm deeply convinced that this sort of thing will work out eventually, and my hope is that I know enough about what I'm doing so that the experiment has a fair chance." She then proceeded to record a conversation she had with a group of fifth graders, trying to help them to see their responsibility for cleanup and care of materials.

ME. Look at these brushes. What do you think we can do about it?

ROGER. Everybody should wash their own.

ME. Yes, we know they should, but they don't. Do you know how a brush should be cleaned and why?

BETTY. You should wash it and put it away.

ME. Yes, but it isn't being done.

MARY. You should make them.

ME. If I have to be a policeman for everybody, what time will I have to help you? Is this my brush or yours? Do I use it? Or am I a maid?

TOM. Make the ones who leave brushes clean up for everyone.

ME. Well, then you want to appoint a maid. If this were your house and someone came in and left a mess, would you put it in order or would you leave it because you didn't do it?

TOM. Yes, but it isn't fair to us to clean up for the other guy. I won't do it!

ME. Well, what can we do about it?

HELEN. Sometimes we haven't time to clean up well. The bell rings and we have to get out.

ME. But you are given five minutes' warning.

BILLY. Let's make everyone stop and post watchers to see that everyone cleans up. They can remind the others.

ME. How do you feel about that?

CLASS. Let's try it.

ME. Let's watch and see how it turns out. Maybe we can work things out so that everyone will watch himself instead of the other fellow, and without being told, help the ones who have ?. lot to clean up. The more we help others, the more they will help us. The better we keep our materials, the better they will work for us. Let's go! How about trying it out right now!

Results: Fair.

It was a long and slow process for Mrs. Tambling to build the attitudes she thought important, as her diary over the next months attests. But in January she was able to evaluate progress in these terms:

The children get their own materials and put them away without being told. Socially they are group conscious in that they want their class to do a good job. Within their smaller groups they borrow back and forth, assist each other, discuss common problems, and evaluate each other.

PLANNING IMPROVEMENT PROJECTS

In addition to planning ways of caring for routine housekeeping duties connected with a classroom, many special opportunities for improving the physical environment occur.

Cleanup—A Special Event

Cleanup may be a special event which can be used as the occasion for worth-while cooperative procedures. The plans for a work period quoted in the preceding chapter[1] included cleaning the window seat and the art-supplies closet, raking around the kindergarten door and the terrace. This was only part of a larger spring cleanup project involving that group and the whole school over a period of time.

Another occasion for making cleanup and room decoration a special event is a scheduled visit of parents. The annual parents' night was impending in Miss Naughton's school. She asked eight of her

[1] See page 27.

children who were finished with another job to take over the responsibility for making the room attractive. Her account of the way the children worked is a good illustration of informal group planning in a situation and in terms of materials at hand.

> I enjoyed the next hour and a half; the children worked without much attention from me, and they worked with a will. Beatrice and Margaret straightened cupboards; George and Donald first framed pictures and then arranged book covers on our new bulletin board which Peggy's father made for us. Margaret and Tonita chose the book jackets of some of our favorite books in the library. They hung them on a clothesline in the front of the room. Nancy and Bonnie arranged the window sills. Sharon and Suzanne worked on panels showing scenes from prehistoric panels. As the children in the activity room finished their puppet heads, they joined us and set to work.
>
> They continued to mount and put up pictures this noon and several stayed after school to help.

Such drive to do a good, complete job is evidence that the children felt that this classroom was theirs.

Planning Seating Arrangements

The seating arrangement in a classroom is another good subject for group consideration. Miss Brainard had part of her sixth grade group meet with her. They "planned a new arrangement for the desks, to afford more floor space and make the room less formal."

Miss Grossman did not plan the informal arrangement of her classroom with her first graders but found it necessary to discuss the matter with her children after their mothers had visited the school one day in early fall. She describes the incident in these words.

> When several mothers came in and looked around one afternoon, they were shocked to find the room arranged so differently. The desks are in groups instead of the traditional rows and the teacher's desk is moved over into an inconspicuous spot. The mothers couldn't get over the grouped desks. "Won't the children talk?" was the immediate reaction.
>
> The next day one of the children remarked that he thought our desks ought to be in rows. Apparently there had been some discussion at home. We had a little talk about it and the majority of the children said they liked the desks in groups. We decided to leave them that way. "It's more friendly," was one comment.

Making School More Attractive

Making school a more comfortable and attractive place to spend time together offers many opportunities for group cooperation. Miss Wilson looked about her little one-room school in the South one day and was not satisfied with what she saw. "The school was insufficiently light," she later wrote. "There were no bookshelves; the inside was unpainted; there was no place to hang wraps; seats were screwed down so that light came from the right; and there was no play equipment nor shrubbery on the sandy yard." Miss Wilson decided something should be done about all this. Her story continues.

One morning at the close of devotion period, I asked the pupils to look at their school and school yard all day long and ask themselves, "What needs to be done?" At the end of the day, time was given to discuss the questions and their findings. I had an upper-class pupil write the suggestions on the board. We then discussed what we could do. The question of obtaining money, materials, and help was considered. I won't go further into the detailed planning, but in the end some suggestions were given immediate attention; others were to be worked on gradually and hoped for in the distant future.

The next day screwdrivers and hammers were brought from the homes and the seats were turned so that the light came over the left shoulder. (This was discussed in the health class.) The blackboard was moved to the opposite end of the room and windows were washed. This made little improvement in appearance but the difference in the amount of light reaching the children's work was immediately noticeable.

After the girls had scrubbed the desks, floors, and walls, several boys visited local automobile service stations after school and obtained quantities of burned motor oil that darkened the floor and reduced dust produced in cleaning.

To provide a place for wraps, a nail parade was planned for one morning. Children who could brought nails and marched around the room singing and depositing their nails in a container. One family contributed two wide boards that were nailed on a level with the window sills. Beneath this the nails were put, one for each child, with a hanger also brought from home marked with his name. Pennies were contributed for bright material and girls made a curtain to conceal the wraps. This added some to the appearance and comfort of the room by removing wraps from the desks and seats.

Meanwhile, the central office had been asked to paint the interior. It was found that they would furnish paint but no labor. We sent letters asking parents to reply if they were willing to help. Nobody seemed to have time because the work had to be done in the daytime. We next approached the agriculture and shop work instructor of the high school. He and a class of boys devoted a period a day to painting and taught the larger boys in our school to use the brushes. Between the two groups a coat of white paint was applied that increased the light and improved the general appearance.

Orange crates and discarded lumber were brought from home and from the nearby high school that had recently been built. Bookshelves were assembled by the boys, and a low table was constructed. The girls painted the table and several small chairs were made from the crates. Books brought from homes supplemented the few that were bought with a supplementary reader fee required by the office. Thus a reading corner was developed.

A discarded window shade was placed over an unused piece of blackboard and framed to form a bulletin board. That served as a decorative feature as well as a source of information. Grades took responsibility for planning display materials and information monthly.

A plea to a community group for pictures to be placed on the wall brought a variety of pictures from which three were salvaged—a scene, a portrait of George Washington, and one of Booker T. Washington. These were mounted in frames from the five-and-ten-cent store and placed on the walls, in addition to classroom charts and children's work.

Meanwhile, the Parent-Teacher Association and school had been sponsoring programs in the high school auditorium and had gotten enough money to buy material for swings, teeter-totters and a spinning ginny (merry-go-round). The high school shop class did the construction work.

In February when the farmers began preparations for planting crops, one or two parents contributed loads of manure to serve as fertilizer. A group of boys went into the nearby woods to see what evergreen plants could be found that would serve as shrubbery, and reported their findings to the class. Matured heights, blooms, and physical needs of the plants were discussed. The drawing class drew plans. An afternoon was used for setting the shrubs. Later flower settings and seeds were brought from home and put in places best suited for them.

The children were delighted with each improvement and their delight seemed reflected in their work, behavior, and appearance. Needless to say the school looked more "lived in" and attractive.

From Miss Wilson's brief account, it is impossible to judge the quality of cooperative planning that accompanied this development. We can be sure that there were innumerable opportunities for group planning whether or not all were capitalized upon. The account does tell us several things about the teacher, however. First, she did not ask children to give suggestions for improving their school until they had studied the situation for a time. Second, she provided time for discussing suggestions and, later on, for carrying out plans. Third, she gave a pupil the opportunity to record the suggestions where all might see them. Fourth, she encouraged the pupils to divide their plans into two groups—immediate and long range. Fifth, Miss Wilson helped the children to turn to many sources of help—the high school, the central office, parents, a community group. If one source

failed, they turned to another. Sixth, she helped the children to secure needed supplies—by encouraging small donations by each child,
finding uses for discarded material, using nearby woods. It is to be
expected that these steps taken by the teacher contributed to the
children's learning of cooperative procedures.

Planning for a Work Period

The details of planning missing in Miss Wilson's record
may be illustrated with a description of one planning session in Mrs.
Hannum's fourth grade room in a different part of the country.[2]
Mrs. Hannum's children were also interested in improving the appearance of their room and school. During the fall they had made chair-
back covers; painted the hall, the activity room, the kindergarten
room, the bulletin boards; scrubbed walls and radiators; and painted
flowerpots for the room and the hall. One piece of unfinished business
was to decorate the chair backs they had made earlier. The job to be
done in the session observed was the making of designs and stencils.
The discussion was divided into three parts, which Mrs. Hannum
probably had planned in advance.

During the first phase of the discussion, the group addressed itself
to this question raised by the teacher: "What materials are needed
for making a stencil?" The children listed scissors, construction
paper, newspaper to cover desks, paintbrushes and paint for the stencils, jar tops to put paint in. They discussed why brushes were hard
to get and why they were expensive. On the list the children also
added old cloth to practice on and boards to which to tack the cloth.
One child suggested water for cleaning brushes. The teacher had the
group discuss differences in oil and water-based paint and then asked,
"How will we clean the brushes that we use for oils?" The child
changed her suggestion to turpentine.

The second phase of the discussion began with the teacher's
question, "What standards do we have for an indoor work period?"
The children listed "talking softly," "not disturbing others," "cleaning up your mess," "doing your own job," "sharing," "wearing special clothes," "working neatly." The teacher suggested "being satisfied only with the best" and "using newspaper to protect the place
where you are working and to prevent mess." The children then
added "know where materials are," "learn how to use material," "put
away material."

---

[2] This description is based on a record made by an outside observer.

The third phase of the discussion centered on subjects for designs. Suggestions were insects, stories, animals, toys, birds, and flowers.

Here were a group having the earmarks of skill in planning. Their suggestions came quickly, as would be natural in this instance of "review" planning. Long ago these children had learned important lessons about careful preparation for doing a job. They had learned that certain ways of working are necessary when many people are sharing the same room and facilities. One might ask whether this planning was necessary. A teacher must guard against using group time as a period for children to repeat mechanically the steps in a well-known procedure. In this case, it was apparent that the group had not made stencils for some time. Many in the group probably needed certain reminders. For example, it could not be taken for granted that all children would have thought about the properties of oil paint. Perhaps the group did not need to be reminded of its standards of behavior, but the rules were offered sincerely and sounded as if they were those the children lived by because they had meaning for them. It is quite likely that individuals became more creative in their designs by having some broad suggestions not likely to hamper individual choice. Mrs. Hannum used a good technique in dividing the problem into parts so that the discussion would not wander back and forth between designs, preparation of materials, and work habits.

Mrs. Hannum's school was not like Miss Wilson's. The building was in good repair. The board of education could afford to furnish painters and custodial help. Yet school officials valued opportunities for children to experience useful work and to do the planning required to make the work progress efficiently. Time for indoor and outdoor work was provided as a part of the regular school program. One need not teach in a dilapidated building to have opportunities for children to plan for more comfortable and attractive living.

Naming the Goldfish

For Mrs. Austin's kindergarten children, choosing names for their goldfish was part of improving their room. Mrs. Austin's record of how the children went about the job of naming their fish shows that a teacher may utilize an opportunity which she might not have anticipated.

Several children were watching the goldfish.

BRENDA. Let's name our goldfish.

JIMMY B. O.K. What'll we name 'em?

GARY. How about Gary?

LARRY. Or Larry LeRoy Eugene Smith?

CHARLENE. What do you think, Mrs. Austin?

TEACHER. Why not ask all the boys and girls to help us plan names for them?

CHORUS. All right.

It was the second week of school, and the kindergarten children were very much interested in two goldfish which swam obligingly back and forth among the green moss above the white sand and bright-colored marbles in a large glass bowl. The teacher requested that the children gather in a group, and asked Brenda to tell the children of her idea. The children agreed enthusiastically that it was a good idea to name the fish. Mrs. Austin's record continues.

TEACHER. How shall we decide on the names?

CHARLENE. Larry and Gary have thought of some names.

TEACHER. Shall we ask other children to suggest some names too? Then we can decide on the two names that seem to fit the best.

Several children offered suggestions at the same time.

TEACHER. Shall we take turns to offer our suggestions? We can't hear if we all talk at once. What was your suggestion, Ronald?

RONALD. Jack.

Other suggestions followed rapidly. The teacher wrote on paper each name as it was given: Jack, Ronnie, Larry LeRoy Eugene Smith, Gary, Raggles, Sandra, Sandy, Peggy Sue, Jimmy, and Martha Ann.

TEACHER. Many of you have suggested your own names or names of your friends. We have only two fish but we have a great many children. It would be hard to decide which children to name them after, wouldn't it? Let's look at our fish for a while. Perhaps we can think of names that would fit them better than children's names. How do they look? What do they do?

JOHN. They swim.

LARRY. They wiggle their tails when they swim.

PEGGY. We could call one of them "Wiggle-tail."

TEACHER. That's a good suggestion. (Writes name.)

FARRELL. They both wiggle their tails.

TEACHER. Yes, they do, don't they? Perhaps we could think of a name that tells how they look? Do they look just alike?

EDDIE. No, one of them is gold and the other one has speckles.

CHARLENE. We could name one of them "Goldy."

EDDIE. And the other one "Mr. Specklefish."

LARRY. Or just "Speckles."

TEACHER. Are there any other suggestions? (None) Then I'll read all the names and you be thinking about which one seems to suit our fish.

When Mrs. Austin had read the list, several children offered their choices. Then the teacher suggested that they vote. She reports that the results of the vote favored Goldy and Speckles, but that Wiggletail and Mr. Specklefish also received a great many votes. It was finally decided to name them Goldy Wiggletail and Mr. Specklefish. "But we'll probably just call them Goldy and Speckles, because you don't always say your whole name," one child said.

Mrs. Austin noted on her record that when it was time to vote she began with the names at the bottom of the list and proceeded up, knowing that early in the year children have a tendency to vote for the first name read.

Mrs. Austin played a skillful role throughout this discussion. First, she seized the opportunity to turn a chance discussion into a valuable experience in group thinking. Second, she allowed Brenda to restate her idea herself. Third, she gave all children an opportunity to offer suggestions within ordered freedom. Fourth, at a time when she would not interrupt spontaneity, Mrs. Austin herself offered a suggestion for the group's consideration. Her suggestion was in the form of questions which caused the children to turn to a new source of ideas for names—the habits and appearance of the fish themselves. In other words, she widened the range within which choices might be made. Fifth, she treated each suggestion with respect—Peggy's and Farrell's—using a further question to help them resolve a difficulty, "Do they look just alike?" Sixth, Mrs. Austin reviewed all the ideas that had been given and suggested that the group vote. Knowing the habits of young children, she maneuvered matters so that the children would be likely to select one of the names suggested after they were applying more intelligence to their procedure. Seventh, she did not let the matter rest with a slender majority but encouraged the group to persist until they had found a solution pleasing to everyone. All in all, Mrs. Austin's children had a most fortunate experience with making a group decision.

Deciding Where to Store Bottles

In no two classrooms do precisely the same opportunities arise for solving little or big problems. In Mrs. Austin's kindergarten there were goldfish to name. In Mrs. Upton's second grade there were some bottles to be stored. While a child served as group leader, Mrs. Upton made a record of the discussion, adding, "This sounds very 'grown up' but I took it down as they said it." The analysis was later added by an outside consultant as part of a cooperative study of running records as an aid to teachers in improving cooperative procedures.

Record	Analysis
TEACHER. Our art teacher gave us a problem yesterday. Do you remember what it was—and would you like to talk about it? John may be the leader and ask for the problem.	Teacher helps group get launched, selects leader, and sees that he knows where to begin.
LEADER. What is our problem?	
PUPIL. We need a place to put the bottles we brought for the art teacher.	
PUPIL. We could use the orange crates until the easels come.	Leader allows free flow of suggestions.
LEADER. Is that good?	Leader asks group to evaluate the first suggestion given. Leader might better wait until a group of suggestions has been given so no one child's suggestion is being attacked.
PUPIL. That is not a good place because we need it for our ferns we planted.	
PUPIL. We could use the teacher's locked cupboard.	
PUPIL. We could use the bottom part of our book cabinet.	
PUPIL. We could change the readers from our reading cabinet and put the readers in the teacher's cabinet—then we could put the bottles in the reading cabinet.	
Pause—	
TEACHER. Is there any reason why the last suggestion might *not* be a good idea?	Teacher might wait until all suggestions are out and then, if the leader needed it, give him advice about having the merits of *all* suggestions discussed.
PUPIL. If we move the reading books they will be too far away from the reading classes.	
PUPIL. We could use that box in the corner—we don't use it for anything.	
PUPIL. We could use the windows.	
PUPIL. The bottles might get broken when we open the windows.	Leader might help pupils to withhold such comments until the evaluation time. (It is important that an accepting atmosphere be maintained while suggestions are being given.)

Record	*Analysis*
TEACHER. Several good suggestions have been made. You might ask the children to think them all over and decide on the best.	Teacher helps leader move along to a new step.
LEADER. Which do you think is the best?	
PUPIL. The box in the corner.	
PUPIL. There is not enough room in the box.	
TEACHER. I can think of a way we might change *that*.	This might have been put as: "Can you think of a way. . . ?"
PUPIL. We could stack them inside and underneath and on top.	
PUPIL. We could use some cardboard and make another shelf.	
PUPIL. I could bring some boards and I can nail them too.	
PUPIL. I could bring some steel.	
LEADER. You can't *nail steel!*	
Recess bell	Bell apparently prevented a proper close to the discussion. The children probably did not leave feeling that a decision had been reached.

The analysis accompanying this record shows the useful role played by the teacher. Even though comments in the analysis regarding the gathering and evaluating of suggestions may seem negative, they are made only for the purpose of further improving an already good planning period. Observation of a number of planning periods in Mrs. Upton's room furnished convincing evidence that relationships among children and between children and teacher were excellent. The leader was able to operate skillfully because his teacher had set an example of good leadership on previous occasions. Group members were able to offer their suggestions freely and without prompting because they had been encouraged to develop that kind of initiative. A word of caution is in order, however. In many classrooms the use of the group time to solve such a minor problem as where to store bottles for a short period would be wasteful. A large group should discuss matters involving important policies or requiring direct participation in order to secure understanding and a sense of commitment. These criteria hardly apply here. The problem was simple enough for a child leader to handle, and the teacher likely felt that this added value justified the use of time.

CONCLUSION

The physical environment in the classroom offers many opportunities for planning together. To care for and improve this environment gives one a chance to observe tangible results of one's planning. There is a place for every type of individual and enough responsibility for all.

The amount of time to be spent on such planning depends upon cases. Establishing the idea of shared responsibility and helping individuals to learn to carry out the jobs they undertake are of primary importance. Teachers must be sure that individuals know how to do, or get help on, the tasks they assume.

As soon as possible, planning for routine chores should be handled with dispatch and time saved for more creative planning, such as that involved in special projects designed to add to the comfort, attractiveness, or interest of a group's surroundings.

CHAPTER IV

Planning Conduct in

Specific Situations

SCHOOLS HAVE always been concerned with the conduct of the pupils; discipline is often a teacher's biggest problem and the criterion most often employed in judging teaching success. Teachers who have learned something about working cooperatively with pupils have discovered that appropriate conduct for individuals and groups in specific situations is an excellent subject for group discussion and decision. These teachers have found that so-called misbehavior often stems from lack of understanding of what is required by a situation, especially an unfamiliar one. Misbehavior also stems frequently from lack of understanding of how other people are affected by one's conduct.

Teachers cooperating in this study used a number of approaches to group planning for better conduct. One was setting up standards to cover general or specific situations. A second was discussing a situation in which behavior problems had arisen. A third was anticipating in various ways the conduct that would be best for a coming occasion. A fourth was planning ways to maintain friendly relations with other people. These approaches are discussed in turn in this chapter.

SETTING UP STANDARDS OF CONDUCT

A favorite approach with some teachers, as they plan with pupils ways of behaving when passing through the halls, eating in the lunchroom, enjoying an assembly, going on a trip, or having some other experience, is to help the group develop a set of conduct rules or "standards." This practice, in and of itself, is neither good nor bad. The results may be ways of behaving to which group members are genuinely committed. An illustration of this is the "standards for a good work period" used by Mrs. Hannum's children in preparing to make chair-back designs.[1] The results may, however, be a set of teacher-like, abstract rules that appear to have been motivated largely by a desire to produce expected responses. Let us see how one teacher worked to secure standards of conduct that were the group's own.

Mrs. Tambling, the art teacher who almost despaired of ever getting children to accept responsibility for the appearance of the art room shared by so many groups, had a similar problem of getting them to accept responsibility for their conduct there.[2] She decided to invite members of her classes to make up their own rules and had a most unusual experience as a result. "What's important for the art room?" was asked each class in turn. "Here's how the ideas came," she reports.

> No throwing anything.
> No running.
> Clean up your own mess.
> Don't handle other people's work.
> No shouting.
> No interrupting.
> Listen when Mrs. Tambling talks to the class. She means *you*.

Mrs. Tambling's report continues.

> It all sounded good—until the last period. I built it all up just the same as before. Jim said, "We don't want any rules." The room came alive with "No rules." We took a vote: no rules, rules made by ourselves, rules made by Mrs. Tambling. The vote was nine to fifteen for no rules.
>
> "O.K., let's try no rules for this period." ("Oh, fool," whispered my inner self!)
>
> The result was instantaneous. There was a rush for the clay bin; a clay fight started. Three minutes later one of the boys was biting his lip to keep from crying; he leaned against the wall glaring. Somebody tripped. Somebody got a wad of clay on a drawing. The noise was terrific; there was confusion everywhere. One boy got his foot stepped on. All good fun!
>
> A girl asked me to stop it. "I can't. There are no rules. They are within their rights!" said I.
>
> A boy came up. "Gee whiz! Enough is enough! Make them stop!"
>
> "Can't do it. I'm no better than you are. Do something about it if you don't like it!"
>
> Finally, a girl got up and wrote on the board: "All those who want

[1] See pages 40–41.
[2] See pages 34–36.

rules sign here————." At five minutes before the period was up, there were eleven names out of fifteen on the board.

I stopped the class. "Eleven people want rules. Four people don't. We haven't time now to make rules so write a letter to me, a personal letter, and tell me these things: 1. What did you accomplish this period? 2. What did you learn? 3. What rules are important? 4. What can you do to make the rules work? You had a choice of democracy and you didn't want it. Some of you asked during the period for dictatorship but that wasn't what you voted for. You voted for no rules or anarchy. Now you know what that word means. We've had our party. Is it fair now to leave the mess for me? Let's all clean up together."

Oh, it was wonderful. Such effort, such helpfulness, such saintliness (or contrition). I do know that that period made a deep impression and I still think it was a good, if extreme, idea. I took a chance. The letters should show plenty.

Two days later, Mrs. Tambling continues her report.

The letters came in today. Some were just crude lists. Others were written on good stationery and addressed in sealed envelopes. All were honest. For instance:

1. I never had so much fun in all my life. I don't know how to make *good* rules. I learned how to duck.
2. We never had such a good chance to see why we have to have rules.
3. I accomplished a lot because I wasn't going to let them stop me. (Passive resistance.)
4. It wasn't fair because only a few boys had any fun. It was dangerous. If we are in a group, we have to have rules so that no one will get hurt and because we want to do our work.

And so it went on. The rules followed the same general pattern as the others, so I lettered them into a composite sign and we now have rules for the art room. It will be fun to see if they enforce them! Everyone heard about the famous last period and other classes asked for a repeat performance, but once is enough. I referred them to the class that went through it.

Mrs. Tambling took some risks when she allowed the children to test their extreme idea, yet it must be admitted that the pupils had an unusually realistic learning experience. As some of the letters of the children show, there was a new appreciation of the need for law and order in groups. It is quite possible that school is just the place to arrange for opportunities to test the consequences of behavior, because limits can be set and the group can be protected from danger while the learning is taking place. The teacher could count on the fact that most groups contain reasonable and well-balanced individuals whose leadership would come to the fore. The chief problem would be to secure the understanding and cooperation of parents and colleagues, which Mrs. Tambling did not have time to do in the present instance.

An opportunity which Mrs. Tambling missed was to have a representative committee finish the job of making a composite list of rules and of lettering them for the group. Even so, the pupils could feel that the product was genuinely that of the group. Mrs. Tambling could hardly be accused of overdirection.

In general, teachers should proceed with caution in using the "standards" approach to improved conduct. There is a tendency for both children and adults to verbalize their ideals easily but to find it hard to live up to the standards they set. Schools must exercise care not to encourage this tendency to divorce acts from avowed intentions. Therefore, a very few simple statements growing out of a need for a guide to conduct on a particular occasion usually have more meaning than long lists of rules covering every contingency. Standards developed for real use should serve the group frequently and not remain as a wall decoration in the classroom or corridor.

HOLDING DISCUSSIONS ON TROUBLE SITUATIONS

Establishing long-term conduct goals is not the only way in which pupils can be helped to accept group responsibility for improved behavior. When troubles arise in groups, matters may be smoothed out through group discussion.

Unscheduled Discussions

Such discussion need not always await a set time. Miss Martin used little incidents as they arose as opportunities to help her first and second grade children use increasingly better judgment in situations. In her attractive classroom each table and group of chairs was painted a different pastel color. The children had just carried their chairs from their discussion circle back to their tables when the teacher asked them to pause a moment while she asked their leader this question: "Did you like the way the chairs were put away, Joe? You know, if you're the leader, you appreciate a little help."

Joe started to make several different points. "Let's take one suggestion at a time, Joe," the teacher advised. "What is one thing that would make it better?"

Ronny gave his opinion. "The leader called 'green chairs,' 'blue chairs' too fast!" Sarah thought they should carry their chairs properly the way it said in their big book. (She referred to a large book illustrated with line drawings by the teacher.)

"Do you think we've given some good suggestions?" Miss Martin asked. When the children agreed, she came back to Sarah's suggestion. "Do you think we need to practice carrying our chairs, or shall we just try to remember?"

This record shows a teacher trying to help children do clear and constructive thinking. The emphasis was not on scolding or building feelings of guilt over bad conduct, but rather on planning better ways of handling a situation that had not gone smoothly.

Mr. Yates also provided needed discussion when an occasion arose. An argument had developed when one of his sixth grade boys, lumbering to the pencil sharpener in a careless manner, bumped into another boy. Since the incident occurred during the weekly activity period of a boys' club, the teacher allowed the argument to continue for a short time. When it reached the point of "You did it on purpose!" "I did not!" "You did!" he restored order and asked the group what they thought of an argument of this kind. Mr. Yates reported the discussion that followed.

> One boy commented, "They are acting like a bunch of babies." Because I wanted the discussion to be kept on an objective plane rather than concern itself with this particular case and the personalities involved in it, I asked the group, "How many of you have ever found yourselves arguing like that at one time or another?"
>
> One by one the hands went up until finally every hand in the room was raised. "Why, then," I asked, "don't we see more of this kind of arguing going on in the subways, for example, where people are often pushed or bumped by others?"
>
> One boy answered, "Well, those people are always in a rush. They haven't time to argue." Another boy said, "I sometimes hear people say 'Excuse me.'" "Yes, that's right," I replied. "Why don't we do that in school?" "I'm no sissy," came a low, unrecognizable voice.
>
> Evidently this summed up the entire group's feeling because there arose a chorus of yeses, accompanied by a nodding of heads throughout the room. It was obvious that all of them were sure only a sissy would ever say "Excuse me."
>
> Believing that all of them should have an opportunity to express their views openly, I asked why they seemed to feel that a simple apology such as that would make any one of them a sissy. Their comments on the matter were interesting. George remarked that if you were pushed you had to push back or else you just weren't a regular fellow. Bill didn't agree because he recalled that during a fight he had seen on

a newsreel one boxer pushed the other by mistake and then apologized for it, and the boxer certainly wasn't a sissy, was he? Another boy remembered that he had seen a similar occurrence during a hockey game on television. A few more fellows recalled incidents of "regular" men apologizing for their mistakes.

The group quieted for a few moments, and I could gather from the expressions on their faces that the boys were thinking that it was possible to say "Excuse me" and still be very much of a young man.

Mr. Yates had not tried a group discussion with these boys before, and he was pleased with their constructive thinking. "It might have been simpler for me to stop the argument when it began and to tell the boys what would have constituted acceptable behavior on their part," he added in his record, "but I have grave doubts that such procedure would have had anything but a very fleeting effect. By group discussion they tackled their own problem themselves and derived satisfaction from forming their own conclusion."

Mr. Yates's comment leads to the observation that individuals can undergo a change in attitude and feel committed to a different way of behaving without verbalizing the commitment as a definite plan. In this instance the students changed their attitude; they did not voice a definite plan to say "Excuse me" when bumping into people in the future. It appears that it was easier for these boys to come to a new conclusion with regard to sissiness as a result of pooling their experiences than it would have been for any one of them to make this shift by himself. Although the group did not set about to make a plan, this definitely seems an instance of group thinking.

Special Conference Periods

A group conference time is a valuable aid in helping pupils to feel continuously responsible for ironing out difficulties arising as they work and play together. When Miss Grossman introduced this idea to her first grade children, it did not take them long to learn that this was a constructive way to handle problems. The teacher's diary for October 8 reads:

Our independent work periods are pretty noisy, so today we had a conference. I explained to the children what I meant by a conference, that it was a meeting in which to talk over our problems. They thought it an excellent idea and we really had a fine chat with good results. A little later we were short two bottles of milk. Emilio discovered this and came bursting in with, "Miss Grossman, we need another conference. We have a problem—two bottles of milk are missing!"

Mrs. Wardell found it was effective to use the group conference when a discipline problem arose in her eighth grade mathematics and science class two days before Thanksgiving. In recording the incident in her diary, Mrs. Wardell wrote: "This turned out to be an outstanding incident in many ways and has had the most lasting effect of anything I can recall in my relationships with this eighth grade and in their attitude toward each other in the classroom." This is her description of the affair.

A math and science period the day before had ended on a very disagreeable note. The passing bell rang just as something had been thrown, followed by a tussle; and the class left amid guffaws, reveling in the fact that something had been put over on the teacher.

Believe me, "teacher" did a lot of thinking and evaluating that evening. In itself the incident wasn't much, but it was certainly symptomatic of underlying attitudes which were undesirable. From past experience I've learned that such incidents are forgotten by the children, but that indirectly the children build on them in the future. This afternoon, when I next met with the group, was certainly no time for lectures or punishment as it was just before the early vacation dismissal; and yet I felt some use should be made of the climax reached the day before. The crux of the whole thing for me was leading the individuals to see their responsibility in the matter.

Class opened as a conference period, a time to check up on our aims and accomplishments before vacation. I frankly stated that I had done the same thing the evening before. It was gratifying to see the group state their aims, with social factors at the top, and they concluded with (1) social habits and (2) work habits. I asked that they take yesterday afternoon as a basis for evaluating. They seemed sincere, understanding, and even concerned that they were not accomplishing either aim. For the first time they had been made conscious of the importance of learning to live together in school.

Perhaps it doesn't sound like much, but to me it represented growth since September, when a similar conference brought forth the frank remark that it was *my* job to *make* them work and behave. And we're still building!

It is not easy for Mrs. Wardell and others like her to help students take their first fumbling steps in group ways of working after years of experiencing a different relationship with teachers. The job of building new expectations and inner sources of control is a gradual process, as Mrs. Wardell shows in a January entry.

My big problem this week has been "talking" in eighth grade math. We planned before Christmas to have helpers and checkers with talking permitted. Somehow the talking seems to outweigh everything else, and there has been a lot of time wasted. I had so hoped that there was an individual sense of responsibility developing and, so help me, I believe there is! I'm afraid the effectiveness of conferences will wear off. There must be another way for the group to develop in itself a realization of its needs and aims. Maybe this was too abrupt a change for the group; if so, I mustn't be afraid to backtrack a little.

Mrs. Wardell evaluated carefully as she went along so that she could note any encouraging signs of progress and change her procedures if it seemed wise to do so. It is a good idea for teachers to be aware of the fact that they may misuse a procedure like the conference and lead pupils to look upon it as an ineffective bore. This is especially likely to happen if during the conference the teacher harangues the group about being "steady," "taking care of yourselves," "being quiet" (stock phrases that children's ears tune out when overused by a teacher), instead of planning definite steps with the members for shouldering individual and group responsibility.

Miss Turner's records of two conferences with her kindergarten children illustrate the way two common problems—taking things that belong to others and fighting—might be handled with very young children. One day she found Dolores, Johnny, and Dennis carefully going through the pockets of children's coats hanging in the cloak-room. She also saw them take a powder puff from Hall's pocketbook. Johnny's mother had told Miss Turner that everyday the boy was bringing something home from school, but so far the teacher hadn't seen Johnny or any of the children taking things. Miss Turner brought the group together and conducted the following discussion.

> TEACHER. Whose pocketbook is this?
> HALL. That's mine, Miss Turner.
> TEACHER. Does this coat belong to any of you children?
> JOHNNY. Yes, that's mine.

The teacher went on holding up quite a few articles, some belonging to the children and some to herself. The children talked about playing with someone else's toys and decided that when they were through playing, they should give them back or put them where they belonged, and that they shouldn't take things that didn't belong to them.

Lionel said, "People who take things haven't learned to share. But we can play with other people's toys if they let us." The group agreed that Lionel was right, that maybe some of them forgot and didn't return things that belonged to other people. "This has worked so far," Miss Turner reported.

It should be noted that the word "stealing" was not used, that no accusations were made, that no one was made to lose face with the group. Miss Turner acted on the assumption that at least three of the children needed help in distinguishing between "what is mine" and "what is yours." She made this lesson concrete and then encouraged the group to verbalize certain generalizations about conduct that very likely had more significance because the children arrived at them together.

On another occasion there was difficulty with three boys in the cloakroom. "They were always fighting," Miss Turner wrote, "and just didn't seem to get along with one another. We talked it over as a group and got the following story from the children."

> James should have been in the room, at work. Dennis had his coat off, James came over and kicked Dennis and Dennis kicked back. Johnny on his way to the bathroom was attracted by the disturbance in the cloakroom and entered. Johnny told Dennis to get out and started to chase him. Dennis came crying.
>
> SUSAN. Miss Turner, these boys just don't know how to take their things off. They need someone to watch them.
> HALL. They fight all the time.
> JOHNNY. Well, James started it.
> SUSAN. You are big now and can take care of your own clothes.
> SALLY. Mother doesn't take my clothes off.
> Several others echoed this sentiment and added that they didn't fight either.
> TEACHER. Well, what can we do to help these children remember not to fight in the cloakroom?
> LIONEL. Well, maybe they will remember now.

The three fighters thought they would. Miss Turner was not sure that this resolution would carry over, for Easter vacation was arriving and the three boys were immature socially. But she was confident that such discussions were a help. "I have been trying to let the children decide more of their problems," she commented, "and they certainly have a great respect for their fellow students' decisions."

Miss Turner was taking more risks in this discussion than in the previous one. Three boys whom she described as "immature socially" were made the center of attention. Other children were put in a position to harangue them and to boast about their own model conduct. The three "culprits" were given no help in making a specific plan for conduct on future occasions. However, the teacher was setting a good precedent by having the group get the facts straight before discussing what should be done. Also, it is possible that the three boys might have felt that the group was taking a friendly interest in them. Perhaps a few seeds of doubt about the desirability of starting fights in the cloakroom were planted.

Miss Hogue believes that such seeds of doubt may be the beginning of a change of attitude and offers an example occurring in her kindergarten at Halloween time.

> We had considerable talk today about Halloween and the celebrations prevalent on the nights preceding. One little boy spoke up in the beginning of our conversation to tell us that tonight was "break-window night." I had never heard of such a specific kind of celebration myself, but I could believe it possible, knowing the number of windows that are broken regularly in the school building. Anyway, a discussion was started about damaging property, which lasted about ten minutes, with only occasionally a question from me, the children themselves keeping it going by their comments. I think it was well worth the time spent because the children were apparently able to convince the boy who made the remark that it really was not a good idea. At any rate a few seeds of doubt were planted in his mind, and I'm sure in others' too, which I hope bore fruit.

Groups discussing a trouble situation may not always work out plans that are best in the teacher's opinion. Miss Foguely's third grade children were tackling the problem of their conduct in an overcrowded library. General discussion of how to behave in the library and resolutions to be better next time had proved ineffective. Therefore, even though the teacher doubted the wisdom of the solution finally reached when early failures were evaluated, she was willing to let the children try it, maintaining an attitude of "wait and see." Her report reads:

> Nathan thought a committee should be appointed to "watch" the children. In view of the fact that Nathan was one of the most serious offenders, I was more than surprised. I questioned whether they wanted to be watched and Joan said she thought in third grade we should be able to take care of ourselves. Nathan still wanted a committee and was joined in this by several others. The class supported them and thought the committee should do something.
>
> When the committee had been appointed they wanted to mark people, but the class didn't favor the idea. Joan again spoke, saying why couldn't they decide for themselves how they behaved. They decided on having a self-evaluation chart. Being hesitant about the use of stars and other such rewards, I wasn't too much in favor of the idea but the class was so anxious to try it that I agreed.
>
> The committee asked for help in the correct spelling of names and

then went ahead and made a large chart with the names in alphabetical order. I felt that much was gained by the committee in planning the chart, in both the social and the subject matter field. Correct measurements were needed for the spacing of names.

It was agreed that each child should judge his own behavior in the library beginning with the following week. Also if he thought he was a good citizen he would so indicate in whatever manner he wanted on the chart after his name.

So we shall wait until next Wednesday.[3]

The children in this instance had made a definite plan which dramatized the acceptance of individual responsibility for conduct.

When problems are brought to the attention of some groups, the solutions proposed tend to take the form of punishments. Miss Quayle tells of the way in which her fifth and sixth grade children discussed what to do with three boys in their class who had broken the window of a teacher's car when aiming at a wasps' nest. The principal had said when he angrily brought the boys in, "Shall I attend to them or do you want to?" This is how the teacher "attended to" the boys.

> The class held a meeting and decided that the three boys should have extra work during recesses for a week to remind them that laws were made for the protection of all children. One youngster thought that they should have a longer reminder because of the "terrible results" that would have occurred if the wasps' nest had broken. Another said, "No, it wasn't thrown in temper."
>
> All were quite serious, which is rather unusual for this group. The class chairman did a good job by not allowing too much to be said about the boys.

Dealing with the problem in a simple class meeting seems preferable to copying adult courts elaborately, as is the practice in some schools. It is commendable also that the children in this instance focused on the deed done and not on the personalities of the guilty parties. One would wish that the boys themselves might have had some part in working out the solution and also that other alternatives beside punishment might have been considered. The teacher reported that the car was insured, so the problem of reparations was not under consideration, although the observation was made that someone had to pay for such damage. An opportunity to consider the feelings and the inconvenience of the teacher whose car was damaged was entirely missed. It is the teacher's right as a group member and his responsi-

---

[3] The story of Marshall's use of this chart is told on page 462.

bility as a mature status leader to introduce considerations the group is overlooking.

A Scheduled "Problem Time"

Some teachers, like Miss Oliver, seem to be able to create an atmosphere where children solve problems reasonably and cooperatively. "Problem time" in her second grade classroom was a time when children could bring their troubles and disagreements to the group. Miss Oliver has furnished three illustrations of the use of this time in her room. The first has to do with Peter, who asked the teacher privately whether he might bring up something that happened on the way home the night before.

PETER. Last night when I was going home John jumped on me and threw me into the hedge. I wasn't doing anything to him. I wasn't even saying anything.

FRANK. That's a safety rule. You shouldn't jump on people. You could hurt them.

RICK (the leader). Johnny, do you want to say anything?

JOHNNY. Yes, I did it.

RICK. Well, at least you're honest about it.

JOHNNY. I just jumped on him a little bit. We have a club and I was testing my strength.

PETER. John has done it to me before last night but I never reported it. But last night he knocked me down.

TEACHER. It sounds as though you and Peter are not very good friends. I wonder how we can help them?

JOHN. Well, I like Peter, but if I'm nice to him my brothers will beat me.

TEACHER. Well, Johnny, if you say that you like Peter, do you think you could treat him as though you did on the way home and in our room? Do you think you could try to be his friend?

BARD. You're supposed to walk home without having people hurt you.

BETTY. That's one of our agreements—we should help other people —especially when they are not touching you.

JOHN. I think I can. I'll try, Peter.

Peter seemed much relieved.

Noteworthy in this record is the fact that the pupil leader early turned to John for his side of the story. The teacher came in at points where she could help the group focus on a friendly solution. She chose to ignore John's rationalization that his brothers would beat him, but made capital of the boy's statement, "Well, I like Peter . . ." She helped Johnny to have a positive picture of future conduct in his mind, treating Peter as a friend outside of school. Other members of the group emphasized their "agreements" in ways that were real guides to conduct.

The second incident occurred in connection with a regular Friday afternoon story hour for which the children prepared all week and signed up on Friday morning. Just as Diane, the leader, was about to begin, Robin and Cynthia jumped up and came over to the teacher, weeping. Cynthia had just discovered that her name had been erased from first place on the list and that Robin's was there instead. Robin denied all guilt.

> TEACHER. We really have a problem to settle if we are to have our story hour. Can we settle it without wasting time?
>
> HENRY. What's the sense in crying? That won't help. It doesn't make any difference if you are first or not.
>
> TEACHER. Henry is right. Crying has never helped settle a problem.
>
> CYNTHIA (still weeping). Yes, but I want to read my story today. If I'm last there might not be time for me.
>
> DIANE (the leader). We could vote whose story we wanted to hear first or—Eenie, meenie, minie, mo, Catch a bunny by the toe . . .

Cynthia's story was voted first. Both girls, now smiling, went to their places. As far as they were concerned, the difficulty was settled. Miss Oliver, however, was not satisfied. She thought the children should discuss the matter again, since it tied up with the problem of "snitching" prevalent in the community. Too, she thought that Robin really had erased and changed the names. And so Miss Oliver said:

> Sometimes I've said that we would only have time for one more story when some children haven't had their turns. This seems too bad when they have prepared them for us. Let's go on with our story time now but let us try to think what we could do so we wouldn't have this problem again. I think Cynthia would have been glad to be last if she just knew that she would have time to read today. Think it over for problem time.

When the matter was discussed in "problem time" the following Monday, it turned out that Sharon had accidentally erased Cynthia's name.

> TEACHER. How could we make sure that this wouldn't happen again?
>
> MARY LEE. Why don't we write our names on paper instead of the board? Or if we are going to use the board, put a sign, "Do not work here," 'cause I don't think Sharon meant to erase the name.
>
> TEACHER. A very good suggestion, Mary Lee.

PAM. Why don't we let the leader just choose who she wants to read from the names?

RICK. No, 'cause some people just would choose their friends.

SANDY. We could choose which story book we wanted to hear instead of taking the names as they are on the board. (Children place books they are going to use on the ledge before story time.)

CYNTHIA. Maybe the children who don't have time could be first the next week.

MARY LEE. Why don't we try writing the names again and the leader keep a list on paper too. See how that is.

The teacher added: "All children seemed to agree to this. Since the discussion we have had no difficulty."

Again here is an example of a discussion in which the effort was not to fix blame but to work out a solution agreeable and fair to all. Furthermore, there was emphasis on preventing difficulty in the future.

The third illustration from Miss Oliver's records shows how much practice her children were having in looking at all sides of a question and in planning constructively to remove causes of trouble. Henry thought his problem couldn't wait until "problem time," so when he went before the group at "sharing time" the children were ready to listen to him.

HENRY. The other day I was painting at the easel. I left the easel to throw my paper in the basket and when I came back Leland had my place. I tried to tell him that I just wanted to put my paper in the basket but he wouldn't listen to me. So today when I went up to the easel Leland came and wouldn't let me paint again. He said that he just threw a paper in the basket. He made me let him have the easel the other day, but when I did the same thing today he still wouldn't let me paint. I don't think he's being fair about it. It isn't right.

SANDY. Leland, if you made Henry give it to you, you should have done the same thing when Henry wanted it.

LELAND. Yes, but I had started to paint and I wanted to finish.

TEACHER. Henry wanted to paint too.

HENRY. Leland, you could take your picture off and finish later.

CYNTHIA. Henry, why didn't you put your name on the paper, then no one could paint on it?

TEACHER. A very good suggestion, Cynthia.

PAMELA. Could we move the wastebasket over near the easel, then you wouldn't have to leave your place? I think it would be better anyway 'cause you wouldn't have to walk so far in quiet time.

TEACHER. We could try that. Leland, what do you think about this problem?

LELAND. I think maybe I should have let Henry paint.

TEACHER. But you are not quite sure?

LELAND. Yes, I am. If I did it to him I should let him have it. I'll take my paper off, Henry, and finish later.

HENRY. I think that's only fair, Leland.

TEACHER. Did you notice how Henry acted when Leland wouldn't give him the easel?

DIANE. He just let him have it and did something else.

TEACHER. What do we call a boy like Henry?

BETTY. He was thoughtful because even when he knew he was right he just didn't disturb us then.

TEACHER. Henry was a good sport. Henry was right. He was helping too by not disturbing us.

This record shows three concerns of the teacher—an interest in preventive measures, a desire to have Leland leave the discussion with a clear commitment for future conduct, and a wish to reinforce the idea that a time and a procedure existed for settling differences. The children in Miss Oliver's room seemed to be discussing their problems impersonally, yet with real interest in reaching constructive solutions.

Discussions with Concreteness Added

Often it is possible to make a discussion of a trouble situation more concrete by visiting the place where the problem occurred, meeting the person especially concerned, or re-enacting the difficulty.

Miss Bellin reports on the use of on-location planning in connection with an accident which happened to one of her second grade girls.

Joyce was hurt on the playground today. It was found that it was due to carelessness on her part since she played too close to the wall. While we were talking the matter over, June suggested that we go out on the playground and pick out the best places to play. We agreed to do this.

We decided to keep away from the cement walls since they were low and not a safe place to play. We chose the best places to play—those that were flat. We cleaned some sections of pointed stones.•

It is probable that better solutions occurred to the group when they were on the scene of the accident than if they had talked the matter over in their classroom. Again the emphasis was not on blaming Joyce for being careless but on making a better plan for the future.

In Mrs. Lardner's case, when trouble had arisen between some of her upper grade children and one of the other teachers in the school, she arranged for a chance for the problem to be talked out together.

Several of my children go to the music room twice a week for instrumental lessons. Lately they have been returning after a time and complaining that Mrs. Fortune never came to the music room and so they missed their lesson. After this had happened many times, with the children becoming more and more discouraged, I tried to help them solve this problem. I suggested that we ask Mrs. Fortune to meet with us and talk over the matter. I myself was definitely on the children's side but felt it would do them no good to know that and that just grumbling about the matter was getting them nowhere.

After a lengthy discussion, in which Mrs. Fortune's reasons for not meeting her appointments were never clearly given, but in which she gave the impression that the children were not practicing, thus coming to class unprepared, we arrived at what, so far, has proved an agreeable solution to the problem. The children saw that if they failed to do their share, the teacher's interest in helping them would not be very great. They promised to practice daily; she in turn promised to be on hand for the lesson.

Mrs. Lardner helped both her colleague and the children to save face as they planned jointly what each would do to make it possible for them to work together. Discussion can be more concrete and constructive when all interested parties are present to reach a common agreement.

Discussions can also be made more concrete through use of role-playing to re-enact different examples of behavior. Through this device the discussion can be focused on the particular problem before the group and fitting solutions can be seen.

Miss Deutsch used role-playing in an unusual way with her kindergarten group one day. She decided suddenly at story time to take some roles before the children in the hope that this would crystallize something she had been working on all year. As the teacher tells it:

When the usual arguments and pushing of one another began, I asked one of the boys to come up by me and pretend that he was sitting in such a way that I wouldn't be able to see a book held by another child. I then asked in a very pleasant tone if he would please move over so that I could see the book. Next, in a gruff, hostile voice I told him to get out of my way and pushed him simultaneously.

This brought laughter from the group at first, but then we eagerly discussed which way of speaking to each other made us feel friendlier and less apt to hit rather than comply with a justifiable request.

The next day the teacher had a chance to study the effects of this discussion.

At story time today one of the children spoke hastily to another. At once one of the children asked him if he had forgotten how we had decided yesterday to talk to each other. Another child immediately told him exactly how he should have spoken, and I didn't say a word during all this.

Miss Deutsch used role-playing to help teach a new language of courtesy; following the role-playing, discussion was used to deepen understanding and to foster a commitment to desirable forms of communication.

ANTICIPATING APPROPRIATE CONDUCT

Behavior in a New Situation

Constructive use of planning conduct may be made in anticipating behavior that will be appropriate in a new situation. Miss Miller saw the necessity of this kind of planning before her kindergarten children attended their first assembly. She recorded the discussion as follows.

TEACHER. Today instead of going to the gym for games, we are going there for an assembly. Do you know what an assembly is?

The children gave various answers but no one gave the right one.

TEACHER. You've all tried but let me explain to you what an assembly is. It is a group of people or children gathering together in one room. You have a speaker (a man who talks to you), a movie, a show, or singing. There are many different kinds of assemblies.

When we go to the assembly we will sit on the floor just as we do here. When there are so many people in the room, what do you suppose we will try to do before the assembly starts?

TOMMY. Be quiet.

JIMMY. Sit still.

CORAL. Cross our legs.

JEAN. Keep our hands in our laps.

TEACHER. That was very good. Now the assembly is going to begin. What do we do?

JOHNNY. Turn our eyes so the speaker can see them.

ALICE. Be quiet and listen.

TEACHER. How will we walk up to the assembly?

MARY. On our tiptoes.

JEAN. With our lips locked.

YVONNE. In a straight line.

PAULINE. No running down the hall.

Miss Miller's children already showed the effects of previous discussions of how to behave. As the teacher added, "The ideas of the children were picked out by themselves from knowing how we act in the room and when walking down the hall." Going on tiptoe and with lips locked are concepts picked up from overzealous adults perhaps, but the record shows thoughtfulness on the teacher's part. She broke the discussion into segments, helping the children to anticipate three different problems involved: going to the assembly, waiting for the program to begin, and being a good audience. She also helped the children to know what to expect when their gym was being put to a use that was entirely new to them.

An alternative procedure might have been for Miss Miller to take her children to the assembly room where they could plan "on location" and thus better visualize the situation. However, because these children had used the gym previously, it was possible for them to plan adequately for the new experience without actually being at the spot where the assembly was to be.

When Miss Jones's first grade group was about to present their first auditorium program, they planned "on location" twice. The teacher's diary says:

> Our first visit was one of exploration. We explored the stage, backstage, saw how the curtains and lights worked and walked around the empty auditorium. We had seen the place only from the viewpoint of the audience. This was something new.
>
> Later, when we started practicing parts, we learned to speak clearly because half the class sat in the last rows and listened to the others to see if they could hear. (In an earlier discussion they had decided they didn't care for plays they couldn't hear.) Then the groups changed places and soon all parts were spoken clearly.

Such trips to the scene of the future activity make planning conduct more realistic.

Miss Franklin reports two instances of careful advance planning with her first grade children in order that they might do their part to make the all-school Thanksgiving and Christmas programs a success. The first step in planning conduct at the Thanksgiving program was to have a clear idea of the program. As the teacher wrote later, "I was happy to see that my children were ready to enter into every part of the program without looking to me because they knew what was to happen." In the conference period on the day of the program they discussed the affair.

> I pointed out that the success and beauty of this program depended upon all classes taking part in it and being quiet all through it. Since we are a restless bunch, we planned to have a good time before going into the auditorium. Then we would sit quietly during the talk and songs. We had learned the Thanksgiving songs and were anxious to

sing with the entire school. It was decided that Judith would sit on the end, as she could go up on the stage without causing disorder. We planned to put our seats back quietly and leave the auditorium in orderly fashion so that the solemnness and thankfulness of the program would not be lost.

Miss Franklin adds, "The children were not restless and wiggly as they have been at other programs. In this instance it clearly bore results to have the children participate in the planning." It may be noted that the planning included not only anticipating everything connected with the program itself, including the way of leaving the auditorium, but also a scheme of preparing themselves for sitting quietly.

Planning for the Christmas program presented even more complications.

In our morning conference period, we discussed seating arrangements. All the primary classes had been asked to bring chairs and sit on the stage because our auditorium will not hold both the elementary and junior high schools. It's a long walk from our room in the new wing to the auditorium. We were asked to leave our room at two o'clock so that all the classes to sit on the stage would be seated before the others came at two-thirty. We talked about, and practiced, carrying our chairs, holding them off the floor. We decided to sit up and be ready to take part in the singing because the rest of the school would be watching us.

In this case there was actual practice of one feat that is difficult for young children—carrying chairs safely and comfortably for a long distance.

Miss Bellin helped her second grade children make a good plan for receiving a visit from Santa Claus. Because there had been a near riot on such an occasion the year before, Santa was to visit each group in its own classroom. The teacher's account of the planning reads:

This morning when we got together I asked my children if they thought we ought to make some plans for Santa's visit to our room this afternoon. They agreed that we should. Many suggestions were forthcoming out of which evolved some plans: we'd each design a place mat for our place at the tables; we'd say "Merry Christmas, Santa Claus" when he came in; we'd sing "Santa Claus Is Coming to Town"; we'd take turns talking to Santa; we'd try to be polite at all times; we'd laugh and have fun, but we'd remember the rights of others.

Of the results, Miss Bellin writes: "I am glad to say it worked out very well. It certainly helped to have the children participate in the plans. A child just seems to resent doing what he's told to do, but will do the same thing willingly if he has some voice in making the plan."

Giving a Group a Second Chance

When children participate in planning for their future conduct, the results are sometimes a little unexpected, as Miss Altberg found out. Since September this first grade teacher had been trying to establish self-direction. As she reports:

> This is especially necessary in my room, as my supervisor visits me frequently and usually talks with me for several minutes. Not having any textbooks, my children cannot sit and study and they can't just sit still for long. Therefore, I presented the problem to the class and asked for suggestions.

Miss Altberg goes on to tell that the group suggested getting paper from the closet and drawing, using pegs and beads, and reading library books. These means and others were to be used when visitors came into the room to talk with the teacher.

Then came the test. One morning the supervisor entered. Immediately no less than fifteen children rushed to the bookcase. Miss Altberg writes: "The tumult was unbearable and my supervisor asked the children to be seated. In their effort to do the right thing they had caused confusion and disorder.

"After the supervisor left," the teacher continues, "we discussed what had been wrong. We agreed that for safety purposes not more than three children were to be at the bookcase at one time." Miss Altberg really wanted her children put to the test. "I am anxiously awaiting a visitor so that I may see the result of this discussion," she concluded. A later entry in her diary contains the sequel.

> This morning my supervisor visited me again. While he spoke with me I threw furtive glances at the children. Then it began. Not more than three children appeared at the bookcase at one time. I saw Stanley stand and start to leave his seat. He counted the number of children and sat down. Since he sits in the fifth row he had to wait several minutes before securing a book.

Both supervisor and teacher were greatly pleased with the result. The teacher mentions "the satisfied look on the children's faces" after the supervisor left.

This series of episodes illustrates the point that in matters of conduct teachers must not expect quick or easy success.

Miss Brainard had an experience with sixth grade children which taught her the same lesson. She thought she had provided for sufficient planning with her group so that they might be left on their own while she was busy with a small group elsewhere. Events proved otherwise as an entry in her diary shows.

> This was the day to prepare the auditorium for the Book Fair. I had been asked to take charge of arranging the flowers. After our planning period, when I thought the children understood the various tasks they needed to work upon, I took a group of six children to help arrange the flowers. I had expected such grand cooperation from the youngsters, for they have been working very nicely when I was in the room. But all my hopes were shattered! They did not work nicely. They resorted to much of the customary nonsense and they accomplished very little.
>
> We were not finished with the flowers at the game time, so the children were allowed to go outside for their play period. Even here they were quarrelsome and didn't get along nicely.
>
> When they came in we took the time usually devoted to checking work to talk over the causes of our troubles. (After reading Julia Weber's *My Country School Diary*[4] I know this idea of democratic living is not going to be a smooth, steady road of progress, but I wondered why everything should have gone so terribly.)
>
> In thinking back over the situation, I believe I missed an opportunity to use this activity as a valuable experience in group living. I assumed too much of the responsibility. The children had practically none of it. I knew I would have the flowers in school on Monday morning. It would have been much better, I believe, if we had taken time last week to talk over the plans for decorating the auditorium, discussing arrangement of flowers, color combinations, etc. The children would have realized that thirty-one couldn't work efficiently on the actual arrangement. I believe they would have suggested a committee to arrange the flowers and would have assumed more responsibility for working unsupervised. Perhaps someday I'll learn not to try to put the cart before the horse.

We can learn two things from Miss Brainard's experience. First, when things go wrong, and even when they go right, it pays to reflect upon the factors that might have caused the failure or the success. This gives a better basis for planning operations in the future. How much better it was that Miss Brainard looked to faults in her planning rather than merely held a moralistic discussion on "how we be-

[4] Julia Weber, *My Country School Diary* (New York: Harper and Brothers, 1946).

have when the teacher is out of the room"! Second, these sixth grade children showed that they needed more than a plan for the use of their time when they were on their own; they needed to understand and accept the reason for their being left without teacher supervision so that they might feel they too were helping, even though not in the flower-arranging group. It is possible that children might reach the point where such careful planning and full explanation would be unnecessary, but Miss Brainard's children had not had long experience in assuming responsibility for themselves.

An entry in the diary of the following day shows that Miss Brainard did not leave the matter with scolding herself and making resolutions for the future.

After yesterday's experience, we decided one thing we needed to do was to have some practice in playing games by ourselves without a teacher in charge. We divided into teams. One team was to organize and play its game independent of any help from me. (They had selected the game before leaving the room and knew the order for their turns, but they had to select their play space, arrange their circle, and start their game.)

I worked with the other team on a game they should be able to play hereafter by themselves. (I'm hoping too that some of these games will be organized and played by the children before school when we seem to have so many complaints from the playground. Much of the trouble seems to be that the children don't know what to do, so they resort to teasing.)

The plan worked wonderfully. The children who played by themselves were justly proud of their achievement. They had had a good time and everyone had several turns.

Here again, Miss Brainard's good sense is evident. Planning conduct did not consist of confessions and promises. The group analyzed one cause of the difficulty and planned to remedy it. In other words, they set about training themselves for self-leadership in group games.

Planning to Meet a Danger

Miss Potter discovered that her fourth grade had a concern which planning together might help. The subject of recent murders of children in the city was brought up when news events were being discussed. Many of the children seemed puzzled and a little alarmed, and several asked what they should do. The teacher was helped by an F.B.I. broadcast asking teachers and parents to advise children of precautions they might take to protect themselves. Miss

Potter decided to discuss the matter with the children. This is how the discussion proceeded.

> We set up a plan of conduct for safety and decided that it was best at all times to play in groups of three or more, and to be sure that parents were always informed of children's whereabouts. It was further decided that at no time should any of the children accept money or candy from strangers or go off to assist strangers in search of "lost articles" or accept a ride in a car.
>
> The children agreed that it would not be wise to go with strangers who might tell them that their parents or friends wanted them and that they were to be accompanied by the stranger. They also agreed that at any time when they might be molested or when any person behaved in a peculiar or indecent manner in their presence, they would report it to their parents or teacher and seek immediate aid of nearby policemen or storekeepers in their neighborhoods in emergencies.

Even though this discussion may have been highly directed by the teacher, the children were helped to have a clear plan of action for their own safety.

Anticipatory Role-Playing

Planning how to operate in an anticipated situation may be facilitated by role-playing. Miss Van Alsten found this a useful way to help her third grade children check in advance on their ability to handle the problems that would arise in connection with a tea they had planned for their mothers. The teacher's diary account reads:

> Time which had been set aside for English was devoted to reading in the English books how to make introductions. We then had role-playing to show how they would greet their mothers when they came to the door, how they would lead them to the name-tag committee to have their names pinned on them, then how they would introduce their mothers to me and finally take them to a chair and introduce them to the person sitting next to them before getting them tea and cake.

On the following day Miss Van Alsten's children checked on their plans carefully and further tested them with additional role-playing.

> This was the big day for the children. Before school closed for the morning session the children held a short meeting for final checks on what was done and what still needed to be done. Virginia wanted to make sure that the introductions would be made correctly, so as the name tags were finished they were placed on my desk. The children then put them in alphabetical order so that they could get them quickly. I moved my desk by the door and Virginia stood by it as she would do

in the afternoon. Two other children volunteered to help "play" the introductions. One played herself and the other played her mother. I was included in this role-playing as myself.

The little girl introduced her "play" mother to Virginia, who hunted up that name tag. After Virginia had carefully pinned this on, the little girl brought her "mother" to me and introduced her, then showed her to her seat. Some children giggled, but the idea was well portrayed. The meeting was closed with last-minute reminders given in excited tones.

Testing plans in advance is a technique of cooperative planning that is well worth while in helping pupils to learn.

PLANNING TO MAINTAIN FRIENDLY RELATIONS

Teachers cannot take it for granted that children and youth will always be spontaneously thoughtful and helpful. Experience in working out ways by which a group may show consideration pays dividends.

Keeping in Touch with Absentees

Planning to keep in touch with children who must be absent from a group for some time gives a splendid opportunity for developing friendly feelings. Miss Orson has a story to tell of experiences of her kindergarten children that really is four stories in one. "The carry-over from one experience to the other has been remarkable," the teacher writes. In her account Miss Orson shows well the kind of planning five-year-olds can do when thinking of things they could do for others.

Kindergarten Children Learn Generosity

A. It began when Freddy became ill with rheumatic fever and left school. The children's curiosity led them to ask, "Where is Freddy? Why is he in the hospital? What will they do to him?" We discussed these matters, stressing the good care and fun which the doctors and nurses give to sick children.

The teacher went to visit Freddy in the hospital and told the children what his room and new playmates were like.

The children wanted to help Freddy to get well and several suggestions were made. The final decision lay between buying a book or making a book. It was agreed that those who wished to do so would bring a few cents to school to buy a book and, whether they brought money or not, all would help to make scrapbooks for Freddy. These included original drawings, pictures from magazines, and the children's stories about the pictures. As there are no stores in the area which could be visited as a group, the teacher offered to buy the kind of book the children had decided on.

At Christmas time we made plans to play Santa for Freddy. Good toys were brought from home and wrapped in gay paper. We had so many (some duplicates) that we decided to send some to Freddy and the rest to his hospital friends.

B. In the spring, James fell from a tractor and broke his leg. Again the children consulted their piggy banks and toy shelves and sent gifts with personal letters to James. This experience was highlighted by the increased independence in making suggestions and decisions and a finer appreciation of the plight of a child confined to the use of his hands. Their gifts were chosen for "looking at, listening to, and holding."

C. We had a siege of mumps, and as a result Lidy lost her hearing. For several weeks there was a question whether or not she would return to school. Again, the children, more spontaneously even than before, said, "What can we do for Lidy?" The types of things a girl could enjoy using by herself were considered. Someone suggested a doll's house, so a carton, paint, cloth, wood, thread, and glue were assembled.

In a few days' time, although Lidy was about to return, the house was ready. We gave it to her to show her we understood. It was a proud little girl who carried a new doll's house home that day.

D. At the last P.T.A. meeting of the year the kindergarten won the dollar reward for having the most parents present. The next day the teacher explained the situation and said simply, "What do you want to do with your dollar?" Without further comment the children came forth with the following suggestions:

Buy something that we can all use (a book, toy, or plant).

Buy a new toy for Lidy, Freddy, or James.

Buy refreshments for our mothers to eat at our program.

Send the money to hungry children in Europe.

What a thrill! Not one selfish suggestion in the lot! The class talked about their ideas for a few moments and then voted. The majority voted for the fourth suggestion and the teacher raised the question, "To whom will our money go? We could send it to a group of children like ourselves or to one child." Juliette said that her mother has friends in France with a little girl Juliette's age. Could we send it to Arlette? the children wanted to know. The teacher explained how CARE packages are sent and told the children that she would add to their money if they wished to send a package to Arlette.

Miss Orson concludes by saying, "I feel that the children learned several social concepts and skills through these experiences: sympathy for infirmities of others, understanding of the problems which invalids face, understanding the role of doctors, nurses, and hospitals, sharing one's own blessings, and holding discussions and reaching conclusions and decisions."

Planning thoughtfully for others, as Miss Orson's children did, surely can be expected to increase understanding of how others feel and appropriate ways to be kind to them. Some teachers give their groups opportunity to plan together ways of keeping in touch with a member who is to be absent for some time because of travel. Plans often include ways for the traveler to get the most out of his trip and to contribute to the group upon his return. One third and fourth grade group gave these suggestions to a classmate who was leaving on a trip to Florida: (1) Write a diary. (2) Make a map of your route. (3) Watch for interesting things. (4) Write letters. (5) Bring back souvenirs. Such planning promotes group solidarity and makes it easier for the absent member to find his place in the group upon his return.

Groups may also plan to receive an absentee back into the class in such a way that he will quickly feel part of things again. For example, Miss Rezny's sixth grade followed the suggestion of one of their classmates and appointed three children to inform absentees about work missed.

There is similar value for building group solidarity and thoughtfulness toward others in the planning of a farewell party or some special attention for a child who is moving away and leaving the school. Planning correspondence with the child after he is established in a new school is another opportunity that should not be missed in building friendly relations with people other than those one meets frequently face to face.

Planning Friendly Relations with Adults

Giving some attention to the problem of relations of pupils with substitute teachers is an opportunity that should be cultivated in all schools. Miss Murphy, a fourth grade teacher, had such an opportunity thrust upon her one day.

> I was out of school one day and on my return asked a few questions about the work covered the day before so that I would know where to pick up. Volunteers told me what had been done in reading, arithmetic, and so on, and we proceeded to begin the day.
>
> Suddenly someone said, "Miss Murphy, we had a little trouble yesterday." At that snickers started, grins appeared, and all of a sudden everyone began to tell me of the "fun" they had had. From it all, I gathered that the poor substitute had put in a terrible day.
>
> I closed my book, settled back, and said, "Want to talk about it awhile?" More tales, and finally I said, "Well, how do you feel about

it today?" Silence, then a few weak murmurs of "Ashamed." One child said he thought we should write a letter and apologize.

"No," said another, "that would make us feel silly and embarrassed."

"We *should* feel silly and embarrassed because we made her feel silly yesterday, and if we don't do anything about it she will think we act that way all the time and that will make Miss Murphy feel embarrassed." Richard was very positive about this need for action so I turned the group over to him.

After a long discussion, during which the chairmanship changed several times (while I sat back, listened, and said nothing), it was finally decided unanimously that we should compose a group letter and all sign our names to it. I wrote at the board as they dictated. Brains were racked to select the words and phrases that would express just what they wanted to say. Finally it met the approval of all.

The teacher states that this activity took from 9:15 to 2:00 with time out for assembly and lunch. The children, aware that the day's work had been ignored, suggested that the teacher "count the letter for English and writing so we really aren't missing *everything*." Is it worth the time taken, the teacher asks herself?

As for concrete results, I won't know until the next time the children are faced with a substitute. From other aspects, I think the affair was highly successful. For one thing, it is the first time we have ever had a discussion that was truly handled by the class. I was extremely happy to see my quartet of mischief-makers take an active part in atoning for their "sins."

The unanimous consent gained on several points that started out in violent discord thrilled me. In respect for leadership, cooperation, and listening to the person who has the floor, they made huge strides.

A teacher does not always know when he is to be absent, but he can prepare the way for better experiences with substitutes in two ways. He can make sure that children have had a share in planning for their education and can carry on independently and help the substitute be effective. He can also lay plans with the children for pleasant dealings with any adult who is called upon to guide them, and he can help them to evaluate such an experience afterward. Role-playing to anticipate situations and to relive an experience would be useful discussion aids in such an undertaking.

Mrs. Gates used the approaching Christmas season to help her third grade children plan thoughtful behavior toward adults. A running record of part of the discussion shows also the way in which this teacher received and made positive use of the contributions of each child.

TEACHER. How can we help others at Christmas time?

CHILD. Saying "Excuse me."

TEACHER. Yes, being courteous. You know Harry almost always says "Excuse me."

CHILD. Seeing paper and picking it up for Miss R. [the principal].

TEACHER. That's part of Christmas, isn't it? Now there is someone who has been here only two or three weeks.

CHILD. Janitors.

TEACHER. They are here all the time, but how could you help them?

After the child had answered, the teacher went back to the other question about "someone who has been here only two or three weeks."

CHILD. The painters.

TEACHER. What kind of Christmas could we give them?

MICHAEL. Don't get yourself all painted up.

REID. Stay away from the boards the painters stand on.

TEACHER. Do smiles help?

It may be noted that Mrs. Gates's children were thinking in terms of thoughtful behavior rather than material gifts.

Studying Others' Feelings Through Role-Playing

An excellent way of helping young people understand the feelings of others is the role-playing technique already referred to.[5] Mrs. Uvak, a fourth grade teacher, tells how she was prompted to try role-playing one day when she had ridden on a bus used by many of the children coming to school. She found that the children rushed for seats before adults could get on and were rowdy besides.

We talked about this in our class. We decided to "play it out" and had certain children take parts of adults and of children. We played the wrong way to do it. We asked the "adults" to try to "feel" how adults feel when being pushed around and to tell the others how they felt. Then we did it the right way. The children enjoyed this acting and I believe it has done some good.

Mrs. Banning reports the use of role-playing as a basis for discussing all sorts of situations in which her fourth grade children are involved.

Not only have we used role-playing for occurrences in the schoolroom, but we have used it in discussing reports received from the buses, on the streets, and at the corner store. Yesterday I introduced it in our Mothers' Club. Children and parents seem to get a different view of a scene after seeing it acted and they realize that often, if we could see

[5] See page 69

ourselves, we would make an already bad situation better instead of worse.

Miss Radcliffe, an elementary school principal, gives a rather full report on the process of role-playing used in her school after a program, carefully prepared for their mothers by sixth graders, was marred by the antics of a few boys.

> The chairman acted the part of his mother, another child the teacher, another me, another the music teacher (who had just assigned the principal part of the Christmas play to the chairman). Other children re-enacted enough of the program for the class to recapture the feeling of the thing. After the re-enactment, the answers to my questions, "How did you feel as so and so?" indicated that the children had had a good many feelings of the people they had played.
>
> scotty. I was absent Friday. Just now, as my mother, I thought it was pretty silly.
>
> carmen. As my mother I did not feel anything.
>
> antoinette. Well, I looked around at his mother the day he gave his speech. She was smiling. She felt something.
>
> mary. As the teacher I was nervous and embarrassed.
>
> frank. As the music teacher I could not see Frank.
>
> miss radcliffe. But you knew what Frank was doing. What did you think about the others? The chairman, for instance?
>
> frank. I could not see Frank from where I sat. ("Emotional block," Miss Radcliffe notes in her record.)
>
> chairman. I did not want to admit it, but Friday afternoon my mother shot me a look and made me straighten up.
>
> tommy. I think the chairman should not have been fooling before the program started. He should have been thinking of his part and getting ready.
>
> eleanor. As my mother I could see what was going on and it bothered me. I forgot to listen to the speaker.
>
> mary. Antoinette certainly makes a good actress. She played the chairman very well.
>
> mary c. When I pretend I'm my mother it makes me angry to see people act smart.

Unfortunately, Miss Radcliffe's record ends without giving information on results of the role-playing. However, she has made it clear that role-playing is an important technique in cooperative planning for better human relationships. Through this technique, people have an opportunity to develop greater understanding of the effect of their actions on their relationships with those about them, and the teacher is given a new basis for understanding his pupils.

Mrs. Washington reports a use of role-playing to help her twelve-year-old children understand the points of view of people of other races.

> One day a boy related how a white man and a Negro man got into an argument relative to the dividing line between two farms. The white man struck the Negro first. A fight followed. To make a long story short, John, another boy in class, said that this Negro should have gone home, got his gun, and killed the offender. The majority of the class disagreed.
>
> I allowed free discussion. One of the questions brought up by the members of the class was: What would be the result if there were shooting and killing every time there was an argument between two people? "Negroes should not deal with white people in their stores," said Tom. A friendly debate ensued with children who were in favor of both sides each trying to show that the other was wrong.

Mrs. Washington then proposed that they imagine they were living in a community and were seeing what would happen if they could not get along together. Some took the part of Negroes and some of whites. The teacher summarizes the discussion as follows:

> Those who were acting as Negroes were convinced that they were dependent upon whites for many things, and those who were acting as whites were convinced that they too needed the Negro to help carry on their business and other activities. They all "got it off their chests." Then they were in a frame of mind to admit that all people must live and work harmoniously together; that they must share and cooperate, have self-control and ability to make intelligent decisions; that they must face reality and have initiative. They realized the importance of being neighborly and settling arguments legally, for nothing is gained by physical fighting.

One of the values of role-playing is the quality of the discussion it provokes. People look at other people and their problems differently after they have tried to put themselves in another's place.

A rather elaborate and long-term example of experiencing the role of another person is offered by Miss Rye, who reports the follow-up of an astounding statement of one of the older boys in her school. When the class was asked, "What do you really have fun doing?" this boy said, "Do you really want to know? Well, we have fun going into people's backyards and taking tomatoes off the vine. Sometimes we eat them; other times we just throw them at each other."

"Well, I'd asked for it," Miss Rye comments. She goes on to relate how she interested this fifth grade group in a tomato-growing project. In the fall they were to bring back reports of the cultivation, growth, and final production of the tomatoes. The teacher concludes:

In September what experiences were shared! Some experiences were very similar to those that had been encountered the year before by their neighbors. A much richer discussion of respect for another's property ensued. The children had come to understand what lies behind the appearance of a tomato upon a vine. Visits in the community revealed the fact that the children had turned to more desirable play activities.

Attempts to help pupils be more thoughtful of others are more likely to succeed if these young people can take the place of the other fellow and learn how *he feels*.

CONCLUSION

It is sometimes necessary and desirable to make general plans for conduct. Dismissal procedures, appropriate conduct in an assembly, ways of working together in an art room—such matters have to be worked out and understood by all. Agreements have to be reviewed occasionally as someone forgets or is thoughtless. This type of planning easily degenerates into empty verbalization, however, and should be used sparingly.

It seems preferable to anticipate as far as possible the kind of behavior that will be required in particular situations and to help young people make specific plans for such behavior. Planning on location and anticipatory role-playing are aids in increasing the effectiveness of such resolutions for better behavior in the future. This kind of planning will reduce but not eliminate the difficulties that all groups encounter as members have misunderstandings. Planning to settle difficulties in such a way that they may be avoided in the future is another responsibility of the school. Here it seems best to avoid dealing in personalities and instead to concentrate on the general type of problem illustrated by the occurrence. It is important to give interested parties a chance to give their view of the affair under consideration and then to work out a constructive plan to better conditions in the future. All parties to the discussion should leave with a feeling of commitment to an improved way of operating.

Another important responsibility of the teacher is to help young people to make all plans in terms of the best interests of the individuals affected.

CHAPTER V

Planning Studies

AN ESPECIALLY useful opportunity for learning cooperative procedures in schools is to plan extended or intensive studies going beyond the information possessed by members of the group at the moment. A study may have as its purpose the furthering of understanding of the group on some topic or issue, or it may be designed to prepare the group to solve some problem requiring intelligent action.

Pupil participation in mapping out and following through on a study is commonly misunderstood. Some persons, believing that this inevitably includes pupil selection of what is to be studied, voice disapproval of cooperative procedures in schools on the grounds that learners are not qualified to make such decisions.

From the variety of illustrations presented in Part One of this report, it should be clear that even if pupils are given no chance at all to plan in relation to areas of study in the curriculum, many other opportunities for use of cooperative procedures remain at the disposal of teacher and class. Furthermore, as this particular chapter demonstrates, there is much room for young people to plan studies even though they and their teacher may be operating within rather fixed course of study limits. If on some occasions the pupils can have the additional experience of choosing freely what they will investigate, that is all to the good and will give them a valuable opportunity to consider the many factors that must be taken into account in curriculum planning—timeliness and significance of the study, suitability for their own group, feasibility from the standpoint of resources for learning.

The teacher working in a departmental setup will find that cooperative planning of studies offers him the best opportunity to capitalize on the drive and increased understanding that come when pupils are learning cooperatively. Cooperative learning is a special application of the process of cooperative planning. It involves working together to set learning goals, to find means of reaching goals, to pool findings, and to evaluate and use results. A teacher of a subject may not feel that he can use cooperative procedures to any great extent, especially at first. He may wish to start by holding some orienting discussions as to the value of the subject and the nature of its discipline, and he may help the pupils to explore together the textbook and other materials they will be using. These may be steps toward fuller participation in planning studies later on.

This chapter is divided into two parts: (1) planning within the limits of a course of study or subject and (2) cooperative learning outside a course of study or similar limitations. In the examples given in each section pupils are seen planning what they will find out about a given topic or problem, what resources they will use, who will investigate what, how much they will accomplish in a given length of time, and how they will share information. There are illustrations of general, long-range planning and of specific, short-term planning.

PLANNING WITHIN LIMITS OF SUBJECT AND COURSES OF STUDY

Many teachers find it necessary to confine pupil-teacher planning of studies to limits imposed by a course of study or by the boundaries of a particular subject. Still, these teachers find it possible to utilize the power and drive that come from group consideration of the most fruitful ways of meeting requirements.

Sixth Grade Helps Plan Social Studies and Arithmetic

Three entries in Miss Rezny's diary for early fall show how she and her children found room for cooperative planning within the limits of the course of study. They provided for individual choice.

We are working on chosen topics about primitive man, trying to do things of interest to the individual, yet keeping within the limits of the course of study as we are expected to do.

They decided how they would study a country and how they would tie their study with modern times.

The children have decided to study Egypt by topics, this time not only learning about ancient times, but comparing what news there is about the topic *today*. Arthur's Aunt Mollie was there years ago. He is going to find out if she will tell us about her visit.

They took responsibility for making their arithmetic more meaningful.

> We have been making up our own examples in arithmetic, using newspaper ads, scores, etc. Children seem to be interested, have been building a bulletin board around them.

Planning to Learn in the Area of Science

It is common practice for teachers to encourage children to begin a study by listing the information they would like to have. As Mrs. Kingsley's third grade children were about to begin a study of birds, she asked them to decide first how they would like to list their questions. The children suggested individual lists, a list on the board, a list on tagboard to be checked off as they found answers. The winning proposal was the listing on tagboard of the important things the children wanted to know.

When the group started to contribute questions, it was not long before the list had grown to thirty items, including such topics as kinds of nests, how birds fly, what kinds of birds lay eggs in water, what are the danger signals of birds, how and where they get their food, and why is the owl so wise. The kinds of questions asked show considerable previous knowledge of birds, which raises a nice point. The children might be merely turning into questions facts already known. On the other hand, they have to have some background or do some exploring of a subject before they know the best questions to ask. Also the questions one individual asks may lead to a new interest for another.

An excerpt from the question-gathering process will show that Mrs. Kingsley was trying to help the children be thoughtful in phrasing their questions.

> JOHN (giving the first suggestion). Nests.
> TEACHER. Will you explain that a little more?
> John discusses his point further.
> TEACHER. How do you want us to word that?
> JOHN. Kinds of nests and where they build them.
> This is written down as No. 1.
> RONALD. Kinds of food. (Written down as No. 2.)
> KENDALL. How they build their nests.
> TEACHER (pointing to No. 1). Is this the same? Can you think of another suggestion?
> KENDALL. Kinds of birds.
> TEACHER. Do you mean we should be able to name them or how to tell them? Can someone help him?

CHILD. Ways of telling birds. (Written down as No. 3.)
CHARLES. Materials used in building. (Written down as No. 4.)
JOHN. Where they live.
TEACHER. You'll have to make that a little clearer.
JOHN. North or South Pole . . .
RONNIE. Number four is like number one.
TEACHER. We'll have to see later if there is overlapping.

After thirty questions had been gathered Mrs. Kingsley turned the attention of the group to the problem of overlapping, which gave Ronnie a chance to make his point again. Throughout this discussion, she made children feel comfortable about participating. Most of her own contributions were questions turned back to the group.

As Mr. Tanner was beginning a study of insects with a fifth grade group, he gave a brief talk, then held an exploratory discussion before asking the children to make certain decisions about their study. The first decision was that since the children could not study all insects, they would limit themselves to a list of seven insects proposed by Leslie. The teacher then said, "Perhaps there are some questions in your minds about these insects that you would like answered. If so, I'll write them on the board." Beverly and Willie each gave one and Tommy added five more at once—all dealing with food, protection, friendliness to man and the like. Edward added his which came out of an earlier argument. "Do grasshoppers spit tobacco?" The teacher's record shows how that day's planning was completed.

TEACHER. Now we have a list of insects we would like to study and certain questions we want answered. What do you think is the best way for us to study them? Shall we have different committees study about different insects and report to the class or shall we all study as nearly as possible the same insect or insects? Maybe you have some other suggestions.
BETTY H. Mr. Tanner, I think we would learn more if we all studied about the same insects together.
EDWARD. Yes, Mr. Tanner, let's study about ants first.
TEACHER. If it is agreeable with the class we will become familiar with the books on the back table tomorrow and begin our study of insects (ants first) on the day after tomorrow.

Had Mr. Tanner been a little more experienced with cooperative planning, he would not just have let Leslie list the insects he wanted to study and then assumed that these were the choice of the entire group, nor would he have treated Betty's and Edward's proposals as group decisions. Furthermore, he would have encouraged Tommy to let someone else have a chance to propose some questions. However, he served a useful function when he made sure the children had a background for planning and when he divided the discussion into parts —insects to be studied, questions to be answered, and procedure.

A record of observation in Miss McNulty's fifth grade illustrates how a rather loosely organized, free exploration of many possibilities in a study of the solar system can serve as a preliminary kind of planning. Such a discussion has value, but it may lead to poor habits in group planning if it is not followed by more exact planning at the earliest opportunity.

In the course of the discussion these suggestions were given by various children, with three pupil secretaries at work taking notes.

> PAT. We could draw a mural of the solar system and put names on. . . .
>
> NORMA. It would be nice if we could all make a booklet. . . .
>
> JOHN. If we work everyday we get more in the habit than when we work now and then. . . .
>
> THOMAS. I would like to get the name and address of an astronomer, write and ask him questions you don't know anything about. . . .
>
> JANE. We could get pictures.
>
> THOMAS. We might see if we could see some different signs in the stars that we haven't read about. . . .
>
> JIM. I am going by plane this week end. If I had binoculars I could get a better look at the stars. . . .
>
> JACK. We could put something in the P.T.A. paper. . . .
>
> CHARLES. We could make a lot of stuff, have the sun in the center, have things fixed to turn. . . .
>
> ALVIN. I could bring some films to school. . . .
>
> ARNOLD. I could bring puppet string like when I was in first grade we made many pictures. Maybe we could do that. . . .
>
> HARRY. We could make fog and show what scientists see. . . .

The complete running record would show that, for the most part, these suggestions were not even picked up for discussion, to say nothing of their being adopted. There was considerable discussion of the booklet idea, for the children returned to it several times even after the teacher suggested turning to something else. There was some questioning also as to how to make a model of the solar system. But Miss McNulty left unchallenged such unclear statements as those of Arnold and Harry, and she raised no question about Jim's being able to see the stars better from a plane. Without clinching any decisions, she closed the discussion abruptly with Harry's suggestion about fog. A desirable next step would have been to have the secretaries organize their notes and bring back a list of suggestions so that the group might evaluate them and decide which ones they would carry out.[1] However, Miss McNulty encouraged children to contribute freely in the group, and this procedure for opening up a new study is a refreshing change from the almost stereotyped way in which groups often begin discussions—producing an impressive list of questions about which no one is greatly excited.

In all three of these examples there is a lack of planning to experiment and test hypotheses, which is an experience to which the area of science especially should lend itself.

Planning to Learn in the Area of Social Studies

When Miss Rademacher was introducing a new unit on Mexico, she too gathered questions from her fifth grade children. They were the stock kind that were easy to put into an outline doing justice to any textbook: *History,* with subheads *Explorers, Settlers, Growth; People,* with subheads *Religion, Sports, Homes, Customs; Climate; Land; Government; Transportation; Products; Inventions; Location; Occupations; Trade; Communication.* After gathering these suggestions and organizing them logically, the teacher asked the group where they would find answers to these questions. A list of seventeen sources was quickly suggested, including such items as interviews, newspapers, travel bureaus, souvenirs, encyclopedias, geography books, and maps. The next steps, the children replied when asked, were to be "study" and "divide into groups." The children seemed to be going through some familiar steps and the questions suggested for investigation seemed to the observer not very genuine. The teacher listed with each question the name of the questioner, which may have prompted some to produce a question merely to earn this recognition. It is so easy to fall into meaningless routines in planning a study that teachers should be on the lookout for ways of varying procedures and of making plans that grow out of real interests and concerns.

A report from Mrs. Percival shows the many opportunities she found for students in her junior high school English—social studies class to plan for their learning even though there were course of study requirements to be considered. In the following outline she relates the steps taken in choosing the topic of investigation and deciding on sources of information and procedures of study.

[1] For a record of such a secretaries' meeting held at the observer's suggestion, see pages 392 ff.

I. Arriving at the topic to be studied by:
   A. Asking children which of the remaining areas of man's life they wished to explore next
   B. Agreeing on transportation
II. Discussing possible angles of approach and means of securing information
III. Deciding to search for "ads" in magazines; locating addresses in phone directories, visiting all possible travel information bureaus, checking files in classroom and library, in order to obtain information
IV. Writing letters requesting information and materials
V. Setting up reasons for studying transportation, such as:
   A. Gaining an understanding of the development of transportation through the ages
   B. Learning the influence of natural resources, geographical barriers upon land and water development
   C. Appreciating the work done by pioneers in transportational development
   D. Realizing the value or the influence of railroads upon the development of our early history
   E. Noting the use of the simple tools as means of aiding in transportation in earlier times
   F. Following the progress made in transportation by men and machines to note the effect of the Machine Age on transportation
   G. Learning different countries and making studies and comparisons of their modes of life, climate, weather, and effects on their transportation
   H. Discussing reasons for progressive and retarded methods of transportation
   I. Gaining an over-all picture of the importance of all means of transportation in order to develop a better understanding of nations and our shrinking world
VI. Deciding upon the procedure (how to study it) by:
   A. Hearing many children submit ideas
   B. Listing five that seemed most reasonable
   C. Voting on one idea (Majority voted to take an imaginary trip)
VII. Preplanning for the imaginary trip by:
   A. Seeing the need
   B. Deciding how long I can stay
   C. Planning the destination
   D. Seeing all possibilities of travel
   E. Examining the possibilities for:
      1. Time; cost; clothing
      2. Pleasure to be derived; weather
   F. Deciding how to go
   G. Mapping out full plan of trip

    1. Getting tickets, making reservations, passports, visas
    2. Getting checkups, tests, health certificates
    3. Buying appropriate clothing
VIII. The trip
    A. Keeping daily accounts
    B. Writing letters home, to friends
    C. Sending cablegrams, telegrams
    D. Collecting for hobbies
    E. Observing scenery, people, customs, climate, methods of transportation, industries, products, elevation, rainfall, and population

Mrs. Percival's report shows that her pupils chose their area of study from a limited range of choices; they planned means of carrying out the study; and they decided upon the form in which their findings would be reported. The outline does not indicate that the children had the experience of evaluating the worth of their work or of planning to put their results to any particular use. However, it illustrates the many opportunities available for cooperative planning even when choice of studies is limited.[2]

Planning to Learn in the Area of Mathematics

Two teachers in one high school found that even a subject like high school mathematics yields opportunities for pupil-teacher planning. Many of the things they tried could be applied to any subject.

Mr. Rufus describes his way of operating with his tenth grade class and gives his evaluation of it in the following report.

Problems or projects were suggested by members of the class. Those suggestions which contained enough mathematical operations to be worth attempting were listed on the blackboard. We then considered the list and after a period of discussion selected the problems we wished to attempt. Majority vote of the class determined the selection.

Our method of attack on a project was first to divide the projects into logical units of work. Next a group leader for each unit was selected. The leaders then assembled their group by selection of classmates to work with them. Each group headed by its leader proceeded to gather its data. The leaders reported to me for instruction, then passed the help on to members of their groups as needed. After data were gathered, the groups fitted their units together and drew up conclusions as a class.

This method is no cure-all; it is subject to a lot of evils, the same as

[2] For another account of group planning of a unit in social studies, see pages 271–272.

any other. I will say, though, that if one could eliminate the indifferent student, the system is then far superior to the old method.

Miss Fielding, another mathematics teacher in Mr. Rufus' school, used even more cooperative procedures. Her detailed account shows the many opportunities she made available for her students during one semester.

I tried to encourage and to allow more opportunity for student participation in planning and doing work this last semester than I had ever done before. My five classes were tenth grade general mathematics, tenth grade plane geometry, and three sections of eleventh grade business arithmetic.

Whether the students liked this way of working or not depended upon individuals. Some preferred to be told what to do, but the leaders and, in fact, a large majority of students have seemed to appreciate the chance to make suggestions to the group and to do more individual planning too. The following are some ways that have been attempted in my classes:

1. Planning the arrangement of furniture as far as possible.
2. Deciding where and how to keep all material that will aid in the work.
3. Volunteering to assist in making out absence slips. (I check these.)
4. Selecting a host or hostess for the room for a short period of time.
5. Bringing material for use in class and for the bulletin boards.
6. Determining where to commence at the beginning of the semester. The Lee Clark test was taken.
7. Deciding upon certain policies concerning assignments, correction, keeping notebooks, and recording marks, as indicated by a survey we made.
8. Deciding what is fair in general as to marks in mathematics.
9. Planning by groups when they are ready to advance to new topics. (I guide mostly in long-range planning and order of topics.)
10. Deciding when tests are needed. (They frequently impose tests upon themselves.)
11. Doing numerous outside activities, such as measuring the playground by the building in order to help visualize an acre of ground, etc.
12. Having opportunity to discuss likes and dislikes and the fairness of final examinations.
13. Suggesting sources of information and following them up.
14. Naming situations to be investigated, that is, helping to build the course and make it more interesting and more meaningful.

About the same type of pupil-teacher planning was attempted in each group, especially regarding procedures, planning and content of the course, the order of topics for consideration, number and length of assignments, choice as to the type and amount of work that individuals hoped to accomplish weekly. This was planned with me. I encouraged no weekend assignments at all.

However, the class in general mathematics used no text and we built our own course based on their own findings. They made personal contacts with people engaged in various occupations in the community.

This was all planned carefully and the group organized with a secretary who recorded with whom each made an appointment, and also recorded a summary of the final report of each one. In a few cases, it was necessary for the visit to be made in school time. If the teacher consented, it was permitted. After the contact was made, a report was submitted by each one. It was then discussed.

The success of Miss Fielding's venture may be judged somewhat by the quality of the discussion her students carried on one day in March before a group of visitors including the principal, the head of the mathematics department, a history teacher, and an outside observer.

The room was attractive with growing plants on window sills and pictures appropriate to the season. On the rear bulletin board there were charts showing uses of mathematics, bank and insurance forms, and graphs of various kinds. The class began with Marie, the hostess, introducing the visitors and turning the meeting over to Gordon, the chairman. After Doris presented a summary of the work done the previous semester, Mark reported the work of the present semester. A record of what transpired during the following class period will make clearer the procedure Miss Fielding has described briefly in her account.

Record	*Analysis*
CHAIRMAN. This week we have been working on insurance brokers. Friday is the time to plan ahead. Is anyone ready for a test? (No one.) Then there will be no test on Monday. Since we have a committee that has planned rather far ahead, we know what we are going to do. Any questions from a chairman of a committee? (Pause, no answer.)	
The teacher urges the same question. The chairman of the investment committee asks about a trip to the bank.	No doubt the teacher knew that it would take a little more courage than usual to speak up on this day.
CHAIRMAN. Shall we go to the bank before or after our study?	

Record   *Analysis*

A boy and a girl give contrary
views.

CHAIRMAN (of another committee). Does anyone know the cheap-
est way to get farm equipment?

GIRL. I saw in the paper last
night about an auction. I think
that would be a good way.

TEACHER. Do you mean used or
new?

BOY. Used.

TEACHER. It would make a difference in what you would have to
invest.

Another boy suggests government surplus property.

BOY. Sales come in the spring.

TEACHER. Is that your problem,
how to equip a farm? If it were
new equipment, where could you
get information?

CHAIRMAN. I don't think you can
get anything new now.

TEACHER. I think you are quite
right. I was talking with a man
from the farm implement factory.
He said they were turning away
men because they have no material.
I think the *Farm Journal* might
have information.

BOY. The Farm Bureau might
help.

BOY. You are not going to find
plows in war surplus.

BOY. You can get plows and discs
now. It is tractors and threshers
and big machines you can't get.

BOY. I don't believe the average
farmer uses these machines. He has
his threshing done. He has just
simple machines.

CHAIRMAN. He can hire a combine and have it done in one operation.

BOY. Yes, there are people who
just go around like hay balers.

The chairman is not quite skillful
enough to urge that the previous
question be answered before the
new question is considered. Group
membership skill has not been developed to the point where a new
question will be held until it is time
to introduce it, or where, if one
member does exercise poor judgment, another member will suggest
holding the question in reserve.

Teacher helps the group (or the
visitors, at any rate) to see the
background out of which the question of cheap equipment was raised.

The teacher contributes as any
group member might. Throughout
this record there is free, circular
discussion with teacher, chairman,
and group members joining in as
they have an idea to add. However,
because the chairman so often takes
the role of a group member, he
soon lands in difficulty.

Record

CHAIRMAN. It is the little machines. You can get all the big machines you want.

BOY. Farmers do not make much. Machines are high.

CHAIRMAN. I find farmers quit farms and work in shops downtown.

BOY. Most of the farm tools are going to other countries.

TEACHER. I wonder if you want to save farming until that committee has done more work?

GIRL. Talking of investment, aren't you doing more than banking?

GIRL. I said "just banking" but I meant insurance and all that. We have those books back there. We want to find out more.

TEACHER. Shall we go to the bank or have a man come here?

BOY. He could talk to all of us.

GIRL. We couldn't see them doing their work, using adding machines and so forth.

BOY. We can get more information if the banker talks to you as a group.

BOY. We can get questions, see what we want to find out, make a big list of them, and have two people get down the answers.

Another boy mentions a movie that would show them everything.

CHAIRMAN. We would have to go at different times or we could not all see.

BOY. The movie might not be up to date.

TEACHER. May I express this? Last semester we went to the bank first for over-all ideas. Then we had a banker come up here. Do you like that idea? How many would like to go instead of sending a few? (Four or five hands.) Maybe we

Analysis

Notice that the chairman has stepped out of his role and has been prolonging a rather scattered discussion, with many statements made that are not examined and do not clearly contribute to answering the original question.

After giving the chairman plenty of time to sense what is happening, the teacher raises a question which causes a shift in the discussion.

Teacher returns to the problem that had been left unsolved.

Another illustration of the group's lack of skill in finishing one point before introducing another. Notice the order of discussion: trip to the bank—movie as a substitute—trip—movie—trip.

The teacher is serving the function here of contributing from her previous experience. She helps the group see the choices available, but she does not press them to follow the plan of a former class.

Record

had better leave that until the committee has done more study.

CHAIRMAN. Any other questions?

Lyle, chairman of the renters
committee, asks the chairman to
allow time for their panel.

CHAIRMAN. I think we better
stop this now because we have a
group with Lyle and Marie as co-
chairmen who have the floor for the
next ten or fifteen minutes. . . .

Nine students then came up for a panel for which extra chairs had
been provided ahead of time. One girl went to the board to serve as
secretary and wrote headings for two columns: "Owners," "Renters."
As points were made for either side she listed them. This device helped
the audience to follow the discussion. After some minutes of debate,
the chairman of the homeowners group intervened:

Record	*Analysis*
MARIE. We will have to stop. We have had a good discussion. What can we do to find out more?	Marie shows awareness of need to plan next steps.
CHAIRMAN (Gordon). Find costs of repairs.	
MARIE. We can also have some-one come to talk.	While the rest are suggesting *what* to find out, Marie introduces one suggestion of *how* to find it.
DORIS. Find out the costs of in-vestment.	
CHAIRMAN. Find out how much taxes you have to pay, such as school, and so on.	
BOY. Also insurance.	
TEACHER. Can you talk a little more about how to find out these things?	The teacher steps in to help Marie get an answer to her original question.
BOY. We could make a census of owners and renters.	
BOY. We could see a real estate agent.	
GIRL. We could do some problems in the book.	

Throughout this last discussion the board secretary recorded the
suggestions given for future study. The chairman then suggested
that they stop to give another group time to organize.

Record	*Analysis*
TEACHER. Shall we have a summary?	The teacher's question serves to help the chairman examine the wisdom of turning to a new group.
CHAIRMAN. We have only five minutes, so maybe there is not time for another group to organize. Does Lyle want to do anything more?	
LYLE. You will get assignments for next week.	
MARIE. I don't think we know what kinds of problems we can use.	Marie, the teacher, and Martin all see the importance of more time to plan what assignments the class will carry out in connection with the problems being explored by the homeowners and the renters.
TEACHER. Do we have time to decide what we have to study first?	
MARIE. The costs of home-owning and renting?	
GIRL. How about taxes?	
MARTIN. Why don't we find answers to some of these questions? We can get into deep water.	
CHAIRMAN. I approve that suggestion.	
TEACHER. I like that suggestion of Martin's too. Maybe we'd better take another day to discuss.	The period ends with a plan for the next day.

This record shows a group which is on its way toward greater skill in cooperative learning. Although loose ends were left dangling at the close of the period, the group had a clear impression that there were many leads to follow, that there were numerous ways to follow these leads, and that more specific plans would be made before anyone would be expected to carry out a definite assignment.

The students showed that they accepted responsibility for planning how much they would accomplish, when and how, and that they had well-established procedures for making decisions, dividing responsibility, and keeping the large group informed of developments. The teacher let the students carry out the responsibilities undertaken, coming in just at points where she could help them make necessary decisions.

Eleventh Grade Plans Study of Hygiene and of Occupations

Mr. Rice too found that he could give his students a large share in planning what they would undertake in his courses and how they would proceed to learn. In his diary he describes his customary practice in this regard.

> When I meet with my hygiene classes each year, the beginning weeks are used to plan the year's study under the title of "Health Problems of Society." I try to guide them in their planning, but also try not to dominate. At the end of two weeks this year we had included the following topics: juvenile delinquency, poverty, crime, venereal disease, sex education, etiquette, and vocational information. I think that the above demonstrates that a class, with guidance, will want to talk about topics which are important to society. In many instances they will probably make a wiser selection than many adults.

Mr. Rice also reports how one class took over more detailed planning—the trips which the class would make.

> One of my classes (eleventh grade) planned a unit on occupations. As we were suggesting ways of attacking the problem, one boy mentioned it would be good to make some trips to see how various men did their work. Some boys immediately volunteered ideas:
> 1. Visit father's potato farm
> 2. Visit father's mink ranch
> 3. Visit the post office
> 4. Visit a veterinarian
> 5. Visit a chain grocery store
> 6. Visit mother's nursing home
> 7. Visit automatic-screw machine factory
> 8. Visit a second father's farm
>
> We made all the above-mentioned trips as suggested by the boys. These were the occupations on which eight of the boys had reported. With the help of other students, each one involved arranged the trip (time, transportation and other details) to his father's or employer's place of work. In each case, the parent or employer explained the work adequately, and in some cases the boys did part of the explaining.
>
> While I'd had five trips in mind for the class, the above worked out much better. The whole group was enthusiastic and they learned many things and acquired greater appreciation of various occupations. They benefited from the group planning.

COOPERATIVE LEARNING WITHOUT
COURSE OF STUDY BOUNDS

Teachers who are not confined to a particular subject or subjects, who do not have certain units or other material to cover with pupils, or who feel free to take even occasional excursions outside the course of study can go far in cooperative planning of learning opportunities. In such situations teachers and pupils are free to deal with problems of school and community living. They are free also to pursue a learning experience intensively for a day or two or to give a course of study intermittent attention over a long period of time. Both of these practices are departures from the typical unit of work or the sequence of topics in a textbook.

Studies Initiated by Teachers

When a teacher and children are not made to feel that an area of study, such as community helpers, is the exclusive property of the second grade, they may make useful studies along this line whether they be in first grade or sixth.

First grade children plan a year of social studies. Reference has already been made to the way in which Miss Daly helped her first grade children work out a social studies program for an entire year.[3] Miss Daly has prepared a brief description of one of the studies planned and carried out by her group one year as a result of taking walks around the neighborhood and building a list of community workers whom the children wanted to know more about.

First Grade Studies the Barber Shop

One segment of the child's experience in the community is his periodic visit to the barber shop. We planned to study the barber and the service he renders. Questions were recorded and a visit was made to the barber shop down the street.

Then a desire to build a barber shop (with a beauty parlor attached) was expressed. Together we listed what we would need in our barber shop. I transferred these to a large chart which I illustrated with line drawings to give clues to such words as "barber chair" and "hair drier." Instead of using group time to decide on division of responsibility, the children divided themselves into informal work committees by signing up under the various jobs to be done.

Work was done cooperatively. Equipment was constructed for the barber shop and the beauty parlor adjoining and a price list was posted. Our questions were answered and checked off. Experiences were recorded. Many were illustrated by children's drawings. Original stories were written. (Yes, I have discovered that my first graders *can* do this kind of writing by spring.) The dramatic activities within the barber shop established the obvious health learnings: clean hair, clean fingernails, and haircuts.

Miss Daly's story illustrates the fact that young children do a great deal of their planning in the presence of concrete materials. With the aid of such materials and of trips to get firsthand informa-

[3] See page 26.

tion, they can do a creditable job of planning for cooperative learning.

Sixth grade children plan to learn about peanuts. Often a useful study can grow out of a group experience if the teacher is imaginative enough to see some of the possible educational values inherent in the experience, and if teacher and children are free to spend time on a subject of their choice. Miss Brainard's sixth grade had spent considerable time for two days bagging peanuts for a sale the P.T.A. was holding in their school.[4] The teacher's diary relates how the study was launched.

> We had been doing so much handling peanuts, selling peanuts, counting peanut money, that I asked the children yesterday what they knew about peanuts. They discovered that they knew surprisingly little. They outlined some topics they thought they should look up.
>
> We were in our discussion group and had been talking about the various uses made of peanuts. We were about ready to summarize the work when I was called from the room. I asked Virginia if she would do the writing on the board and asked the group to see if they could summarize in outline form the various uses of the peanut which had been mentioned. It just did my heart good to come back and see how the class had carried on independently. I was out of the room only a very short while, but they had made a very good start. As I entered they were disturbed because someone had mentioned candy as a use of peanuts and Virginia had put it down, but the topic under which it was placed said "Uses of peanut oil." They realized the need of revising the wording of the main topics and the outline was completed as follows with explanatory subheadings: Uses of Peanuts: Peanut oil, Food for people, Food for animals, Other uses.

Sixth grade children plan to learn about nutrition. An excerpt from a running record of a planning session in Miss Long's sixth grade room shows in a more detailed way how a study may be launched. The group had become interested in nutrition after a talk by the school nurse. The day before the record was taken, a boy had offered to bring some white rats "tomorrow." The teacher had headed his proposal off until the group could get ready for the rats. Now the group was planning the preparation needed.

Record	Analysis
The teacher first asks the children what is the purpose of having the rats. They answer that it is for nutritional experiments. The	Teacher makes sure large purpose is clear and that purpose of the day's discussion is understood.

---

[4] For a description of this activity, see pages 186–187.

Record

teacher writes this on the board. The teacher then writes the word "problems" and asks the question, "What problems will we run into?" The teacher records as problems are given:

1. Where will we get a cage?

TEACHER. Shall we solve this now as we go along?

CHILDREN. No, let us get the problems out first.

2. How will we care for the rats over the week end?

CHILD. I can solve that now. We will need to ask about food.

TEACHER. What about the temperature?

They decided to question Mr. Edwards (the custodian) as to how low the temperature gets in their room over the week end. The teacher asks for a volunteer to talk to Mr. Edwards about it.

TEACHER. Anything else?

3. What kind of food?

4. Where are we going to get it?

Teacher says she has another question that she thinks should come next. Children offer, "When to feed them," "How to feed them." Finally the teacher makes it clear that she means money.

5. Question 5 becomes "How are we going to get food?"

CHILD. We ought to have someone responsible for cleaning out the cage.

CHILD. How long are we going to keep them?

The teacher postpones these suggestions to talk more about the food. She tries to get the children to talk about the source of vitamins.

Analysis

Teacher accepts suggestion as given. Teacher makes sure group is agreed on plan of current phase of discussion.

By a question, teacher shows the solution will not be a simple one. Here the group departs from its plan of just getting problems out but quickly goes back to the main activity.

Might it not be better for the teacher to contribute her suggestion just as other group members do rather than cause children to guess what is in her mind?

The teacher has a responsibility for helping children learn to deal with one point at a time during a discussion. She must be sure that

Record   *Analysis*

those making "premature" suggestions will feel comfortable about
having introduced them.

TEACHER. Somebody tell me how   Teacher gives children the op-
to say this about feeding different   portunity to help with wording.
foods.

6. How to feed the rats that we
   wish to grow to be healthy?
   CHILD. Are we going to feed it
with an eyedropper?
   Teacher does not hear and calls   This can happen to anyone under
for another problem. . . .   the stress of leading a discussion.
                              To avoid losing contributions,
                              teachers may help group members
                              learn to take responsibility for re-
                              peating a lost contribution for
                              themselves, or for a fellow member,
                              at a point in the discussion when
                              there is suitable opportunity.

As this discussion went on the teacher gave children chances to
make their own points, checking with them to make sure they understood. Suggestions postponed earlier were given a chance to come in.
The last question, No. 25, was: "How can we get the wisest answers
to these questions about the rats?" This was a good question to promote an intelligent approach to solving the problems raised.

Planning to learn about the Community Chest. Parts of a running
record of a discussion of the Community Chest in Miss Wells's fifth
grade room give further opportunity to study some details of cooperative learning. This record has been analyzed in terms of the role
played by the teacher. The following information was on the board
when the observer entered.

Community Chest Questions   How to Find Out
1. Where does the money go?   1. Read the paper.
2. Why do we give the money?   2. Ask questions.
3. Where is it kept until it is used? 3. Read the posters.
4. How is it used?   4. Listen to the radio.
5. Where do we give the money?   5. Keep your eyes and ears open.
6. How much should we give?   6. Listen to what others say.
7. How much do they want?   7. Talk together.
8. Is it going to be used well?   8. Call up the different agencies.
                                       9. Go to the movies.

10. Call up the Community Chest office.
11. Visit the agencies.
12. Write and ask.
13. Have someone go see them and come back and tell us.

Two mothers were also present. They had been asked to get some information for the children on the agency selected for special study and were on hand to find out what the children specifically wanted of them. After some preliminary discussion of the size of the goal and the uses to which the money in the Community Chest was to be put, planning for the mothers' visit to the agency began.

Record	*Analysis of Teacher's Role*
PARENT. We'd be glad to go to the Goodwill Industries.	
TEACHER. Now what do you want them to find out about that?	Raises question.
CHILD 1. What it is.	Allows free flow of suggestions.
CHILD 2. What it does.	
CHILD 3. How it looks.	
As soon as these suggestions started to come, a child voluntarily went to the board and started recording them.	
CHILD 4. I think that would come under what it does.	
CLAIRE. How they divided the money.	
TEACHER. What do you mean? We know we are talking about the Goodwill Industries. What do we want to know?	Helps child clarify thinking.
CHILD. Where they send it.	
TEACHER. Let's wait until we settle Claire's question. There's a good question we could ask about money. Who can state it?	Helps keep discussion on the track. Helps to get Claire's question in usable form.
CHILD. How does the money help?	
TEACHER. What money?	Raises clarifying question.
The statement finally put down as No. 3 on the board is "How does the Community Chest money help the Goodwill Industries?"	

Record

TEACHER. May I suggest a question that maybe you hadn't thought about? What is an industry?

CHILD. People working.

TEACHER. You know you have to have people working. Would you like to ask a question?

CHILD. Who works for it?

This goes down on the board as No. 4.

TEACHER. There is another question. If it's the Goodwill Industries, what would you like to know?

CHILD. How do they help?

This is added to the list on the board as No. 5.

CHILD. Who they help.

Put down as No. 6.

CHILD. How do we help them?

Put down as No. 7.

Analysis of Teacher's Role

Raises clarifying question.

Helps group formulate question.

Helps group formulate further questions.

Two more items were added after some leading questions by the teacher. To achieve No. 8, "How could we help them?" the teacher had to resort to hinting questions and succeeded in getting the children rather confused. The last item, No. 9, "How they make money," came as the result of a direct and helpful suggestion: "We said the Community Chest pays some institutions some of their money. Would you like to know if the Community Chest pays all of the expenses of the Goodwill Industries? How would you ask it?"

The teacher then gave the children an opportunity to evaluate the list as a whole by suggesting that they "read them all and see how they look." The record continues.

Record

GIRL. It doesn't balance.

TEACHER. Why?

GIRL. The last one isn't a question.

Teacher reads the list: "*What is it?*" "*What* does it do?" etc. Children remake the last item into a question.

CHILD. When will the mothers come [to report]?

Analysis of Teacher's Role

Helps group study its product.

Teacher fails to use this suggestion for needed planning.

Record	*Analysis of Teacher's Role*
TEACHER. What do we want to do tomorrow?	Leads thinking to future planning.
CHILD. Give money.	
TEACHER. If we give money, what do we want to think about?	Leads to future planning.
CHILD. How we get it.	
TEACHER. How *do* we get it?	Encourages suggestions.
Child makes suggestion.	
TEACHER. How else can we get it?	
Another child makes suggestion.	
TEACHER. Any other way? You haven't any of you said you would ask your mothers. (Storm of protest from the children.)	
TEACHER. Perhaps we can talk about this tomorrow and what is in the paper—how they are getting along.	Clinches tomorrow's plans.

In general it may be seen that Miss Wells played a useful role, giving children plenty of chances to do their own thinking, yet striving to enhance the quality of contributions made.

Learning about "Our New Tasks." Excerpts from a second running record from Miss Wells's fifth grade room a month later show the way in which the same group of children approached a very different kind of study, "Our New Tasks," which interestingly enough had grown out of a study of colonial times. Again the record is analyzed in terms of the teacher's role. The following information was on the board when the observer entered.

Discoveries and Inventions That Make New Tasks

1. New World Dangers
   a. New bombs
   b. Jet propulsion
   c. Rocket
   d. Insects
2. New Transportation
   a. Airplanes
   b. Boats and ships
   c. Automobiles
   d. Trains
   e. Busses
   f. Submarines
3. Radar
4. Radio
5. Television
6. New ways of writing
7. Telescope
8. Heating inventions
9. New types of lights
10. Cosmic rays
11. New uses of materials

How These Affect Our Living

1. We go places faster.
2. We go more places all over the world.
3. We get news more quickly from all over the world.
4. We have more dangers.
5. They bring countries more closely together.
6. They give us more things to learn.
7. We have more things to learn.
8. We have new material in different ways.
9. We have a chance for better health.

Our New Tasks

1. Help prevent world dangers
   a. Know about other nations
   b. Understand them
   c. Be friendly with them
   d. Use the atomic energy usefully

2. Learn about the new inventions and discoveries
   a. How they are made
   b. How they are used

The period opened with a rehearsal of a program planned for parents that afternoon. As the last talk was finished one of the boys called attention to the second and third items on the list, "How These Affect Our Living." "Miss Wells," he said, "I believe we shouldn't say those two things the same way." This launched the group on a consideration of their list thus far and on the need for possible additions. The children began a free interchange of opinions on the point raised, and the teacher asked several to state their suggestions. Reference to the record will show how the discussion proceeded.

Record	*Analysis of Teacher's Role*
TEACHER. Is that all we want in our list?	Gives opportunity for further suggestions.
CHILD. I have some more, Miss Wells—learn how the different materials are used.	
(Girl goes to the board and starts recording these suggestions under the heading "Our New Tasks.")	
BOY. "Materials" is spelled wrong.	
TEACHER. How would you spell it?	Pays attention to a suggestion.
He writes on the board "materails."	
TEACHER. Why don't you look it up? It's nice that you notice these words.	Suggests reference to authority. Gives praise.

Record	*Analysis of Teacher's Role*
Boy looks up the word, then with a smile says, "You were right the first time."	
A boy new to the group had trouble seeing why this new item, "Learning how the different materials are used," needed to be in the list when they had No. 11, "New uses of materials," in their first list. The teacher let various children explain it to him until he saw the difference in the two lists.	Encourages pupils to help one another understand.
TEACHER. Look at your list of "How These Affect Our Living" to see if we have any more new tasks.	Helps group turn to source of further ideas.
Item 4 is suggested: "Be careful when going places." Item 5 is suggested: "Keep healthy."	Allows suggestions to flow freely.
Another child suggests: "Keep clean."	
CHILD. We could write a, b, c under "Keep healthy."	
This suggestion is followed. The list becomes:	
a. Keep clean	
b. Eat the right kind of foods	
CHILD. Brush your teeth daily. (This is put down as c.)	
TIFFANY. I should think brushing teeth would be a part of "Keep clean."	
A slight argument develops between two children. Teacher steps in: "Tiffany thinks this way; what do the rest of you think?"	Helps get argument out in the open.
TEACHER. Then what do you want to do about c?	Helps clinch decision.
By common consent it is erased. Children go on listing items.	Allows suggestions to flow freely.
c. Go to bed early.	
d. Get plenty of fresh air.	
e. Go to the dentist twice a year.	
When the suggestion comes to "Dress warmly in winter," the board secretary starts to put it down as No. 6.	

Record	Analysis of Teacher's Role
TEACHER. Use your eyes.	Causes group to think.
ELEANOR. I think "Dress warmly in winter" would go under "Keep healthy." (It is put down as f under No. 5.)	
Teacher suggests that they read through the entire list to see if it is balanced. Child suggests changing No. 5 to "How to keep healthy."	Causes group to review accomplishments. Helps them to think for themselves.
Teacher has them read through the list several times, noticing the first words.	
Finally child says, "If we change to 'How to keep healthy' it wouldn't balance."	
So it is left as it is. . . .	

The group then turned to planning how to receive their mothers in the afternoon. It can be seen from this record that Miss Wells helped the children to make an orderly plan for their study.

Study sponsored by an inter-school council. In Ventura County, California, high school students were given an unusual opportunity to take part in curriculum planning as a result of foresight on the part of county educators.[5] When the entire state was working on a framework for the curriculum, the planning committee of the Santa Barbara–Ventura Inter-School Council held a meeting on a "Consideration of the Purposes of Education in California." The committee members decided to get reactions and suggestions from councils of member schools. A check sheet was furnished which listed proposed purposes and gave students a chance to answer three questions with regard to them: (1) Are we satisfying the needs of the students? (2) What do we need to do? (3) How do we do it? Each student body president was asked to meet with his school's administrator and select a committee of two or three outstanding students who would give their impressions of the list of purposes proposed. A summary of conclusions was to be sent to the State Curriculum Commission.

The following report on procedure coming from member schools will show how each center went about involving different individuals in the project.

[5] Reported in *Students Frame the Framework*, compiled and edited by Charles E. Neuman, administrative assistant and director of secondary education, Ventura County Schools, California, March, 1949. Mimeographed. In this particular example place names used are real.

Member Schools	*Procedure Used in the Study*
Carpinteria High School	Student committee, senior problems class discussion, special consultant, principal and committee evaluation.
Fillmore High School	Four members of the student council first filled out the framework questionnaire and discussed its questions with the chairman of the curriculum committee, the student council adviser, and the principal of the high school. It was then decided to ask all the seniors and all members of the faculty to fill out the survey. The faculty report is still incomplete, but the trends in both groups have been noted.
Moorpark High School	A group of twelve students (three sophomores, four juniors, five seniors) acted as a group to consider the framework. This group compiled the summary with the help of the vice-principal. It made a special attempt to leave the personality of the teachers out of the survey. The survey is now before the faculty.
Nordhoff Union High School	The student body president, vice-president, secretary, and commissioner of finance acted as a study group to consider the framework. Working with our vice-principal, these four students compiled a summary of the framework.
Oxnard Union High School	The student government class worked as a group in formulating the conclusions for Parts C and D of the survey. Parts A and B were analyzed by a committee composed of four students and three administrators.
Santa Paula High School	A committee appointed by the student body president which included students from the various ability and interest levels met several times to discuss this report. The committee ended its survey with a three-hour summary meeting.
Simi Valley High School	Each senior student filled out the survey form. A committee of five was chosen to summarize the survey. This work was done with no adviser. The faculty is now filling out the survey form as we did.

Member Schools	*Procedure Used in the Study*
Ventura Junior High School	Scored by a tenth grade English class.
Ventura Junior College	The persons involved in the study of the framework were several members of the council, several faculty members, and the senior citizenship problems class.

The splendid quality of the results which were included in the full report shows the value of planning carefully for wide and thoughtful participation in such a venture.[6]

Following Leads of Pupils

As was stated in the introduction to this chapter, cooperative planning of learning experiences does not necessarily mean that the teacher asks the children directly what they would like to study. In fact, some of the best studies, from the standpoint of meeting needs, grow out of leads furnished by the children in the ways they behave, the questions they ask, the things they show an interest in or a concern about. Miss Donnal reports how three different learning experiences of her fourth grade were inspired by leads furnished by the children's behavior.

1. Study of Indian Life

    I had noticed that for over a week the children had been playing Indians while outdoors. Also, during our work period many were busy at the workbench constructing bows and arrows. Thomas brought to our discussion group a page torn from a comic book which had illustrations of Indian sign language. I asked the group if they would like to learn more about Indians. There was an enthusiastic affirmative response.

2. Study of Negro History and Culture

    We had just finished listening to a record, "Jazz Band," the story of how the Negro slaves were taken from Africa and brought to New Orleans. Charles, a very aggressive child, said to Mary Lou, "Was your mother a slave?" "No," said Mary Lou, "was yours?" "None of my people were ever slaves," Charles replied.

    This touched off much talking among the group. After they quieted down, I said that the chances were that many of their ancestors had come from Africa and had been slaves. The group was not willing to accept this. When I asked them where they thought their great-great-great-grandmothers came from they said, "From God."

    I let the discussion drop there, seeing how sensitive they were on

[6] For an additional account of group planning of a study initiated by a teacher, see pages 290 ff.

the matter. It was evident, however, that there was a great need for helping them to eliminate the shame they felt concerning slavery and Africa.

My approach to this study came quite accidentally and without any preplanning. We were in the city visiting the planetarium. Some of the children asked if we couldn't stop in the museum to see the wild animals. This desire brought us to the African rooms.

The children were fascinated with the exhibit. After coming out they made the observation that many of the African things were superior to the Indian things (for which they had had a great deal of admiration). It was quite obvious that they were a little less self-conscious now about this topic of Africa. They were able to talk unemotionally about this place and its peoples. I asked if they would like to find out more about Africa. The reply was "Yes."

3. Sex Education

As a preface to this I would like to point out that the children already were familiar with the fact that the egg must be fertilized for the mother to reproduce young.

Charles asked me one day, "Where does the baby come out of the mother?" James followed with, "How does the father put the sperm into the mother?"

Calvert immediately replied to Charles's question, "Why, they cut the mother's stomach open and take it out."

I corrected Calvert's answer and asked Charles if he could figure out where there was an opening in the body for the baby to come out, remembering that this hole could get larger. I then asked James if he ever saw dogs or cats mating. He said that he had. I then told him that there was a connection between the mother and father.

James said he had some pictures of men and women that he would bring to school.

Miss Donnal's stories illustrate three types of study all inspired by children. The study of Indian life met an interest the children were revealing. It is significant that this interest soon led to the production of a play about Indian life which, as the teacher says, was not just a concluding activity for a unit but actually a new interest. However, interest in finding out information about Indians did not cease when something new was started, which may be a good sign that the interest was not imposed in the first place.

The study of Africa met a real need of children to "eliminate shame they felt concerning slavery and Africa." Again there was a definite verbal agreement to pursue a study. The teacher reports, "Though newer interests have displaced our concentrated study of the Negro, the children continue to bring in new information when they find it."

The third illustration differs in that it reveals no verbal commitment to the study at any time. The study was an ongoing one, engaged in intermittently as children showed a desire for more help on this important problem. In all three cases, however, the children were true partners in setting learning goals.

Miss Murphy too followed the lead of a pupil, although she could have led the group in another direction by using the fourth grade geography book. One day as a small reading group was enjoying a story about Mexico, someone asked, "Are we going to study about Mexico this year?" The teacher asked how many wanted to, and since all did, she suggested that the matter be brought up later before the entire class. The teacher's account says:

> It turned out that everyone wanted to study Mexico because "it's right near us and we ought to know about it." So there we were but we were faced with many difficulties. None of our supplementary geography books touched Mexico. How could we study it if we couldn't find information?
> "We could look in the encyclopedia," Mary said.
> "I have a book at home that tells about it."
> "I could get a book from the library."
> That point seemed settled. We would *find* some information. Actually we also wrote to Mexican cities, railroads, airplane companies, Mexican consuls, and the United States Office of Education for additional information.

Miss Murphy did not have entirely smooth sailing. The parents of some children thought they should not be asked to buy extra books. The principal declared that the teacher should not have started a study unless there could be a book for every child. But the children did have a chance to participate in an important phase of their learning—locating sources of information.

In Miss Olliphant's case some unexpected studies came into being because she and the children were free to follow the logic of experiences they were having together. Her fourth grade group had spent the early weeks of the term on problems of food supply and rationing. Miss Olliphant next led the children to a consideration of kinds of homes many years ago and how past ways of living help us today. One committee decided to make a study of some early poems of the Negro that they had found in their research. This soon became an interest of the entire group. A program of individual and choral reading of various poems was prepared and presented in a chapel in another school.

One boy was so impressed by this experience that he asked one morning if he might write a letter in class telling his brother, serving in the armed forces in England, about the program. Soon many in the group wanted to do the same thing. There was discussion of whether parents should address the letters or whether this step could be taken at school. Different kinds of mail service to soldiers were considered. One child proposed that they review ways to write letters.

Replies to the children's letters and souvenirs sent by the grateful soldiers led to a display with the whole school taking part. Even ninth and tenth grade students housed in the same building became interested and helped the younger children in their search for information on the countries where fathers and brothers were stationed.

Miss Olliphant arranged a meeting between these high school students and one of the fourth grade committees in which the younger children could say what kind of help they would like. The high school classes agreed to prepare some illustrated reports on different parts of the world that would include items the fourth grade children wanted to know.

Miss Olliphant states that although these studies lasted for the remainder of the school year, other things of interest came up that required their attention for a while.

This teacher's report reflects the enthusiasm of the children and of those to whom the interest spread. The older and younger pupils all had experiences in making plans for learning together which could hardly have been anticipated by adult preplanning.

CONCLUSION

Those fortunate teachers who have no course of study bonds to hold them back have a world of opportunities for cooperative learning. They and their children are free to select from the many problems of living in a modern world those that appear most important and inviting. What learning can be like for groups with such opportunities has been well illustrated in this chapter. The chapter has, moreover, offered examples of many degrees and kinds of pupil participation in planning to learn. Many of them are available to teachers and pupils working within numerous restrictions imposed by the planning of others. The teacher who truly believes that learning is enhanced in quality and amount when people help plan for it themselves can find many opportunities, great or small, for cooperative planning of this nature.

The successful practices described in this chapter have at least two things in common. The teachers were genuinely committed to following the decisions of the group, and they realized the importance of careful and definite planning of all the steps along the way through a learning experience. A promising practice illustrated in a few of the examples is that of continuing to discover new questions to be answered in a study rather than of attempting to build an exhaustive list at the start.

CHAPTER VI

Planning Products

A WHOLE HOST of opportunities for learning cooperative procedures lies in the interest young people have in
turning out some more or less tangible product. Whether the product
be designed for the use of the makers or intended for the pleasure of
others, the focus of the group's attention is on the product itself.
The teacher, however, must watch out that learnings of the group are
not sacrificed to his own desire for a quick result, pleasing in the light
of adult standards. As a group plans and carries through the production of something useful, the members are having chances to learn
just as certainly as they are if they map out a study of Africa or of
mathematics or of water supply.

In this chapter experiences of pupils and teachers engaged in cooperative planning of products are examined. The chapter is divided
into two sections; (1) planning to make tangible objects, such as
butter or a playhouse or gifts or a piece of writing, and (2) planning
less tangible productions, such as parties, programs, and trips.

PLANNING TO PRODUCE
TANGIBLE OBJECTS

There are many values in planning to make various
kinds of tangible products—in planning what to make and how to
make it and how to secure materials and the necessary facilities.
Individual initiative is encouraged, and there is much opportunity to
plan "within materials." Following leads given by the materials
themselves is a type of planning which is useful for all and which is
especially satisfying to less vocal individuals. In this kind of activity
the results of planning are quickly and easily tested.

Planning to Make Butter

Mrs. Austin tells how her kindergarten children planned
to make butter after discussing a story in which a churn was men-

tioned. A picture in the book reminded one of the children of the churn the little pig had used to fool the wolf. The teacher then brought out a small glass churn from the cupboard and let the children examine it.

"Could we use it to really make butter?" one of the children wanted to know. Since other children showed interest in the proposition and the project seemed feasible and worth while, the teacher agreed and plans were developed.

> TEACHER. What will we need to make butter? (No response.)
> TEACHER. What did the farmer's wife in the story use?
> GARY. Milk.
> SKEETER. No, cream.
> TEACHER. I will bring some cream tomorrow so we can make butter. What will we need to put it on?
> EDDIE. Some bread or crackers.
> TEACHER. How would you like to have graham crackers? (General agreement expressed.)
> TEACHER. There's another way to make butter besides churning it. Does anyone know what it is?
> CAROL FAYE. You can get some oleo and color it.
> TEACHER. Yes, but there's another way to make it from cream, by shaking the cream in a glass jar. Shall we try both ways?
> CHILDREN. Yes.

Mrs. Austin's story illustrates several good techniques in planning with younger children: (1) Pictures and objects were used to build the background necessary for intelligent planning. (2) A vicarious experience (a story) was used as a source of suggestion. (3) The teacher accepted (for the time being, no doubt) an erroneous concept as expressed by a child—making butter by coloring oleo—and described in simple terms the second way of making butter which she had in mind. In her description she emphasized the correct concept, making butter from cream. (4) Since these children were in early stages of experience with planning, the teacher simplified the process as much as possible by offering to supply the necessary materials and by stating a concrete plan of action for the children to react to, for example, "Shall we try both ways?"

As far as the record shows, Mrs. Austin did not give the children a chance to commit themselves as a group to the butter-making project. When one child asked if they might make butter, the teacher assented and the project was adopted. The teacher missed the opportunity to help the children learn the difference between a proposal by one group member and a decision by the group. Mrs. Austin did, however, decide for the group in terms of criteria: apparent interest of the group and feasibility and probable educational value of the project.

The teacher goes on to describe how the chances to participate in the churning process were divided and how the product was tested and enjoyed. This part of the enterprise apparently was teacher-planned, a perfectly defensible procedure. No teacher and group can make use of every opportunity for group planning that presents itself.

Planning How to Build a Church

The building of a church by Mrs. Austin's class is an excellent illustration of the concrete type of planning which must be done with young children. As the teacher tells it, the first grade teacher gave the kindergarten a church front that had been used in a program. This piece of stage property had doors that opened and a bell that swung back and forth when a cord was pulled. The doorway was tall enough for children to enter erect. The church front itself seemed to suggest building the rest of the church. The children began to plan.

JIMMY. Let's make sides for it.

TEACHER. How shall we do it?

JIMMY. We can put the front here and put some of that long brown paper over to here [south wall] for the sides. These two windows can be the back.

CHARLENE. Yes, they could be windows in the church.

TEACHER. Let's try it. Jimmy and Ronald, will you help me move this, please? (The front of the church was moved to the place designated by Jimmy.)

TEACHER (to the group). What do you think?

EDDIE. I don't think there will be enough room.

TEACHER. Why?

EDDIE. Well, we need room for the choir and the minister, and seats for the people who come to church.

TEACHER. Shall we move it back a little farther? How is this?

EDDIE. That ought to be all right, I think.

JIMMY. Yes, that's better.

TEACHER. How can we fix it so that the front of the church will stand up without our holding it?

DON. Nail it to a heavy box.

TEACHER. Can any of you bring some boxes tomorrow? (Several volunteered.)

The teacher's leadership in this instance was of two sorts: (1) helping children test suggestions through actual manipulation of materials, for example, placing the church front in different spots; and (2) raising questions which caused children to see the need for further plans, for example, "How can we fix it so that the front of the church will stand up?" Mrs. Austin's record continues the story.

> And so it was arranged. Every day a committee was chosen to work on the church until it was finished. Other plans were worked out. Patty suggested that we have windows like a real church (stained-glass windows). After discussing the possibilities of painting the windows or painting pieces of paper to paste on the glass, we decided to paint the papers but to paint the space between the papers with black paint for the lead between the panes. Many children participated in painting the papers. Then we selected the ones that looked well together.
>
> We found we needed a pulpit, choir seats, seats for the congregation, song books, a Bible, a minister, a deacon to welcome people at the door, and a sexton to ring the bell (singing "ding-dong, ding-dong" as the bell moved back and forth)—cardboard shrubbery was painted and placed at each side of the front. Plans also included what the minister should do.
>
> RONALD P. He should let the choir sing "Silent Night" and then let the audience sing.
>
> TEACHER. We call the people who go to the show an audience, but what do we call the people who go to church?
>
> PEGGY. The congregation.
>
> TEACHER. Yes. How should the minister let the congregation know when to sing?
>
> RONALD R. He could say, "Let us stand and sing 'Away in the Manger.'" And then everybody could stand up and sing.
>
> TEACHER. Then what would the minister do next?
>
> EDDIE. He could preach a sermon.
>
> LYLE. Then he could say a prayer.
>
> JIMMY. And then the sexton could ring the bell again and everybody would know church was over and it was time to go home.

This part of the teacher's report shows how the group was helped to carry the project through to the point of using its product.

Planning to Furnish a Playhouse

The next construction project upon which Mrs. Austin's kindergarten group embarked was that of furnishing a new playhouse. The children's increased skill in planning is apparent in the way one suggestion followed another with little encouragement from the teacher. Mrs. Austin reports that after the children returned from the Christmas holidays they were presented with a playhouse. Aware of the coming event, the teacher had visualized moving furniture from a nook used as a playhouse into the new structure. However, after the children had exclaimed in delight, said their "thank you's," and settled down to sober thought, it was soon evident that such would not be the plan. One of the first remarks was, "Oh, now we can have two playhouses and one family can visit the other family sometimes." Mrs. Austin records the conversation that ensued.

TEACHER. Do we have enough furniture for two playhouses?

CHILDREN (disappointedly). No.

TEACHER (encouragingly). What could we do about it?

PEGGY. We could buy some furniture with some of the paper-sale money.

EDDIE. We could make some furniture.

DAVID. I could bring some boxes.

TEACHER. Fine. What kind of boxes?

DAVID. Some milk cases and orange crates.

JOHN F. Up on my mantel is my little bank and I have some money in my bank. I could bring it and we could buy something for the playhouse.

GRAY W. I could bring a board for a bed and some steel for a bathtub.

RONALD R. I have some tools I could bring to help make the furniture with.

PATTY T. I could bring some dishes.

CHARLENE. I could bring a box to make a cupboard to put the dishes in.

PATTY MC C. My daddy has a truck and he could bring us some boxes and lumber.

After a few more such offers, the teacher summarized by saying, "We can make some furniture and buy the things we can't make." Every offer was accepted except John's. John was thanked but was asked to leave his money in his bank since paper-sale money could be used for the purpose. Mrs. Austin's record continues.

TEACHER. Shall we plan what furniture we need? Gary has suggested a doll bed; Charlene has suggested a cupboard. What else do we need?

JANICE. We need a stove.

EDDIE. We ought to have a dresser or maybe a vanity. My mother has a vanity.

JIMMY B. Mine does too, and it has a little skirt around it. Does yours?

EDDIE. No, but it has a little bench you sit on.

TEACHER. Olna Jean, what do you suggest?

OLNA JEAN. A table and some chairs.

TEACHER. These are all good suggestions. If you bring some boxes tomorrow we can begin work. We can use our kindergarten tools and Ronald's; and if we need any help perhaps Mr. Wall, the industrial arts teacher, will help us.

As children started to bring materials, work began. The teacher's log of the building of the stove illustrates how well these young children worked with materials. Cooperative procedures include more than discussion by people sitting together in a group.

Wednesday. Jimmy, Eddie, and Bobby washed boxes and removed paper. Took third box apart, removing nails and washing pieces to be used for oven doors and board across the top at the back of the stove. Measured the box to be used at top of stove.

Thursday. Roger and Katherine M. sandpapered the wood to be used for oven doors. Richard, Marvin Lee, and Gary hammered boxes together, fastening board on top and lower front.

Friday. Ronald P. and Judy sandpapered the top and front, measured board for brace in back, marked in pencil place to saw. They planned what needed to be done tomorrow and reported to group: "Tomorrow you can saw this board here where we made this pencil mark and nail it to the back of the stove. Then you can put the hinges on the oven doors."

Monday. Walter, Ronald W., Martha, and Patty P. sawed the board and fastened the brace across the back. Then they planned how to put the hinges on the oven doors. They measured and made pencil marks where screws should go, wondered how to put screws in. Patty suggested hammering in a nail a little way to make a hole and then pulling out the nail and putting the screw in. She said her brother did it that way. They tried it and were delighted with the result. Finished with the screwdriver. Reported to the group.

Tuesday. Skeeter and Buddy put hooks on oven doors so they could be fastened to the top. Practiced opening and shutting oven doors. Hammered nails in coffee-can lids to make holes for burners. Made designs with pencil first to plan where to make holes.

Wednesday. Owen and Farrell fastened four burners to top of stove and nailed board across the top at the back. Did a little more sandpapering. Announced to the group that the stove was all finished and ready to be painted.

Thursday. Eddie and Peggy put on first coat of paint (white).

Friday. John and Charlene put on second coat of paint.

When children are planning "within materials" they seem to have a ready source of suggestions in the materials themselves. Credit must be given, however, to the earlier experiences with planning which Mrs. Austin helped this group to have.

Planning to Build a Toy Store

Excerpts from a record made in Miss Fanetti's first grade classroom show the kind of construction planning that an age group with considerable experience in group thinking can do. The children were planning to continue work on a toy store in the corner of their room. For a time the roof was the big problem.

JOHN. When people go in, their heads would hit a flat roof.
TEACHER. That's something to consider.
JIM. We could raise sticks up and make it just as good.
TEACHER. Are you saying you want to raise the walls of the store? Could we find out right now if the roof would be tall enough?
ANN. We could go in and see.
TEACHER. Good. Let's choose someone tall to make the test for us.

When Sally stepped into the roofless frame, her head was well above the present walls. "Gee!" came a chorus of voices. After that all suggestions for solving the problem were explained and tested by using the store frame as a point of reference.

When the children were considering spaces to be left in the walls for doors and windows, the teacher helped them to reflect on one another's suggestions.

TEACHER. What do you think of Donald's suggestion, Linda?
LINDA. I think it's a pretty good suggestion, but I think we should have a window on one side, one on another side, and one by the door.
TEACHER. How many would that be?
SALLY. I was thinking about one big window and one little door.
TEACHER. If you don't understand Sally's idea I think this is the time to question her.

Several children asked questions and Sally explained further. Miss Fanetti asked Sally where, if she had her way, she would put the window and the door, thus helping the group test the idea.

JIM. I think that's a good suggestion.
CARL. I think I understand what Sally means now. I thought the windows were going to be bigger than the door.
TEACHER. A window could be wider than a door, but the door doesn't need to be wide.

Again the teacher had the children plan by using the specific materials. "Diane, let's see if you and Lewis can get in and out of that space."

The children showed that they knew the value of a careful plan when the teacher asked a little later, "Are we ready to plan the inside now?" "No," was the reply, "we have to know *this* doesn't work, and *this* doesn't work . . ."

"That's why we're planning," Miss Fanetti said. "It's pretty valuable time we're spending right now." Later, when the group decided to carry out the plans made that morning rather than go on planning the inside of the store, the teacher commented, "One day we decide what we are going to make, the next day we are busy working."

Even this brief glimpse at planning construction in a first grade classroom shows that the teacher was helping the children to listen carefully to the suggestions of others, to test ideas directly through use of the materials to be worked with, and best of all, to value a plan before plunging into work. This is a step in maturing beyond that illustrated by Mrs. Austin's report on the construction of a stove.

Planning to Construct a Birdbath

A complete running record of a discussion when Miss Peterson's second grade children were deciding how to construct a birdbath gives an opportunity to observe the complexity of ideas with which some seven-year-olds are prepared to deal. The children had found a large shallow pan with a hole in it, the discarded top of a birdbath. It was this find which had prompted them to think of constructing a new birdbath on the school grounds. It is likely that the children and teacher could have worked out the problem more easily had they planned with concrete materials from the very start.

Record	*Analysis*
TEACHER. Let's think about our problem for a minute. It's a big one—constructing a birdbath.	Teacher states problem, implying an invitation of suggestions for solving it. Group members give suggestions freely, drawing on past experience in some cases.
JOAN. We could fill up the hole with cement.	
JOHN. We could do like Miss Macon did last year, fill it up with stones.	
JACK. I know how you could have some cement left over. Put it in and scrape it off.	
TEACHER. Show us what you mean.	Teacher attempts to make the discussion concrete by encouraging use of sketches on the blackboard.
JACK (drawing on the blackboard). The hole is here. You can pack the cement in there.	

Record	*Analysis*
TEACHER. Your idea isn't to cover the whole thing with cement?	Teacher asks questions for clarification.
JACK. No.	
TEACHER. Curt, you come up and show us your idea.	Teacher makes certain that the group will have opportunity to choose from a wide range of suggestions.
Curt draws a picture of a hollow in the ground with the pan resting in it.	
TEACHER. What do you think of that idea?	Teacher asks for group evaluation of suggestions.
CHILD. I think it is good.	
TEACHER. Go on with that idea. Do you remember what happened last year?	Teacher encourages children to state their ideas fully.
Dorrance starts to explain.	
TEACHER. Start at the beginning, won't you?	
DORRANCE. You dig a hole and then put the cement in.	
TEACHER. If you put the pan in, how can you put cement in? I don't understand.	Teacher tests her own and the child's understanding.
DORRANCE. I don't either.	
TEACHER. Go on. You have a good idea.	Teacher encourages child to have respect for his own idea.
GIRL. You could put the cement in the pan.	
TEACHER. What about that, Dorrance?	Teacher suggests that Dorrance evaluate this amendment to his idea. Teacher allows discussion to pass freely from one child to another.
DICK. We wouldn't need to use the pan at all.	
JACK. If we fill the whole top, it might run down the sides.	
BOBBY. We could dig a hole, put the pan in, and use cement only to cover the bottom.	
TEACHER. We have the cement, but that is a good idea to save cement.	Teacher is encouraging children to be neither niggardly nor wasteful with materials.
TOM. We could fill the hole, then put rocks on the inside, and then cement over them. That would be more attractive.	
TEACHER. And not use the pan?	Again teacher tests her understanding.

Record	*Analysis*
TOM. Yes, but put rocks in the pan and around the sides. We could whitewash the stones.	Tom merges several suggestions incorporating a new one of his own —the rocks.
The group shows enthusiasm. (They have the same thing around flower beds in front of the school.)	
CHILD. That's a good idea.	Children show willingness to praise the ideas of another.
CHILD. That's the best idea yet.	
TEACHER. Now let's get some more ideas.	Teacher might have helped the group to settle on this generally favored idea, but on this occasion she chose to see how much further the group could go in suggesting alternatives.
ANN. My aunt did it this way: she used colored stones and cement.	
TEACHER. Did she dig a place in the ground?	Teacher uses question to relate Ann's description with the suggestions before the group.
ANN. She dug a hole, put cement in first, and then the rocks, and she has no insects in her garden.	
TEACHER. What keeps them out?	
ANN. The birds eat them.	Teacher is wise enough to see that Ann's apparently irrelevant remark about insects actually is pertinent.
TEACHER. Now let's get some different ideas.	
BILL. Couldn't we mix the cement in the pan and leave it?	
TEACHER. Joan, can you understand Bill's suggestion?	Teacher sees importance of testing whether or not one child is communicating with another.
JOAN. I can't understand but I have another suggestion.	
TEACHER. Just a minute. Let's understand. Bill said we might mix the cement in the pan and leave it. Let's get the top and look at it.	Teacher makes sure that each idea gets a hearing before new ones are introduced.
Child goes to get pan.	Very likely it would have been helpful if the top (pan or lid as it was variously called) had been brought in sooner.
CHILD. Maybe Joan can bring her birdbath.	
TEACHER. We have a top, let's use it.	Teacher brings group back to original problem.
MARY. We should dig a hole and put the pan in.	
TEACHER. Could you hear? Mary had a very good suggestion.	Although Mary is actually repeating an earlier suggestion, the teacher makes sure that she gets the attention of the group.
Mary repeats.	
TEACHER. Let's just look at the top awhile.	A time for just thinking during a discussion often is a good idea.

Record	*Analysis*

CHILD. That's too little.

Teacher allows free musing. The change in tempo of the group at this point was useful as a way of resting.

CHILD. People have stepped all over it.

It is interesting also to note that children were viewing the problem with a fresh look.

CHILD. We will have to hammer it.

TEACHER. Just look and think.
Andrew comments on the hole.

TEACHER. It doesn't matter about the hole, does it, because we will fill it with cement?

JANE. We have a cover at home that isn't being used. It is perfectly good. We don't know what to do with it. It's just lying around the yard.

Actual viewing of the lid under discussion no doubt reminds Jane of the cover she could bring.

BOY. If we put cement in, it will take up most of the room.

Viewing of the lid also causes this group member to be more realistic about the limitations of the material around which the group was planning.

TEACHER. We have two ideas.

BOY. Just two?

TEACHER. (1), we can get rid of the pan; fill the hole with cement. (2), we can dig a hole and put the pan in and put cement in the pan. Or there is a third. Jane could bring a new top. Now think. Which is the best idea? Think why your idea would be better. We have three suggestions.

Teacher decides it is time to summarize the suggestions made up to this point. Here the teacher recognizes the boy's questioning of "just two" ideas and also picks up Jane's offer, which seemingly had been ignored.

JACK. I think we should dig a hole and put cement in.

TEACHER. With the stones?

A question to clarify the proposal.

DONNY. I think we should get a real big garbage can and put cement in.

Apparently the smallness of the lid prompted this new suggestion.

DORRANCE. A whole garbage can?

DONNY. We could fill it half with cement and then with water.

DORRANCE. We don't have enough cement.

The suggestion calls forth the critical powers of several in the group, and Donny is forced to revise his idea somewhat.

LARRY. Won't it be too deep? Birds can't swim.

Record	*Analysis*
DONNY. I didn't mean that deep.	
TEACHER. How deep, Donny?	Teacher strives for accuracy in presentation of ideas, then asks for an evaluation.
Donny shows the group.	
TEACHER. Now, how about Donny's idea?	
DORRANCE. We don't need to do that. Just the top is enough.	
TEACHER. Nicky, what do you think of Donny's idea?	Teacher tries to draw in a child who had not participated actively.
NICKY. It's good.	
TEACHER. What is his idea?	She tests his understanding.
Nicky doesn't know.	
Jackie shows how a deep garbage can could be used. Puts drawing on board showing that they can put dirt in the bottom, then cement, then just a little water at the top.	A convert to Donny's idea works out a creative solution.
TEACHER. Why a whole can?	Teacher asks questions but does not evaluate.
JACKIE. It looks better.	
TEACHER. Now we have had good ideas. Dorrance says there's no use making it any harder. Larry said it must not be too deep for the birds. Tom gave a good suggestion about digging a hole and putting in cement. What would be the easiest?	Teacher summarizes the later discussion and ties it in with the earlier suggestion that had met with such favor. She ends with a question that may at this point lead to consensus.
JOAN. Dig a hole, put in cement.	
TEACHER. How many agree with Joan?	A group member states the proposition most likely to be favored. The teacher is testing for consensus, not taking a formal vote.
There are many hands.	
TEACHER. Are you going to use any stones?	Teacher raises a strategic question which leads to some important discussion from the standpoint of making a workable plan.
JOAN. I don't think so.	
TEACHER. Is there any reason for stones?	
Teacher makes two or three tries at questioning on this point. Finally a boy says that cement won't stick to dirt.	
TEACHER. I am glad someone said that.	
CHILD. We need stones to spread the cement on.	
A boy tells about concrete reinforced with metal rods. (He had seen a bridge being built.)	

Record	*Analysis*
TEACHER. So we can use what method? Michael is not sure.	Teacher tests understanding.
ANOTHER BOY. Stones.	
TEACHER. So, let's write what we have decided.	This, the third summary, is put in writing on the blackboard.
JACKIE. Stones to hold cement to the ground.	
PRINCIPAL (who was observing). Do I understand you won't use the lid (pan)?	
MICHAEL. No, we will put stones in the lid and around it.	
Teacher has Michael come up to demonstrate.	Teacher encourages child to interpret his ideas for himself.
MICHAEL. We can hammer this up and that will be the shallower place.	
TEACHER. Then we are going to use this lid? Do you agree? What will we need?	Teacher makes certain of decision. Teacher launches new phase of discussion.
BOY. Cement will spread.	
TEACHER. Then what will we need? Are we ready to do it today?	
BILL. No, we need to mix the cement. We can't mix it in the lid. We could use that box.	
TEACHER. Will that cardboard box be good for mixing cement?	While Bill's personality probably was not severely damaged by his being in the spotlight for a time for suggesting an impractical idea, group leaders and group members have to guard against the temptation to "ride" someone who may wish he could take back his words. In this case, it might have been better to say, "You probably forgot that cement is mixed with water and a cardboard box wouldn't work very well." No doubt, if the teacher had been left to handle the situation alone, the affair would not have been blown up to such proportions and Bill could have been given a quiet moment to think.
PRINCIPAL. What goes into mixing cement?	
BILL. Cement and water.	
PRINCIPAL. So will that be good?	
TEACHER. What does water do?	
Several children also "attack" Bill on the same point.	
TEACHER. Can we do it now?	
ANN. No.	
BOY. We could use a flowerpot.	
ANN. I could bring something to mix it in.	
TEACHER. Can you bring it Monday? Then it's settled.	Teacher converts an offer into a definite commitment.

Record

Teacher writes: "How To Make a Birdbath."

TEACHER. What are we going to do, Bill?

Teacher writes as Bill dictates: "1. Dig the hole."

TEACHER. What is the second step?

CHILD. Put the pan down in the hole.

TEACHER. Is that all right? While one committee is digging, could another be doing something else?

BOY. Mix cement.

TEACHER. Could we do it at the same time?

The children agree and the teacher adds to No. 1: "Mix cement."

TEACHER. One committee will do this while another committee does that. Now what is the next thing to do?

Teacher tries to get Janet to tell, but Janet does not know.

CHILD. Pour cement.

TEACHER. Where?

CHILD. On the rocks.

TEACHER. What is the next thing to do?

CHILD. Put in the top. (Put down as No. 2.)

CHILD. Put stones around and in the top. (Put down as No. 3.)

TEACHER. Michael, will we put cement over or between the stones?

MICHAEL. I think between would be best.

TEACHER. Read this now. What is next, Larry?

LARRY. Pour in cement. (Put down as No. 4.)

JOHN. We would need to put water in. We need that for a birdbath.

MICHAEL. Are we going to mix

Analysis

Teacher gives Bill a chance to cancel out his unfortunate contribution.

Teacher tries to draw in another non-participant.

Perhaps because of a desire to cut a fairly long discussion short, the teacher ignores these contributions that are premature.

This definite plan undoubtedly helps the children who have been active in the discussion to be clear as to next steps. It probably helps some others who have been some-

Record	*Analysis*
all the cement at once? Maybe we would have some left over and it would go to waste.	what at sea during the entire discussion to get an idea of what the discussion had been about. These latter children will no doubt achieve complete understanding only as they work through the project.
Teacher has a child read the first four points.	
TEACHER. Then after the cement gets in, John says put water in.	

This lengthy record has many interesting features. The skillful role played by the teacher is well worth careful study. It is interesting to observe the way in which she helped the group reach a consensus. The children under her guidance were being challenged to do critical thinking. Miss Peterson did about as well as one could to make a verbal approach to a problem of this kind by young children concrete and meaningful.

Planning to Make a Book

A joint meeting of the three upper grade groups (fifth, fifth and sixth, and sixth) in Robinson School for the purpose of planning the cooperative production of a large book yielded a record that throws some light on the way in which ten- to twelve-year-olds can handle a problem. With the principal acting as chairman, the group first reviewed the plans for the book as agreed upon the day before. As pupils named items that had been planned in detail, Miss Hallum underlined them in a list requiring large group agreement before individuals and small groups could prepare pages for the book.

Record	*Analysis*
PRINCIPAL. What is your next most important thing to do? What should we decide on today?	Leader has group select aspect of problem to work on.
The group agrees on margins, kind of paper, and media for illustrations.	
PRINCIPAL. Who could report on what we decided yesterday about size of paper? (Small scattering of hands.) If that is all we shall have to review what we decided.	Leader provides for a review of previous planning. Too often there is an assumption that all who have been present when a plan is formulated are clear as to the decisions reached.
Principal calls on Mary, who can't remember the number.	
PRINCIPAL. Do you see any paper that size in this room?	Leader suggests concrete object as an aid to recall.

Record

A boy points to some. Then most of the class knows the answer.

LARRY. 18 by 24.

PRINCIPAL (kindly). Did somebody tell you?

LARRY. No, ma'am.

PRINCIPAL. What is the reason for using this size?

CHILD. Paper is already cut to this size. It is a good size because you can get more on the page.

PRINCIPAL. What about writing?

BOY. Manuscript writing. (He reports sizes of letters agreed upon.)

PRINCIPAL. Can you add anything?

CHILD. Use a black pencil. Crayon is messy; it smears.

PRINCIPAL. Anything else on writing?

GIRL. A committee from each room is to write a chapter.

PRINCIPAL. What shall we work on in discussion today beside the topic?

GIRL. Just the children talk, not the teachers.

PRINCIPAL. Remember, I wasn't going to dangle you on strings like puppets? Where are we going to start?

Group in front answers, "Margins."

PRINCIPAL. Are you going to let this group run you? You might as well have me. Any other place to start beside margins? How many of you want margins? (Many hands.) I am going to call on someone to start. . . . Douglas.

DOUGLAS. One or one and a half inches wide.

Analysis

Recorded words sometimes give an impression of severity that was not present. Throughout, the leader's tone and facial expression were kindly; there was good rapport between leader and group.

Leader encourages thoughtful answers.

Leader is helping children to keep an eye on their discussion process as they plan. A suggestion had been made by the observer on a previous occasion that circular discussion be encouraged. The teachers and principal had shared this suggestion with the children.

Record	*Analysis*

GIRL. We should have more than that so the cover won't cover up some of the writing.

BOY. Four inches on the right-hand side, I mean left hand, and two on the right.

BOY. We should have two inches all around.

PRINCIPAL. Show where you want the four inches and where the other margin. (Draws a sketch on the board, marking off margins all around. This drawing is used frequently in the ensuing discussion as children attempt to explain their ideas.)

Except for this concrete aid to discussion, the leader allows a free flow of opinions.

BOY. I think there should be one inch on the left side and one-half inch on the right-hand side.

MRS. CHARLES. That doesn't tell us anything.

A boy defends the four-inch margin on the left.

The role played by Mrs. Charles, one of three teachers present, is reproving.

SHIRLEY. Two on the left, one on the right.

GIRL. But Shirley, the cover might cover the writing. With two inches on left there wouldn't be any margin.

GIRL. The cover would take two inches. If you had one inch on the other side, it wouldn't balance right.

BOY. One inch would look better and leave more room for pictures.

GIRL. How can you read the book if the cover is covering up half of the writing?

PRINCIPAL. Half?

Although the children had been encouraged to speak in turn without waiting for recognition or comment by the leader, this procedure was still so new to them that this kind of communication between pupils was rare in this record. Usually contributions were given as more or less isolated answers to a common question rather than as one person trying to communicate with another.

Leader is working for accurate statements.

GIRL. Some of the writing.

BOY. You wouldn't start writing on the margin. Look at that book. (Points to one made by a previous class.) That isn't so bad.

BOY. That's two inches.

Again a concrete aid to planning has been provided, this time in the form of books made by previous classes which have become a part of the school library.

Record   *Analysis*

GIRL. The rules of the school system say to indent and start at the margin.

PRINCIPAL (getting a ruler and starting to measure). Who's measured this? All right, you two girls measure.

The girls report on margins in two books with hinged plywood covers made by previous classes.

PRINCIPAL. How can you tell whether you are right? Turn the pages.

GIRL. They pasted papers on. We are going to write on the pages.

PRINCIPAL. Was that decided? Let's decide that. Bobby, do you want to start a discussion on that? (Much discussion favoring writing on the pages. They stay on better and you get more on a page.)

Leader is alert to unwarranted assumptions and judges that decision on the point raised is a prerequisite to a decision on margins.

MRS. CHARLES. Can you use that paper if you have half-inch letters?

GIRL. I think we should write directly on the paper. (Two others agree with her.)

PRINCIPAL. We're repeating a little. Any more discussion?

Leader protects group from wasteful discussion.

GIRL. We can get more on a page but suppose we make a mistake. We will waste good paper.

PRINCIPAL. Shirley is doing some good thinking.

When a valid new point is made, leader allows full discussion of it.

GIRL. We can correct mistakes. . . .

GIRL. We can write first in pencil and then check.

PRINCIPAL. Would you do any practicing first?

SAME GIRL. Practice, use pencil, then check.

PRINCIPAL. How many are ready to vote?

There are hands raised and children call "Question!" Principal calls for vote. There is a minority

Leader takes responsibility for bringing group to the point of decision.

Record	*Analysis*
of two or three in favor of writing on a separate paper. When asked for reasons for separate paper, Arthur did not know.	The minority is given one more chance to state its case.
PRINCIPAL. Are you willing to give in if you have no reason?	
ARTHUR. Yes.	
PRINCIPAL. What will you do then?	Leader tests the understanding of the minority on the point conceded.
ARTHUR. Write on big paper.	
After more measuring they discover there is a two and one-half inch margin on the book they are examining.	
BOY. Four inches doesn't give room for pictures.	Examination of the product of others' planning helps to clarify the issues.
BOY. The cover will take two inches of it probably.	
PRINCIPAL. Probably? Did it in that book?	
BOY. No.	
PRINCIPAL. Why are you talking against this plan (two and one-half inch margin)?	Leader is working for sound reasoning.
Boy is uncertain.	
GIRL. We thought four inches. That is four there.	Group members are helped to learn the value of checking supposed facts.
There is a discussion of whether they measured right. Upon remeasuring, they found the margin to be two and three-quarter inches.	
PRINCIPAL. I guess it has grown a quarter of an inch. Somebody is sticking out for four. Why?	
MRS. CHARLES. If you can't give a good reason—	
GIRL. We thought we needed two inches for the cover, but we didn't.	A climate where one can admit mistakes without losing face is indicated here.
GIRL. I think they have talked me into two inches.	
PRINCIPAL. Two?	
GIRL. Three.	
PRINCIPAL. I'd talk against two and three-quarters for one reason.	Leader is operating as group member here.
MRS. CHARLES. Personally, I think that would be hard.	

Record   *Analysis*

PRINCIPAL. Of course it would give us practice in arithmetic methods.

There is a chorus of "No!"

PRINCIPAL. Any more discussion or comments? I don't know whether there was any agreement. How shall I find out?

Leader does not take a decision for granted.

CHILDREN (calling). "Question!"

PRINCIPAL. How many want three inches?

Most children do.

PRINCIPAL. Does anyone want something else?

Leslie raises his hand.

MRS. CHARLES. Go ahead if you want to talk.

LESLIE. Two inches on the right.

Leslie has actually opened a new phase of the discussion.

PRINCIPAL. Any reason?

Leslie answers.

MRS. CHARLES. Shirley, go on. What are you waiting for?

Teacher is aware of an individual trying to summon the courage to speak.

SHIRLEY. Covers take two inches, so—

GIRL. What has the cover to do with right-hand margin?

PRINCIPAL. Shirley, you have a point; come on up and show us.

Leader protects the right of an individual to be fully heard.

Shirley shows that there will be an uneven margin if they use a three-inch margin (two to accommodate the cover, plus one inch) on the left and a two-inch margin on the right.

People begin to agree with Shirley.

Mrs. Charles shows on one of the model books how the three-inch, two-inch suggestion would work out.

PRINCIPAL (holding up a printed book to show that the outside margins are wider). How would you explain this?

Another resource is employed.

GIRL. That book doesn't look too bad.

Record	Analysis
PRINCIPAL. Do you want it just "not too bad"?	
GIRL. No, as good as we can get.	
A vote is taken: many are for two inches as a right-hand margin; many are for one. Four people are asked to count hands.	
MRS. CHARLES. Come on, Bruce, get counting. Come on over here.	This teacher often seems to be hurrying someone.
Forty-five children voted for two inches, thirty-seven for one.	
PRINCIPAL. Shall we go by this? Are the thirty-seven willing to abide by two inches?	Again there is opportunity to help children value consensus rather than a slender majority.
They agree.	
PRINCIPAL. How about the top and bottom?	
Two girls support two inches.	
PRINCIPAL. Are you ready for the question?	
Two-inch margin is approved. . . .	

At this point the group turned to a new problem, selection of type of paper. Consideration of the media to be used in lettering and illustrating was, with group consent, postponed until the next day. The leader then had the group review decisions made.

Record	Analysis
PRINCIPAL. Someone summarize for us on the margins. We had two widths.	By waiting until many had formulated their summary mentally, the leader increased the number of active though silent participants and was able to call on one of the less ready talkers.
Principal waits until there is a number of volunteers.	
PRINCIPAL. Eddie, how wide will the left-hand margin be?	
EDDIE. One inch.	The need for a summary is indeed apparent.
PRINCIPAL. How many agree?	
BOY. Two inches.	
PRINCIPAL. How many agree?	
GEORGE. Four inches.	
There are groans.	
SHIRLEY. Three inches.	
PRINCIPAL. How many agree with Shirley? (Most.) How many inches will it be, Edward?	This confusion is an indication that in that large group (about seventy-five children) there were some who could not follow the in-
EDWARD. Three.	

Record	Analysis
PRINCIPAL. How many think some other size? (None.) What size shall we use for the right-hand margin?	tricacies of the discussion. One would want to know more about the extent of the confusion and the type of group member who tends to become lost.
Everybody agrees on two inches.	
PRINCIPAL. Who is to find out about heavy paper?	
CHILD. Miss M. (the supervisor).	
Miss M. offers to get the paper, but asks whose responsibility it is for writing a note about it and getting a sample.	
CHILD. The three secretaries (one from each class represented in the joint meeting).	
PRINCIPAL (to secretaries). Will you work that out?	Responsibility is definitely fixed.
PRINCIPAL. Who would like to evaluate the discussion? Remember what we were going to work on. That is what we are going to evaluate. Mary Lou, we haven't heard from you.	Leader suggests evaluation of group process.
Mary Lou gives a summary of the margins.	The first reply is in terms of the group product. The confusion at the time of summary is not mentioned. The group is as yet inexperienced in this type of evaluation.
JEAN. I think we have stayed on the subject.	
PRINCIPAL. Without so much pulling from me?	
JEAN. Yes.	
PRINCIPAL. I think more participated than yesterday. How many did participate today?	The leader is highlighting one type of participation.
A large number raised hands.	
PRINCIPAL. There is one thing I was thinking. I go around and call on people. I am going to suggest next time that groups seat themselves differently. Those in the front of the room get more chances to talk.	The leader's suggestion about seating was a good one as the group in whose room the meeting was held was seated together nearest the front.

From the Robinson School record it can be seen that the principal was conscious that there had been overdirection in discussion. The problem was shared with the children so that all might work on improving the discussion pattern. Other noteworthy features of the principal's leadership were the attempts to foster straight thinking partly through use of concrete aids to planning, through the opportunity given to minority opinion to have a full hearing before the group, through the protecting of individuals' ideas until they had really been listened to, and through the useful summary and evaluation at the close of the meeting. Of the three teachers present, only Mrs. Charles took a hand in the discussion. Although she was no doubt trying to be helpful, her contributions usually were of the "come on now, hurry up" variety. If all the teachers had tried to function as group members, they might have found a useful place in the discussion.

Planning a Room Mural

The making of a mural or frieze is a project frequently engaged in by school groups, perhaps because it lends itself so well to group planning and execution. Miss Sudbury describes planning for a room mural by her second grade children.

After Christmas plans for a room mural were made. Jimmie, who has unusual artistic ability, was selected by the group as chairman to get ideas from the group.

JIMMIE. What shall we put in this picture?

JACQUELINE. Some children and flowers and grass.

KENNETH (who is alert and sensitive to seasons and the world around him). This is winter and you can't see much grass.

TEACHER. If you want a winter picture, what story might you be telling?

FLOYD. Some kids feeding the birds. (We were studying animals, birds and insects at the time.)

ARLIN (who always has worth-while suggestions). You could have other animals too, like squirrels and dogs. (This was agreeable to the group.)

TEACHER. Who wants to be Jimmie's planning helpers?

Since too many children volunteered, Jimmie was asked to choose his "chalk figure" committee. He chose three children who were perhaps the most capable for that particular job. To sketch trees, a house, bushes, and a feeding tray, five children were chosen by various members of the group because they had previously displayed ability to do their particular jobs well.

After the "chalk committee" had completed their work (of figures grouped together and feeding a squirrel) the mural was found to be incomplete. Other figures and bushes were added. The group then checked the mural for filling all empty spaces, or in the words of our art supervisor, leaving "no places for playing football."

Then the painting committee, with the help of all others in the group, decided upon colors. Again the suggestions of the art supervisor were reviewed: (1) repeat color (do it again), (2) light against dark, (3) dark against light, (4) bump the edges, (5) clean colors.

Colors were tried for effectiveness on other paper. Our principal was asked for help in selecting a color which would go well with colors already decided upon. She brought us some art magazines to help us decide on colors.

During the painting of the mural use was made of the list of names on the board, which were suggested by the children for definite jobs, such as painting house, faces, shirts, trees, bird, etc.

In analyzing the techniques she employed, Miss Sudbury listed three. (1) Use of children with special talents to draw out the talents of the others (Jimmie, with marked artistic ability, to plan the mural with the group). (2) Teacher's leading question: "If you want a winter picture, what story might you be telling?" (3) Use of list of names to help establish definite responsibilities. A fourth might have been added, the use of advice given by the art supervisor on a previous occasion.

Planning to Make Christmas Cards

In making articles like Christmas cards, it is important to plan for a neat product as well as for the ideas to be expressed. Miss Franklin reports both kinds of preparation in her first grade group.

December 10. We spent most of our time today planning and making Christmas cards. During the morning, we went over the symbols and colors. We decided to write "Merry Christmas" on the inside of the card and sign our names. We talked about spacing and keeping the cards clean. We planned to put newspaper on the tops of our desks to keep paste off. We discussed the steps necessary to do a neat paste job. I demonstrated the steps and many of the children did too. First, the children were to lay the design on a clean piece of newspaper. Then they were to pick up the design and lay it on a piece of colored folded paper in the right place. The next step was to lay a piece of newspaper on it and press down. The rest of the morning was spent examining Christmas cards.

The teacher goes on to describe how successful the finished cards were. "Even Bernard who usually makes a mess of everything did a neat job. Our results prove the importance of children knowing what to do and how to do it."

Planning to Make Christmas Gifts

The quality of planning which a group of seven slow-learning children were capable of is shown in a record kept by Mrs. Fitzpatrick. Planning to make Christmas gifts grew out of a discussion of whether or not to have a Christmas party.

LEONARD. I don't want no party.

TEACHER. Why?

LEONARD. I need my money for my Christmas presents.

MINNIE. We don't need much, and Mrs. Fitzpatrick, can't we make some things for Christmas?

WILL. Like what?

MINNIE. Oh, things like dolls and doll clothes and chairs.

WILL. Oh, girl, we can't make no chairs for our mothers.

TEACHER. Perhaps we don't have the things we need for making chairs but there are some other things we could make that won't cost much, if anything at all.

CORINNE. How can we make a doll?

TEACHER. Well, have you ever seen a sock doll?

MINNIE. I have.

CLARK. Oh, Minnie, you haven't.

MINNIE. I have too. Mrs. Fitzpatrick had one on her desk one day, didn't you?

TEACHER. Yes, they are easy dolls to make and they wouldn't cost anything. How many would like to make a doll?

ALMOST ALL. Yes. Uh huh. (Etc.)

TEACHER. What about you, Calvin?

CALVIN. Uh huh.

The teacher then told the group what supplies she had on hand, such as thread and needles, and what things the children would need to bring, such as socks and cotton. She also showed them pictures and patterns of other gifts they might make. After several minutes of examining these, the children continued the discussion.

CLARK. Mrs. Fitzpatrick, can I make this (a wooden toy rabbit)?

TEACHER. Sure, Clark, but what about wood for it? I have an empty apple box we could use, but I'm sure it won't be enough for everyone.

LEONARD. I can bring some boards. I got a lot of them at home.

MINNIE. Can we start on these right now, Mrs. Fitzpatrick?

CORINNE. I want to make a doll.

TEACHER. All right. How many would like to make dolls? (All agreed.) How about the working time? Do you think we'll need any more time on this?

WILL. We won't need any more time than our work period. Maybe some time.

MINNIE. Let's work all day.

LEONARD. No, girl, I gotta read too.

WILL. We have to work in our store.

TEACHER. As Will said before, maybe sometime we'll need more time than others, so we'll have to arrange things so we can get our other work done at a different time. Then our work periods can all be in one.

LEONARD. Tomorrow I'll bring the wood.

CORINNE. What about the cotton?

CLARK. I can bring some cotton.

LEONARD. I can too.

TEACHER. All right, let's go over what we have to bring for our project. . . .

This record shows that these mentally handicapped children were capable of showing initiative in this kind of concrete planning. They had ideas about the allotment of their time; they volunteered materials; and one child recalled an item, cotton, that had not been provided for.

Planning Articles for Sale

In addition to giving children a chance to decide what articles to make and how to make them, a projected sale gives the additional educational opportunities of pricing articles and of making arrangements.

In Burnwald School the kindergarten and primary grades were to have a big Christmas bazaar in their auditorium-playroom. Although it was a faculty decision that the bazaar be held, all the children in these groups met in the auditorium to lay general plans. Each group was then to plan particular items to furnish for the bazaar, with the understanding that in case of duplication plans would be changed. An observer took a running record of discussion in three classrooms on the day when bazaar items were decided upon. The three records give an opportunity to compare discussion of the same problem by children five, six, and seven years of age under the leadership of three different teachers.

The record taken in Miss Fallon's kindergarten class offers an example of exploratory discussion which opens up ideas but which does not make definite plans.

Record	*Analysis*
Teacher asks the children for suggestions about making things to sell.	Teacher states purpose of discussion.

Record	*Analysis*
PAUL. A toy sword.	
TEACHER. Could you bring one to show us?	Teacher attempts to keep children on reality level.
CHILD. A boat.	
CHILD. I thought of a little teeny boat of cardboard.	Allows free flow of suggestions.
CHILD. My mother said she could make a hot pad out of paper.	
NANCY. Christmas tree decorations.	
CHILD. A toy fire engine.	
CHILD. I made a wagon last night.	
TEACHER. What did you make it of?	A way of checking on the reality of the comment.
Child explains.	
CHILD. I made a toy ball last night.	
TEACHER. You didn't *make* one, did you?	Again, the teacher pushes back to reality.
JIMMY. Wooden sword.	
TEACHER. That was Paul's idea, but if you think you could, you bring it.	Teacher gives a kindly reminder while still encouraging Jimmy.
What could we make in here? What did we say yesterday?	Teacher attempts to link discussion with a previous one with little success.
CHILD. Pie.	
CHILD. I can make all kinds of things. My Grandma sent me some high-flyers.	Teacher faced choice of pointing out the irrelevancy of the contribution or of ignoring it. She chose to ignore it.
CHILD. Beanbags.	
CHILD. Christmas tree decorations.	
TEACHER. That was what Nancy mentioned.	It is difficult for group members to keep all contributions in mind without a written record (impractical in this situation). Teacher's comment was matter of fact.
CHILD. I have two paint sets. I only need one. I'll sell one of them.	
TEACHER. When we go home at noon we can ask what our mothers can help us with.	Closes discussion with an action suggestion.

Discussion in Mrs. Winston's first grade group was already under way when the observer entered. The teacher spent some time building a background for the day's planning.

Record	*Analysis*
TEACHER. Why are we having the bazaar?	Teacher helps group review the purpose of the planning.
CHILD. So we can get money for the school.	
TEACHER. Is that a good way to make money for our room?	
CHILD. Yes.	
TEACHER. Where are we going to have the bazaar?	Teacher ensures understanding of arrangements.
CHILD. The auditorium.	
TEACHER. Why are we having it in the auditorium?	
CHILD. Because it is big.	
TEACHER. Billy, do you know why we are having it in the auditorium?	
Billy does not know.	
TEACHER. Another reason is that the first, second, and third grades will be there. Harris, how about you? Who else will be there?	Rather than start a prolonged guessing game, the teacher supplied the answer she had in mind.
HARRIS. The mothers.	
TEACHER. If we can't make things, maybe mothers will help.	
CHILD. How about lanterns of paper?	This child, who is ready to start listing suggestions, is ignored. This readiness might well be a sign that the teacher was protracting these preliminaries past the point of usefulness.
TEACHER. When we left the auditorium, Miss Peterson asked us to send her a list of the things we could offer.	Teacher now states purpose of present discussion.
CHILD. Things we can make!	
TEACHER. Are we going to make the same things as the second grade?	
CHILD. No.	
TEACHER. What are we going to make?	
CHILD. Lanterns.	
TEACHER. Could we make something different?	Child tries again to register his suggestion. The teacher does not seem to approve.
CHILD. In nursery school I made a snowman out of cotton.	

Record	*Analysis*
TEACHER. Could we make that here? You made that at home. Child repeats "nursery school," but teacher does not hear.	Case of misunderstanding. Child does not succeed in communicating to teacher.
TEACHER. Well, could we make some stuffed things here, some animals? How many could we make?	Teacher picks up from snowman suggestion only the idea of cotton and twists that to using it for stuffing.
CHILD. We could do what you suggested yesterday—the candles. TEACHER. You brought some already, we ought to use them. CHILD. My mother wants to keep hers. TEACHER. We do not want the best ones. What kind do we want? Children mention used ones. CHILD. We could make cartons.	This suggestion and ones that follow show that the stuffed-toy idea was not immediately appealing.
TEACHER. Could we make them all by ourselves? Does anybody know? Why? Just answer if you have an idea. They wouldn't be strong. CHILD. We sewed in kindergarten. TEACHER. What did you sew? CHILD. An elephant.	Teacher helps group evaluate a suggestion.
TEACHER. Would you like to make something you could sew and stuff? Remember it has got to be good and strong, something people will want to buy. (Children raise hands to vote.) Norman, come up and count the people. When over half of the people want to do something, we do that, don't we? (Group approves stuffed animals.) What do we need? CHILD. Cotton. TEACHER. What else, to sew? CHILD. Needles and thread . . .	At the earliest opportunity the teacher reinserts her favorite suggestion. The use of the vote, always popular with children, no doubt won the day for the teacher's idea.

At this point Mrs. Winston set the discussion on a different track. At the end of the period she said, "Now, let us see what we are going to make," and she wrote on the board: 1. Candles. 2. Toys—wood. 3. Stuffed animals. She then made sure the children understood that their plans might be changed if there were too many duplications by other groups.

Included in the plans for the day in Miss Peterson's second grade room was the item: *"Discussion*—Things We Can Make for the Bazaar."

Record	*Analysis*
TEACHER. If you have anything for discussion, will you get it right now?	Throughout this discussion there is much planning around concrete objects.
Note: This gave the children a little stretch because they were postponing their playtime to hold this discussion to suit the observer's convenience.	
TEACHER. What are we going to discuss?	Teacher makes sure that everyone understands the subject for discussion and has time to prepare to contribute to it.
Child states the problem.	
Teacher puts on board: "Things we can make."	
Several children report what they did the night before.	Teacher allows free flow of discussion but also sees to it that children get a chance to make the contribution they are prepared to give if invited.
TEACHER. Caroline, let us see what you brought.	
CAROLINE (showing some spool knitting). Mother did this much.	
TEACHER. What are you going to do with it?	
CAROLINE. Make a pot holder.	
TEACHER. Do you know how to sew it together?	
CAROLINE. Yes.	
TEACHER. Show us.	Gives child a chance to demonstrate a process.
JOAN (showing a Christmas book). I started this book, but I haven't finished it.	
TEACHER. Did you make this book yourself? Does anybody want to ask any questions?	Teacher encourages group to linger on one contribution until they have received full value from it.
MARY. I have a magazine that tells things you can make—Santa Clauses, and things like that.	
TEACHER. What is the name of the magazine?	
BETTY. Is it *Child Activities?*	
MARY. I don't know. I'll bring it tomorrow.	

Record	*Analysis*

TEACHER. Let us go back just a minute. I want to see the book Joan has made.

Now, Mary, can you tell a little more about your idea? It sounds interesting.

Analysis: Teacher does not scold Mary for taking discussion off on a tangent but politely draws the discussion back after a moment.

Teacher then shows that the intruding idea has a place.

A few moments later Harvey showed a toy he had made of notched spools and rubber bands. Miss Peterson had him explain how he made it, and the children asked questions. The record continues.

Record	*Analysis*

TEACHER. Could you help the children make these, Harvey?
HARVEY. Yes.
TEACHER. What do you call it?
HARVEY. I call it a little tank.
TEACHER. Should Harvey name it?
CHILDREN. Yes.

Analysis: Teacher builds a child as a leader for the group on a certain job.

TEACHER. I have some suggestions; would you like to hear mine? Someone told me yesterday about a napkin ring. (The teacher has to explain what a napkin ring is.) How many have them at home? (A few children do.)

Analysis: Teacher has a right and even an obligation to contribute suggestions. The question is how to make the adult's suggestions take their rightful place among all suggestions given rather than receive special consideration because they are the teacher's. One way is to suggest the idea casually and then see if it comes again from a child. That would be a real test that the idea had taken hold.

Two attempts are necessary before communication is established in this case.

Do you want to know how to make them? (Children are obviously not as interested as in their own suggestions. The teacher has Joan explain what napkin rings are.)
CHILD. Oh, now I know.
CHILD. We could make some pot holders.
TEACHER. Good, I wanted you to suggest that. Can you hold it just a minute? (She goes back to the napkin rings.) Tomorrow I'll tell

Analysis: Children still are more concerned with their own suggestions.

The teacher follows through on her idea.

Record	*Analysis*
you how to make them. Shall we put down napkin rings?	
The children are asked to read to themselves as the teacher writes on board:	Helpful to have a summary.
Things we can make 1. Little tanks 2. Sailboats 3. Stuffed dolls 4. Floating candles 5. Napkin rings 6. Pot holders	
TEACHER. Will this be all we will make?	An attempt to clinch a decision.
CHILD. A teensie pillow.	Children's ideas still are not exhausted.
TEACHER. Maybe we could add to it. Will you read what we listed so far?	The teacher wisely leaves the way open for further ideas.

It is not always easy to determine whether variations in discussion patterns are due to differences in maturity and experience of group members with cooperative procedures or whether they are the result of differences in skill on the part of leaders. It is probably safe to conclude from the three examples given that discussion, and therefore the job of leadership, was most complex in the oldest of the three groups. The seven-year-olds carried their planning further in one period than did the others. While this may have been due partly to the fact that they came to the discussion better prepared than the younger children (as a result of good management on the part of Miss Peterson), the additional maturity of the children was undoubtedly an important factor.

All three teachers used some leadership techniques worth noting. Miss Fallon tried to have her children be realistic, and she gave them time to explore ideas and to get further help from their mothers before deciding what article to make. Mrs. Winston and Miss Peterson provided for a summary at the end of the period, and in addition, the first grade teacher left the children prepared for a change of plans. Miss Peterson made sure that the children would come to the planning period with concrete ideas, and she helped the group to give thoughtful attention to each contribution. However, both the first and second grade teachers were a little blinded to children's reactions by their preoccupation with their own suggestions. In Mrs. Winston's case, this affected the course of the discussion in a major way.

Planning a Written Product

The writing of a letter, story, or play by a group calls into use talents other than those required for planning in terms of concrete materials. Miss Sudbury describes the composing of a group letter of thanks by her second grade children.

Planning a Cooperative Thank-You Letter

On Mary's Birthday, Mary's mother had sent a cupcake for each child in the room. So thrilled were the children with their pretty cakes that most of them didn't eat them but took them home to share with their parents.

On the following morning the teacher asked how many had enjoyed the cakes and before she had a chance to say anything else, a thank-you letter was suggested by Jackie.

TEACHER. How shall we write it?

KENNETH. Choose people to make up the letter.

FLOYD. Then we will put it together.

TEACHER. Who would like to take charge?

Many hands went up. The teacher chose Peggy because she felt that Peggy, who had a hearing defect, needed help in leading a group.

PEGGY. Who wants to say something?

Four sentences given by Pauline, Larry F., Robert, and Judy were chosen by a majority vote to make up the body of the letter. The sequence of sentences was obtained when the teacher asked, "Which sentence do you think comes first? Second? Third? And last?" As each choice was made, the child whose sentence was thought to come first placed himself first in line, and the second, third, and fourth child stood in consecutive order.

PEGGY. How shall we write it?

GLENDA. Choose other children to write it on the board.

GLEN. Let the children at each table have a turn at spelling words.

When the four children who copied the letter on the blackboard had any difficulty, other children helped with the spelling of words, the one whose sentence it was, dictating it as we went along. Glenda suggested that the word "yellow" could be found in a book that her group was reading. Precocious Pauline suggested periods at the end of sentences when they were omitted. Attentive Larry called attention to the omission of the "little mark at the top after the y in Mary's name" (in the phrase "Mary's birthday").

After the completion of the writing of the body of the letter, the following four choices for the endings were suggested by many children:

Your classmates in Room 15
Your friends in Room 15

From the class in Room 15
Mary's friends in Room 15

Because the recess period was at hand, not enough time was given for the discussion of the best endings. "Your classmates in Room 15" was eliminated because "we are not Mrs. Cole's classmates." "From the class in Room 15" received the majority vote.

After recess Peggy asked, "What are we going to do with the letter?" Robert said, "We should copy it and send the best one to Mrs. Cole and keep the other one for the book (of class experiences)." The class voted to do this.

Mary delivered the best copy to her mother.

Miss Sudbury concludes her evaluation of the experience.

While many children took part in the writing of the letter by spelling individual words, I feel that this procedure is not advisable for small children. The continuity of the letter would have been maintained and much less time would have been consumed had the four children whose sentences made up the letter been helped over the hard places while they themselves wrote it.

However, this has been one of the most satisfying cooperative planning experiences that we have had, due in large measure to the children's feeling of a need for action. There was interest and cooperation from all and actual practice in oral and written expression.

1. Teacher's leading questions: How many enjoyed the cupcakes? Which sentence do you think comes first?

2. Active use of children: In leading group. In writing on board. In helping with spelling.

An illustration of group writing from Miss Sanborn's fourth grade classroom offers suggestions for making this kind of planning more efficient. Decisions that had been made by someone prior to the planning described here were:

1. Each child would make a Thanksgiving booklet.

2. Each chapter in the booklet would be composed by the whole group and copied by the individual for his own booklet.

3. The chapters would be:
Why We Have Thanksgiving
Why the Pilgrims Came to America
Life of the Pilgrims in Holland
Voyage to America
The First Thanksgiving
Thanksgiving Today

The problem for the day was to write the third chapter on "Life of the Pilgrims in Holland." The first step was to think out the ideas to be incorporated. These were listed as follows:

1. Happy at first
2. Houses different
3. Children spoke Dutch better than English
4. Didn't have church of their own
5. Children were not healthy
6. Heard that America had land for all
7. Children liked Dutch ways

The procedure was then to formulate, polish, and agree upon the chapter, sentence by sentence.

While one might wish to question the restrictions placed on creativity by each of the preliminary decisions, one sees that once these steps had been taken, the pooling of ideas to be included in a chapter proved a sound technique for implementing the decisions. There is some value also in group experience in weighing words and judging expressions in terms of effectiveness in conveying ideas. These values, however, might be sought in other content and in relation to other purposes.

Miss Sanborn's group also had the experience of writing a play. The class was observed one day discussing the problem of "listing scenes." First, there was a discussion of dramatic elements—action, dialogue (conversation and expression), plot (continuous story), scenes (episodes), costumes, scenery. The children then made the following list:

1. Discussing the Voyage
2. Talking on Board the Ship
3. Meeting of the "Ark" and the "Dove"
4. Finding a New Home
5. Buying of Maryland
6. Settling in Maryland (Life in the Colony)
7. Giving Up of Land
8. Changing the Capital
9. Making the Boundary Line

The principal, who was visiting the group, asked the children what was to be their next step. "Choose the scenes we will use and put some of them together" was the answer. The observer noted during the period that the teacher kept the discussion on the track, gave wide opportunities for participation, welcomed a suggestion that the new settlers have some excitement on board ship, related the scene "Finding a New Home" to the experience of a boy who had just moved to the school district. It was obvious that the children had engaged in a great deal of research before undertaking the planning of their scenes.

Planning to publish a newspaper at school is another worth-while enterprise for children and youth. Miss Brainard's diary gives a detailed account of the development of a newspaper in her sixth grade group. Briefly, these were some highlights of the experience.

1. By decision of the group, the real interest of the class in having a newspaper was determined by the response to the first call for contributions.
2. A representative committee inquired into the matter of costs and reported to the group.
3. Shares of stock were sold to finance the paper.
4. Children were helped to learn proofreading through the use of an opaque projector, which made it possible for a group to focus attention on articles submitted.
5. The goal of an issue every two weeks was reached through the use of two staffs, giving each staff more time to take into account past mistakes in preparing a new issue.
6. Profits were figured after each issue.
7. Editors who had had experience conducted training periods for new staffs.
8. Reporters from each class in school were added to increase reader interest.
9. Steps in printing a commercial newspaper were compared with steps which the children employed; other comparisons were made.

All of these steps involved a great deal of planning together, as Miss Brainard's detailed account shows.

Planning School Gardens

Garden plots at school open up manifold possibilities for cooperative planning that provides its own tests of effectiveness—in results that are tangible, like radishes and tomatoes and flowers.

A half-day spent in a school in a rural setting yielded much evidence of how an entire school may cooperate on a gardening project that has the worthy aim of supplying the school cafeteria. The fifth grade children in this school were in charge of the whole garden, and in their room was a map of the triangular garden plot available for their use. The map was drawn to scale and showed the ground allotted to each grade, as well as the crops for which each group was taking responsibility. A list of what each group had planted had been lettered on a large poster near the garden map.

First Grade—Radishes
Second Grade—Parsley, carrots, radishes, lettuce, pumpkins
Second Grade—Carrots, lettuce

Third Grade—Onions
Fourth Grade—Carrots, tomatoes, late cabbage
Fifth Grade—Tomatoes, beets
Sixth Grade—Onions, string beans

The fifth graders had decided to delay the planting of their tomatoes and beets so these would be ready for use after school opened in the fall. They were buying some of their plants. A large chart on the wall showed that these children were making an intensive study of vegetable gardening. These were the chart headings:

WHEN AND HOW TO PLANT VEGETABLES

Name	When to Sow	How Deep	Width of Rows	Plants Apart	When Come Up	Days Needed to Mature

The children were also learning to classify vegetables into seed crops, stem crops, fruits, bulbs, root crops, and leafy vegetables. Out of thirty-five children in the group, the teacher explained, eight had had actual experience in planting tomatoes. Around the experience of the eight, the whole group had built their plan for planting their tomatoes at school. On the day of the visit, the children were discussing how to "draw" the tomato plants for transplanting. They decided that the soil should be wet so it would cling to the plant, that evening or early morning was the best time, that the plant should be shaded from the sun at first, and that at some time the plant would have to be staked up.

The third grade, which had elected to raise onions, had worked out standards for choosing a crop.

Standards for Choosing a Crop

1. Will it mature before we leave school in June?
2. Will it be good to use in the fall?
3. Is it a crop that is suitable for us to plant?
4. Is our climate suitable for the crop?
5. Can it be used in the cafeteria?
6. Does our soil suit this crop?

On the board was a story which was a progress report showing some of the group's plans for the future.

Yesterday we went to the garden.
We saw that the onions were coming up.
When they get a little larger we will have to work the soil around them. This will keep the weeds out.
Some radishes were coming up too.
The first grade planted them.

The first grade children had been very much occupied with the garden, and their room was full of stories about it.

We will have a school garden.
We will plant vegetables in it.
The boys and girls will work the garden.
Gardens must be planted in the spring.

. . .

We need many things to have a garden.
We need a rake to make the soil fine.
We need a hoe to make holes.
We need stakes to show where the seeds are.
We need labels for the different stakes.
We need a watering pot if it does not rain.
We need a garden plow.

. . .

Our garden will be in small plots.
Each class will have a plot.
They will plant it and work it.
Each class will have a different size plot.
Each plot will have a different vegetable.

. . .

We will make the soil very fine.
We will plant our seeds at the end of the garden.
Our class will plant radish seeds.
Radish seeds are small and round.
We will be careful to drop the seeds in the rows.

. . .

Gardens must be kept clean.
Weeds grow best when the sun shines.
We will have to keep the weeds out.
The best way is to work the soil often.
Vegetables grow best when there are no weeds.

. . .

Our radishes are up now.
The plants are very little.
The ground is wet now.
When the ground is dry we will work them.
That will make them grow.
We will give them to Mrs. Edison.

The second grade's stories gave some additional angles to gardening.

Our Garden

We're planning to have a school garden.
We will give the food to the school cafeteria.
Mr. Day has plowed the ground. Then he slabbed and
harrowed the ground to break the clods. Mr. Day
then put manure on the garden.

Things We Will Do

First we will pick up the stones and carry them
away. Then we will rake our garden. We will rake
it several times until the soil becomes fine. We
will make some rows and drop the seeds in the rows.
Some children will then cover the seeds lightly.

The fourth grade had been considering helpers needed to make a garden.

What Helpers Do We Need to Make a Garden?

Rain	Rake	Horses
Plow	Shovel	Garden Tractor
Harrow	Wheelbarrow	Sun
Slab	Manure Spreader	Spreading Forks
Hoe		Birds

The children in this rural school were learning to garden scientifically by using the best information they could get and by making careful plans as to what steps to take, what tools to use, and proper timing.

PLANNING PRODUCTIONS

Results of group planning may be in less tangible form than gifts or murals. They may be in the form of productions, such as a party or play. Here, too, there is opportunity for much concreteness in planning and a chance to test results in terms easily understood by the planners.

Planning Parties

Mrs. Austin's account of planning for a Halloween party with her kindergarten children shows how well five-year-olds can handle such a problem.

Record	Analysis
One of the children had brought a pumpkin to school. Following a discussion of Halloween, the	Teacher makes use of opportunity to hold background discussion. Teacher poses problem.

Record	*Analysis*

teacher asked: "What shall we do for Halloween in our kindergarten?"

CHARLENE. Could we have a Halloween party?

TEACHER. Yes, we could have it on Halloween day. How many would like to?

Teacher gives group opportunity to register opinion.

Unanimous assent.

JIMMY B. Could we dress up in costumes and wear masks?

TEACHER. Shall we have just the ones who want to wear a costume? If you don't have a costume, what could you do?

Teacher encourages development of original ideas.

LARRY. You could dress up like a girl!

SKEETER. You could be a hobo.

RONALD. You could wear a sheet and be a ghost.

EDDIE. You could make a hat and a mask and just wear those.

Four children give pertinent suggestions without interruption by teacher.

TEACHER. Yes, we could make hats and masks at school in our work time. What else shall we plan to do for Halloween?

Teacher makes a suggestion for carrying out child's idea, then by a question, launches a new phase of the discussion.

WAYNE. We could make a jack-o-lantern out of our pumpkin.

TEACHER. How shall we make it?

By a question the teacher encourages child to go further with his suggestion.

WAYNE. Cut eyes, nose, and mouth and put a candle in it.

PEGGY. We could decorate our room with Halloween things.

TEACHER. Yes, we could begin working on the decorations right away so we would have them finished in time for the party.

In the permissive atmosphere created by the teacher's ready acceptance of children's ideas, children take initiative for suggesting new problems for group consideration.

GRAY W. Will we have anything to eat at the party?

Another example of pupil initiative.

TEACHER. How many would like to have refreshments served at the party? Do you know what refreshments means?

EDDIE. It means something to eat.

TEACHER. What shall we plan to have for refreshments?

Record	Analysis

CHARLENE. Ice cream and cake.

TEACHER. Usually people have ice cream and cake at birthday parties, but Halloween is a special kind of day. Wouldn't you like to have something special for your Halloween party?

Teacher encourages further suggestions by her statement and question.

MARTHA. Sometimes people have apples at Halloween parties.

TEACHER. Yes, that's a good suggestion.

PEGGY. Popcorn would be good.

CHARLENE. And let's have some candy.

TEACHER. How many think apples, popcorn and candy will be all right for our refreshments?

It was agreed.

Teacher gives group opportunity to register opinion.

TEACHER. We have planned to wear costumes, to make a jack-o-lantern, to decorate our room, and to serve refreshments of apples, popcorn, and candy. Do we need to decide anything else?

Teacher summarizes plans made so far and gives opportunity for the children to think of other items requiring consideration.

RONALD P. We could guess who everybody is.

Five children respond freely.

RONALD R. We could play a game.

PEGGY. We could say those poems about the pumpkins and jack-o-lanterns and brownies.

SANDRA. We could sing some Halloween songs.

JIMMY. We could trick or treat.

TEACHER. When do children usually play the trick-or-treat game?

Teacher challenges suggestion with a reasonable question.

EDDIE. You do that on Halloween night when you dress up and go around the neighborhood.

TEACHER. Yes, shall we save that for Halloween night? If you are treated, what could you do for the people who treat you?

Teacher helps children to be ready with a plan of conduct for future use.

PEGGY. Say a Halloween poem or sing a Halloween song.

CHARLENE. That's a good idea.

At this point the teacher judged it was time to terminate the planning period, for signs of fatigue and restlessness were beginning to develop. Since young children have a short span of attention, Mrs. Austin kept planning periods down to ten or fifteen minutes in length. Her record continues with an account of later planning.

Another day, baskets for popcorn were decided upon in preference to plates or sacks. Other planning resulted in the decorations.

The cutting of the pumpkin to make a jack-o-lantern was great fun and everyone had a turn to help draw the design, to cut, or to scoop seeds. It was decided to save the seeds and plant them in the spring.

The decision to save the seeds and plant them in the spring is an example of how children learn to do long-range planning.

An account by Miss Franklin shows in detail the careful planning her first grade children engaged in before enjoying their Christmas party.

December 8. We wanted to create the real Christmas feeling for our Christmas party so we talked about the things that make a good party. Veronica said we should make the room look like Christmas. Several children volunteered to decorate the room. Carl said we should have fun at our party. We decided to plan games that could be played indoors. Mary said, "Let's plan for some entertainment at our party."

We had been listening to parts of the "Nutcracker Suite" since the first of December, so we chose the parts we liked best to listen to at our party. This meant we had to send a note immediately to Mr. L. to see if we could have the phonograph for a half-hour on the day of the party. I explained to them we might not be able to get the machine because many other classes wanted it too. Gwendolyn spoke up and said we could borrow hers for the party. We thought as a part of our entertainment it would be fun to sing our Christmas songs. The children asked me to read them a Christmas story as part of the entertainment. Several children were chosen to lead the games and others to see that the entertainment went off all right.

The next thing we discussed was refreshments. In evaluating our Halloween party, we thought that we had had too much food, because most children brought in refreshments. Lots of it was the same, and we had to save it for the following week. We thought it wasteful to have so much when there are so many starving people in the world.

After much discussion, we decided on a simple menu of red and green jello, gingerbread men, and Christmas candy. We planned to make our own jello and gingerbread. The children were enthusiastic about this. Jean said, "This will make it just like Christmas to make our own refreshments." The children planned to bring the ingredients for the cookies and the jello. Each one would bring something. I volunteered to supply the candy and the containers for the jello. We planned to decorate plain white napkins to look like Christmas napkins and make place mats for our desks.

In checking over our plans, we discovered that provision had not been made for arranging the desks for a party, for serving the food, and for cleaning up after the party. We decided to have a cleanup committee and a serving committee to take care of these jobs. After discussing the duties of these committees, we selected our children to work on each of these committees.

As far as can be discovered from the teacher's report, the planning for the party was divided into distinct parts and each problem brought up by the children was thoroughly dealt with before a new problem was discussed. The final checkup on plans proved to be a useful device.

Miss Franklin goes on to comment on further preparation and on the party itself.

The different committees met with me several times before the Christmas party, but naturally, with so many things going on, the day of the party was one of real excitement. We would have been lost without our careful planning.

Like Miss Franklin, Mrs. Nugent wanted her second grade children to plan their Christmas party by making use of their previous experience in planning a Halloween party. The difficulties she ran into are those that group leaders frequently encounter if they are too attached to a preconceived outline of plans. Only some means of studying the actual progress of discussion will reveal such difficulties. A running record of part of a planning period in Mrs. Nugent's room will serve to illustrate pitfalls to be avoided in group leadership.

Record	*Analysis*
TEACHER. What is the first thing we should do in planning for a Christmas party? Let's think what we did first for our Halloween party.	The teacher's idea of making use of past experience was a good one. However, her question was not clearly enough defined to secure the response she desired, and she was not flexible enough to take the children's guesses and turn them to constructive use. When "played games" was suggested, the teacher might well have accepted the contribution, perhaps asking, "Shall we have a few people plan some games for us?"
CHILD. Played games.	
TEACHER. I mean in planning. What is the first thing in planning?	
CHILD. A program.	
TEACHER. That would be part of it. (Waits for another suggestion.)	
Didn't we have a group of people? What did we call it? (She "fishes" for some time for the answer she has in mind.)	

Record

Analysis

Didn't we call it "program committee"? You have mentioned different committees we should like to set up. What should we have up here on the blackboard first? Committee to work on what?

CHILD. Program.

TEACHER. All right. (Writes "program.")

CHILD. Cleanup.

TEACHER. That would come later. What else? (Although the teacher rejected the suggestion in this way she did enter "cleanup" on the board record later.)

CHILD. What we eat.

TEACHER. What would that be called?

CHILD. Refreshments.

TEACHER. Now think what would you like to have?

BOY. I think food.

TEACHER. Maybe the refreshment committee could do that or do you want a special group?

The children want a special group.

TEACHER. What shall we call them?

CHILD. Passers.

TEACHER. I think we can find a better word than that.

CHILD. Servants.

TEACHER. Shall we call them servants?

The children like this term.

TEACHER. Do you need something like napkins and place cards? What would you call that kind of committee?

The children are not sure.

The teacher's questions tend to be confusing because vague.

The teacher wisely accedes to the wishes of the group.

Teacher rejects suggestion by her evaluation of it.

The teacher at this point was amused and good-naturedly gave in to the children. She might have accepted "passers" as one suggestion, then asked for several ideas and finally suggested choosing the best of the whole group of terms. If promotion of clear thinking and a vocabulary to express ideas accurately may be considered as possible values of group planning, it would seem that a good opportunity had been lost at this point.

Record	*Analysis*
TEACHER. What committee would get our room all ready, some special things up? Are you going to leave this room *undecorated?*	Again the teacher has the children playing a guessing game. After a broad hint, someone hits upon the right answer.
CHILDREN. No.	
TEACHER. Well, what do you need?	
CHILDREN. Decorations.	
TEACHER. Do you need any more on the list? How many do you want on each committee?	
CHILD. Seven.	
TEACHER. That would be too many. You would get in each other's way.	Teacher makes arbitrary ruling instead of encouraging the children to work out a reasonable number.
CHILD. Three.	
Teacher chooses chairmen and has each chairman choose two others.	
TEACHER. Think what suggestions we can give these people so they will have them right in their minds.	As the observer left, the teacher was asking the large group to give a few suggestions to each committee. This might or might not be a wise use of the large group's time.[1]

"Party Plans" (as recorded on the blackboard).

> Program
> Cleanup
> Refreshment
> Servants
> Decoration

Party-planning in school calls for other preparations also, as Mrs. Malden's report shows.

September 15. I opened for discussion with my fifth graders the possibility of having a tea party for their mothers. The purposes would be to have their mothers become acquainted with their new teacher and new classroom and to give all of us a chance to have a social hour together. The boys and girls were excited over the idea of a tea party and were most anxious to learn how to give one. We discussed the meaning and purpose of a tea party and decided on refreshments—tea, punch, and cookies.

Later in the day we used our English period to learn how to make

[1] Ways of saving time for the large group are discussed on pages 386–387.

introductions between children, between adults, and between adults and children. The boys and girls loved "acting out" introductions with their classmates.

September 16. We found a punch recipe and tripled proportions. Then we made out a shopping list for our shopping committee. We figured up the total cost for refreshments and divided by twenty-five pupils. The boys and girls decided they were giving the party and they would pay expenses from their spending money. Mothers would not be asked to contribute money or refreshments for their own party.

September 17. The tea party was a great success! At 1:15 the children and I went to the cooking room and made the punch. . . . Then to the library where we learned to set a tea table. There was plenty for everyone to do. . . .

Mrs. Malden's story shows that a party can be made the center for many useful learnings but that it need not consume many days of preparation.

Planning with Parents for a Party

Miss Reisner formed a committee of first grade children and parents to help plan a party for all the mothers of her group. In Miss Reisner's school there was considerable interest on the part of principal and teachers in encouraging planning in such mixed groups. A running record of the joint planning on this occasion serves to illustrate some of the values and difficulties of planning with a group representing such a wide difference in age and experience. Three mothers had come to plan with Miss Reisner's committee of six first graders. Others in the group were a fellow-teacher who wanted to study the procedures, the principal, a family life counselor, and an observer. The children first showed their mothers a health chart the teacher had made and duplicated. Each child had made a cover for his chart, following his own ideas of decoration. The children were to check the chart at home with the help of their mothers.

> TEACHER. We want the mothers to help plan a party so we can tell all mothers what we are trying to do.
> FAMILY LIFE COUNSELOR. Do parents know the basic foods, the amount of sleep children should have?
> PARENT. Yes, they know the basic foods.
> PRINCIPAL. They know these things, but don't follow them.
> PARENT. We tell our children that they grow when they are asleep.
> TEACHER. Should we be specific or keep it general?
> PARENT. This chart is enough.
> TEACHER. Do we need an expert or can the children tell it?
> PARENT. Children have a way of putting things.

It was decided that the children would put on a short dramatization to be followed by a luncheon. Other suggestions were that leaflets describing a good school lunch might be handed out and that parents might like to exchange recipes. The next problem was to plan the menu. A parent asked the children what they wanted.

> CHILD. Food.
> CHILD. Milk.
> CHILD. Sandwiches.
> CHILD. Banana sandwiches.
> PARENT. Carrots.

It was further decided that the mothers would take the responsibility for getting donations of food and for managing the luncheon. The next problem was that of setting a time for the party. The parents wanted the party on Friday so it would be easy to get away from home. After considerable discussion of this and other points, the mothers' committee decided to meet at a later time, and the meeting was adjourned.

It may be noted that the meeting sometimes provided a place for the child members of the committee and again left them untouched by the discussion. Since this was the case, the children grew very restless before the meeting was over. One suggestion prompted by this experience is that the business related to adult-child enterprises be divided as carefully as possible into two parts: (1) those matters in which the children can have a genuine share and (2) those which will be decided by adults. In this case, planning for the children to make a definite contribution (show their health charts) early in the meeting was good. However, this contribution on the part of the children did not result in interaction with the adults; the children were merely *talking to* the parents. The children were also active participants when the menu was under discussion. There was a little interaction at this point which the abbreviated record does not show.

The parents actually took over the decision-making with respect to the program. This the children could have done well by themselves. Probably there could have been adult-child interaction during this phase of the discussion if adults had been a little more skillful in their group techniques and more thoughtful about helping the children to participate. It may be assumed that the children would later plan the dramatization with others in their class.

It seems quite apparent that the children might better have been excused from the deliberations as soon as the details of the luncheon, including setting the day for it, were taken up by the adults. Again, these are matters which the children could have settled had the party been for them alone. It is to be hoped that there was opportunity later for the children to help plan the serving for their group.

One might ask whether there was any point in having the parents and children meet together for any of the planning. Two potential values come to mind. One is the motivating effect of participation in planning. For the children and parents who were present, and for those to whom they could communicate their feelings, there was very possibly a greater identification with the project as "ours" rather than as a "party we are giving for you" or a "party you are giving for us." A second possible value is that adults and children may come to understand one another and have greater mutual respect as a result of cooperative thinking. This value would exist only if the adults and children found themselves able to operate as interacting peers on some points at least. To what extent such interaction is possible with six-year-olds and adults is a matter yet to be determined.

A second example of adult-youth planning of a party comes from a junior high school where the Hi-Y and Girl Reserve groups were holding a joint meeting. The year before, these groups had sponsored a highly successful "Ma, Pa, and Me Night." Their purpose was to plan a second such affair. Others present were a few parents, the secretaries of the local Y.W.C.A. and Y.M.C.A., the advisers of the two school clubs, and an observer. The Hi-Y president acted as chairman.

> CHAIRMAN. What did you like last year?
> PUPIL. Singing and speeches.
> PUPIL. The girls in the cafeteria made a mess.
> CHAIRMAN. We need someone to take this down. What didn't you like?
> PUPIL. We didn't have enough time.
> GIRL RESERVE ADVISER. Which part?
> PUPIL. The gym.
> PARENT. It helped community spirit.
> GIRL RESERVE ADVISER. Let's consider the purpose first. Why do we plan to have young people included? I think there are four reasons: one, to introduce parents to teachers; two, to give returned veterans a chance to get reacquainted; three, to give the family something to enjoy together; four, to help parents become acquainted with their children's friends and school.
> Y.M.C.A. SECRETARY. Are there many fathers back from the service and war plants?

HI-Y ADVISER. Yes, and older brothers.

PUPIL. We could use two gyms and have square dances for parents in one. The kids didn't know how to square dance.

ADULT. Should we have the parents in one room and the students in another?

PUPIL. Should we dance in the same room with other activities?

CHAIRMAN. Let's go to plans for this year's program.

Y.W.C.A. SECRETARY. What kind of songs should we have? Those that parents know?

GIRL RESERVE ADVISER. Do you want a speaker or a panel?

Y.M.C.A. SECRETARY. The students might talk on "How I Would Run My Home."

Y.W.C.A. SECRETARY. Is there anything you'd like help on—like having your parents see the importance of bringing your friends into your home? Or would you like to put on a skit?

GIRL RESERVE ADVISER. Let's see how many want discussion. (Favored by most.)

They decided on dancing in one gym, games in the other. They decided on food at the end of the evening. They set up committees for publicity, fun, food, and program.

This brief record does not do full justice to the contributions made by some of the students. In general, however, the professional adults were the most active in the discussion. It may be noted that their participation was largely in the form of questions—questions that were suggestive and that helped the group reach decisions. Undoubtedly the pressure of time caused the adults to try to hurry matters along. Still, the plans that resulted clearly expressed the will of the group, were based on the experience of the year before, and were definite enough to allow small group planning to ensue.

Planning Programs

A program may be planned as a holiday observance such as Miss Merlin, a fifth grade teacher, describes in her diary.

"Do we ever have Halloween programs?" was June's question one day. Although I knew she very likely had some ideas ready for such a program, I asked the group if they would like to think it over. Later they decided to make their program one of Halloween poems. The remark of mine that influenced them in this direction was that most of the Halloween poems have fun in them.

The boys and girls planned to work together in small groups on various poems. Some of the poems are those which I had mounted for the bulletin boards, but the children sought others too. As we had had some informal choral speaking this year, that was the choice of two groups. Another group decided to dramatize their poem. A fourth group came to me for suggestions. They had only to be shown some slides to get an idea that satisfied them. Several boys who were not interested in performing preferred to make scenery.

The teacher, without design perhaps, had helped build a background for the planning by bringing attention to poems of the season and by giving her class experience with choral speaking. She then brought the suggestion of one child before the group, giving time to think up ideas. She helped further with direct suggestions to the large group and to a committee. The teacher's full report also included an account of how the children selected the audience for their program.

Miss Naughton's children planned a poetry-listening hour, inviting a guest reader and turning over to two classmates the job of selecting poems to be read. The teacher was rather dissatisfied with the audience courtesy displayed, especially during the latter half of the hour-long program.

This very concern for audience courtesy shows what an excellent opportunity for many kinds of learning is afforded by such a program. Besides having an opportunity to enjoy the poetry itself, the children could evaluate this experience in planning an even more enjoyable poetry hour on some future occasion. For example, they might decide that the program had been too long even though the quality was good. They might decide to try a different way of selecting poems to be read. They might work out ways for some kind of participation by themselves as a variation from straight listening.

Many other types of listening experiences can be planned by groups also, such as listening to radio programs or recordings.

Planning Plays

Sometimes circumstances force groups to produce a play with extremely limited time for preparation. Miss Brainard found herself in this situation, but she made it possible for her group to have the experience of selecting the play they would produce and of planning how to meet a deadline. The teacher reports the affair in her diary.

November 27. Now that the Thanksgiving program was over, we thought we should reach some decision about our presentation of a Christmas play. Reports on stories which would be suitable for our use were made. (I was rather disappointed by the response to the suggestion to look for stories.) Cathy got some plays from the library. Bob was quite anxious that we use Dickens' *Christmas Carol,* so he brought in a book containing a version of that story. All the other books were ones I brought in from the main library, or ones we brought up to our room from our school collection of Christmas stories. (I didn't go to the neighborhood branch library because I thought that source was easily accessible to the children.)

After Cathy and Bob had given their suggestions, I mentioned "The Voyage of the Wee Red Cap" as a story suitable for us to dramatize. We are going to have to consider these three possibilities when we return from the Thanksgiving holidays.

Personally I'm getting a bit concerned about the time element, for if we give the play for the school program it must be presented for the P.T.A. on December 17. Twelve days doesn't allow much time to reach decisions through group discussions. Perhaps I'm crossing bridges before I reach them. It may all work out smoothly.

December 2. Today was the day to make our decision about a Christmas play. I brought up the matter of the time we had. That didn't seem to baffle the children at all. They were all for a play, so we proceeded with the idea of which one it should be.

The play which Cathy brought in we noticed required the payment of a royalty. Some children immediately thought of little ways to circumvent the payment. Others thought the play should be discarded from our choices because of this fee. (It was only three dollars, so it wasn't prohibitive.) I suggested that we consider it among our choices since Cathy had presented it, but that, if we selected it, the payment of the royalty would be the only honest practice we could follow.

Cathy had read her play to the group previously. We asked her to review the characters needed and to present the possibilities for our staging the play. Next I read completely "The Voyage of the Wee Red Cap," having the children list the characters as I read it. They also listed the scenes needed in dramatizing it. In the afternoon, I brought in the records which I had brought of Dickens' *Christmas Carol.* We listened to the recordings and the children listed the characters and the scenes needed.

When the three choices had been presented, we discussed them as possibilities for our play. We had a pretty lively discussion. (It was not all question-answer procedure with me seeming endlessly to prime the pump, as so often happens.)

The story already in play form (the one requiring a royalty) was discarded as being rather difficult to stage. Many of the children expressed their preference for Dickens' *Christmas Carol,* but they thought it would be difficult for us to stage some parts. They also thought it was an impractical one for us to select since there was such a preponderance of boys' parts and we have eight boys and twenty-two girls in our class. Several expressed their choice for "The Voyage of the Wee Red Cap," and after discussion, this story became the almost unanimous selection.

Since Cathy and Bob had been the only ones who had brought in stories, I selected them as the committee to see the principal. They were to find out if she would like us to present the play for the P.T.A. meeting. They were also to ask if the clerk would type the parts for us when we had the story dramatized.

We realized we had to work quickly. Two of the books from our school library contained the story. Two girls volunteered to go to the branch library to see if the story was contained in any books available there. I offered to look in the main library when I returned the books that we were not using. Another teacher who had an errand up at State Teachers College offered to inquire in the library up there.

Our many sources produced only one additional copy, but we got busy in three small groups and dramatized the various scenes.

December 4. With our time so short, we thought we had better choose committees to work on the various phases of our project. We have selected a scenery committee, a costume committee, a program committee, and one for stage properties.

The scenery committee began functioning almost immediately. We had decided to show the Spain scene and the Holland scene as tableaux. Jean took her committee and they went down to the auditorium "armed" with a fifty-foot tape measure, pencil, paper, and window pole. (The orchestra was practicing, but we thought if they closed the curtains they could get their measurements without disturbing the rehearsal.)

They did quite well. Then they went to the office and cut off two lengths of paper from the large roll. They brought it upstairs and, using the corridor floor for their workshop, fastened it together. Tomorrow they hope to get the Holland scene planned out.

December 5. It always amazes me what some youngsters are able to do in art work. Jean, Janet, Dick, and Virginia worked out in the corridor. Janet could draw figures well, so she was given the task of drawing the central figures in the picture. Dick started working on two windmills which were to appear in the scene. Jean started on a house and Virginia, a tree. They accomplished a great deal in that work period.

We couldn't leave the scenery on the corridor floor and since it is twenty-one feet long, moving it into our room presented a bit of a problem. When we got it in, we fastened it across the front of our room.

"Don't you think we could work on it here tomorrow, Miss Brainard? It's an awful job to move it," was Dick's query.

"We might be a little crowded, but we could move our desks closer together and leave work space at the front of the room," one person suggested. That seemed an agreeable plan, so we shall shift furniture tomorrow to make room for our scenery painters.

December 12. As the date for the presentation of our play nears, the children are ever more conscious of the responsibility which is theirs since they promised to put on the Christmas program. They have been working like the proverbial beavers. There have been so many and such varied jobs to do that we are seldom all in one place at the same time.

Those working on the Holland scene have given up their game periods, worked before and after school and at lunch time. They were quite pleased today when Mr. R. helped the boys arrange it on the stage. Their comment was that it was an awful lot of work when it would be in view only a few minutes. I suggested that we might ask the principal if there were some place in the school where we might display it for a while when we return from the Christmas holidays. I agree with them that it deserves a longer viewing. However, from the number of heads that popped into our room while we were working on it, I think their work was being seen.

December 18. The play is over and now the excitement due to that will subside. Working against a "deadline" for giving a performance is a very lifelike situation, but personally I often feel that a great deal is lost educationally by such a procedure. One of the good purposes which the play has served is that several children who have done outstanding work on the scenery are ones who have been rather retiring in class. It has also stimulated some lively discussions and has presented real problems which had to be solved.

Miss Brainard's account contains several useful suggestions for other teachers. She herself took a stand for fair dealings—just consideration of Cathy's play and payment of the royalty if the play were used. She encouraged intelligent listening as plays or stories were presented by having scenes and characters listed for use in evaluating the material later. Even though she had some misgivings about rushing the play through, there was admirable use of divided labor and responsibility which gave opportunities for growth to many children.

Casting a play presents both a problem and an opportunity. Some teachers assume the responsibility themselves. If casting becomes a group activity, care must be exercised in order that damage may not be done to personalities. What happened in Mrs. Graham's third grade group can occur all too easily.

TEACHER. Let's choose girls of different sizes for the three sisters. I think Betty would be good for the smallest one. (The children groan in protest, but one boy supports the teacher. Teacher puts Betty's name down.)

TEACHER. Why would Melvin be good for the Mayor?

CHILD. The Mayor was fat.

CHILD. Melvin is getting fatter all the time.

Mrs. Graham had very likely started this trend of judging characters in terms of size and appearance when she suggested a basis for choosing the three sisters. Quite to the contrary, play casting should give children the experience of deciding the many things that go into playing a role and the possible value to a person of playing a certain role.

In Miss Naughton's sixth grade, tryouts were managed entirely by the children. Although the teacher did not always concur in the children's judgment, she let group choices stand. She was willing to let the group test its decisions for itself as work on the play progressed, and she was able to say, "How much better it is for the children to manage affairs like this!" It is certain that she had opportunity to learn much about her children from observing them in operation in this way. The teacher probably helped the group first to set up criteria for selecting various characters. She also had the responsibility of helping them evaluate the wisdom of their decisions later.

Planning costumes is another valuable experience which play-giving affords. Mrs. Bassett's second grade children went into great detail in planning costumes for a dramatization of "Little Red Ridinghood." An excerpt from a running record of this planning shows how a plan for the costumes of the daisies was arrived at.

> TEACHER. All right, what should we plan next?
> CHILD. The daisies.
> TEACHER. What do daisies look like?
> Teacher and children discuss color and description of daisies.
> TEACHER. How could we have daisies have these colors?
> CATHERINE (after other suggestions from children). We could have white petals sticking out around the neck.
> TEACHER. What else do they have?
> CHILD. Green stems.
> TEACHER. How could we do this, Catherine?
> CATHERINE. The children could wear green dresses and pants.

At the end of a long and rather tedious period, the following plans had been recorded on the board.

Costumes for Our Play

Red Ridinghood—red cape, basket
Daisies—orange cap, white petals, green dress or pants
Grandmother—nightcap, curlers, nightgown, bedsocks, bathrobe
Wolf—artificial nose and teeth, brown costume with fur
Bo Peep—blue dress, apron, hat, crook
Fairy—white gown, wings, wand, star headband
Woodman—shirt, leather jacket, hatchet
Bunny Rabbit—white suit, pink ears, cotton tail

Before spending as much time on large group planning of costumes as Mrs. Bassett's group did, one would want to consider first whether or not elaborate costumes are required or desirable. How likely is it, for example, that these second graders would be able to carry out some of their plans without a great deal of adult help? Secondly, one might consider individual or small group planning of costumes as a first step, with children bringing their plans and problems to the large group for checking and for help.

Planning a Circus

An enterprise as large as a circus may grow from very simple beginnings. Mrs. Remington tells how her second grade happened to plan for such an event.

One of the three reading groups was discussing the circus stories they had read. They had shown such interest and enjoyment that the teacher asked if they would like to share these stories with the other members of the class. The children suggested many ways in which this sharing could be done. The teacher put these suggestions on the chalkboard. Some of the suggestions were: make a big picture (frieze), write stories, read stories aloud, learn some circus songs, find stories for the others to read, and give a play.

The suggestions were evaluated as the teacher asked the children questions. Which of these things can be done in a day? Which will take a long time? Which can you do alone? Which must several people do together? It seemed that they might use more than one way of sharing. By this time it was evident that the group was most interested in giving a play.

The teacher then asked that an elephant costume be brought from a storage cabinet. This concrete example immediately brought to mind other animals they might use in a circus play. Their suggestions were again written on the chalkboard. The teacher mentioned that a circus also had people and the children then named the people in a circus.

By now excited children were saying, "I'd like to be a camel" and "I'll be a clown." But the teacher pointed out that they had listed many more animals and people than there were children in the group. This problem was solved by the suggestion that they ask the other members of the class to help give the play and invite other classes as an audience. The remainder of the class when consulted were quite willing to help with the play and began to offer ideas of their own.

The first discussion period with the whole group ended with the making of specific assignments. One child was to write a note asking the librarian for reading materials. Another was to tell the music teacher about the plan. Some were to locate stories and read them. Others, the teacher included, were to find pictures for the bulletin board.

For three or four days the children read stories, told of circuses they had seen, examined pictures and began to give interpretations of circus animals and performers. They were now ready to decide on the parts for the play. Whenever possible, a child was given the part he preferred. If several wanted the same part, there were tryouts and the selection was made by voting.

The teacher called to their attention the fact that performers did not speak but that the ringmaster made all announcements. Each child was to help the ringmaster by telling what he wanted said about himself. This called for further research. You couldn't talk about how much an elephant weighed unless you knew something about elephants. These speeches were written, read aloud, evaluated by the class and sometimes rewritten. Any child having difficulty was given assistance by the teacher or by another child. All speeches were put together in order and given to the ringmaster.

The children wanted a popcorn man and a balloon man. After some discussion of the additional work involved in such an activity, they decided to have only the balloon man. He was to sell balloons to the visitors after the show and to the school children at the noon hour. Several hundred balloons were obtained from a wholesale house and posters advertising their sale were put up in the corridors.

For several days the large colored chalk frieze outside the classroom door had announced the coming event. At the end of three weeks the parents and children laughed and applauded as the show ended with a parade through the audience.

The teacher helped the children's planning by (1) encouraging suggestions for sharing circus stories; (2) proposing criteria for evaluating suggestions; (3) displaying a costume to stimulate a flow of ideas; (4) pointing out the need for more participants; (5) leading the group in making specific assignments to various members; and (6) offering information about the duties of the ringmaster.

Planning Exhibits

Exhibits of various kinds give children an opportunity to learn how to plan and organize with both space and materials. Exhibits can be planned for schoolmates or adults or both. They can include collected articles or articles made especially for the purpose. Miss Naughton's group of sixth graders decided early in the fall to have a one-day "museum" where all sorts of interesting curios from far away and long ago could be displayed along with the children's hobbies. Sally, for example, could bring an 1899 doll and an old iron toy stove. The teacher's diary for September 25 shows a busy day of preparation, and clearly reflects previous planning.

This was certainly "Museum Day" in our room. We lived and breathed museum from morning until night. About 8:20 hurrying figures began to come into our room, most of them burdened with strange-looking bundles. Russell, Arthur, and Ray opened the ticket-selling booth. Suzanna and Bonnie escorted Margaret, Lin, Lucretia, and Beatrice to the retiring room, where they costumed themselves as old-fashioned women, a Chinese girl, and a Mohammedan Indian woman.

We started to work on the exhibits for the museum. For an hour and twenty minutes our classmates showed us what they had brought and talked about the objects. This would help us to explain the exhibits to the children who were to attend the museum. Then it took us over an hour to print labels for the articles. When several boys and girls had finished their own labeling, they cheerfully helped their classmates and the teacher.

Noontime was even busier than usual. Ray started to sell tickets early. The printing was completed and tables were borrowed from other classrooms.

At one o'clock we proceeded with our treasures to the auditorium. We worked like Trojans for an hour and a half and had just about finished when our first customers arrived.

Miss Naughton's neighbor across the hall, Miss Rezny, reports another kind of exhibit which her children sponsored in November. The children had planned to have a hobby show, only to learn that a fifth grade class was preparing one. The teacher's diary tells how the group hit upon and carried out another idea.

When the children heard they could not have their hobby show, their faces were so downcast that I suggested we think of something else to do—perhaps something that would show what people can *do* instead of *collect*. No response. I hinted that some of them had talents they could share. Fred, Henry, and Harry popped up with "I could draw pictures!" Lawrence said, "I could make a wood carving," and Elizabeth added, "I like to draw dogs' heads." And so the idea for an art show began to expand. The first thing to be done, we have decided, is to make small posters advertising the show. The best three will be enlarged for hall display.

The day of the art show, Miss Rezny's diary reflected the details that had been planned by the group.

We had fifty articles and pictures on display in little Room 207. Six children fixed the room in the morning. Gloria brought a decorated ballot box from home. Each class came at the time designated on its poster. A host and a hostess, changing with each class, greeted the visitors, who were invited to cast their votes for the picture or object they liked best.

A few days later, parents of Miss Rezny's children had a chance to see the art show on open-house night. Miss Rezny had used the occasion as an opportunity for the children to plan what they would like their parents to see when they came to visit. Her diary gives a good picture of the preparations.

> Tonight was "Open House." I rather think I was on just as high a plane of excitement as the children. They were excited because they thought their room just right for guests and because they were running their art show again. I was truly pleased because the execution of our simple displays climaxed a week of planning, first with the entire group, then in committees. Our room was the result of the children's thoughts about what they believed would be of interest to visitors. Nothing was displayed that was not "of the children."
>
> First, we decided to feature Book Week, which was a natural choice. The children wanted more than an exhibit of good books and posters, so they decided that book reports, original stories—anything that might be connected with "literature"—should be shown. We then listed the display areas and volunteers signed up for the particular spot they wanted or wrote what they wanted especially to do for the group. . . .

From Miss Naughton's and Miss Rezny's accounts it appears that children were encouraged to exercise initiative, to produce original ideas, to take into account the many details associated with a group enterprise as well as to assume a share of responsibility for it.

A running record taken in Miss Hawkins' third- and fourth-grade room, when preliminary planning for an exhibit was in progress, puts one segment of such planning under the microscope.

Abbreviated Record	*Analysis*
TEACHER. Let us think of the big questions we need to answer as we think ahead in planning our exhibit.	The children apparently have had previous experience with setting up such questions.
As children make suggestions, the teacher lists them on the blackboard: (1) Where shall we put the exhibit? (2) When shall we have the exhibit? (3) How? (4) Who? (5) What? (6) Why?	
TEACHER. Which should we plan first? Then others will follow.	In some cases the choice of items to take up first is of real importance and the experience of making the choice is of value in itself. In this case, the children appear to be giving meaningless guesses as to what the teacher wants.
CECILE. Where shall we have the exhibit?	
BOY. What are we going to have?	
TEACHER. What do you mean? I don't follow. Explain a little more.	
A boy tries to explain.	

Abbreviated Record	*Analysis*
TEACHER. We have different opinions on what to do first. Think of a party at home. What do you have to do first?	This kind of question is confusing. It soon appears that the teacher has a definite choice in the matter and that she means to keep pulling until she gets the desired answer.
JEANNETTE. What are you going to have?	
TEACHER. It is tied up with something else to do, with where to have the exhibit.	
HOWARD. How or what to have?	
TEACHER. I am thinking of the space in which to have the party or exhibit. That helps decide whom to invite.	
GIRL. Decide where to have the exhibit.	This same suggestion was made earlier by Cecile. The teacher's question could just as well have come at that point since the intervening remarks in no way represented evaluation of suggestions as a basis of choice among several possibilities.
TEACHER. Do you accept that? The children give assent.	On the basis of common consent, the teacher opens a new phase of the discussion.
TEACHER. What are various places or possibilities for the exhibit?	
JOE. The auditorium, the hall, or our room.	
TEACHER. What are the advantages and disadvantages of having the exhibit in the hall?	Teacher encourages evaluation of suggestions.
CHILD. Too many people passing.	
TEACHER. It is not private, is that what you mean? Which has space large enough?	
CHILD. We need space for lots of things.	
BOY. I have a three box model. I'll need a table for that.	After allowing contributions which give examples of need for space, the teacher helps the group come to a definite decision.
GIRL. We need a stage for puppet stage.	
TEACHER. Where will you put your long poster?	
Have we settled where to have the exhibit?	

Abbreviated Record

BOY. Have it in the auditorium because it is larger.

TEACHER. Can you think of any way to delegate these jobs? Should I say *who* will do them? Who will know best about the models?

CHILD (low). You.

TEACHER (laughing). Don't say me, either.

BOY. The committee that worked on the puppets will know best where the puppet stage should be.

GIRL. Let each committee do their job.

TEACHER. Job?

HARRY. The exhibits committee (all school) should go down and decide the space needed.

TEACHER. It's your exhibit, your class. You have your own committees.

GIRL. Let each committee go down to the auditorium.

Teacher records on blackboard:

Where—Auditorium

What —Each committee go to the auditorium to decide where their space is.

CHILD. We might choose the same one.

TEACHER. After the committees go to the auditorium to decide, what should they do?

CHILD. Get things ready.

GIRL. Tell the whole class where you decided, report to the class.

TEACHER. Now bring up your questions.

JEANNETTE. Take a vote.

GIRL. Talk it over and then decide.

Analysis

It is impossible to tell whether the teacher based her judgment here on the basis of advice of one individual or of a member speaking for the group. At any rate, acceptance of a decision is assumed and discussion is opened on a new phase of the problem.

Instead of taking offense, the teacher treats the suggestion as a joke.

Teacher shows her evaluation of Harry's suggestion. She might have asked the group's opinion instead.

Teacher records decisions she believes are agreeable to the group.

Group member foresees a difficulty.

Teacher prompts group to solve the new problem.

Teacher gives a chance for expression of further problems seen by the group. Group members answer in terms of suggested solutions to the anticipated problem (two

Abbreviated Record	*Analysis*
DONALD. Discuss who needs a certain space most—like the puppet committee, they'd need the stage. . . .	committees wanting the same space).

Miss Hawkins had greatest difficulty getting the discussion launched. She decided to give the group the experience of setting up their agenda, yet allowed her own preference for one approach to prevent the children from making any real choice. After the group agreed to work first on where to have the exhibit, the teacher exercised useful leadership, helping the members to come to decisions when they had held sufficient discussion of a problem. She was quick to pick up a problem introduced by a child (two committees might want the same space for their exhibits) and to invite the members to help in the solution of the problem.

Planning Trips

When pupils are preparing to go on a trip they must think of several things—what they want to see or find out about, their route and means of transportation, their conduct in transit and at the destination point, and how to share and use findings. Many of these steps are illustrated in an account by Miss Tate of planning a trip to the grocery store with her first grade children.

We had an opportunity for several cooperative planning periods during the week of Valentine's Day. Our first grade group had been studying grocery stores for some time, and several children had expressed a desire to visit one of the stores in our community. We wanted the experience of going to the store together to purchase some refreshments for our Valentine's party. As there were several different grocery stores in the neighborhood, there was an opportunity to choose the type we wanted to see. We selected the supermarket as the one offering the most interesting possibilities.

There were several things we had not been able to find out in our discussions and reading about grocery stores, so we made a list of questions we would ask at the store. We also talked about things we had read about that we would look for in this store. The teacher offered to make arrangements for the most convenient time to visit.

Our next step was to decide upon our purchases for the party. Many ideas came from the group, but with some guidance it was decided that milk and cookies would be best. We figured out the number of quarts of milk we would need and the number of cookies.

The day before we were to go we talked about acceptable conduct for the trip and the kind of a partner with whom we would like to walk.

One of the mothers was invited to go with us. We went over the questions we wanted to ask and the children eagerly volunteered to ask specific ones. We also selected the children who were to carry the milk and the cookies and the child who was to give the clerk our money. Children who might have been reluctant to ask a question were found to have good qualifications for carrying our purchases.

Our visit was a great success. The general manager happened to be in the store and answered all our questions satisfactorily. He also showed us many interesting things about the store that we had not known before. The children were well mannered, attentive, and very enthusiastic. They knew what to do, what to expect, and what was expected of them.

After the trip we evaluated our experience and found that it was very worth while. Many pictures were made telling about incidents at the store, and a letter was written thanking the manager for his thoughtfulness. We had a greater appreciation of the contribution made by the grocery store.

According to Miss Tate, pupil-teacher planning contributed a great deal to the trip's success in creating greater pupil interest, better conduct, and greater participation in the study.

A group of fifth grade children in Miss Tate's school system had a valuable experience in planning a train trip to a distant metropolis. Because they had been studying astronomy, a visit to a planetarium was included in their schedule. They secured books from the library to prepare themselves for getting the most out of the planetarium. They also planned what pocket money would be reasonable, investigated fares, and arranged for parents to accompany them.

CONCLUSION

In this chapter the examples of planning tangible objects or less tangible productions have served to show how numerous and varied are the opportunities in all schools for learning through planning and managing cooperative enterprises. Again and again it has been evident that when pupils plan in terms of definite materials and space they are creative and imaginative and use extremely good judgment. Surely the pupils undergoing the experiences reported here are learning the value of having a plan and of working things out together. The records as analyzed have also shown ways in which teachers can facilitate group planning and ways in which they sometimes can become obstacles to clear group thinking. Most of the examples have shown teachers sincerely wanting pupils to learn as much as possible when they are in the process of producing something.

CHAPTER VII

Planning Service Projects

CHILDREN'S SERVICES can be employed thoughtlessly just to get a job done, or, with appropriate planning, they can be used in ways that ensure educational value for those participating.

During World War II paper sales, clothing drives, and other efforts were well used by some educators as opportunities for pupils to plan ways of being of real service to others. But educative service opportunities clearly need not be confined to wartime projects. In all schools there are many opportunities for a class or a smaller group to carry out projects that are primarily service-centered. Some of these projects may be pursued for the benefit of another group in the school; some may serve the whole school. There are many possibilities also for groups to render service to the wider community. Opportunities for service sometimes come as a request for help from an individual, such as the school principal, or from a group, such as the school council. At other times the pupils themselves think up ways to be useful. Planning to render a service gives special opportunity to select a project, set goals, and assign responsibilities.

This chapter illustrates all these variations, dealing in turn with the planning of service projects of a temporary nature and with the planning of continuous service over a period of time.

PLANNING TEMPORARY SERVICE PROJECTS

Service projects that have a well-defined beginning, middle, and end are included in this section. The first group of illustrations shows pupils undertaking various projects to benefit their school as a whole.

Planning to Contribute to a Science Exhibit

In one school a request from the science teacher gave Miss Hogue, the kindergarten teacher, a chance to plan with her

children what form their contribution to the science room would take
and to learn what others in the school were doing in the same connection.

> The children and I talked over the request together and we decided
> that we would like to send in the robin's nest we had along with a pic-
> ture we had of a robin, some shells from the seashore which some of the
> children had brought in, and a chart we had made from the rabbit's
> feet and tail another child had brought in. We talked about sharing our
> things with the rest of the school, and after labeling our exhibits we
> visited the science room to place them. The children were greatly in-
> terested in the contributions other classes had made.

Planning for a Safer Playground

One week five of Miss Isaacs' second grade children were
involved in playground accidents. For two days conference time was
used to discuss the causes of accidents. The teacher's diary shows
how these discussions led to the performance of a useful service.

> The children at first tended to be very personal in placing blame. In
> order to guide the discussion into more constructive channels, I sug-
> gested that we think about which accidents were due to careless use of
> equipment and which to failure to share the equipment. On Monday
> we plan to go out to the swings to see if we can discover why the acci-
> dents happen.

Later the teacher writes in her diary:

> Some constructive ideas came out of our actual observation of other
> children using the swings. During conference time we listed the follow-
> ing safety suggestions: (1) Mark a danger zone around the swings.
> (2) Have children wait for turns in lines behind each swing. (3) Have
> someone from the playground committee see that children take turns.
> The children have now identified their problem as "How can we help
> make our playground a safe place to play?"

Miss Isaacs resolved that next she would try to get the children to
see what people were concerned with safety on their playground and
who could help them put their new ideas into effect. Some results of
her resolution are recorded in her diary.

> One of the highlights of the day was the activity resulting from the
> reply to our letter to the student council asking for an opportunity to
> talk over our playground plans with them. One seventh grade and one
> eighth grade member sat in our conference circle today, listened atten-
> tively and asked questions as the committee on swings, the committee
> on tree branches, and the committee on holes and rocks told of their

plans. Now we must wait for the student council and the school principal to give us the go-ahead signal on our plans to remedy playground
dangers.

Miss Isaacs' account of the children's later activities reveals the
nature of the plans made.

> This week we have spent much time out-of-doors. Older children
> have been cutting low-hanging branches on the playground while my
> second graders carry away the twigs and branches. The committee on
> swings is digging narrow shallow trenches and sinking yellow-painted
> two by fours in a rectangular space around the swings to mark off a
> danger zone. The rest of the class has filled in marble holes and re-
> moved dangerous stones.

The teacher's first mention of the safety problem was dated September 30. On November 3 she reports the completion of the children's project to inform the rest of the school concerning playground
safety measures.

> Today my second graders presented their playground safety program
> to the primary and upper grade assemblies. The crayoned pictures they
> put on the opaque projector told the story of our problem and how we
> solved it.
> 1—Child with a cut on forehead
> 2—Class conference about the accidents
> 3—Our trip to the playground to look for dangerous spots
> 4,5,6,7,8—Pictures of the dangers
> 9—Conference with student council
> 10,11,12,13,14—Pictures showing how we improved the dangerous
>   places
> Children told about each slide and were very proud of their contribu-
> tion to the safety of the school.

This plan of reporting the steps in the solution of a problem was a
useful type of summary and evaluation for Miss Isaacs' class and
served to spread a concern from one group to a wider society.

Solving a Problem of Ethics

Often a service project presents unexpected opportunities for group thinking. In rendering a service to their school, one
fourth grade group ran straight into a problem of ethics. Mrs.
Spain's children had decided to put on a snack sale to raise money
for the school microphone fund. They had received permission from
the student council to sponsor the sale as a way of supplementing
receipts from the school paper drive.

When the room representatives reported to the council that proceeds of the snack sale had been $10.40 and that their group proposed to donate five dollars of that amount toward the microphone, other members of the council objected. Mrs. Spain made a record of the discussion her children carried on when David reported the dissatisfaction of the council with his room's decision.

> DAVID. The student council thought by our posters that we meant to give all we made.
> BETTY. It wouldn't be fair if we gave all and others give none.
> WILMA. Why?
> BETTY. Others wouldn't think they had to help.
> CARL. They are helping as well as we are by bringing in paper.
> CHRISTINE. We said we would give all, so let's do that.
> BETTY. Oh, no, we didn't.
> CHRISTINE. Our motto was "A Microphone for Easter" so we meant the money for that.
> WILMA. I think we should give all, because we'll probably win the paper prize, so if we want to buy something for our room later we'll have money without this (snack sale) money. Besides, everyone helped us earn so much. The students and the teachers both did.
> KENNETH. Why not give all since we said our sale was for that?
> TEACHER. How much did we expect from the sale?
> CHRISTINE. Not more than five or six dollars, but we said the money was for the microphone so we should give all.
> VELMA (the president, who previously reported to the student council about the five-dollar gift). Oh, let's give it all and settle it.
> TEACHER. That's not the idea, is it? Don't we want to be sure we are settling it in the right way?
> STUDENTS. Let's vote.
> VELMA. All in favor? (All are in favor but one, Betty.)

Mrs. Spain noted that she stayed out of the discussion except for clarifying a point. To her the children seemed well satisfied with the decision.

Perhaps the greatest value of the sale for these children was the experience of facing a moral issue and working out for themselves the position they would take.

Planning to Sell Tickets

When Miss George's fifth year class was asked to sell tickets for the operetta produced by the junior high school section of the school, the teacher wondered at once how this experience could be of most value to the children. She reports the way the group prepared for their task.

The class discussed the meaning of the word "operetta" and learned a bit about the one being produced. They sang a few of the leading songs. The cost of the tickets and what the school could do with the money earned was discussed. Then the best way to sell tickets was reviewed. Children advised each other about the good manners a salesman must have and to whom they should try to sell tickets. The purpose of a receipt, the care of money, the methods of figuring the cost of tickets sold, and how to calculate change were reviewed. A ticket booth was made from orange crates. Committees took care of selling the tickets as the children brought their money to school.

This description shows preparation that takes into account the need for members of a group to be well informed with respect to a service they plan to render.

Planning a Christmas Bulletin Board

Mrs. Nestor's sixth grade had a continuing responsibility, the school library. A running record supplied by the school principal of a discussion in their room shows the process of deciding to plan a special Christmas bulletin board as part of that service.

Record	*Analysis*
TEACHER. Let's bring ourselves up to date. We have been working on school service. What has been ours?	
CHILD. Library.	
TEACHER. How many have ever gone to an outside library and seen anything interesting there besides books? (Hands up.)	Teacher ties up the job for the day with outside experience.
CHILD. Story time.	
CHILD. Puppet shows.	
TEACHER. For what purpose was this done by the library?	
EDGAR. For the public.	
TEACHER. But why for the public?	
SONNY. So they will want to read the books.	
TEACHER. That's right. We want to advertise.	Teacher makes transfer from other libraries to the purpose of the day's discussion.
The problem was then formulated as "How can we interest the children in extra Christmas reading?"	Although apparently there has been preparation for this discussion, the teacher makes sure the problem is clearly defined.

Record	*Analysis*
TEACHER. Margaret Anne has made a list from her survey of the class.	This preliminary survey by one of the group is an interesting device for saving time in the large group and might well be used to encourage participation by a less vocal child.
MARGARET ANNE (reporting). Fix bulletin boards. Talk to the children about books. Preview books for interest. Display books on the table.	
TEACHER. It's easy to say we're going to do these things. Now, let's look at these and see which ones we can actually do.	Teacher points out the need for detailed planning. The next four contributions show that the children are talking about different items in the list.
L. M. We have some good drawers in the room. Pictures would almost tell what the book was about.	
M. A. Someone could explain the bulletin boards.	
JOYCE. Posters would explain.	
B. M. What should we have for the table?	
TEACHER. Instead of taking all of these at once, what could we do? Should we do all, some, or one of these?	Teacher helps to divide the discussion into parts.
The children vote. All except one child voted for *all*. One child voted for a single one.	A vote is taken without discussion of the issue. There is no attempt to hear from the minority. Perhaps on this occasion the issue was not crucial enough to warrant spending time on it.
B. M. Let's plan one, then go to the others.	This child may have sensed what would meet the objection of the one dissenter.
TEACHER. Now, which one should we do?	Teacher falls in with the suggestion of one group member.
JOHN. We should do "Fix the bulletin board."	
STANTON. It reaches more people.	
B. M. It would take too much time to plan a whole bulletin board.	
TEACHER. How many think it takes more planning to plan a bulletin board than to plan a good preview of a book?	Teacher uses appeal to authority of other children's experience. Teacher's own opinion is rather obvious, however.
Vote of group is that it takes more time to plan a good preview.	

Record	*Analysis*
TEACHER (to B. M.). Did you not know enough about previewing books to know? B. M. Yes.	One would have to hear the tone of voice and see the facial expression of the teacher in order to determine whether this was a question seeking for information or a reprimand. (The writer was not the observer on this occasion.)
TEACHER. How many think we could take bulletin boards? Vote is in favor.	Teacher tests to determine whether consensus had been reached.
TEACHER. There is the bell. What do we do now? CHILD. Go to lunch. TEACHER. What do we do from here? CHILD. Plan again tomorrow.	Although time has run out, teacher closes discussion with the thought that it will be continued.

In this instance time was used (1) for building an understanding of the general service to be rendered (publicize the library) and (2) for deciding upon one particular service project to plan first. These are important steps to take, because no group can serve well unless there is understanding and a feeling of commitment.

Beautifying a Barren Hillside

In a neighboring elementary school the sixth grade children undertook the beautifying of an eroded bank on the school grounds as a service to the school and community. Part of their service was to prepare a cooperatively written report on their project. The report, which is reproduced in part here, was written by eleven sixth grade children, a sixth grade teacher, the principal of the school, a neighbor, and the general supervisor. Each new heading indicates not only a new phase of the problem but also a new reporter. The material was assembled by the teacher, Miss Ronald. The teacher's introduction shows how the group formulated the purposes to be fulfilled through the project.

The two sixth grades of the school total seventy-five children. Their social studies theme for the year is "Conservation." Their school building sits up on a hill and all of the land leading from the school is terraced. On the east side of the primary playground is a bank. Last year sturdy white cement steps were built by engineers. Prior to the building of the steps, all school children and other pedestrians climbed a steep hill as the short cut to two school buildings. Naturally the installation of some new steps did not entice all bank climbers to use them. The soil beside the steps became so firmly packed from the weather and the walkers that this one entrance to our school was a most unpleasant sight. What better conservation problem could we desire?

Just one hike around our school grounds was all that was needed. Simultaneously the children said, "We are the oldest children in the school; it is our problem." But what to do? How should we start? Children, teachers, and principal realized the need for study, research, and expert guidance. What should be our plan of approach? What should be the organization?

All cards were laid on the table. Discussions followed and little by little our problem was forming into words and was stated. Problem: How can we get a better understanding of the condition of the soil beside the new steps and the plants that will grow there so that we can conserve the bank and aid in its beauty?

Then we worded two purposes: 1. To save the soil beside the new steps, 2. To beautify the bank.

Our course was laid and our study begun.

The report continues with stories on "Our School Bank Before" and "The Bank After." Committee reports on facts about soil and plants are included next. The story is taken up by a writer who describes how the children were organized for working.

After we started the work on the bank we knew we would have to know more about the soil which was there and the plants that would grow on it. We decided to divide into groups. One group would study plants and find the kind that would be suitable.

Following about two weeks of study both sixth grades came together for discussion and the exchange of ideas. By this time it was too cold to work outside, so we dropped the problem until spring.

Seventy-five children are too many to work on an outside problem at once. So we divided once again into two groups. This division worked out very well since we had another unit, "Minerals and Metals," to be covered in our social studies. The outside group worked on the terrace while the inside group made a booklet on some mineral or metal. The groups changed every other day so everyone would have a chance to work on both activities. With this organization we finished our outside work in one month.

As the work progressed, the cooperative report shows, it was necessary to consult various experts. Grading the bank, having the soil analyzed, contouring, seeding certain areas, putting in rocks and bushes to protect the hillside from trespassers, and cleaning the area after other work was finished are various steps described in the report. The account also includes a list of expenditures.

The principal's contribution was to summarize the skills and techniques practiced by the children as they worked on their project. Among other things, she writes:

> Some skills and techniques were consciously worked on while others were used without any particular emphasis given to them. The number of times most of these skills were practiced was so great that the facility gained in their use was noticeable.
>
> Perhaps the outstanding technique practiced over and over again was that of planning. There were many occasions for the technique of pupil-teacher-principal planning. There were the over-all plans that had to be set up each time a new problem was opened up, or when a new phase of the work was started, or when replanning was necessary because of new insights, or when weather interfered and it was necessary to revamp our plans.
>
> There was the day-by-day planning for details. This was when we decided precisely what was to be done, who was to do it, what materials were needed and what was available, when we were to work, how long, and what standards were to be reached.
>
> There were so many activities going on in so many areas of the school grounds that the groups were left on their own a great deal. Thus opportunities were many for taking responsibility, cooperating, pooling ideas, ironing out difficulties; in short, practicing the skills of democratic living.

After commenting on learnings with regard to use of tools and skills related to landscaping, the principal concludes by saying, "Evaluation of the work each day in the light of the standards set up gave the children many chances to learn how to take inventory and then chart the next work."

Evaluation in children's words is found in a section of the report entitled "Comparing the Banks."

> At the beginning of the year we had two very unattractive gullied banks by our new steps. The two sixth grades have worked on one of those banks this year.
>
> We have planted flowers and grass. We have made contours so rushing rain water would not make gullies. There are also a small rock garden and thirty forsythia cuttings. We have a border of rocks with sedum planted between them. There are barberry bushes at the top and bottom of our bank. We put them there so that people and bicycle riders would not go down it.
>
> The other bank is no comparison to the one we have worked on. It still has very firmly packed soil and is gullied badly. We hope the sixth grades next year will try to beautify it.

In his final sentence the writer of this section shows the forward-looking nature of the group's evaluation, a measure of the concern that had developed.

Planning to Make a Cathedral Window

Miss Beach, a teacher of mathematics for eighth and tenth grade students, gave her classes an opportunity to help plan and make a cathedral window needed for an Easter pageant. The time available for the project was too short to allow all the participation in planning which the teacher would have liked. The pupils accepted the problem and decided to do textbook work at home to allow time to work on designs in class. From designs worked out by individuals the group selected one. There was student participation also when dimensions were decided upon. The students first decided to cut out their designs and trace them on plywood but revised this plan as soon as it was tested.

Planning to Move for a Day

Kindergarten children frequently are asked to serve others by giving up their room for a meeting. Miss Hogue saw this as an opportunity for her children to plan their moving. Her diary relates what happened.

October 23. Tomorrow is a big day in our school—the day of the P.T.A. Carnival. Our kindergarten room is used and we have to move to another room for the day so that the parents can get ready. The gymnasium and the music room are also used, so there is considerable activity about.

The children of course knew about the carnival—we had had notices and other publicity for days—so they understood when I explained about moving to another room. We asked questions back and forth about the reasons why, and about the new room. We made a list. We listed things we would need to take with us, counted the children to see how many chairs we would need to take, talked things over with the janitor and some older children to plan what we could do to help move.

Well, the whole thing turned out to be fun for all of us, whereas if I had not included the children in the planning, I am certain they would not be ready for the change tomorrow. We will have time tomorrow morning to do the moving with the help of the janitor and the upper grade helpers.

October 24. The big day arrived and is behind us. The moving was done quite easily and I was very pleased with the children's response. I had dreaded it but the children were grand about it and we had a happy day in spite of the confusion.

We were further rewarded for our moving because we are to have some of the profits from the carnival—about $100. The carnival was a huge success and worth the strenuous effort. I must let the children have a share in planning what we will buy with our windfall.

Miss Hogue and her children were able to maintain their serenity under trying circumstances because all had planned for the change. And already the teacher's mind was leaping ahead to a fresh opportunity for her children to plan together.

Planning to Survey First-Aid Supplies

Second grade children in Mrs. Upton's room were given a chance to help the P.T.A. with first-aid supplies. A running record of the group planning for this service brings up several interesting points. First the teacher made sure that terms were understood.

TEACHER. What do we mean by first-aid supplies?
BOBBY. It means Band-Aids that help us.
TEACHER. You remember, Bobby, we helped you one morning.

Later the teacher helped the children to see that only some of them should go to survey conditions in the two centers where supplies were kept, the first-aid room and the principal's office. The teacher used this opportunity to develop a concept.

TEACHER. What would we call this if part went one place and part to another and came back to report?
CHILD. A committee.
TEACHER. You will want to find out all the important things.

The group that went to the health room came back rather quickly, and the teacher had an opportunity to help the children see the importance of their mission and gave them a suggestion to bolster their self-confidence.

TEACHER. Are you ready to report? What did you see?
CHILD. We saw a cabinet.
TEACHER. Is that all you saw?
CHILD. Two ladies were in there and wouldn't let us in.
TEACHER. The children want to know the condition of the bed. Is there a warm blanket? Was the bed made neatly? Go back and tell the ladies you are a committee helping the entire school and you need to see what is in the health room.

Mrs. Upton was helping her children to be intelligent about their chosen service by visiting and surveying the locations in question. She also was building morale by making them feel that they were helping the whole school.

Planning to Beautify the Community

With Mrs. Banning's middle grade children, an approach to rendering a service was through discussion of needs and of ways of helping their community. In her diary the teacher presents the situation.

> The community in which I teach is an all-colored war-project one. The houses are small. The streets are paved and lighted. Most of the people are from farther south. Very often the yards are a bit untidy and broken glass is found in the street.
>
> I have talked about these conditions with the children. I have told them that everyone who sees these things points his fingers at our race. We have discussed together ways of helping to make a more beautiful community. As a means to this end, I have offered a prize of a two-dollar bill to the boy or girl who has the best-looking flower garden before school closes.

Although the wisdom of such a prize to motivate community service may be questioned, the useful function the teacher was performing in helping her children face a real problem cannot be questioned.[1]

Planning Thanksgiving Donations

At Thanksgiving time in Robinson School, the sixth grade had an opportunity to plan to be of service to a community institution. Under the leadership of their teacher Mrs. Charles, the children were planning donations for a hospital. The following information was on the board when the observer entered.

> Plan Program of Donation Day
> Select Committees for:
> 1. Decorations
> 2. Taking donations to hospital
> 3. Writing invitations
> 4. Making poster for hall
> 5. Delivering "verbal" invitation
> 6. Arranging gym for program

> *Problem*

> How can we celebrate Thanksgiving at Robinson?
> How can we help the General Hospital?

[1] For the way in which an entire school engaged in a school-community beautification project see the film *Learning Through Cooperative Planning* (New York: Bureau of Publications, Teachers College, Columbia University).

Activities

Plan how to receive donations
Get someone to receive the donations
Plan to get donations to the hospital

A running record of the planning period follows.

Record	*Analysis*
The teacher brings up the question "How can we help the General Hospital?" and suggests that the children should decide what they need to work on this day.	Teacher helps group become clear on purpose of discussion.
TEACHER. What have we completed?	Teacher helps group review progress to date.
. Children suggest different things, but when the teacher challenges them they finally agree that their items really have not been completed. Finally, Item 4, "Making poster for hall," is checked off.	This checking against previous plans ensures follow through.
TEACHER. Where would you like to start?	
CHILD. I'd like to select the rest of the committees.	
TEACHER Are you sure you're ready? I don't believe you are.	Teacher evaluates and rejects or accepts suggestions herself. Alternate procedure here might be to get two or three suggestions from the group as to starting place, having the group evaluate them and then make a selection—or the teacher might make the selection in the first place if saving time is more important than giving children this particular chance to make choices.
TEACHER. What other suggestion?	
CHILD. Hear the invitations.	
TEACHER. All right, let's have the three people read theirs. Oh, Gail is working on the lunch order. Let's start planning to receive the donations. Does it make any difference where we start?	
Child suggests a parade.	
Teacher writes on the board: "Parade to bring donations to stage." She asks in what order the parade should go.	Teacher adopts suggestions without asking for alternatives or without receiving group approval.
CHILD. Older children first.	
TEACHER. Any objections? (There are none.)	
CHILD. I thought we decided to invite Miss Jenkins.	

Record

TEACHER. What has that to do with the plan?

CHILD. Oh, I didn't know.

TEACHER. We are talking about how to receive donations.

GEORGE. I think the younger children should come first.

TEACHER. George, you didn't object when you had a chance, now you're out of luck.

Child suggests order for the grades.

Teacher writes on the board: "Older children first, 7, 8, 6, 5."

TEACHER. How would we manage it?

CHILD. Have Miss Hallum (principal) to call out rooms.

TEACHER (with friendly smile). Who's Miss Hallum? Is she planning the program?

CHILD. One of us could do it.

TEACHER. Well, that's better.

SUPERVISOR (who is observing). Would the donations be taken up when the children first come in?

Two children try to explain. One is unable to, the second shows he has misunderstood the question. Teacher repeats the question.

CHILD. Should we have the donations after Mrs. Adams (president of the hospital board) is introduced?

TEACHER. Would we want her to thank us before she received the donations? I give you this piece of chalk; when do you say "Thank you"?

TEACHER. How many want donations delivered to the stage as soon as possible?

ALL. Yes.

Analysis

Teacher is often a little brusque with the children, although in a good-natured way. This way of receiving contributions might easily close up a more timid participant, however.

Teacher clarifies present problem under discussion.

Teacher rules a suggestion out of order, again rather brusquely.

Raises question to push group on to more detailed planning.

Often it is easier for someone not in the leader's chair to spot a point on which group members may not be clear. The supervisor was serving a useful function here.

Teacher clarifies point herself. She might have asked for group reaction.

Teacher helps group make decision by breaking question into parts.

Record	*Analysis*
TEACHER. Which of two suggestions do you want: One, when we enter the gym? Two, after we are seated, call each group up? Are you ready for the question?	This way of making the alternatives clear is very helpful to a group.
Second plan wins. Teacher writes on the board: "Be seated and then take donations." Teacher introduces the question whether the donations should come in all "hodgepodge" or separated.	Raises further point for discussion.
Child suggests they be separated.	
TEACHER. Anyone else want to talk on that?	Gives opportunity for further discussion.
Different children give their opinions.	
TEACHER. Anyone else an opinion on that? How will Lee in the first grade know where to put his things?	Raises a challenging question.
CHILD. We could have a picture of a can and so forth.	
TEACHER. Anyone else?	
CHILD. We could have signs.	
CHILD. Better have pictures. The first grade can't read.	For the first time in this session, the group approaches a circular discussion (one member talking directly to another member on a point he has made).
Teacher asks for other opinions.	
CHILD. We could have signs and pictures.	
CHILD. Tell them.	
TEACHER. Could they remember?	
CHILD. Can't we have some of everything in a different place on the stage?	
CHILD. The older children would come first. They could show where things are to be put.	
CHILD. I thought that was Mrs. Amos's job.	
TEACHER. You think so!	This was said jokingly yet it might have carried a little sting.
Two children explain that this is their job.	
TEACHER. Let's talk more about donations. Jewel?	
JEWEL. Sounds all right to me.	
TEACHER. What do you mean?	Encourages a clear statement.

Record	*Analysis*
JEWEL. I mean the separate piles.	
TEACHER. How many agree the donations should be marked in some way?	Helps group clinch decision.
All agree.	
TEACHER. Do you want to settle it now or give it to a committee?	
CHILDREN. Committee.	
TEACHER. Do you have a committee on this list that could handle this?	This is a wise step—seeing if a responsible group is already available.
CHILD. Decoration Committee.	
Children agree.	
Teacher writes after "Decorations," "Signs."	This use of records should help the committee to remember its duties.
TEACHER. Have we gone as far as we can on that?	The leader senses that the group may be ready for a new problem but consults the group on the matter.

Mrs. Charles's group next evaluated and decided among the three letters that were being prepared by individuals. The teacher then had the group go back over items, review plans, and check off matters that had been turned over to a person or committee. The children went on to plan how and when donations would be taken to the hospital and how introductions on the program would be handled. The period ended with a listing of things that needed to be planned or accomplished the next day.

In Mrs. Charles we see an experienced leader of children's planning. Although she tended to be overdirective, she helped the group move through their planning in an orderly way and make some clear-cut decisions.

Planning to Bag Peanuts

When the P.T.A. in Miss Brainard's school purchased a large lot of peanuts which were to be bagged for sale, the sixth grade children were asked to help on the project. The teacher was determined that the experience should be used for educational purposes, and before the peanuts arrived she discussed the job with the children.

I said that if we were going to use our school time to take part in this project there must be some things we could learn from such an activity and I asked for their opinions as to its educational value. (I didn't phrase it just that way.)

Their suggestions showed consideration, I thought. Some things they mentioned were as follows: (1) It gives us a chance to work with others. (2) We have to be trustworthy and not take or eat any of the peanuts, because they don't belong to us. (3) We have to be fair in bagging the peanuts—putting too few in the bag would cheat the customer; putting too many in the bag would be unfair to the P.T.A. and cut down their profits. (4) We have to stick to our job and work as a team.

The children also helped select people for various jobs, and as they worked they found ways of operating more efficiently, showing that they were planning within space and materials. The children also evaluated the way they had worked.

We felt we had done most things rather well, but we had erred on the quantity put in the bag in some cases. We decided that part of our trouble was that some children made a race of the job. That was not the object. We wanted to work quickly, but if the job wasn't done right it was of no help to anyone.

On the following day Miss Brainard's children had the good fortune to put their evaluation to a test through a second opportunity to plan and carry out plans. The teacher's diary continues.

We had a rather unexpected opportunity to check our evaluation of our job yesterday. The peanuts were still with us. Miss F. (the principal) asked if we'd be willing to take another turn bagging them. It provided a chance to try again in the areas where we had failed. Most children preferred to shift to a different job which we did quickly up in our room.

Before going downstairs, we recalled the phases of the work we had not done so well yesterday. We decided to pick out sample bags at random to check on our quantities. We were to remember we were helping with a job, not racing with anyone. Everyone worked nicely.

Surely Miss Brainard's children were learning the discipline of useful work and of planning for efficient cooperation.

Planning to Do a Favor

Because Miss Sinclair's sixth grade children had been interested in trees, a letter from a fifth grade class in Vermont made its way to their room. The children in Vermont were making a large map of the United States out of wood one-half inch thick. Each state was to be cut out with a coping saw and fitted into the large map like a puzzle. These children had sent letters to other children in every state in the Union asking for a sample of the wood for which the state was famous. They needed a piece six inches square to make the state of Pennsylvania. When Miss Sinclair's group agreed to do this favor for the Vermont children, they found that much planning and investigating and doing were required. The teacher tells how they proceeded.

We turned to history to consider our famous trees and why they are famous. After writing to the Commercial Museum in Philadelphia and to the Department of Forests and Waters at Harrisburg, and consulting the almanac, we decided that we might send:

1. White pine, because more of it had been cut in Pennsylvania than any other wood.

2. Oak, because more of it is now being cut annually than any other wood.

3. Hemlock, because it is the state tree.

4. Elm, because of the part it played in the treaty between William Penn and the Indians.

After making their choices, the children decided to contact a nearby lumberyard by telephone, and after deciding on the qualifications of the person to do the telephoning, they selected two of their classmates for the job. The class also wanted to telephone Vermont, the teacher reports, but changed its mind when it discovered the cost. The story continues.

Four other children of the class visited the lumber yard with me. We were able to obtain all the required kinds of wood except elm. When the manager of the lumber company heard our story, he very kindly donated the wood and allowed the committee to see the wood being cut to the specified size.

When the committee gave its report, the class chose white pine and hemlock to send. They wrote letters giving reasons for their choices and asking the children in Vermont to make the final decision.

The experience was completed when the package was wrapped, addressed, and taken to the post office by another committee of four. Every step in this service project seems to have been planned with the children.

Planning to Improve the Reputation of a Community

The stimulus for a group of nine- to fourteen-year-old boys in New York City to serve their community came when several reported in a meeting of their Youth Builders Club that they were refused part-time jobs when they gave their address as Harlem. Confronted with discrimination due to residence, they decided to call a conference of delegates from Harlem elementary schools to discuss "How can we improve the reputation of our community?" They invited a number of members of the community to take part—the captain of the police precinct, the superintendent of schools, several parents, and a reporter from a paper that exploited the district by its sensational treatment of Harlem crimes. A visitor at the meeting has furnished a brief report.

The discussion ran rather informally, with suggestions and remarks by the boys that showed excellent thinking and a good understanding of the problem. Unfortunately, a few adults present began to monopolize the conversation and direct it into channels other than those the boys were choosing. Consequently, when the period ended, no great progress was visible.

However, the group did decide to meet again and elected a committee of boys and adults to visit several newspapers and attempt to gain their cooperation; to investigate the possibility of requesting a city examination for playground supervisors; and to report back to the group at a future date.

Sitting in on this conference was one of the greatest thrills of my life. It gave me new insight into the kind of thinking that young people are capable of doing.

This example highlights the difficulty of holding joint discussions of adults and young people, yet it also emphasizes the need for the two groups to learn to plan together.

Planning to Send a Parcel Overseas

Ninth grade pupils in a social studies class found a way of rendering service to people overseas. Their teacher Mr. Grace describes the way in which the project was started and carried through.

The students read in their *Young America* the plight of the people of Europe. Someone suggested that we send boxes of food. They all agreed. One girl offered to write letters to reliable agencies for names. Names of ten needy families were received.

A sandwich sale was planned in order to raise money. This netted sufficient funds to pay for mailing costs as well as necessary materials. Pupils did the planning of the contents of the boxes. They studied the postal laws and regulations. They negotiated the mailing, including weights, size of boxes for overseas mailing, declaring of contents, and writing the forms. The pupils divided into groups to write letters, which they translated so the families would understand them.

The enthusiasm exhibited was beyond belief. Now they are anxiously awaiting replies from their friends overseas.

Learning through cooperative procedures occurred for the pupils of Mr. Grace—learning that was heightened by the glow of doing something for others.

PLANNING CONTINUED SERVICES

A number of schools make it a policy for different groups in the school building to undertake responsibility for a particular service over a period of time—a year, a semester, or less. In some schools it has become a tradition for each particular age group to have a particular service. The plan at City and Country School in New York City is well known: the eight-year-olds operate the post office, the nine-year-olds operate the supply store, the ten-year-olds do hand lettering, the eleven-year-olds run the printing presses, and the twelve-year-olds have charge of the kilns.

At Corpus Christi School, also in New York City, there is a similar tradition but the details vary: grade 3 is responsible for the lost-and-found department, grade 4 has charge of the school museum and radio-program announcements, grade 5 has charge of the bank and the store, grade 6 has charge of the leisure-time program and of placing school news on the bulletin boards in the corridors, grade 7 has charge of the library and the picture file of famous characters and events. The enterprises of grade 8 are the safety patrol, the hall cadets, and the usher squad.

The discipline of carrying a real responsibility over a period of time makes the planning of continued services a real opportunity for learning. In this part of the chapter examples of such planning are presented and analyzed.

Planning for a Lost-and-Found Center

Setting up and managing a lost-and-found center was the job undertaken by Mrs. Bassett's second grade children. There are many opportunities in such a project for learning to exercise good judgment. A study of the running record of preliminary planning for the lost-and-found service will show opportunities utilized and missed by the teacher.

Record

Analysis

TEACHER. Why do you think we need a lost-and-found?

CHILD. So people won't lose things.

TEACHER. Yes, but if we find them, then what?

CHILD. So we can give them to the people.

TEACHER. Now let's write them on the board.

It would be well to use a complete phrase like "lost-and-found center" or "department." The children might decide on the term.

Teacher accepts suggestion and calls forth another with a question.

Teacher writes: "Why do we need a lost-and-found? 1. We need to keep things from being lost. 2. If we find something we can return it."

TEACHER. Now what can we do?

CHILD. I can bring in a box of cotton.

To help develop vocabulary, teacher might say, "Let's write on the board our two *reasons* for having a lost-and-found center."

The teacher has apparently reworded the reasons without help of the children.

TEACHER. We are not talking about Christmas presents now, Elliot. Where should we have a lost-and-found department?

CHILD. In the auditorium.

Teacher's question is not suggestive enough. A better question: "If we are going to have a lost-and-found center, what will we have to decide?"

Other ways of handling this might be: (1) "How would we use a box of cotton in our lost-and-found center, Elliot?" (2) "Are you thinking of our lost-and-found center or of Christmas presents, Elliot?" There are some advantages to giving Elliot a question so he may think this through.

TEACHER. Any other suggestion?

CHILD. Outside.

TEACHER. Where else?

CHILD. In Mrs. N.'s room.

TEACHER. Yes, but Mrs. N. will be back next week.

CHILD. Here, in this room.

TEACHER. Yes, we could have it right here. Let's list where we might have it now.

This is good technique, to gather all the suggestions, and then consider the whole group of them.

Teacher rejects a suggestion, giving a good reason. She might have asked the contributor, "Shall we drop your suggestion then?"

The record does not show whether or not the suggestions were discussed and evaluated before the decision was made. Apparently "in our room" won. (The writer was not present on this occasion.) The record continues.

Record	*Analysis*
TEACHER. How can we let people know where the lost-and-found is?	Teacher may perform this function of raising questions that introduce the next decision to be made or he may give the children a chance to think what else they will need to plan for.
CHILD. Put a sign on the door.	
TEACHER. Where can we put lost-and-found articles?	
CHILD. A box for each thing. Like a box for money, a box for clothes, and other things.	
CHILD. We could have boxes in the hall.	Here for the first time the participation pattern of teacher-child-teacher-child is broken.
CHILD. We could put signs on it.	
TEACHER. We should, I think, decide on a time when people could bring lost-and-found articles to the room.	Teacher introduces a new problem before there is a clear decision on the previous question.
CHILD. From nine to twelve.	
CHILD. From ten to eleven.	
CHILD. During recess.	
TEACHER. When can the people be in charge?	
Suggestions from children.	
TEACHER. Who can do this?	
CHILD. Let the people who have to stay in from recess be in charge.	
TEACHER. I don't think this would be much punishment. It would be rather much fun, I think.	Teacher's point might better have been that they would want everyone to have a part in the project at some time. She might have asked for group evaluation of the suggestion.

After a decision had been reached as to times when the department would be open, the teacher reviewed the plan.

Record	*Analysis*
TEACHER. Now we shall be open from 10:15 to 10:30, 1:30 to 1:45. Now when can people bring things to me?	". . . to *me*"—it is such slips that show that the teacher herself is not thinking of this as *"our"* lost-and-found center, *"our"* room.
TEACHER. We'll have to continue deciding about this another time.	Often advisable to cut the planning into smaller "doses," especially with younger children.

This problem apparently was within the capabilities of these younger children, and a fair preliminary plan was found on the board at the end of the period. The test would come as the lost-and-found center went into operation, when further planning would surely be needed.

Planning to Take Charge of Junior Red Cross

When Miss Tremont was given a responsibility in her school, she found educationally useful ways to share it with her fourth grade children. Her account shows the opportunities utilized for group planning and concludes with an evaluation of the worth of the experience for the children.

I was appointed by my principal as building chairman for the Junior Red Cross. I asked my pupils if they would like to be in charge of the activities and told them briefly some of the phases of the work. They were very enthusiastic in their response. They chose a room chairman who called for suggestions for carrying on. Two volunteers were chosen to go to each room to tell the pupils about the Junior Red Cross and to take supplies to them.

Someone asked, "What are we supposed to say when we go to a room?" Together they outlined a talk which could be given, divided and organized the supplies, then had each one practice his talk before our room. They brought out many helpful suggestions for speaking before a group.

Then came the follow-up work, giving out additional supplies as needed, suggesting new activities for the school, making reports, packing finished articles for the county chairman.

Miss Tremont's evaluation after a period of time was, "So far we feel that the group has been unusually interested in doing Junior Red Cross work, and that all the pupils have developed in initiative and dependability." Taking pupils into partnership yields results in interest and responsible behavior.

Planning a School Supply Service

Running a school supply store is a service that middle grade children often enjoy rendering. Miss Ingham's fourth graders in the Brookton School operate their store in a rather unusual way. Actually they conduct an order department. They make an illustrated catalogue (with index) showing the items they deal in and giving prices. They take orders on specially developed blanks, secure the goods, and on sales day, dispense the orders. This scheme requires an extensive organization—the store order department alone has a bookkeeping department, a mailing department (for handling orders from rooms), an information department (for checking on errors), a sales department, and a banking department. The executive department gets the total order ready to be sent to the business house where the children secure their goods. The art department illustrates the catalogue, including the new sheets that must be added from time to time. The position of store manager is a coveted one. The store is a non-profit organization, and the children protect themselves against loss by their system of advance orders.

On the day an observer was present to study this system, there appeared on the blackboard the following chart.

Today's Store Plan

1. Preparing the school order
2. Writing the news bulletin
3. Making more order blanks
4. Making more envelopes
5. Banking department, keeping records
6. Making new pictures for catalogue

A sample news bulletin issued periodically to other groups in the school contained these items.

1. Kindly bring catalogue to store on next sales day. We have a new page.
2. The Funny Face marking pencils are now in stock. Cat. No. 137.
3. The black crayon chart pencil is now in stock. Cat. No. 513 or 115.
4. Can you figure our sales total for last week?

a.	113 pennies	d.	10 quarters
b.	13 nickels	e.	3 half dollars
c.	9 dimes	f.	2 dollars

Total $——.——

Prominently displayed in the store was this declaration:

Our Guarantee

Truthful advertising
Prompt delivery
Sound advice
Dependable service
High quality supplies
Satisfaction or refund
To aid kindergarten in ordering

There are many simpler ways of running a school store, but the Brookton pupils are having quite an education in economics and are getting experience in organizing and managing a complex enterprise.

Other Types of Continuing Service

Other opportunities for long-term responsibility exist in many schools. Some may be more appropriate for elementary schools, some for secondary; some opportunities may be appropriate for both. A group may plan to:

Take charge of displays or exhibits, keeping the school informed of new additions, inviting other classes to contribute, acting as guides.

Write stories and prepare to read them to younger children.

Take charge of health problems, checking on absentees, studying causes of absence, assisting the school nurse, giving first aid.

Help the kindergarten teacher dress the children for going outside early in the year when the children are less independent.

Prepare the auditorium for assemblies.

Handle milk orders and distribution.[2]

Take over responsibility for the appearance of a certain section of the school grounds.[3]

Take charge of the costume closet, keeping an inventory, maintaining costumes in good order, checking costumes in and out.

Write notes for kindergarten children to take home to parents whenever there is need.

Take charge of projecting motion pictures and other types of films and slides.

Act as teachers' aids in lower elementary grades.

Assist with the intramural program of sports, coaching, refereeing, managing.

Handle school publicity, making posters and using other means of advertising school events inside the school and in the community, preparing newspaper releases to inform the community of educational progress.

Handle interschool relations, planning visiting days for prospective students and their parents (sixth grade children about to enter junior high school or ninth grade pupils about to enroll in senior high school), arranging interschool conferences for those serving on student councils, school newspapers, athletic boards.

To this list one might add dispensing supplies, serving as office helpers and guides to visitors, and taking care of rooms shared by many, such as an arts-and-crafts laboratory.

[2] See pages 406–407 for an account of the way this service was handled by small groups in one teacher's class.

[3] See pages 212–213.

In an elementary school these continued services may be handled either by one class or by an all-school committee, depending on the nature of the service. In secondary schools the most common arrangement is for the service to be put in the hands of a standing committee responsible to the student council. In any case, a teacher-sponsor should feel responsible for more than getting a job done well. He should be aware of all the possible learnings accruing from careful cooperative planning of the service. He should also help the group to see ways of enlarging and improving a service.

CONCLUSION

In this chapter attention has been focused on the possibilities of pupils learning more about cooperative procedures through a group approach to serving others. The services rendered by a group for the school as a whole or for the community are not just a matter of giving with no return. Rendering service is a matter of sharing in the jobs to be done so that living will be better for all. In addition, it is a matter of seeing new services needed by many and of creating the means to render them. The world has need of many persons who wish to share work on jobs for the common welfare and who have experience in planning and acting cooperatively.

CHAPTER VIII

Planning to Solve

All-School Problems

WHEN A SCHOOL is taken as a unit of operation, problems of living are more complex than those encountered in one classroom. The age span is greater, the organization more intricate. As is true in the wider community, there is great likelihood that "what is everybody's business is nobody's business." Careful planning must be used to take care of problems that are school-wide. These problems may be met as they arise; even better, some may be anticipated by planning ways to prevent many occurrences that are common to large organizations.

In this chapter examples are given to show various ways of attacking all-school problems: (1) the school council, (2) constituent groups aiding on all-school problems, (3) forums, (4) all-school committees, (5) participation with adult organizations. Each of these approaches is discussed in turn.

PROBLEM-SOLVING IN SCHOOL COUNCILS

The school council, made up of representatives of the student body and faculty, and sometimes of parents, is an excellent device for coordinating adult-youth planning for an entire school. Such councils are more common in secondary than in elementary schools. They are equally appropriate at both levels. In setting up a council each school must make decisions about representation: in secondary schools representatives may be elected in first-hour classes, homerooms, grade or some other groups; in elementary schools representation may extend from kindergarten through the highest grade, or may start with first, second, or even third grade. The problem of maintaining communication between the council and the constituent groups is real in all schools. But one of the greatest

problems is giving the council jurisdiction to plan in certain areas
without adult veto.

Beginning a New School Council

Organizing a school council where there has never been
one is not so simple a matter as it may appear. An organization set
up in advance of recognized need will find little of worth to do. Even
if there is much need for a coordinated attack on school-wide problems, teachers and students may not be aware of it or of the usefulness
of a school council in planning together ways to solve such problems.
Building this awareness must often be a gradual process. Therefore
it is well for a new council to start with limited but well-defined functions and to expand from there.

Miss Fenstrom, an assistant principal, and her principal were
both new to a school the same year. They wished to improve student
participation in all-school affairs but decided to begin with groups
and traditions that were already started. As Miss Fenstrom noted:

> During the first part of the year, it was necessary to reorganize the
> safety council and patrol groups. It had been the custom to permit
> just volunteers to serve on these groups. We felt that since safety
> education is a definite part of our course of study, every pupil in the
> upper grades should participate to some degree in these activities. It
> took quite some time and no little effort to effect this complete change
> in thinking and doing since we believed in approaching it only from an
> educational viewpoint and we wished to continue voluntary participa-
> tion. Imagine our gratification when, at the turn of the semester, the
> pupils wanted to know when it would be "their turn" to serve on a
> patrol group or in the lunchroom (which we included in an all-school
> participation program).
>
> As for the student organization, it had been an entirely formalized
> affair: monthly meetings of the entire student body in the auditorium,
> very formal parliamentary procedure used to consider not very impor-
> tant, not very interesting school problems. This was followed by a quiz
> or a play. We didn't feel that to bring the school together for such a
> program once a month was really justifiable. Upon questioning a group
> of the teachers at random, we learned that their pupils didn't know what
> it was all about. We decided, therefore, this year to work through a
> representative student group beside carrying the safety organization.
> When any occasion arose that seemed worth while, we had an assembly,
> the president of the student group presiding.

Miss Fenstrom and her principal saw the need of enlisting the
support and understanding of the teachers before such a "representa-

tive student group" could be launched, so they submitted a question-naire which gave the teachers an opportunity to indicate whether or not they felt a student organization would be helpful. The teachers could indicate also which ones on a list of proposed committees they would approve and the degree to which they thought their own pupils could participate actively.

Most of the teachers favored the idea but saw few committees as appropriate. "So our organization from the first lacked scope and interesting, challenging topics," Miss Fenstrom writes. "Neverthe-less we called our group together. Three to five representatives were sent from every room, first through seventh. Officers were chosen and we began work." Her account illustrates the fact that one successful piece of planning is a good way to convince members of the worth of their organization.

Perhaps the only problem we really settled with fair success was the one of the playground. The playground entirely surrounds the build-ing, and presents an ever-present problem of children coming into the building at will, through all entrances, and running through the halls. When asked why they entered, they always give the same answer, "I don't know." The first discussion of this was interesting indeed. At the end of the period one of the older girls from the ungraded room made the astute comment: "There is just one thing to do: the older children must just set an example for the younger ones, and look out for them." I really felt then that the children had begun to see the problem in its true light. Following the children's suggestions we shifted groups on the play spaces and placed girls from the fifth grade rooms in charge of all games in the primary rooms before school and at the noon hour. This latter plan has been a real success and has been greatly appreci-ated by the primary teachers.

Beyond this the student organization was used as a means of deal-ing with school problems as they arose during the year.

When a call from a neighbor came early this spring informing us that pupils were trampling her lawn, our property committee was asked by the principal to "take over." It was decided to have groups of older pupils visit each room and discuss the situation with the pupils. It was decided to appeal to them on the basis of wanting to live in a well-kept-up neighborhood and that it was everybody's business to help keep it attractive. The talks were made, suggestions given, and coop-eration asked. The plan must have worked, for after that very few calls were received about trespassing by school children. Children seem to know what to say to other children and how to say it. They speak the same language.

Pupil control of the school lunchroom and pupil presentation of all notices to go home were other responsibilities which the new council undertook and on which some progress was made. The sponsor did not expect too much the first year.

It has been our aim to lay the foundation for a worth-while organization with real problems to solve and we hope the ultimate result will be a feeling of responsibility on the part of the pupils for their own conduct and self-control. It probably was a good idea to have begun in this small way in a new situation, tackling only the most outstanding problems at first rather than spreading out over a large area. Our plans for next year include pupil-planned lunchroom arrangement and direction; more school activities, such as Red Cross, health, and assemblies, under pupil planning; continuation of playground and hallways program; progressively better safety work; and development of ability to work with existing rules by periodic participation in making those rules and by participation in places of authority where those same rules are carried out.

As Miss Fenstrom has pointed out, it is better to make simple beginnings and let organization grow as students' concerns widen.

An Experienced Elementary School Council Meets

The following report of a council meeting in the school where Miss Fenstrom and her principal had worked for several years previous to their transfer shows a group of pupils fairly mature in group procedures. Room mothers, who were invited to attend every other biweekly meeting of the council, were present at the meeting.

Record	*Analysis*
After the usual preliminaries, each room is asked to give citizenship reports, beginning with the seventh grade. There are reports on papers brought for last Friday's sale and on stamps sold. Reports are in terms of percentages (of children contributing). The fifth grade representatives have their report written out and recorded on a large chart which they use in reporting to the group. Reporting ends with the third grade.	Children came with well-prepared reports. The reports showed planning and work back in the classrooms, an important requisite for a successful council. There was, however, no opportunity for the youngest children to participate.
The president asks all citizenship chairmen to put down the following dates: February 7—fats	Announcements were clearly given and representatives came prepared to take notes.

Record

collection, upper grades; February 8 and 22—paper sale. When the principal reminds them that the twenty-second is a holiday, the date is advanced to March 1.

The president then asks if the mothers have any suggestions.

MOTHER. Would you like a bulletin on student council activities and plans?

PUPIL. We have one now.

PRINCIPAL. This mother means one for the home.

MOTHER. Neighbors often call for information.

PRINCIPAL. Maybe we should send the bulletin to non-parents also.

FIRST MOTHER. This would be good publicity for the student council.

PRINCIPAL. Other items could go in also.

ADVISER. Would you have to follow up on the collection?

FIRST MOTHER. Could we use block captains?

PRINCIPAL (to sixth grade room mothers). Could the sixth grade do it because of last year's experience?

MRS. W. We could put a pep talk on sales in the first bulletin.

ADVISER (to chairman of room mothers). Would mothers help with cars? Papers could be brought any time. We could put this in the bulletin. The office could take the addresses and children could classify them.

FIRST MOTHER. What activities are there besides paper and grease collection?

ADVISER. Only money-making.

PRINCIPAL. Also stamps and other drives like clothing. (The principal explains that the use of

Analysis

At this point there ensued a fairly lengthy discussion among the adults present. Unless the problem was one which adults could discuss *with* children instead of *in front of* children, might it not have been better to save it for a room mothers' meeting?

Record

paper-sale money is reported to the executive board of the P.T.A.)

PUPIL. We might offer a prize.

ADVISER. Then we would have the bulletin on dates of drives.

PRINCIPAL. Could we put in the campaigns like safety and respecting lawns?

At the adviser's suggestion the president asks for reports from the property chairman. The president asks the property chairman to take notes about cutting across lawns, although he allows little time for this activity. A girl gives a well-planned report on the following of rules for throwing balls on the school grounds. She rereads the rules agreed on in school. The next question is that of keeping on sidewalks. What will help? The children discuss flower beds and shrubs along the edge of the walks.

MOTHER. What is the rule about children returning to play after school?

PRINCIPAL. Parents and children must take the responsibility. There is a rule that children must go home and report.

THIRD GRADE BOY. People should tie up dogs to teach them to stay home. (There is much discussion of the problem of dogs on the playground.)

At this point pupils are asked to bring notes for the school paper up to the secretary. . . .

Analysis

This child was trying to relate himself to what he thought was the problem under discussion: How to encourage more cooperation on collections. The child's suggestion was seemingly ignored.

At last the adviser helps to turn the discussion back to the pupils.

On this problem both parents and children made contributions, talked *with* one another.

The adviser and the principal in the foregoing record were attempting two things that are difficult in school council work—they were trying to induct the younger children into the business of the school and to find points at which parents and children could plan together. In the first case there seemed to be little success, at least at the meeting observed. In the second case a problem shared by both groups was finally brought up for discussion. Both aims are worthy and possible of fulfillment if there is careful planning.

One arrangement which might help would be to have the younger children in the school attend council meeting less frequently or for a shorter period than the older children. Plans could be made for simple but active participation on their part while they are present. They, too, could be asked to come with some report or other. Their opinions on certain matters could be asked directly. They could be helped to take simple notes. Older children could accompany them to their classroom after council meeting to assist them in making their reports.

The parents' role in a school council meeting might well be that of observers part of the time. But during another part of the meeting there should be discussion that is mutually engaged in. Purely adult discussion should be saved for another occasion.

Elementary School Council Coordinates
Christmas Decorating

In Miss Brainard's elementary school the council considered how the Christmas tree in the auditorium should be decorated. Should the tree be trimmed with commercial ornaments or with decorations made by the children? As Miss Brainard reports:

> Most of the older children preferred the commercial decorations because, as they said, "Our tree looked too junky last year." However, their preference was not accepted. The idea of having one class responsible for the selection of the ornaments made by children developed in the hope that some theme and order could be developed.

This is a good example of making a plan with features appealing to all.

A Meeting of a Junior High School Council

Compared with the record of a meeting of Miss Fenstrom's council, a record of a junior high school council meeting shows a great deal of business transacted in one session and a more intricate web of interrelationships in school and community. From the record it can be noted that representatives are selected from and report to their social studies class. Apparently teachers make provision for council business to be discussed in these classes. The record also reveals that this school council is represented on an all-city council which handles certain city-wide problems. Study of the record enables one to see a rather skillful student president in action, a principal who contributes usefully to the discussion without dominating it, and group members who show initiative in discussion and who realize the value of making exact plans to care for problems raised.

Record	*Analysis*
After minutes and committee reports are out of the way, the president says they have a letter from the senior high school asking students not to attend the dances there. The vice-president reads the letter.	President early shares responsibility with another officer.
PRESIDENT. Any discussion of this letter?	
None is forthcoming.	This lack of responsiveness in the early part of the meeting may have been due to the unexpected presence of the observer.
Principal reads from a neighboring city's paper an article having to do with a similar problem.	The fact that the principal had the article with him is evidence that he had some foreknowledge of the agenda, which allowed him to be more useful to the group.
PRESIDENT. Any discussion of the letter? Do you feel the decision is right? Or that there isn't anything we can do about it?	The president's response is accepting, yet suggestive of other alternatives.
EMMALENE. How about having some senior high people come and hear our problem?	
PRESIDENT. Shall we have them or send someone there? Anyone else? Arthur?	
There is silence.	
LOUISE. We could refer this to the All-City Student Council. Shall we invite some here after next all-city meeting if nothing is done there?	
PRINCIPAL (asking for facts). How many of our junior high students have been going?	The principal does not state an opinion but asks questions which will cause the group to consider other people's sides of the question. These questions, as it happened, sidetracked the group from coming to any definite decision on the matter. The students' comments, how-
Two girls say it is more fun than their own school dances.	
PRINCIPAL. Do you people feel the same about sixth graders at our dances?	

Record

Analysis

ever, show where they feel justice
lies.

MEMBER. It's O.K. if they behave
themselves.

MEMBER. It's fifteen cents more
for the school.

PRINCIPAL. How many go to high
school dances? (Many raise their
hands.) I see some seventh and
eighth graders go. That's like
fourth, fifth, and sixth coming
here.

GIRL. They don't object to eighth
graders.

There is some discussion.

GIRL. Well, we're high school;
we're in the ninth grade.

PRESIDENT. Any other discussion?

The president probably intended
this question to call for further remarks on the dance problem.

MEMBER. It is getting spring.
The bicycle riding and lawns are
getting to be a problem. Another
problem, when you come down the
front walk you have to cross the
lawn to get there. Something
should be done to stop it.

JOE. We talked about that in social studies class; because of erosion and ditches it is dangerous.
If it continues, the front lawn will
be just like the other.

Mistaking the president's intention, a member brings up a new
problem. Evidently judging that
the group had a satisfactory plan in
Louise's suggestion (referral to
All-City Council) though no decision was clinched, the president
allows the discussion to take this
new turn. Often it is well for the
leader to make such decisions as to
consensus. This works well if
members are responsible for pro-
tests when they feel general agreement has not been reached.

PRESIDENT. We could put in
shrubbery where people are making
a path.

GIRL. I think we need sidewalks.
(Explains her reason.)

PRESIDENT. Do you think we can
get a sidewalk from the school
board?

GIRL. How much would it cost?

President turns to the principal.
Principal is not sure, but he agrees
to the need for the sidewalk.

President is operating as a group
member here but immediately returns to the role of chairman.

Record	*Analysis*
PRINCIPAL. I hadn't thought of a sidewalk. Maybe that is the answer.	
PRESIDENT. That is the way they did at the Youth Building. Can we take it up in our social studies class? When you give reports in your social studies class we could appoint a committee to see about the sidewalks. Do you think that will be a wise thing to do?	President shows awareness of need to check with constituent groups but has the group agree on how the matter will be handled if social studies classes favor idea.
Boy shows agreement.	
PRESIDENT. Do you other people feel this way? Do you think we should take action?	President does not act on basis of one member's approval but puts the question to the entire council.
PAULINE. I make a motion that we have a committee to look into the matter of the sidewalk.	
Motion is seconded and passes.	
PRESIDENT. Now be sure when you give your reports you stress that running across the lawns makes ruts.	It was useful for the president to help the group be aware of its responsibility for reporting. (It is good practice also to have a group member rehearse his report at the end of the meeting and get reactions from others, providing a summary and test of communication.)

The subject of grounds reminded the principal of the problem of ball-playing near parked cars. This problem was handled by full review of existing rules, with group members asking questions for clarification and interpretation of rules. A girl in the group brings up the next problem.

Record	*Analysis*
GIRL. In our class we brought up several subjects for noon hour— having one day for dances and dividing the gym.	Representative is carrying out charge of constituent group.
GIRL. There is not much dancing now. People are going outside.	A member and the president seem ready to dismiss the problem.
PRESIDENT. It is taking care of itself now. It's nicer weather. It could have started last fall.	
BOY. In our social studies class, we have boys who don't dance be-	Another member opens up a new angle of the problem.

Record

cause they don't know how. The girls won't dance when asked because the boys might step on their feet.

PRESIDENT. Our social studies class suggested the need for a dancing class. They suggested a special room for dances so it won't get mixed with basketball. We could have one day a week, girls teaching boys to dance.

PRINCIPAL. I wonder if there is any need to teach people to dance. Any suggestions?

GIRL. We tried to teach people in the seventh grade, but the boys didn't like it.

BOY. In grade school Miss Y. "called" dances. We all liked it. That is the best time to learn to dance, when people are young.

VERNE. There is no need for a separate room. If someone wants to learn he doesn't care who is watching.

PRESIDENT. Not all people feel like that.

PRINCIPAL. We could reserve one half-hour Friday afternoon just to learn to dance, no spectators allowed.

BOY. Boys in my room would like that if we could get enough groups together. We could go to Miss M. and ask her to help us.

PRESIDENT. Some of you boys who want to dance and have enough initiative, put an announcement of a meeting of all people who want to learn. Get Miss M. or Mr. R. to help the group arrange to have the room. If you think the student council should do anything, you're free to make a motion and we would discuss it. Any further discussion?

Analysis

President is operating as a class representative here, which is justifiable.

Principal temporarily assumes chairman's role.

Members recall experiences that may help to solve the problem.

Principal is operating as a group member here. Apparently his contributions in that capacity are dealt with on their merits, little influenced by his status as principal. (Observation of the way in which the students responded to the principal throughout the meeting support this statement.)

The president attempts to dispose of the problem by leaving the solution to individual initiative.

Record	*Analysis*
BOY. How about the announcement?	A group member wants definite assignment of responsibility. The president's question suggests a solution and a decision is quickly reached. Members take responsibility for being clear about the scope of the proposal.
PRESIDENT. Would you want to establish a committee?	
BOY. I make a motion that a committee be appointed right in the council to go ahead.	
It is seconded and the president asks for discussion.	
GIRL. Will it be limited to boys?	
PRESIDENT. Anyone who wants to learn to dance.	
BOY. People who know a little but just want to brush up?	
PRESIDENT. Yes. All right, we'll appoint a committee. Is there any old business?	

The meeting closed after the election of another representative to the city-wide council to fill a vacancy.

Outstanding features of this record are (1) the president's skill in helping the group to push through to decisions; (2) the skill group members show in fulfilling their responsibilities, such as supplying pertinent information, asking questions for clarification, and bringing in new problems for discussion; (3) the changing role of the faculty sponsor from group member to expert to temporary chairman, at all times giving the students clear opportunity to do their own thinking and the president a chance to be the true leader of the group.

Maintaining Communication with Entire School

As was stated earlier, one of the big problems facing school councils is that of keeping all the students informed and interested in council activities so that plans made for the school will be followed through. Learning the needs and wishes of the entire school membership in order that the important problems of the large organization may be dealt with is another problem.

Schools have tried various methods of keeping the entire student body close to transactions of the council. One elementary school council holds two meetings a year in the auditorium before the student body. (Once a year this same council holds a meeting before the parent-teacher association.) Another council meets in the various classrooms in turn, with the children acting as observers.

A third elementary school made a special drive one year to help all children become acquainted with candidates for student council offices so that they might vote more intelligently. The device used was a poster on an easel in the front hall displaying a snapshot of each candidate, his name, and the title of the office for which he was running. Even the youngest children in the school studied the chart carefully. On election day, the poster was placed inside the voting booth where children could make use of the pictures and names in finding the candidate of their choice on the voting machine that had been borrowed from the city. Teachers were on hand to help the younger children. The principal states that never before had there been such interest in an election and in the work of the council following the election.

In a fourth elementary school the council issued a handbook on good citizenship in the school, also listing names of officers and room representatives. No school council can be effective unless there is cooperation from the teachers of the school. It is important that each pupil belong to some group where his council representatives have regular opportunities to discuss affairs with their constituents. The next section of this chapter gives examples of solving all-school problems from the standpoint of a constituent group.

PROBLEM-SOLVING IN CONSTITUENT GROUPS

When there is good two-way communication between the school council and constituent groups, all the students in the school may have the benefit of deliberations similar to those engaged in by a small, representative council.

Two-Way Communication

Student council and social studies class. Later in the day on which the foregoing junior high school record was obtained, the observer listened to a follow-up discussion when two seventh grade representatives made their report in their social studies class. The record of this discussion shows the part classroom teachers in this school played in furthering the work of the council. The teacher is serving as chairman.

Record	*Analysis*
The boy representative mentioned the letter from the high	

Record	*Analysis*
school student council secretary saying they could not go to any more dances.	
TEACHER. Have junior high pupils been going there?	Teacher tries to find out size of problem.
BOY. Yes, it used to be you could go if you were fifteen, but now they want to make it that you have to go to senior high.	Two members supply clarifying information.
GIRL. Someone said it was not fair now because the ninth graders have Hi-Y memberships that are good until May.	
TEACHER. What do you want to do about it? Do you want something taken back to council?	Teacher makes opening for action.
GIRL. It is up to the ninth grade.	
BOY. I agree with Jean. The ninth grade will be up at senior high next year.	Two members see reason for dismissing problem.
GIRL. People are lying about their ages.	
TEACHER. That is encouraging people not to tell the truth.	
BOY. What about people that are little but are fifteen?	
TEACHER. They have said that it must be just senior high students now.	Teacher helps members see the problem has changed.
BOY. Mr. R. said that we need more youth buildings.	Member suggests another line of solution.
TEACHER. Do you think so?	
BOY. We need more places for little kids who are not in their teens yet.	
TEACHER. What about the problem of being out late?	Teacher uses questions to help pupils look at other aspects of the problem.
GIRL. It is Saturday and they start early and get out early.	
GIRL. With the present facilities there is not enough room for dancing.	
TEACHER. How many go to the Friday night dances here?	
There are many hands.	
TEACHER. That isn't enough?	

Record	*Analysis*

Chorus of "No!" Reporter from the student council reports on the dancing class idea.

BOY. The boys want to dance but they are bashful and can't dance.

GIRL. If a girl liked a boy, wouldn't she help him?

GIRL. It wouldn't be good to have the class on Friday afternoon. There is a party that night.

TEACHER. Maybe we can find a more convenient night.

The problem of walking on the lawn is brought up.

TEACHER. We can do something about that ourselves but we can't do anything about other people's parties.

REPRESENTATIVE. We thought it would be nice to put cement outside where people are making a path. We have a committee to investigate.

TEACHER. How many think that is a good idea? Do you have anything to suggest for our representative to take back?

BOY. This isn't school, but Parent-Teacher-Student Organization comes on our Scout night.

TEACHER. That's too bad. It shouldn't happen repeatedly.

BOY. We have two troops coming to ours.

TEACHER. How many are usually present?

BOY. One hundred and fifty when they are all there, otherwise about seventy-five.

Girl representative adds information on the election of the new all-school representative.

TEACHER. Anything else?

Analysis:

The fact that the reporter brings in this new proposition at this time shows that he sees it as one way of meeting the problem of being excluded from senior high school dances. Group members have useful questions and suggestions to offer.

Teacher makes a nice point about the group's "power field."

As chairman, teacher opens new phase of discussion.

Member shows he looks upon council as a channel for solving many kinds of problems.

There followed some discussion of sixth graders coming to junior high dances. This was finally dismissed as not much of a problem. The last contribution in the meeting came from a girl who said, "The cafeteria plan is working swell. We don't have to wait long now." This voluntary evaluation implies appreciation of channels for solving problems.

The seventh grade pupils engaging in the foregoing discussion were learning to be participating members in solving all-school problems. They could not help but feel that the council wanted them to be informed, wanted their judgment on new proposals, and wanted their suggestions as to further problems for attack.

School council and sixth grade. A casual description in Miss Brainard's diary for December 4 gives an idea of the relationship existing between group planning in her sixth grade and group planning in the school council. This entry shows a class instructing its delegates before they go to the council meeting and dealing with a problem brought back from the meeting.

> A council meeting was called today. The notice said that topics relating to Christmas activities would be discussed. We talked over the matter in our conference period. Our representatives were instructed to report our plan for giving a play for the school. They were also to express our desire to continue the practice of gathering about the tree in the auditorium to sing carols just before dismissal.
> When the children returned from the meeting, they had some questions about the tree upon which they needed to know our opinion, so we met briefly to attend to this matter.

School council and high school homeroom. In one secondary school the place where students participate in all-school management is the homeroom, the grass roots of the school. An example of consultation with a constituent group in this school was a request from the club activities committee of the council that the students suggest in homerooms how they wanted their clubs and activities organized. As a result of the various discussions held on the subject, the committee worked out a satisfactory procedure.

In another high school a problem of crowded lunchroom conditions was taken up in homerooms, where suggestions were given for alleviating the problem.

Planning to Carry Out Assigned Responsibility

Mrs. Nestor's sixth grade class was assigned one part of the school grounds to clean. Notes kept by the teacher show the kind of preparation her group of sixth grade children made. Steps in preparation as noted by the teacher were: (1) Wording the problem. (2) Sending two representatives to a meeting of the grounds committee and hearing reports from them. (3) With the guidance of these representatives, finding out specific grounds tasks. (4) Making a survey of the grounds. (5) Making individual maps of areas and vegetation, of building and grounds. (6) Reading about related soil use in the United States.

The teacher's notes also contain a detailed plan of cleanup as worked out by the group.

Things We Need to Plan to Clean Our Area

What—Clean up our area by (1) picking up paper, stones, trash, peelings, sticks; (2) removing unnecessary plants; (3) taking trash to proper places; (4) raking the area; (5) mowing the grass

Where—The area runs from the outside of the basketball court to the school grounds boundary on the east. It extends to the north to the edge of the softball diamond in the center of the playground.

When—Friday, May 9, at 9 A.M.

How—Tools: four baskets, six rakes, wheelbarrow, one shovel, one pick, five hoes, two hand trowels, lawn mower, two broom rakes

Who—Chairman and committee listed for each of the following:
1. Picking up (baskets or buckets)
2. Raking up (rakes)
3. Hauling away trash (wheelbarrows)
4. Digging up unnecessary plants (hoes, pick, shovel)
5. Mowing grass (lawn mower)

Preparation—Wear old clothes and galoshes or overshoes.

It is plain to be seen that Mrs. Nestor's children were learning the necessity of planning in detail to the extent of anticipating need of tools and dressing appropriately. They were also learning to check with the group coordinating all-school efforts, in this case the grounds committee of the council.

Planning for Better Care of Lavatories

There are various ways of solving the perennial problem of better care of lavatories. In one school system children planned attractive color schemes for redecorating lavatories and worked out stencil designs which they themselves applied. Children from one school in the system were sometimes taken to see the newly decorated lavatories in another school so that they might gather ideas for redecorating their own.

When Miss McNulty's fifth grade accepted responsibility for improving the use of lavatories in their school, the first step was to make a survey of conditions. A record of a discussion shows the kind of points children brought up with regard to the problem of sharing lavatory facilities.

Record	*Analysis*
TEACHER (after establishing the purpose of the discussion). Now what did you find when you went around yesterday?	Teacher begins by making use of facts gathered "on location" preceding this discussion.
BOY. One drain in the boys' lavatory wouldn't flush. Light wouldn't work. Toilet paper in toilet. Quite a bit of writing on the walls.	Broad report, not concerned only with misuse of lavatory.
TEACHER. Now what can we do to remedy this condition?	Leader raises question to invite suggestions.
CHILD. Erase the marks off.	
CHILD. Have a committee to see that no one writes on the wall.	
TEACHER. We can't be there every time someone is there, can we?	Leader raises question to cause member to evaluate his suggestion.
CHILD. We can pick things up.	
TEACHER. Very good.	Teacher makes encouraging comment.
BOY. Some writing is not only on the wall, but on the tin thing.	Teacher might have helped the boy use more accurate terminology.
TEACHER. That's bad. What else? Would the ones who do this just come from our room?	Leader passes value judgment, then raises question to turn to a new line of thought.
CHILD. No.	
TEACHER. What do you say about this, Willie?	Leader draws out an individual.
WILLIE. Rooms could take turns.	
TEACHER. Good.	Leader is encouraging.
CHILD. We could have different rooms to take care of the lavatories at different times.	Group members make suggestions in turn without leader comment.
CHILD. We could have someone to tell the rooms about these things.	
NORMA JEAN. We could have some kind of punishment.	
TEACHER. That's right. How could we get this across to each person?	Leader makes noncommittal reply and raises questions to turn thinking back to previous suggestions.
CHILD. We could have different	

Record	*Analysis*
rooms in charge each week so they would know. CHILD. We could go around to each room. Have a girl in charge of each girls' lavatory, have a boy in charge of each boys' lavatory. They could report people who do something wrong. TEACHER. Now, if we do these things, do we think there will be better use of our lavatories? Now what do the girls have to report?	 Leader poses summarizing question and turns discussion to a new phase.

A similar discussion followed the report on conditions in the girls' lavatories. The teacher then closed the discussion without providing for a clinching summary or a definite plan for next steps, saying, "That's about all we can do now, isn't it?" After the teacher's closing remark, Norma Jean came back to her point of having some punishment. Again she was ignored.

It can be frustrating to group members to propose ways of solving a problem only to have them disappear into thin air. One of the important responsibilities of a group leader is to see that ideas are kept alive long enough to be looked at, evaluated, and either accepted or rejected. To reach no decisions or to hold out no promise of a time when the ideas will be used is failure of leadership.

Planning for Better Use of the Cafeteria

In schools where a number of children, often eating in shifts, must share a large and frequently inadequate lunchroom or cafeteria, the problems are many. Two groups in Valley School undertook to solve some of the problems. A discussion in Miss Durham's first grade illustrates the approach of one age level.

Record	*Analysis*
TEACHER. Just before lunch we talked about the cafeteria. All of us were going to look for what we do wrong and how we can improve. You know *improve* means do *right,* do *better.* BOY. I saw a third grader with a milk bottle standing up on the tray, and walking with it.	Teacher has provided for concrete preparation for the discussion.

Record

TEACHER. What was wrong with that?

BOY. He should have the bottle down and have his thumb on it.

TEACHER. Couldn't you play it out?

Boy is unwilling. Betsy demonstrates.

TEACHER. What does that do?

Boy generalizes.

ELLIOT. Someone was pushing.

TEACHER. How can we improve on that? What should we do?

ELLIOT. Walk.

TEACHER. I've been noting people coming down queerly. (Demonstrates.) What's that?

CHILD. Jumping.

TEACHER. Do you want me to put these suggestions down? What was the first one?

Boy gives a long sentence.

TEACHER. Exactly. Now can anyone make a shorter sentence to put on the board? What is the thumb for?

CHILD. To hold the bottle.

TEACHER. Now say it.

Teacher writes as child gives sentence: 1. "Hold our bottles with thumbs."

TEACHER. Now what did Elliot suggest?

Teacher writes as child gives sentence: 2. "Walk down the steps."

Ellen demonstrates a tray not being held straight.

TEACHER. How do you want it on the board?

Teacher writes as child gives sentence: 3. "Hold tray straight."

CHILD. I know who that was that jumped down the steps.

TEACHER. Let's not call names. Maybe we'll improve next time.

JAY. I saw someone knocking

Analysis

Teacher invites boy to enlarge on his contribution.

Throughout this record the teacher makes use of concrete ways of keeping the discussion meaningful to these young children.

Teacher does not push an unwilling group member.

Teacher provides for generalization.

Teacher keeps the emphasis on improvement.

Teacher makes use of a written record to focus the discussion and to keep earlier contributions from being lost.

Teacher makes member feel comfortable while helping in the formulation of a simpler sentence.

Teacher helps group recapture second constructive suggestion.

Group member follows teacher's cue in demonstrating her point.

Teacher keeps discussion impersonal while sounding an optimistic note.

Record

over a milk bottle. He had milk all over the table.

TEACHER. What do you suggest to prevent overturning bottles?

JAY. Keep it where elbows won't hit it.

TEACHER. Was that what caused it?

JAY. I don't know.

Teacher asks two other children, then refers to chart developed in the fall, "Standards for Behavior," Item 5: "Keep our hands to ourselves."

TEACHER. Would that help? Shirley, how did it happen?

SHIRLEY. Someone's elbow got too close.

TEACHER. What is your suggestion?

SHIRLEY. Be careful with elbows and hands.

TEACHER. How about other food, the plates?

Child answers.

TEACHER. Who'd like to put it in a sentence?

BOY. Keep hands to yourself.

Teacher writes boy's suggestion: 4. "Keep hands to ourselves."

RICHARD. Today I saw milk spilled all over a tray.

TEACHER. Isn't this what we have already written up here?

JUDY. Everyone was talking too loud. We couldn't hear what each other was saying.

TEACHER. That's a bad idea. How would you like me to write that one down?

Teacher writes as child gives sentence: 5. "Talk quietly."

Teacher asks permission to talk.

TEACHER. I notice some days people have trouble getting food into the trash can. (Children nod

Analysis

Teacher gives help on straight thinking.

Teacher makes use of an earlier product of the group.

Appeal is made to the member most likely to have information.

Teacher helps group to generalize beyond bottles alone.

Teacher kindly refers to record to show contribution is repetitious.

Teacher passes value judgment.

Teacher shows group she is changing roles.

Record

heads.) How do you figure that
out?

DON. I heard a boy drop a milk
bottle and bust it.

TEACHER. And burst it. I think
we've got it straight on the milk
bottles. What do we do?

Don repeats the plan to hold the
bottle with the thumb.

TEACHER. Now back to the trash
can. Why do you have a hard time?

CHILD. It's too crowded.

TEACHER. Lee, do you have any
trouble? Why?

LEE. There are too many people
around.

TEACHER. Too many people. Any
other reason?

CHILD. Some people are taller.

TEACHER. You're getting warm.

CHILD. Too many people.

Teacher calls up two boys of con-
trasting height and has them stand
back to back.

TEACHER. Do you see a reason
here?

CHILD. Lee is too little, Richard
is taller.

TEACHER. What can we do?

LEE. We can get a box to stand
on.

TEACHER. Anything else?

Another child suggests a box.

TEACHER. That's Lee's suggestion. I like that but is there any
other?

CHILD. Put something down.

TEACHER. I don't quite understand.

CHILD. Stand up closer.

CHILD. Bring a little stool to
school.

TEACHER. That's Lee's suggestion. What else could we do?

Child brings up the problem of
crowding again.

Analysis

Teacher helps child hear correct
usage. She is patient about a group
member's need to have a point reviewed, then takes discussion back
to previous point.

Teacher draws into the discussion a child most likely to have a
problem with the trash can. She
accepts reason given but pushes for
further thinking on that point.

Teacher no doubt has a favored
solution in mind.

Again there is use of concrete
illustration.

Teacher shows that the value of
one suggestion is not questioned
merely because additional suggestions are sought.

Teacher tries to encourage member to make his point more clearly.

Teacher patiently points out that
a suggestion has been given previously.

Record	*Analysis*
CHILD. We could put a piece of wood under the table.	
TEACHER (dramatizing difficulty children were having in reaching a tall table). Anything else?	Teacher uses demonstration to help member evaluate his own suggestion.
BETSY. Cut the table legs off.	
TEACHER. That's a good idea. Whom could we get to cut the legs off?	Teacher is acting on the assumption that the idea is accepted by all because it is her favored one.
CHILD. The janitor.	
TEACHER. Let's have Betsy give us a sentence.	
Teacher writes as Betsy gives sentence: 6. "Cut the legs off the table."	
TEACHER. If we are going to do that, who must ask the janitor?	Teacher shows need for assigning responsibility.
CHILDREN. You.	
TEACHER. Oh, no, I don't have any trouble. You are the ones. What do you suggest, Walter?	
WALTER. Lee.	
TEACHER. Lee should? Any other children Lee's size? (Has small children stand.)	There was a little logic in this criterion for selecting children for this mission but not enough to cause the teacher to risk making the smaller children feel conspicuous.
BARBARA. Lee and some others.	
TEACHER. How shall we say that?	
BARBARA. The little children will ask the janitor.	
TEACHER. What?	
BARBARA. To cut off the legs.	
Teacher writes: 7. "The little children will ask the janitor to cut off the table legs."	
The group then reviewed what they had on the board.	Good idea to provide this summary.
TEACHER. I think this will help us a lot in the cafeteria. We won't have to think about big old garbage cans.	Leader helps group have a sense of achievement.

Because of Miss Durham's effective use of dramatization, her first grade children were able to work out a good solution to the trash-table problem. Two previous rules, holding bottle with thumb and keeping hands to oneself, no doubt took on new meaning as a result of the preliminary study of conditions and the discussion of findings.

These young children were concerned solely with their own conduct. In the second record, from Mrs. Whaley's third and fourth grade group, it may be seen that the children were interested in influencing other groups. Punishment was a recurring theme. The record illustrates various ways in which a group may inform itself.

Record	*Analysis*
Child reads list on board ("Things Wrong in the Cafeteria," a list developed in a previous discussion.)	
TEACHER. After we made a list of what was wrong with the cafeteria, what did we do?	Pooling ideas, one way a group informs itself.
CHILD. We went around to the rooms to see what they thought.	Another way in which a group may inform itself.
TEACHER. What do we call this?	
CHILD. A survey.	
TEACHER. Who would like to read our list from the survey?	
Child reads a second list from the board (also compiled in a previous discussion).	
TEACHER. Now we had a committee to go yesterday to Mrs. L. Who can tell us some of the things Mrs. L. thought were the worst things about the cafeteria?	Another way for a group to inform itself. (Mrs. L. is the cafeteria manager.)
CHILD. One thing she said was that children talk too loudly.	
CHILD. She said they talk more than they eat.	
TEACHER. How many things did we find wrong with the cafeteria?	Group might also have taken stock of things that were right in which they were showing improvement.
CHILD. Fourteen.	
TEACHER. What can we do next?	Child makes good statement of the problem. Teacher tries to help him move to thinking of specific solutions but her question is a little vague.
CHILD. What can we do to improve the cafeteria?	
TEACHER. What should we do?	
CHILD. Where my father works when something is wrong they have a committee to find out what can be done.	Interesting comparison from adult world. The teacher misses a bet in not helping the group to see whether this contained a suggestion for them.
TEACHER. But what can *we* do?	

Record	*Analysis*

Child makes further comment about things wrong in the cafeteria.

TEACHER. Yes, but we have decided what is wrong. But have we made any rules? What can we do?

Teacher gives leading question (rules).

NANCY. We ought to take each thing wrong and see what can be done about it. (Gives example.)

Child makes a mature suggestion.

TEACHER. Your suggestion, Nancy, is that we take each one. Have any of you any suggestions as to which one we might take first?

Teacher adopts suggestion of one group member.

CHILD. The trash table. (Gives reasons for this.)

This shows that the child sees his responsibility for explaining a contribution.

TEACHER. Can anybody tell us what Mrs. L. said about the trash table yesterday?

Good to go back to source of information.

CHILD. I don't remember.

CHILD. Mrs. L. said it wasn't in a good place, but where else could we put it?

Child gives explanation of what could be done.

TEACHER. Now we've wandered off again. We were trying to decide which to work on. Is this the one we want to choose?

What to do at such a point is always a problem. The teacher had invited children to go further in exploring the trash-table problem. A child carried discussion on to solution of problem. But the group had not yet decided to start with the trash table first; that was only one child's suggestion. Ways out: 1. Teacher may say, "You are getting us off the track" (which may make the child feel a little uncomfortable). 2. Teacher may let discussion proceed on trash table since it probably doesn't matter too much where they begin. 3. Teacher may say, "We seem to be started on what can be done about the trash table. Is it all right to go ahead on that and then choose another thing to work on after that?" This way a good discussion is not turned off

CHILD. I think we should take the one "the children talk too loudly." If we do this we can take up the other things.

TEACHER. How many think this? (Many raise hands.) Mrs. L. thinks so. She seems to be disturbed by this. Francis, what do you think we can do about this?

CHILD. We can listen to stories on the phonograph.

TEACHER (explaining this). I'll put this down on the board. Is there another one now?

CHILD. I don't know, but I don't think we should have too many children stand around the phonograph.

Record

Analysis

and children see what step they are taking. Actually, when a vote was taken, it was taken only on the second suggestion offered and not on the two that were before the group. Teacher encourages discussion on the problem of "talking too loudly."

CHILD. If anyone gets up from the lunch table we should have them stand up the rest of the lunch hour.

Child suggests a punishment.

TEACHER. Who else has a suggestion?

CHILD. We could be very quiet so the others could hear us.

Teacher keeps way open for other alternatives to come before the group.

TEACHER. Francis?

CHILD. People that sit in the middle walk around.

TEACHER. You would suggest then that we sit at our own table. This is a big problem. Is there any way we can get all children to keep quiet?

Teacher states her version of child's suggestion but does not check to see if she had the right understanding.

CHILD. There should be someone at the end of the table to tap them on the shoulders if they start talking.

CHILD. Some children get mad if you do this.

This is one of the few times in this record when one child reacted directly to the comment of another.

CHILD. Some will start fighting you if you do this.

Child in discussion insisted that if someone at each table checked the table and had the rule breaker punished, it would be effective.

TEACHER. If you think this will work, then we shall put it down. I think we're wandering off again. May I make a suggestion? I wonder if we couldn't this afternoon write a letter in language class telling others what they might do to make the cafeteria quieter.

Teacher accepts contribution, then operates as a group member, giving a suggestion that is apparently assigned no more and no less weight than the suggestion of anyone else.

Child gives another way of keeping cafeteria quieter.

TEACHER. We'll have to have

Record

more than this or we might not be successful in getting the cafeteria quieter.

CHILD. We ought to put in our letter that if anyone talks they will have to write a sentence eight times.

TEACHER. You are all thinking what we might do to punish rather than suggest what they may do to keep quiet.

CHILD. I think we could just say what we want them to do.

CHILD. I don't like that.

TEACHER. I have another idea, but I'm not going to tell you. Let's have someone read the suggestions we have listed.

Child reads the five suggestions:
1. Have stories on records.
2. Set a good example by not talking ourselves.
3. Children sit at their own tables.
4. Every room should have a child in charge of each table.
5. We can write letters to each room to ask them to be quiet in the cafeteria.

TEACHER. Yes, do you have something more to suggest?

CHILD. I think we could send our list around and then ask the other rooms to add to it.

CHILD. I think this is a good idea.

TEACHER. Will you now copy these in your notebooks?

Analysis

Child shows teacher's suggestion was tacitly accepted.

Teacher throws weight on side of constructive measures.

Good when a child feels free to object.

Teacher should have asked child to explain his objection. Little purpose seems to be served by the teacher's mentioning an idea if she does not mean to share it with the group.

Shows good child relationships. The teacher, however, gives no indication that she will follow up on the suggestion.

It is not clear that this is part of a plan agreed upon by the group. Copying in a notebook may be rather meaningless unless need for it is seen and planned for.

Mrs. Whaley helped the group make a constructive plan for getting the cooperation of others in the school, although the group perhaps was not clear as to the relationship between their first four suggestions and the last one. There was never a clear-cut decision to adopt the five ideas, much less a plan for implementing them.

Other problems that have been attacked by grade or class groups, and reported in this study, are (1) making proposals for storage and use of new play equipment (fifth and sixth grade group); (2) deciding what to do about an icy playground (every group in school); (3) planning better use of community recreation facilities (ninth grade civics classes), a study which led to school-council planning of a Saturday morning recreation program for the entire junior high school the following year; and (4) determining pupil rights (ninth grade general education class which had been studying the Bill of Rights and protested a search of their lockers by school authorities).

PROBLEM-SOLVING IN SCHOOL FORUMS

In one elementary school, decisions as to jobs to improve the school grounds and assignment of responsibility for these jobs are taken care of in two assemblies—one for primary grades and one for upper grades. Under the leadership of Miss Casper, the principal, the young children in a planning session in the spring reviewed plans made in the previous fall and checked to see what remained to be done.

They reminded themselves that the fifth and sixth grade group had proposed to stop erosion at one spot by constructing a rock garden, that the sixth grade had agreed to make a bicycle stand, and that the fourth grade was to work on a nature trail. They listed other outside jobs to be done: working in the garden, putting down sod, repairing driveway, cleaning off two picnic areas (cutting weeds and tree limbs), painting and repairing the sandbox, placing and painting benches and tables in the picnic area, putting in new grass, and getting rid of caterpillars.

During the discussion the children talked about tools needed for cutting weeds and tree limbs and decided they were too dangerous for the very youngest children. They decided that the kindergarten children might drop grass seed on the bare places on the grounds. They foresaw that the afternoon kindergarten class would have to be asked not to step on the new grass. They discussed steps in preparing soil and planting and caring for a garden. They discussed DDT and other possible sprays for getting rid of caterpillars. An excerpt from the discussion at this point will illustrate the procedure used.

> PRINCIPAL. We don't know what DDT will do to plants yet. What's one job to do?
> CHILD. Make sure the spray we get won't kill plants.
> PRINCIPAL. So what will we have to do?
> CHILD. Make an experiment.
> CHILD. Ask somebody.
> CHILD. Read about it.
> CHILD. Send for information.
> PRINCIPAL. Are there people in this state who could send us information?
> CHILD. Yes, the Department of Agriculture.
> CHILD. We could send to the United States Department of Agriculture too.

It was decided that the third grade would resume their work on the driveway—putting rocks along it. The need for removing poison ivy from the picnic place was recognized also. The children decided to get help on this from their fathers and the "bigger" grades.

Under the skillful leadership of Miss Casper this large group of young children planned quite efficiently.

Another example of attack on an all-school problem in a student forum comes from the Robinson School where the fifth, fifth and sixth, and sixth grade groups met for a discussion of how safety patrol members and captain would be chosen that year. Miss Hallum, the principal, led the discussion. The record is fairly complete as far as the leader's participation goes, but the observer recorded few of the children's contributions.

In the early part of the discussion children discussed what a patrolman should be like. As suggestions such as "dependable," "good sport," "a leader" were made, the principal helped each child to enlarge on his contribution, by asking, "How does that affect you?" "What difference does that make to you?" "Any other advantages of being a good sport?" Miss Hallum also helped the group to make these terms less abstract by recalling past experiences: "Is there anyone you know who was a good sport last year, who gave up something he wanted to do?" and "Is there anyone who did an especially good job of being a leader last year?"

When one child suggested that a patrolman should have his work in on time, the principal helped him to see that this was not a pertinent criterion but that being prompt on his job was. At one point she tried to prevent the building of an unrealistic list by saying, "We don't want to get too much to live up to. We're all human."

To some contributors the principal would say, "Have we used any word that would take care of that?" or "Have we included that?" These were honest questions, meant not to dismiss the contribution but to have the child examine its usefulness. One child suggested courtesy, and when challenged, said, "I don't remember that we have included it."

"All right, I don't either," Miss Hallum replied, and asked the group, "Shall we include courtesy?" She watched for any signs of disagreement and said, "I believe that will be enough, do you? You don't, Leona?"

Leona believed a patrolman should be a good student. Why? Because he has to make up his work.

Miss Hallum tried to show Leona that she need not be overconcerned about certain values. "Does he always have to make up his work?" she asked. "It is important to be a good student, but if he has other qualities, we might not worry about arithmetic. But would we want someone who had time to do his arithmetic and did not?"

The next consideration was that of points at which patrolmen were needed. When it came to deciding how many were needed, someone recalled that fourth graders were put off the patrol the year before. This led to an interesting bit of group thinking.

Record	Analysis
PRINCIPAL. Was it because they were too young or because the right ones were not chosen?	Raises question calling for judgment.
Children think "too young."	
PRINCIPAL. Do you think there should be fourth graders on? Why?	
Children give reasons.	
PRINCIPAL. Let's have some more comments. Unless we could convince them we had good reasons we might have a pretty hard time. We have gotten two or three opinions. Does anyone else have an opinion? Come on, now, you aren't thinking. Do any of the teachers have any more points?	Provides for thorough discussion of this crucial point.
Child makes an observation.	
PRINCIPAL. I'm afraid you're not answering our question right now.	Shows child his contribution will have a place another time.

Record	Analysis
Will you bring that up later? Will you get good cooperation from children who are hurt? Children think not.	Helps children think of others' feelings.
PRINCIPAL. Let's vote. Do you know what you want? Should the fourth graders be included or not? Put yourselves in their places. The fourth graders are admitted to the patrol.	Makes sure children know the issue on which they are voting.

The next problem raised by the principal was how patrolmen should be chosen. Suggestions were given, including use of the standards set up earlier in the period. The following interchange will show how a decision was made on this point.

Record	Analysis
PRINCIPAL. How did we get those standards? Did the fourth graders help? What if they don't like them? PRINCIPAL. Shall the whole group or a committee choose the patrols? Child makes a suggestion.	Shows importance of participation on the part of those on whose cooperation the children would like to depend.
PRINCIPAL. All right, each group choose your own patrol people, using the standards after they have been checked by the fourth-graders.	Leader settles the point instead of making it a group decision. She was probably operating on an observable consensus, however.

The group then returned to the problem of how many patrolmen would be needed. When this had been decided a member initiated a problem—a role most frequently played by the principal in this discussion. Should the captain be a sixth grader? Another excerpt from the record shows how this problem was disposed of.

Record	Analysis
PRINCIPAL. That is another point. Are we ready to talk about that? Child comments.	
PRINCIPAL (humorously). Will he be a better captain if he has six years instead of five? I think that is a very nice point. Anything else? PRINCIPAL. Who should select the captain? Is it your job or the patrol's job?	Leader gives praise.

Record	*Analysis*
Mary Lee makes suggestion.	
PRINCIPAL. You think if he comes from the sixth grade, the sixth grade should vote? All right, any other suggestions? You want a chance to vote on the captain anyway? Is that your point? How was the captain selected before?	Leader invites alternate suggestions. Again turns to past experience as a guide rather than as authority.
CHILDREN. By the fifth and sixth grades.	
Boy suggests that the patrol elect him.	
PRINCIPAL. Yes, but he sort of belongs to the whole school.	Principal gives a viewpoint, but does it tentatively.
PRINCIPAL. You did not like Mary Lee's suggestion? Could it be someone not on last year? Could you change your suggestion? Would you discuss the captain in your rooms and meet tomorrow just on that? Would you be willing to have the three secretaries who took notes come and talk to the fourth grade? If there is anything else about the patrol we can take it up tomorrow.	Leader wisely postpones a difficult decision until the children have opportunity to think about the matter further. Leader suggests procedure for informing the fourth grade of standards set up for patrols in this meeting.

As a result of this session several things had been accomplished: the qualities of patrolmen, their duties, the number needed, the eligibility of fourth graders, and the process of selection all had been agreed on. A small committee, the secretaries, had been given a definite charge, each grade had a problem on which to do further thinking by themselves, and the way was left open to bring up further problems the next day.

Perhaps because an experienced leader was present, this large forum did planning of a quality to match that of a smaller group. A large group seems to multiply the number of suggestions to be dealt with. In this case the number of repetitive or off-the-track contributions was proportionately but not unduly large.

PROBLEM-SOLVING IN ALL-SCHOOL COMMITTEES

Besides maintaining two-way communication between the entire student body and its representative group, the council, many schools provide additional opportunities for direct participation in all-school problem-solving through the provision of a number of supplementary committees with wider membership than the council.

It is important to keep this supplementary organization flexible, dropping committees as problems are solved, broadening the functions of certain committees when it appears desirable, and creating new committees as need arises. Certain standing committees usually are required, however. Some of the continuing services described in Chapter VII can be put in the hands of such standing committees.

The annual report of one such committee, the order and safety committee in a senior high school, illustrates how a committee sees new problems as it works along and the relationship that must exist between it and the school council. For example, there was a problem of smoking on the school grounds. As the chairman's report states, the committee felt that this was due to ignorance of the school rules. As the problem began to be discussed it seemed best to set aside an area on the school grounds where smoking would be permitted. This solution was taken to the council and faculty for approval.

Through use of a number of such functional committees the arm of the school council can be extended considerably and many persons can have the experience of helping to solve all-school problems.

PARTICIPATION WITH ADULT ORGANIZATIONS

Participation in solving all-school problems occasionally causes children and outside adults to work together. Mr. Rice's diary mentions student participation on the governing board of the parent-teacher association of his high school.

> Our P.T.A. projects have been more successful since student representatives (elected by the student body) were included on the executive committee. When the committee meets it now has the advantage of student viewpoints. When a program is planned it also has the cooperation of the students, and this all brings about a greater harmony and understanding among parents, students, and teachers.

In one city the P.T.S.O. (parent-teacher-student organization) has replaced the usual parent-teacher association.

In Miss Brainard's school elementary children had an unusual and valuable opportunity to plan with a teachers' organization. Her diary relates the incident.

The Elementary Division of the Teachers Association was presenting a puppet show produced by professional puppeteers on three consecutive days in three different elementary school auditoriums. Our school auditorium, with our principal's approval, was selected by the committee as one of the centers. The performance, for which an admission was charged, started at four o'clock. Children from five schools, including ours, attended the performance in our auditorium. Because our school has the largest enrollment of the five and because of the convenience for these children on reaching the auditorium, it was naturally assumed that we should have the largest number attending the performance.

The seating arrangement and the way to spend the interval of time between dismissal from school and the start of the performance presented a twofold problem. Our principal decided to present the matter to the council representatives from grades 3 to 6 (limited to these grades because announcements of the play had stated the performance would appeal to children eight years of age or older). Consequently, as a first step, these class representatives met with the principal. After giving necessary details of the plans she asked their opinions of the best arrangement for seating the children who attended from our school. There was a rather free giving of suggestions—ranging all the way from "first come, first served" to leaving all the front seats for children from the other schools. Several alternative suggestions were made.

Since the children's plans would be tied in with the plans of the committee from the Association, it was decided to select four representatives—one each from grades 3, 4, 5, 6—to meet after school with an Association committee member, the principal, and a group of teachers. The next step was for the class representatives to report back to their classes and discuss the proposals. Each class was to consider the seating arrangements and notify the grade representative of its decision. In the classes, too, there was a free expression of opinion.

After school the committee met. Each child was given an opportunity to report the consensus of opinions gathered. The one proposal of a very long row of seats had to be discarded because of the requirements of fire regulations. An arrangement that worked out rather satisfactorily was reached. The member from the Association reported that our school had bought more than half the tickets. So, it was decided to make a center aisle having ten seats on each side. Our school would occupy the seats from front to rear on one side of the aisle. They would also occupy seats in the balcony. The seats on the other side of the aisle would be occupied by the children from the other schools as they arrived.

The next day the small committee reported back to the council. These representatives carried the details for the seating arrangement to each classroom. At this meeting it was decided to ask the teacher who has charge of our assembly music to arrange some group singing of familiar songs as an enjoyable way to spend the time while the other children were reaching our school for the performance.

The opportunity which Miss Brainard has described gave children a genuine opportunity to plan on a par with adults. The children also learned to plan with the rights and feelings of others in mind. It seems fair to say that the children's participation added to the quality of the plans, and certainly must have helped the children and their teachers over what might have been a tiresome and restless period of waiting for a performance to begin.

CONCLUSION

Participation in problems of a school-wide nature offers opportunities to children and youth to think in larger terms than their intimate class or age group, to learn to work with others of different ages and experience, to tackle problems more complex in nature because they grow out of the living together of many groups. Acceptance of responsibility is dramatized when the whole school depends on the quality of planning and follow-through of one group. Such planning raises the morale of the smaller unit groups, uniting their differences in working for a larger cause, just as it makes for a stronger feeling of belonging in the whole school.

CHAPTER IX

Evaluating Group Processes

and Achievements

As PUPILS use a variety of opportunities to work cooperatively with one another and with teachers, they have many chances to evaluate the ways in which they plan together and the results of group procedures. Cooperative evaluation consists in pooling and weighing feelings, opinions, or evidence as to any one or all of three things: (1) the worth of an undertaking in general; (2) the value of various means used to plan or realize some achievement; and (3) the nature of growth resulting for individuals and the group. Often the evaluation is inherent in plans for a further activity. Judgments are arrived at through direct or implied comparison with other experiences.

In this chapter the experiences of pupils and teachers attempting cooperative evaluation are reported. Evaluation of special undertakings is illustrated in the first part of the chapter. In the last part examples are given of general stocktaking.

EVALUATION OF SPECIAL UNDERTAKINGS

Examples of evaluation of special undertakings gathered in this study fall under three headings: (1) judging how group plans work out when tested in action; (2) discussing the nature of the growth the group observes in itself; and (3) using evaluation as a means of improving plans for further projects.

Judging How Group Plans Work Out

Teachers often hold a general discussion with a group after an event. On the day after a tea for mothers, Miss Van Alsten writes in her diary: "There was a general discussion in the class and all felt that it was a great success and they had had so much enjoy-

ment in having it that they now want to give another one at Easter-
time." [1] Here was an evaluation which showed such general satisfaction with the results of planning that the group wanted to have a
similar experience another time.

A group may also ask others to evaluate its efforts, as Mrs. Malden's fifth grade children did following the production of a play to
which the fourth and sixth grades had been invited.

> We asked the audience for criticisms and suggestions and found that
> they had been very alert to all inconsistencies and flaws and techniques
> of stage craft. A very discerning audience! My fifth graders took their
> comments to heart and added a few of their own. Significantly, their
> burning question was, "Did they like it?" Assured that they had the
> stamp of approval of their schoolmates, they were happy.

An entry in Miss Merlin's diary relates how she resisted the temptation to scold as unfortunate incidents occurred in connection with
the program her fifth grade children gave in assembly.

> A group discussion was held this morning concerning "How could
> we have gained more from our experience?" I thought that some of the
> children had not responded as well as they should have and that several
> others had taken advantage of the situation, but I didn't say anything
> until we had time for an evaluation period.

Evaluation at the secondary-school level may be much more elaborate. When Miss Fielding's high school mathematics classes undertook to plan the policies and procedures by which their work together
would be guided, it was suggested that a questionnaire be prepared
after a few weeks to determine how well their plans were satisfying
the members of the groups.[2] The questionnaire developed by student
and teacher cooperation is reproduced in full to show the nature of
the information gathered. The student replies are included for the
benefit of those who may be interested in the kinds of judgments the
students made.

A Survey of Students' Opinions Concerning Certain Policies in Mathematics Classes

	Text	Collection
1. Do you prefer a textbook or a collection of materials?	80	22
2. Do you like this textbook?	Yes	No
	66	15

---

[1] Planning for the tea is described on pages 69–70.
[2] For a description of the operation of these classes, see Chapter V, pages 86–91.

A Survey of Students' Opinions Concerning Certain Policies
in Mathematics Classes (*Cont'd*)

3. Are you getting the type of mathematics that you desire this semester?	Yes 84	No 22
4. Is there enough review of fundamentals?	Yes 90	No 15
5. Are the tests frequent enough?	Yes 124	No 11
6. Should tests be discussed after the teacher corrects them?	Yes 119	No 14
7. Do you like extra time at the beginning or end of the hour to work on your assignments?	Beginning 57	End 77
8. Do students speak loudly enough in the class?	Yes 97	No 38
9. Should students bring material for bulletin boards and use in our work?	Yes 80	No 52
10. Would you like to have more students as chairmen of groups in our work?	Yes 57	No 75
11. Should our four assignments per week (that we decided upon) be done on M.T.W.Th. or on T.W.Th.F.?	M.T.W.Th. 115	T.W.Th.F. 18
12. Should assignments be decided upon daily or for a week (at least) in advance?	Daily 14	In Advance 100
13. Is there enough discussion about an assignment before attempting it?	Yes 75	No 62
14. How long does it take to do the average assignment? (This includes the class period.) Is it O.K. in length, too short or too long?	20 min.—9 30 min.—42 40 min.—37 O.K. or too short—92	50 min.—4 60 min.—35 Over 1 hr.—6 Too long—41
Would you understand the work as well if fewer problems were done?	Yes 37	No 96
15. Should all students do the same amount of work, that is, should there be a minimum requirement?	Yes 65	No 65
16. Should there be work assigned or suggested by students for which extra or honor credit should be received?	Yes 72	No 62

A Survey of Students' Opinions Concerning Certain Policies in Mathematics Classes (*Cont'd*)

17. Is the work covered too fast (with too little drill)?	**Yes** 40	**No** 93
18. Should you keep together by working on the same unit or work by groups depending upon how fast and hard you want to work?	Together 98	Groups 36
19. Should more problems be put on the board daily for all of the class?	Yes 52	No 82
20. Should all problems be discussed for your group or only by request?	All 42	By request 72
21. Possibilities for correction— which do you ordinarily prefer?		
a. Put all of the problems on the board?	37	
b. Put the answers on the board?	24	
c. A student or the teacher read the answers?	16	
d. Students volunteer answers?	22	
22. Who should correct the majority of the papers?		
a. Correct your own.	45	
b. Exchange papers.	44	
c. Teacher corrects papers.	42	
23. Does the teacher correct enough papers?	Yes 124	No 9
24. Do you like to keep your work in a notebook between marking periods?	Yes 101	No 33
25. Should all marks be recorded in the teacher's class record book?	Yes 84	No 49
26. If you think that a record of marks should be kept, which of the following methods do you like the best?		
a. Keep your own record.	20	
b. Both you and the teacher record.	10	
c. Teacher keep the record.	111	

If the teacher records, the following are ways of getting the

A Survey of Students' Opinions Concerning Certain Policies
in Mathematics Classes (*Cont'd*)

score on papers that the teacher
does not correct.

a. Hand your work in after you correct it.	30		
b. You give your score aloud.	20		
c. A student or teacher comes to you for your score.	61		

		Yes	No
27. Would you like a letter mark for every assignment?		95	10
28. Should work not completed at the time of correction be reduced in value at all?		115	19
29. Should absentee's papers be reduced in value unless the work is brought when he returns or else he returns for seventh hour?		61	74

30. How soon after absence should
work be done? (Depends on
length of the absence.)

a. 1 day	40
b. 2 days	31
c. 3 days	23
d. 5 days	28

It is apparent that as a result of this survey Miss Fielding and her
class had much important information to use in planning ahead.
Most of the replies called for further discussion before an intelligent
and satisfying decision could be reached. It is especially important
that minority views be carefully considered.

If pupils are to have an opportunity to put their plans to a real
test, they must be allowed to make mistakes. By her forbearance,
Miss Rezny gave her sixth grade children a chance to see how adequate were their plans for publishing a newspaper. Like many
teachers, Miss Rezny wondered whether she was justified in keeping
silent when she noticed an omission.

The mimeographing has been done. Martin, Arthur, and Collyn
worked hard on it. The children realized they had made a great error—
the proofreaders forgot to do their job, and no one else had taken the
responsibility. I knew about this but had refrained from telling them.
I wonder if I did right in letting an error be made? I probably will
know by the results next time.

Discussing Nature of Growth Seen

If a teacher is concerned with more than the learning of facts or the improvement of skills in reading, writing, and using numbers, he may give his pupils an opportunity such as Mrs. Remington did at the conclusion of the circus project in her second grade.[3] The teacher began a discussion with the question, "What have we learned about working together?" These were the answers given by the children as recorded on a chart by the teacher.

We need to make plans before we work.
Sometimes we try more than one way of doing things.
Sometimes we have to change our plans.
We get along better when we will share materials.
There are some things one person cannot do but many people working together can do.
We were scared the first time but went ahead and did the best we could. It was easier the next time.
We felt happy because people had a good time.

After Miss Wisneski's fifth grade class had had an opportunity to help plan and carry out a study of the North Central States, they came to these conclusions as to their learning.

1. We are learning to work together.
2. We are becoming skillful in locating information and using it.
3. We know that we must plan before a job can be done satisfactorily.
4. If we have a job to do, we are going to do it even though it may be unpleasant at times.
5. We know how to listen to suggestions of others.
6. It was a pleasure to share our findings with the entire group.
7. We have a better understanding of the North Central States.

It may be noted that only the last item represents factual learning; the other six relate to ways of working and feelings of satisfaction in carrying out a project together.

Evaluating as a Step in Improving Plans

Using evaluation as a direct step in improving plans is illustrated in a report from Miss Oliver. Because of her encouragement, a small group of her second grade children was at work preparing a puppet show. At sharing time one morning Sandy stated that the group would like to present its play and find out if it was

---

[3] See pages 163–164.

good enough for another class to see. The teacher saw that the children would be better able to evaluate if they knew what to look for, so she asked, "What shall we watch for to know whether it is good enough for others to see?" Sandy said, "Well, I'm the reader. See if I speak loud enough and if I have good expression." Toni said, "We could let them see if the scenery is appropriate and if it's done well." Frank added, "Listen for good expression with the puppeteers. Do they know what they should say? 'Cause they should."

The teacher makes this comment in her report: "This evaluation proved worth while since good suggestions for improving the play were made. Because the children were eager to show another class, all suggestions were quickly used."

Later the children decided to make up a new play. This gave an opportunity for further evaluation in terms of "plans for next time." An excerpt from this planning will illustrate the point.

> GAY. If you are going to want more plays you'll have to do something about that box toppling over (referring to an accident when the former play was presented to another class).
> JUDITH. It isn't big enough for so many children. That's why we're having all that trouble.
> BOBBY. I could ask my father if he could get us a box at the refrigerator plant. It would be a wooden one.
> RICK. Good! We could have lights in that one.
> TEACHER. What is your next step, then?

The examples in this part of the chapter have focused on special evaluation periods in connection with specific activities. In the next section are examples of general stocktaking.

EVALUATION AS GENERAL STOCKTAKING

Stocktaking may be a casual affair, occurring rather continuously; it may be done periodically, that is, with some regularity; or it may be done only occasionally as a somewhat special event.

Casual, Continuous Evaluation

Evaluation often is done spontaneously by members of a group who have developed some closeness. Miss Rezny notes an example of this in her diary.

> The children had a class meeting and afterwards remarked how much better it was than the others. The problem of behavior bothered them

now that we have a circle formation. They asked me what was to be done with people who were annoying. I suggested that they decide this, as in all probability they would be annoyed first. This was a new thought; they are thinking it through.

Of the need for continuous evaluation Miss Evans had this to say in reporting on a group study of recreation:

> We found that we must evaluate our work frequently, not only in the classroom, but in the halls and on the playground. We would stop each day more than once to be sure that we were on the right track, and that we were getting the things from our work which seemed of most importance to us. We would discuss the quality of our work and plan ways to do our work more efficiently.[4]

With this kind of attention to evaluation, pupils can learn the value of continuous appraisal of what they are doing and how well they are doing it. This is the kind of behavior that marks the mature individual in a society that leaves much to individual and group initiative.

Taking Stock Periodically

Pupils may be helped to use evaluation effectively if they have a regular time set aside for it. An entry in Miss Green's diary describes evaluation procedure used regularly with her first grade children following the daily work period.

> Some children are interested in building a house out of the building blocks. Children made a list of all the things that they wanted for the house. Committees were formed to carry out these tasks. We checked them off as the jobs were completed.
> Other activities are going on at the same time, such as woodworking, painting, modeling, drawing, and reading. At the end of the work period, each reports to the group of his accomplishments, and what he is planning to do the following day. Suggestions are given by the group.

Miss Sudbury's second grade children regularly evaluate their play periods which they plan in advance and which are conducted under pupil leadership. Evaluation is in terms of standards they have set up for "good" games.

Miss Lambert made plans during a summer workshop to hold weekly evaluation periods in her fifth and sixth grade groups rather than the evaluation at the end of each day that was customary in her school system. An excerpt from a running record of one such evalua-

[4] See pages 290 ff.

tion session, together with the analysis sent back with the record by the observer, shows the nature of Miss Lambert's early attempts at group evaluation.

Record

TEACHER. Pencils down. We are going to think first of our standing appointments, then the things we do not do regularly. Look at the list on the board to remind you. Then if time permits, the boys can take over and we can evaluate the Helpers Club. You have your evaluation standards and get your topics out.

The teacher allows some time to think. The children seem just to be waiting.

TEACHER. Are you ready? All right.

SANDRA. I have done all my work but English. I have done best in arithmetic.

TEACHER. What process in arithmetic?

SANDRA. Fractions.

CHILD. We have done our work pretty well in arithmetic but not English.

CHILD. In social studies we have accomplished quite a bit.

TEACHER. Talk distinctly, please.

CHILD. We have done good in art. I have done good in social studies. I helped over in the meeting. I did better today than before.

Analysis

Could the teacher just suggest that each child get ready for the evaluation, get out the things he will need, and not give so many detailed directions?

Teacher allows much free giving of reactions.

This is the first example of a more objective type of evaluation —the child offers a slight bit of evidence to support what he is saying.

Individual testimony of a similar nature continues for a time. The teacher then tests to see if the present vein of talk is exhausted.

Record

TEACHER. Any more about the experiences you liked?

CHILD. The experience with the class.

TEACHER. Somebody help with the name.

Analysis

Teacher encourages clear and specific use of vocabulary.

Record

BOY. Static and friction in electricity.

TEACHER. Anything else?

CHILD. Everything went well except some didn't get demonstrations done because time didn't allow.

TEACHER. Didn't we do any English?

GIRL. Parts of speech.

TEACHER. Be definite.

GIRL. Writing letters.

TEACHER. Anything else?

BOY. Talking.

TEACHER. Yes, oral.

GIRL. Oral reading, wasn't it?

GIRL. When we were demonstrating we were talking and that was oral.

GIRL. We got in English when we wrote down problems and checked off periods.

TEACHER. What problems?

GIRL. Our social studies problems.

TEACHER. Was that oral English, wording of problems?

Child seems to be in doubt.

TEACHER. Was that oral English?

GIRL. Yes.

TEACHER. What did we plan for English that we didn't accomplish?

GIRL. A test.

TEACHER. Yes, our standardized test. Anything else you didn't get done?

GIRL. Go over our arithmetic tests.

TEACHER. We hoped to get our program books, didn't we? Take your pencils. Now what about next week?

Analysis

Here the teacher introduces a question bringing up the week's opportunities for language learning.

Using the question form would be less abrupt.

This kind of a question, designed to cause "thinking," often has the effect of making a child feel that his idea has been rejected.

The children make a number of suggestions. The discussion that occurred when one boy mentioned art shows how the children evaluated past experience in making plans for the next week.

Record	*Analysis*
TEACHER. I expect we can make that a standing appointment. Do you want a regular period or when you are free?	Teacher gives choice to group.
SANDRA. A regular period. Some don't even get a chance.	
GIRL. Yes.	
GIRL. Yes, because I haven't done anything in class on any media.	

A general suggestion made to the teacher by the consultant on the basis of this evaluation session was that it might be worth seeing if much of the individual testimony could be cut short and more emphasis be put on making sound plans for the next week. This would cut down on the length of the evaluation period, and since the planning ahead for the next week—what to be sure to get in—was really an evaluation, it would appear to be desirable.

In May the observer returned to secure a second record of group evaluation in Miss Lambert's room. Before the evaluation started, the children, at the teacher's suggestion, explained to the observer their recent activities. The responses came rapidly from different children in turn.

> Sanding our desks and putting blotters on them to keep them nice.
> Studying flowers.
> Keeping a chart on the length of days. Every day we look at the *World Almanac* for the time of sunrise and sunset. Before we got the *Almanac* we estimated and were only four minutes ahead.

The last thing mentioned was the sending of a scrapbook to England. (The scrapbook had been sent to the school of an exchange teacher who had worked in America the year before.) Just the day before, the children had received a letter thanking them for it and also some letters from people to whom they had been writing. They decided they would take the letters home for their relatives to see and then they would answer them. Such a review of accomplishments was in itself a worth-while step in evaluation.

After that the group began their evaluation in terms of planning for the next week.

Record	*Analysis*
TEACHER. What are we ready for next week? What do you feel pretty sure of from this week?	Apparently the teacher was following the suggestion given at the end of the previous record. The

Record

GIRL. Social studies.

GIRL. We must work on our fishpond.

The group then pointed out to the observer plans drawn in chalk on the floor the exact size the fishpond was to be.

GIRL. I'd like to get slides in our art work. I'd like to go on to percentage in arithmetic.

PRINCIPAL. Two groups sent in statements on slides but they were indefinite.

GIRL. We plan to make slides on flowers.

GIRL. From the test yesterday I need more work on arithmetic and problem solving but I asked Miss Lambert. I'd like to go to percentages. I'd like to know if others in the sixth grade would like to go on.

TEACHER. Where did you fall down in the test?

GIRL. Roman numerals.

PRINCIPAL. I'm awfully sorry to interrupt, but I'd like to know what the boys think.

BOY. I'd like help in English, pronouns and nouns. I get high scores in arithmetic.

TEACHER. Do you know the next step? What did you work on this week?

WALTER. Yes, multiplication of fractions.

TEACHER. What kind? (Gives example and finally gets the answer, proper fractions.)

GIRL. Next week I would like a spelling bee.

Other children show they favor this.

TEACHER. Are there any special appointments we need to fill?

GIRL. Art.

PRINCIPAL. Related to anything?

Analysis

children's plans reflect unfinished work of the current week.

Throughout this record the principal and the teacher are trying to help the pupils to make more exact plans.

The principal's concern that the boys be given a chance to participate may have been worthy but it cut off the opportunity to get an answer to the girl's question as to whether others would like to go on to percentages. Adults attempting to guide groups must weigh relative values at many points. Could participation by the boys have waited just a little longer?

Record   *Analysis*

GIRL. Social studies.

PRINCIPAL. Shouldn't you say, "Art related to social studies"?

GIRL. Slides.

GIRL. I think it is too early to start slides.

There is much discussion pro and con.

TEACHER. How many feel you are ready to make a few slides?

Teacher tests the group to see if the discussion so far has led to a solution.

BOY. I think we aren't ready until we have studied them some more.

The ensuing discussion shows the division in the group. The teacher allows the different points of view to emerge freely.

GIRL. I don't think that's right. I don't agree with you at all. If we keep on putting it off, school will be out. We can start on flowers. Those who don't want to can make them later.

SHIRLEY. I think we should make slides all at one time.

GIRL. I think so too, but we can look at them.

GIRL. But that isn't all there is. We need to learn a little more first.

BOY. People don't have to make them if they are not ready.

At least eight people make twelve to fifteen very similar comments.

GIRL. We are making slides for education, not just to be doing things.

The weight of opinion seems to be in the direction of letting people make slides when they are ready. The teacher recognizes and reassures those who want to postpone this activity.

TEACHER. How many people need to know a little more first? We will guarantee you will have time to make slides of your choice.

Teacher writes: "spelling bee, art, show slides."

TEACHER. Is there anything else you want to do next week?

At this point many suggestions of individual activity were made, among others: "I'd like to do some splatter work." "I want to finger-paint about trees." "I want to do the next step in multiplication of fractions." "I need more help on the English test. I got only five right."

It is evident from the complete record that plans suggested by the children showed a realistic facing of previous accomplishments and shortcomings. In making their proposals, the children often included evidence. Plans for individuals showed great breadth of interest, reflecting the varied activities the children had had a chance to engage in. The children also learned some valuable lessons about how much they could accomplish in a week, and they showed wisdom in timing their plans in terms of their preparedness for carrying out certain activities, such as slide-making.

Pupil Participation in Reports to Parents

Reports to parents offer a good opportunity for periodic evaluation of group progress if teachers are willing to allow pupil participation in this activity. Since reports to parents are usually designed to help pupils profit more from their school experiences, it would seem that children and youth themselves ought to receive the educational value of this stocktaking.

In some schools students compose a report of group goals, accomplishments, and plans for further work to be duplicated and sent to their parents along with comments by themselves and by the teacher on individual progress. A form for reporting is made cooperatively by pupils in some classrooms. Usually these forms allow room for comments by pupil, teacher, and parent.

On rare occasions students are asked to help evaluate the reporting system in use. An example of this occurred in Miss Longo's ninth grade English class when her students were invited to discuss marking systems and report cards for the benefit of a teacher committee making a study of reports to parents throughout the school system. The present report card in the junior high school had been in use for three years.

At first the students were rather willing to defend report cards and marks.

> We need it to show what we've done.
> It gives us something to work for.
> We need grades for college.
> If we didn't have grades my parents wouldn't know if I didn't work.

There were a few dissenting voices.

> What about the one who tries but still can't get A's?
> A and B in gym isn't fair. We should be marked on effort there. I suggest S and U.

When the discussion moved on to possible types of reports to parents, the students began to be quite discriminating.

Record

TEACHER. One type is report cards. What else?

GIRL. Conference with parents. (Side talk and signs of embarrassment. Teacher suggests three-way conference.)

BOY. In elementary school we got those letters.

BOB. In high school they have cards with S and U.

TEACHER. That would be a system of marking. Any others? Well, let's have a little discussion on conferences.

GIRL. A school this size couldn't have conferences with parents individually.

GIRL. I think students should be independent.

TEACHER. How about parents coming to school?

GIRL. Parents are more interested in us in the elementary school.

TEACHER. Is that right? Would your mother like to hear you say that?

GIRL. I don't know.

TEACHER. Have you ever thought that students do not like to have parents come?

GIRL. Sometimes it is good to have a conference when there is a real problem.

TEACHER. Let's go on to the second point. Keep in mind that we are evaluating these but we should keep an open mind. How about report cards?

DICK. I think I'd rather have written reports. They tell more about what you are doing.

ANNE. They tell more than marks. They tell about attitudes.

Analysis

The board secretary has jotted down: Conferences with parents. Report cards. Written reports.

Teacher helps the group to break the discussion into parts.

Teacher judges that it is time for the group to move to the second point. Actually the discussion moves back and forth between the second and third points, perhaps because report cards had already been discussed in the opening part of the meeting.

Record   *Analysis*

BOY. On the report cards we have now teachers can check work habits, and so on.

GIRL. Some teachers don't check them. I like to know in those classes.

TEACHER. In other words, you are interested in something besides marks. We have a lot of things on this report card.

GIRL. I think parents would be lost without some kind of report.

BOY. Written reports are a lot of work. A teacher has two hundred students a day.

TEACHER. They can be spread over the whole semester. What do some of the rest of you think about written reports?

SKIP. They're a lot of work for teachers in a school like this. I don't think parents would be interested in a letter. A report card doesn't beat around the bush.

BOY. I disagree with Skip on that. My brother is in primary grade; my mother can tell exactly what he is doing in citizenship and so on.

GIRL. Not everyone's average is C. Some have more ability. Marks are so inadequate, they don't mean anything.

Teacher has already had several similar leads to consider the problem of individual differences. For some reason, she chose to ignore each one.

GIRL. I always thought that until now, but when you get out of school you don't compete with yourself but with others. Marks help you find the type of job you should do.

Results of vote: Conference, 0; Report cards, 18; Written reports, 7.

TEACHER. Since report cards won, let us talk about making them better.

GIRL. I like the check list and teachers' comments.

Record

Analysis

TEACHER (to secretary). All right, write down: "1. Check list, 2. Teachers' comments."

GIRL. 'I don't know what to believe about the check list. In Latin they have separate divisions for pronunciation, translation, drill, and so on. You know whether you waste time or not.

JOYCE. I think the check list is all right now.

TEACHER (to board secretary). Write "scholarship report."

Pete asks for separate mark in citizenship.

TEACHER. Doesn't that come in the check list?

PETE. I don't know.

GIRL. Sometimes the teachers mark you down when you talk.

TEACHER. Doesn't citizenship enter into every subject?

GIRL. Well if . . .

TEACHER. Are we interested in subject matter or citizenship or both?

GIRL. Well, both.

GIRL. If both, we should have two marks.

BOY. We should have marks for effort, marks for what we do and citizenship.

TEACHER. Then there should be marks for effort, achievement, conduct. (Asks the board secretary to put that down.) Would you get the same grade in effort and achievement?

GIRL. I'm not sure.

TEACHER. How do you think that is taken care of now in our present marking system?

GIRL. It is not done now to my satisfaction.

GIRL. There should be separate marks.

It is notable throughout this discussion that neither the teacher nor the students even once considered the possibility that students might have any right or responsibility in this evaluation.

Record

HARRY. The high school report cards use 1, 2, 3, 4.

TEACHER. That is a little aside from what we are discussing. We'll get to types of marking systems soon.

GIRL. Those who are at the top of the ladder and don't work hard should get B.

GIRL. Then when we go to college what are you going to do? B is taken down to C and it might keep you out. College is mass production. How will they know your ability?

TEACHER. The time is getting short. I would like to discuss with you the system of grading.

Analysis

Again a lead into study of individual differences is ignored.

The students then pooled what they knew about the marking systems in use in different schools they had attended. The group on a vote showed a decided preference for a combination of A, B, C grades and S and U. The record concludes:

Record

TEACHER. Your comments have been helpful. Jean, can you give us a summary?

JEAN. Report cards are necessary. Most of the students like a combination of marking, check list, and comments.

TEACHER. Anything else?

JEAN. How often should they be issued?

TEACHER. There was no conclusion but you liked a combination of A, B, C, and S and U.

GIRL. If it is an elective, A, B, C is all right, but if it is required and you can't compete, look what happens to the report card.

Analysis

A good opportunity to give a student secretary.

A group member takes the opportunity to give her own interpretation. Because of lack of time this was not checked with the group.

As was noted in the analysis of this record, the teacher chose to exercise her leadership in the direction of staying within the present framework. No new approaches to the problem, such as self-evaluation or cooperative evaluation, were suggested. Nor were the student-offered opportunities to look at the weaknesses of grading systems in terms of differences of individuals followed up. Although this was a smoothly managed discussion, it illustrates the difficulty of trying to dispose of an enormous problem with a superficial discussion in a brief time, using only the prejudices, hunches, and half-truths available to the group. Time for reflection, for interviewing others, for making simple studies of learning and human development could have been provided in ways feasible for ninth grade students.

Occasional Stocktaking

When pupils are learning new ways of working together things may go well or badly. In any case, it is a good idea to stop once in a while to see how the experiment looks to the group. This will enable both teacher and students to do their part in improving the situation.

Mr. Williams had been working with a ninth grade group from September to early November in a core or general education class. The students had come to the high school from various elementary schools in the town. A core class in which there was no straight text-book teaching was a great novelty to them and to the school as well.

On the day when this program was observed, the students had been asked to evaluate their progress in small groups and to be prepared to report ideas for more successful use of "democratic discipline," a topic to which they had given some study. The gist of the reports follows.

GROUP ONE. We should help all the students be in the group. All should do their share.

GROUP TWO. The teacher should be more strict. We do wrong if we are not punished. We should be learning English and history. The reason for the way we act is that others are not behaving and we are "doing it too."

GROUP THREE. We disagree. It is up to the class too. We should have a court. The prosecutor should be someone who dislikes the person.

GROUP FOUR. We can help by following directions, by cooperating, by doing more work, by paying attention. When a person is interfering we can help him understand.

Under the leadership of a student chairman, Paul, an open discussion on the reports was held.

JOHN. We should work with the teacher, not against him.

CHAIRMAN. You find that in any class.

BOY. Some are thinking of the teacher as a policeman. The responsibility is on themselves.

BARBARA. Do they take the responsibility?

BOY. Do you?

BARBARA. I don't see that you're an angel.

CHAIRMAN. No one is good enough to criticize someone else.

BETTY. Do you see the class taking very good responsibility?

FIRST REPORTER. Some are responsible.

JOHN. We have to have policing to a certain extent so we can hear.

CHAIRMAN. We have to know when it is needed.

TEACHER. I need help on that.

LUCILE. Last year we had a democratic class. If all had a chance to lead they would realize what it is to lead.

CHAIRMAN. The teacher doesn't have the respect of the class as a teacher. Outside it's different.

WAYLAND. All these years we've had teachers we've been afraid of. Now we have a different kind and we take advantage.

CHAIRMAN. Any more discussion on that point?

DAN. For eight years we've done as we've been told. This was a quick change. We can't get used to it at first.

ELISE. We're supposed to take responsibility.

JOHN. I agree with Dan. It was a quick change and we're not trying.

JANET. After eight years of being told, you have to govern yourselves.

JOHN. Since September we've made quite a bit of progress. We need to respect the teacher more.

BETTY. A few people are talking among themselves.

CHAIRMAN. Just a few are discussing; the rest are not listening.

JOAN. It isn't just the talking. It's other things they do.

JOHN. The people talking among themselves aren't complaining about the teacher not giving them work.

WAYLAND. I don't think responsibility should all be shifted at once.

GIRL. If you have assignments you can stay after school if you don't get done.

BETTY. It's the time after we finish work; we get to talking.

CHAIRMAN. That's when it's each one's responsibility to keep quiet.

LUCILE. The teacher should discipline us when we get too noisy. He stands and waits and we get quiet. He should show a little more temper.

BARBARA. Some people play with money and other things.

BETTY. The teacher has lost his temper and it didn't do any good.

BILLY. Some people got the impression in grade school that they were bad.

BARBARA. We might try different seating—mix the girls and boys.

GIRL. We've got to learn something before next year.

BARBARA. Most of us signed up for "Ancient Rome." This has been mostly review.

Throughout this discussion there was wide participation. Half of the group contributed vocally, and most of the rest followed the discussion closely, fixing their eyes on each speaker in turn. The fact that the class was seated in a circle helped the flow of discussion from one member to the other without much intervention by the chairman.

A teacher in Mr. Williams' shoes would have much to think about. First, he would do well to value the strength on which he had to build: (1) the students' sense of progress, yet their recognition that young people of their ages should be able to look after themselves better than they were doing; (2) their desire for an orderly situation in which work could be accomplished; (3) their desire to be learning new things; (4) the capable way in which the group members and leader handled their roles; and (5) the basic respect they showed for the teacher in analyzing the situation so frankly. Second, he would do well to look for points where he might exercise the firmer leadership the students were asking for, without giving up his purpose of building a self-directing group. Third, he would do well to have the group help him select two or three points from the evaluation around which they could plan some definite improvements in procedure. Unless this evaluation period were followed up in some such fashion, it could easily result in more frustration on the part of the group, more feeling that they talked a lot and got nowhere.

Another occasion for stocktaking that is available to most groups is the planning of a program for parents. This may occur at graduation time, for example, or during open school week. If the group surveys its activities and accomplishments and decides what aspects of the school program and what successes to report, an excellent opportunity for evaluation is presented. As in the case of many of the examples already given, this type of evaluation through planning future activities in terms of past experience usually results in an accent on the positive and ensures truly constructive criticism.

CONCLUSION

It may be observed throughout this chapter that the emphasis is on evaluation of *group* processes and achievements, on how *we* are doing. This procedure seems to have value in building group morale and in improving group operation. It does not seem to involve the risks to individual personality encountered when individuals must submit their products for formal group "criticism."

The few examples of evaluation of group procedures found in connection with this study show what might be done along this line. Actually, relatively little use is made by teachers and pupils of this opportunity in connection with cooperative planning. Because so little has been done with elementary and secondary school pupils in helping them to analyze and evaluate the processes they use, we know all too little of how to conduct this evaluation so that children will move ahead with respect to their present purposes. We know even less about helping pupils to learn enough about the process itself so that they will carry over generalized insights and conscious skills into new planning situations. There is room for much classroom experimentation here.

While working along this line, teachers must ever be alert that evaluation does not come to be a period in the day or week where a meaningless ritual is carried on. Each experience with evaluation should help the group to be more capable on another occasion.

PART TWO

Trouble Points Met by Teachers

Using Cooperative Procedures

As the records used in Part One and other available records were studied and as discussions were held with teachers, there seemed to emerge some common points of difficulty in helping pupils to learn cooperative procedures. These trouble points are:

1. Getting started with cooperative procedures in schools
2. Planning by teacher in preparation for use of cooperative procedures
3. Developing group membership skills
4. Developing pupil leadership
5. Making effective use of small groups
6. Meeting needs of individuals within the group
7. Record-keeping and cooperative procedures
8. Gathering evidence of pupil growth in and through cooperative procedures

In the next eight chapters (Part Two) these problems are examined in detail in order to find the mistakes that may have caused trouble and to report helpful practices discovered by those taking part in the study.

CHAPTER X

Getting Started with Cooperative

Procedures in Schools

MOST TEACHERS who have taught for any length of time
have developed considerable skill in classroom management. Influenced by their preservice education, by their beliefs about
group control, and by their experience with what, according to their
lights, works and does not work with a group of children or adoles-
cents, teachers have an array of accustomed ways of operating—
ways that give them security in discharging their responsibility in
the school.

Unfortunately, ways of working that give security to teachers do
not always result in the best educational experience for children.
Thus we find many who are not at ease with pupils unless the group
is strictly controlled by the teacher. These teachers may not mean to
be autocratic. Often they *feel* democratic and are *kind* masters of the
situation. They treat their charges well and they desire the best education for them. But they know no other way than to dominate group
situations, and they have not yet seen how this domination robs the
pupils of opportunities to learn some very important lessons in group
self-management.

This chapter is concerned with teachers who realized that they had
been depriving their pupils of chances to learn group leadership and
membership skills. They wanted to correct the situation. They
wanted to build security in new ways of working, because they had
come to believe that these new ways were better. They had become
convinced that *cooperative procedures* should be used in many of their
dealings with their pupils.

Because many other teachers have the same problem of acting on
the conviction that pupil-teacher cooperation is important and valuable, an account of how a few teachers began, the difficulties they

257

faced, and what they learned should be helpful. Every teacher whose work is described in this chapter had something in common with the others—two necessary qualities for getting started with cooperative procedures in school. These prerequisites were (1) a desire to try working cooperatively with pupils and (2) courage to start operating in new ways.

TEACHERS LEARN BY TRYING

Not all were fortunate in their choice of a beginning point; not all chose an opportunity suitable for group planning when leader and members were "green." Mrs. Liebermann was one who was less fortunate in her choice, yet she learned much about co-operative procedures in the only way a teacher can actually learn, by trying them.

Mrs. Liebermann decided to experiment with pupil-teacher planning in her seventh grade English–social studies class. In this undertaking she had the support of a group of teachers with whom she had been studying the process of group work. She also had the encouragement of her principal and of a consultant from the Horace Mann–Lincoln Institute of School Experimentation. In fact, she volunteered to make this trial for the teacher group, with another teacher keeping a running record of the planning session.

The problem before the students on March 24, the occasion of the first record, was that of organizing a study of "The Home." As could be seen from the complete record, this was considered critical territory for group planning. Fear that the young people would fail to make a "good" plan apparently loomed large in the teacher's mind, and she could not be at ease in letting the pupils assume some of the responsibility for this planning. Nevertheless, she bravely added the extra hazard of putting a pupil in as chairman. The record as kept by a fellow-teacher shows what happened in this difficult situation.

Teacher Rejection of Pupil Suggestions

In the forty-five minutes allotted to planning the outline for study of homes, Mrs. Liebermann rejected pupil suggestions ten times. On most occasions, the teacher was pre-empting the chairman's role in making these remarks.

> PUPIL. Let's talk about problems connected with the home.
> TEACHER. Start with a general outline first. A discussion of problems can come last.

PUPIL. Start with the first types of home and then work our way up.

TEACHER. What are the first things we should discuss before we take up types of homes?

SECRETARY. How would you express it (general idea of responsibility) on the board?

TEACHER. Wait. What comes before responsibility?

CHAIRMAN. What is the second suggestion?

PUPIL. Problems.

TEACHER. Let's leave a discussion of "problems" to the last.

PUPIL. Let's start with cave men and why they built homes.

TEACHER. Remember the outline. How shall we word it for the outline?

PUPIL. The reason for homes.

PUPIL. Let's discuss "What do you think of home?"

TEACHER. We're off the point.

PUPIL. We can discuss architecture, the architecture of long ago and of today.

TEACHER. What is our aim? Is it to discuss architecture?

PUPIL. Our aim is to study homes, then and now.

TEACHER. Yes, but what is our real aim?

PUPIL. How to improve the home.

TEACHER. That's right, improvement, not architecture.

TEACHER. What are the three words we think of when we use the word "comparison"?

PUPIL. Past, present, future.

TEACHER. Those weren't the words we used when we took up "schools."

PUPIL. The eighteenth, nineteenth, and twentieth centuries.

TEACHER (to rest of group). She left something out.

PUPIL. Colonial times.

TEACHER. What shall we do first?

PUPIL. Olden times.

TEACHER. Remember our study of the school. What comes first?

PUPIL. The necessity for homes.

TEACHER. What comes first under "homes"?

PUPIL. Responsibility. Each person's responsibility in the home.

TEACHER. No. First, the history of the home. Then, the reasons for the home.

Teacher "Fishing" for Desired Response

There were four examples of the teacher "fishing" for the word she had in mind. These examples of the teacher drawing out particular words are not intended to belittle efforts at building a vocabulary of exact terms for expressing ideas. However, this can be done in a way that will help pupils make judgments for themselves among several alternatives rather than become more and more dependent upon the teacher's flat pronouncement of the rightness and wrongness of a word. Often, the problem is not one of correct wording but of values. What is the *idea* we really want to express?

TEACHER. What is a better word than "duties"?
PUPIL. Responsibilities.

TEACHER. What is a better word, a long word?
PUPIL. Interdependence.

TEACHER. When we talk of responsibility we must depend on each other. What's another word?
PUPIL. Cooperate.
TEACHER. Yes. Another word?
PUPIL. Rely on each other.
TEACHER. Yes, and do what?
PUPIL. Reliance.
TEACHER. I'll tell you. "Share." (Writes word on chalkboard.)

TEACHER. What's another word for "progress"? It begins with *g*.
PUPIL. Growth of the home?
TEACHER. Yes, that's a better word.

Teacher Use of Evaluative Comments

By her frequent use of evaluative comments Mrs. Liebermann gave the pupils further encouragement to accept teacher judgment on suggestions instead of making their own judgments. For the teacher to express her opinion was not undesirable in itself. However, since the teacher had been the dominant figure in the group, she was not helping the pupils to make decisions for themselves on the basis of what the situation required; they were making decisions on the basis of her own approval. Some examples from the record will illustrate this point.

TEACHER. Good.
TEACHER. That's a good word.
TEACHER. I agree. How many of you agree?
TEACHER. We still haven't come to the important ideas.
TEACHER. Well, now we're getting lots of lovely ideas.
TEACHER. A good point.
TEACHER. The order of the outline is bad. Shall we change the order?

Teacher Interference with Chairman's Role

In addition to rejecting summarily a number of suggestions from group members, fishing for the right word, and making evaluative comments, the teacher seriously interfered with the chairman's function at a number of points. Examples from the record follow.

TEACHER. Let's go on with the planning. (After an interruption by the teacher to assign a girl to check on the spelling of "responsibility" in the dictionary and the subsequent fishing for the word "share.")

TEACHER. Go on, chairman. (After teacher's interruption of, "Wait. What comes before responsibility?")

TEACHER. Come to the point. We aren't making much progress with our outline.

TEACHER. How many agree with that suggestion?

TEACHER. We are not getting the whole outline down. What else shall we do?

TEACHER. I agree. How many of you agree with that suggestion?

TEACHER. Let's stop this discussion and get on with the outline.

TEACHER. Well, now we're getting lots of lovely ideas. Put them down, secretary. (Secretary writes: "II. History of the Home.") What can we put under that heading for the outline?

TEACHER. Let's get on with the outline. Chairman, lead your group.

TEACHER. Remember the outline. How shall we word it for the outline?

TEACHER. Where does that belong?

TEACHER. How shall we word it for the outline?

TEACHER. Where shall we put it on the outline?

TEACHER. What's the big topic?

TEACHER. Remember, get it on the outline.

TEACHER. The chairman is too slow. I'll take over.

In a few instances in the foregoing examples the teacher was raising helpful questions: "What else shall we do?" "How shall we word it for the outline?" "What's the big topic?" The student leader had been handed a difficult job and the teacher was obligated to lend him support. However, the chairman might have had a better leadership experience had he been allowed to use his own judgment a little more. His problems of leadership could have been evaluated with him afterward.

A bright spot in the discussion occurred when a group member took responsibility for getting the group back on the beam.

PUPIL. We can study chairs and furniture in primitive times and now. (The class discussed "chairs" for two or three minutes.)

PUPIL. We're getting off the subject. We're discussing outlines, not chairs.

A second encouraging bit of initiative was shown at another point.

PUPIL. I have an idea. Instead of "father," "mother," and "children," why not put down just "interdependence"? (Secretary started to erase items 1.1 and 1.2.)

PUPIL. We're erasing too much. Let's leave those things down and make individual changes in our own outlines.

Teacher Concession

On two occasions the students held out for their point and the teacher gave in.

TEACHER. Wait, what comes before responsibility?
PUPIL. Responsibility comes first.
TEACHER. Okay. Leave it.

TEACHER. How shall we word it for the outline?
PUPIL. Changes in the home.
PUPIL. Comparisons of homes.
TEACHER. Which word do you prefer, "changes" or "comparisons"?
PUPIL. "Comparisons" takes in "changes."
TEACHER. How did we handle this problem when we took up "schools"?
PUPIL. We called it "comparisons."
TEACHER. No.
PUPIL. Let's take a vote on "comparisons" or "changes." (The vote favored "comparisons.")
TEACHER. Why do you prefer that word?
PUPIL. It includes everything. (A vote showed agreement with this opinion.)
TEACHER. Okay. Let's accept "comparisons" for the moment.

Just who the real leader was in this entire discussion may be implied from the following instances of participation: Group members, 65; teacher, 56; chairman, 10; secretary, 2; Total, 133.

Teacher Improvement

One week later, a second running record was made in Mrs. Liebermann's seventh grade English–social studies class. This time she kept the chair, and while she participated almost as many times as all the pupils added together (teacher, 24; pupils, 30), the character of her contributions was of a rather different nature from the week before. First of all, the group had more opportunity to describe the limits within which they would plan. The teacher opened with the question, "What do we have to do now?" and pupils quickly responded.

PUPIL. We've got to plan for the rest of the week.
PUPIL. We must do Lessons Two and Three in the booklet.
PUPIL. We have a choral this afternoon.

During the forty-five-minute period, fourteen of the teacher's twenty-four contributions offered the group opportunity to make suggestions or choices.

What do we have to do now?
What do you want to do tomorrow?
What will we do the second period?
How shall we put this on our plan?
What else, if time allows?
What do we have to do on Wednesday?
Would you like to take up "Narrative Poems"? (Following a suggestion from a pupil.)
Okay. Which narrative poems?
Okay. Then what will we do on Wednesday?
How shall we word it?
Which period would you like to have your spelling match, first or third?
Is there anything undone?
What will you do during notebook inspection?
What will you do during vacation?

Although the teacher still made flat judgments on matters pupils might have been asked to comment on, there was much less arbitrary rejection of student suggestions than during the first session reported. The following excerpts illustrate this point.

PUPIL. Our assignment is to drill on "their-there."
TEACHER. That won't take us very long.

PUPIL. Can we have a spelling match?
TEACHER. Tomorrow is not our day for spelling.

PUPIL. We can make some up (narrative poems)?
TEACHER. You're not quite ready for that yet.

PUPIL. You said you would mark our notebooks.
TEACHER. We can do that on Thursday.

PUPIL. You promised us a spelling match on Thursday.
TEACHER. We can do both. We have two periods.

There were no instances of fishing for the right word on this occasion. In fact, the teacher showed quite the opposite tendency when two alternate suggestions came for wording of their plans.

> TEACHER. How shall we put this on our plan?
> PUPIL. Irwin's Report.
> PUPIL. Master Report on the Home.
> TEACHER. All right. The exact wording doesn't matter.

At one point the teacher thought it worth while to pursue one point where there might have been a difference of conception.

> TEACHER. Let's discuss our vacation plans on Thursday.
> PUPIL. Fine. We can plan our vacation.
> TEACHER. No. We don't want to order anyone how to spend his Easter.
> PUPIL. Well, we can suggest ways of spending vacation.
> TEACHER. That's better. Why "suggest"?
> PUPIL. Don't *tell* people what to do with their own time.

On the second attempt the teacher had improved her own operations in these ways: (1) use of questions to draw more suggestions from the group; (2) a lack of "fishing"; and (3) a more temperate way of disagreeing with pupils' suggestions, revising them or explaining why they could not be used. It is likely that the teacher was helped considerably by discussions in the study group of teachers with whom she was working at the time, since such study would tend to make her more analytical. Suggestions of the consultant probably helped also.

PUPILS ALSO LEARN BY TRYING

Miss Thomas thought that her special case, twenty children physically handicapped, ranging from second to sixth grade, gave her a reason for providing only limited participation in planning. When, early in the term, the principal requested that she take charge of the school milk distribution and added, "The children might help too," the teacher had her own idea of how the children would "help." "They would help me," she writes, "in a way that would not cut in too much on the activities that I had planned and worked out for conducting a multiple-grade setup. None of the children could be considered as average academically. I decided to form committees and let each committee take charge of the work for a week."

Miss Thomas goes on to relate how the first chairman dispatched his committee members to various rooms to collect the money and orders for milk. The chairman checked to see that all the envelopes were in and then turned them all over to the teacher. "I carried them home," Miss Thomas confesses, "counted, verified, sorted the money, and prepared the order for the following week."

After this program had been going on for a few weeks the teacher read a pamphlet on cooperative planning and decided to try a new approach. She describes her new efforts in these words.

> The following week I asked the children if they would like to take over the whole job of supplying the school milk. Then through discussion and a few leading questions on my part, the need for making plans to carry out our work was brought out. We discovered that it was necessary to plan or "think ahead" about the following: (1) selecting a day to carry on our work; (2) selecting the time or period of the day; (3) considering the people concerned with our job; (4) preparing materials concerned with our job; (5) preparing lists of things to do.

Miss Thomas goes on to describe how the children solved their first problem.

> We knew that the milkman had to be paid in advance on Monday mornings. Now the group was asked to choose a suitable day. One child thought that the children should not be asked to bring in their milk money too early in the week. Another said that the work should be done in the latter part of the week. Others suggested the following days: Wednesday, Thursday, Friday. I wrote these on the blackboard and informed the children that they would have to select the "best" day of the three. Before doing this I asked them whom they would have to consider before making their choice. Again, through discussion, and some leading questions, they decided that the convenience of the following people would have to be considered in their selection of the day: (1) The milkman (whose convenience had already been arranged); (2) the children who wished to order the milk; (3) the teachers who had to get the orders ready; (4) our own group, who was to do this job.
>
> Through discussion we eliminated Wednesday because it was our school assembly day and that would leave the morning session too short. Friday was eliminated because of our weekly scheduled visit to the school library. We all agreed then that Thursday was the best day since it appeared to be most convenient to others as well as ourselves.

In a similar manner the children proceeded to solve the other problems they had listed for themselves. Miss Thomas realized that the children would learn problem-solving procedures only by using them, and she gave them the help they needed in taking these early steps.

MISTAKES CAN BE CORRECTED

Mrs. Thurber had been searching for a simple opportunity to try some cooperative planning with her third grade pupils. She hadn't expected that an "oral lesson" on making purchases in a store and figuring the change from a dollar would give her that chance, but as she tells it:

> All but two or three children were completely at sea as to what to do unless they used a pencil. I had a lot of change that day and I spread it out on Judy's desk and showed her how to count it. The class gathered around the desk and several were eager to count out the change. I wrote down the remarks as nearly as I remembered them.
>
> FREDERICK. Why can't we all bring in a lot of change and we could count out our own money.
>
> SEVERAL CHILDREN. No, we couldn't get that much money.
>
> GIRL. I have a box of toy money.
>
> Two more children had toy money, but it wouldn't be enough for everyone.
>
> FRANK. We could make our own money of cardboard.
>
> They liked this idea.
>
> FREDERICK. We ought to make a grocery store over there and have cartons and cans of food to sell. Make a play store.
>
> This is one of the two times I made a suggestion. I have been trying to get the children to eat better lunches and I thought a study of food values might help. I told them of a class I had in Ohio who made a play cafeteria. They liked this idea. We spent the rest of the morning making plans. These suggestions came up and were accepted by the whole group: Form committees—one to cut out pictures of food from magazines, another to paste them on cardboard, a third to put prices on the pictures, and a fourth to make paper money.
>
> The children volunteered for the different committees and spent their spare time assembling a collection. When the cafeteria opened we had two cashiers and the children came up and selected their food. They decided to buy a good breakfast the first time.

Here Mrs. Thurber's account becomes especially helpful, for she shows the troubles the children ran into and what they did about them.

> Things did not run smoothly and we had a period of evaluation the next day. This discussion was much more noisy than it sounds on paper.
>
> 1. There was not enough food. The food committee said the children who had promised to bring pictures and cardboard had not done so.
> 2. The cashiers were too slow. It was decided that we needed cash boxes to keep the different "coins" separated. Three children volunteered to bring in toy cash registers. Only one did so. (This

is the other time I made a suggestion, to make the coins different colors and make them easier to find. They didn't like this; the money wouldn't look real.)

3. The prices were not right for the food. The committee had put just anything on the food just so it had a price tag. The committee on pricing the food said the committee on labels hadn't made enough. This committee said they couldn't spend all their time making price tags or they wouldn't be able to make any money to spend on food. It was decided to take another day to straighten this out.

4. One boy wanted to have a manager with a book of tickets and a punch like they have at Sears Roebuck. Voted down.

5. Another wanted to have waiters to select the food and bring the change to the customers. This was rejected as being no fun.

We listed the difficulties on the board. Too many children were trying to buy food at once. They decided to stagger the buying by having two groups use the cafeteria at a time, one group acting as cashiers and the other as customers.

Mrs. Thurber reports that this plan was successful, though not as true to life.

The class is satisfied with the plan. More children have a chance to practice making change. The other groups work at their desks on problems involving money.

When an especially good meal is chosen I comment on it. We use a chart supplied by the school nurse as a guide to good diet. As a result the committee on pictures decided we had too many pictures of cakes and they are now looking for more salads!

The teacher concludes her account by saying:

This is what I learned so far: (1) Not to be excited by too much noise in the discussion periods. They soon calm down. A few are beginning to think out a suggestion before they make it. (2) If anyone volunteers for a job, put his name, what he promised, and the time it is to be done on a chart. See that he does what he promised. (3) Not to be upset if plans do not turn out as expected. Frequently they are much better than you hoped.

Mrs. Thurber's detailed and honest account shows that while there may be noise and confusion and mistakes when groups of children begin to plan for themselves, the planning process itself may be used to correct those mistakes and improve operations the next time.

PUPILS WILL RESTORE LAGGING FAITH

Sometimes in early stages of learning to work cooperatively with pupils, teachers become discouraged and are ready to give

up, but children themselves will supply the enthusiasm needed to try
again. Once her sixth grade children had had a taste of cooperative
group work they made Miss Overton go on with it. "Why can't we
study Africa as we studied England?" they wanted to know.

"Studying England as we did was the first pupil-teacher planning
we had seriously attempted," Miss Overton explains in her report.
"At the end of several weeks' study, I had decided the trial was a
failure. I didn't think the children got enough value out of the new
way to warrant continuation. I thought we wasted a lot of time and
things didn't run very smoothly."

About the time the study of England was coming to a close, a number of Miss Overton's children went off for a two-week winter camp
experience. Before they left, the group decided that Africa would be
their next subject of study. Negro History week, the British royal
family's trip to South Africa, and the fact that Great Britain had
colonies in Africa combined to make that continent a natural choice.
Thus, according to Miss Overton, the study of England was not considered terminated.

While part of the group was away, Miss Overton thought she
would help the others to get down to business and really learn something about their new subject. So they went back to basic text reading with class discussion. It was when the campers returned and
found what was going on that the question came: "Why can't we
study Africa as we studied England?"

To Miss Overton the question was a welcome one. She too had begun to wonder what was so good about the old way. Maybe they
had not given the new way enough of a trial. Her report gives a
good picture of ensuing developments.

> Thirty minutes after the children asked to study Africa the new way,
> they had posted twenty-five questions they wanted answered about that
> country. We had formed our study groups, appointed chairmen, and
> planned our periods at the library for group study. Since there were
> tables instead of desks in the library, it was decided to do much of our
> group work there.
>
> When the class was brought together for an exchange of information
> and discussion, we decided to summarize our study with a school as-
> sembly.

Miss Overton reports the gist of the children's evaluations.

1. Real fun!
2. Enjoyed the dramatization.

3. Liked planning their time.
4. More interested in African peoples.
5. Want to learn more about early Negro civilization.
6. Many became interested in Egyptian history.
7. Some need help to plan their day.
8. Must learn not to disturb others.

The teacher gives her own evaluation in these terms:

1. More real learning took place. Besides learning the geography of Africa—location, climate, rainfall, mountains, rivers, minerals, government, place in world trade—the children learned to write invitations, to model clay bowls, to work with raffia, and to make scenery and realistic palm trees, pyramids and grass huts.

2. There was a carry-over of interest. Many continued reading about Africa.

3. Even non-readers were able to contribute—perhaps a picture or a clay model, or turning the crank on the movie-box—but a necessary part.

4. Brought individual creative ability to the surface.

5. Gave opportunity for development of social traits—unsocial ones cropped out in some individuals.

6. Every child participated in the school assembly—the first time for many of them.

7. Individual planning is a natural outgrowth of group planning.

Miss Overton concluded her report with some heartening words: "We enjoyed every day of our study of England and Africa and wondered why we had never tried the new way before. It wasn't easy for me after so many years of formal teaching. However, the satisfaction one feels when viewing the enthusiasm of the children more than compensates for the difficulty."

YOU BEGIN WHERE YOU ARE

Several junior high school teachers joined a group on cooperative planning by enrolling in a weekly workshop offered by their school system. In the course of their study of group procedures, each member volunteered to carry out some project in pupil-teacher planning. The reports which they wrote to share experiences with each other show that teachers who desire to try cooperative procedures can find some point at which to begin with their own pupils. Three such reports are reproduced here to illustrate approaches in a variety of school subjects.[1]

[1] The group made use of *A Guide to Study and Experimentation in Cooperative Planning*, published by the Horace Mann–Lincoln Institute. Reports were submitted in response to an invitation in the guide to share findings with others.

In a Seventh Grade Mathematics Class

The first report comes from a mathematics teacher. She begins by telling how the class organized for working together.

In March, I discussed with the group working on cooperative planning one of my seventh grade mathematics classes that I had been unable to reach. I decided that since regular classroom procedure had failed, I would try cooperative planning with them.

We discussed as a class the topics to be covered in mathematics for the year. One of the students listed the topics on the board and the individual members decided what they were interested in studying. The topics were: (1) budgets and family spending, (2) buying and selling, (3) money and banking, (4) geometric figures, (5) measuring time, (6) figuring the cost of things we want to make (boats, wagons, etc.).

We discussed working in groups and settled on a common organization. Each group elected a chairman and recorder. Each group met and made plans for carrying out their work. Reports were made to the class by the recorder of each group about once a week. All students were very interested and the plans as outlined by each group were well thought out.

As frequently happens, plans worked out well for the first two weeks, and then there began to be complaints. The teacher reports how the complaints were handled.

We held a class meeting and listed on the board some of the difficulties. These were: (1) groups were too noisy, (2) not enough concrete work was being done, (3) chairmen were showing favoritism, i.e., taking suggestions from only a few instead of all the group, (4) interest in their topic was lessening. We voted then on whether the class wanted to continue working in groups, to work in the old way as a class, or to form new groups on new topics. The majority favored working in groups. Only *six* of the entire class preferred to work in the old way, doing work the teacher assigned.

We reorganized the groups that wished changes. Some of the students have worked as a group on the same general topic for nearly *five* weeks and are still busy and accomplishing things. The majority, however, have changed their topics. The six who wished the teacher to dominate have slowly drifted into a group and are working on a cooperative basis.

The teacher indicates other difficulties encountered, as her report continues.

Having so many groups working in one room still presents a major difficulty, that of noise. Also, two students have not responded well. One exceptional student has done very little work under this method because he is conditioned to competitive classroom behavior. He has always striven to be the first one through with his work. He admits that he dislikes mathematics. The only pleasure he derived was to be the first one finished. He has been very uninterested in the group work, but has done the minimum required by his group.

A retarded student also has been uninterested. He started out nicely, as he liked to make graphs and he was working with a group on budgets. After making a series of graphs on the cost of living and similar subjects, he lost interest. I have been unable to interest him in working with a group, or even by himself.

The teacher also reports sources of satisfaction.

The other thirty-eight students have been very adaptable and there has been some exceptional work done. Gratifying, too, has been the fact that the parents have become exceedingly interested, as well as the businessmen in the community, especially those dealing with banking, retail selling, car sales, and others.

About once in two weeks I have given a general, routine test. These have included fractions, decimals, per cent. I have found, on the whole, that the class average is higher than when we were having routine drill on these same subjects every day.

The report closes with a note of confidence.

I feel now, as does the class, that, with a new project and more thorough planning, the results will be phenomenal.

In a Seventh Grade Social Studies Class

The second report comes from a teacher of social studies.

My social studies group was ready to study the Revolutionary period in history. The majority of students said the text was too difficult to understand. We decided to plan our work for the month cooperatively.

Students listed on the board all phases of interest in the period. From this list each student selected the topic of most appeal to him. All those having similar interests formed a group. They elected a chairman and recorder, and then set to work to plan their procedure.

They found source materials, made booklets, gave reports, dramatized, constructed buildings, made and dressed dolls to represent the styles of the period, learned songs of that time. After all the work had been assembled, and the entire group had benefited from these activities, a period of evaluation followed. They had also evaluated the work in the groups as they progressed.

This report goes on to indicate that not all students entered in wholeheartedly.

About ninety per cent participated and ten per cent showed resistance. Some were slow to select a topic of interest. Others decided to work with a group of their friends with no intention of contributing. The majority felt that they had acquired more knowledge in this cooperative endeavor than they would have otherwise.

While these mathematics and social studies teachers had a right to be gratified that the majority of students were pleased with the new procedures, they would do well to study those who did not enter in when responsibility was placed with the class.

In an Eighth Grade Home Economics Class

The third report is furnished by a home economics teacher who apparently avoided some of the loss of interest encountered by her two colleagues.

The twenty-two girls in my class meet only two hours each week and the lapse of time between class periods makes it very difficult to keep interest and continuity constant. Earlier in the year the girls had planned their large topics to be covered during the year. Now the question was what was the best procedure for accomplishing the work they had planned.

Since I had joined the group in cooperative planning, I told the girls about that procedure. They were interested and wished to try it. They chose a recorder, and began discussing and attacking the problem before them. They listed several areas that would be included in grooming and personality.

When these were listed, each girl chose her field of study. Thus groups were formed on an interest basis. Each group obtained as much source material as possible. Reading and discussion followed. Later activity groups were formed. Some made scrapbooks on personality and good grooming. Others prepared effective bulletin board displays. Showcases in the halls were used. Girls shampooed one another's hair and tried different hair styles. Reports on personality were given and demonstrations of posture were carried on. Personality tests were run by the students. They also wrote a skit, "The Sad Sacks."

In order to keep up interest and provide a sense of continuity and progress each recorder was asked to give a weekly report of her group in rather detailed form. At the end of the fourth week, the class evaluated their work and procedure. They realized they had made many errors. They listed suggestions for better procedures for their next unit. However, they decided that this cooperative method was really the best way to work. They had fun in sharing interests, materials, and ideas.

It is interesting to note that each of the three teachers in the study group which provided the stimulation for trying out pupil-teacher planning made use of procedures they had learned about and no doubt seen demonstrated. One even shared with her group of students some of her new knowledge of the process of cooperation. All made use of student chairmen and recorders. All started with listing problems, so that students were working on goals they had set for themselves. All, apparently, had carried on some sort of group evaluation of the experience in order to determine student interest in further experiences of the kind and to improve procedures in future attempts. All three reports are realistic in that they reflect problems and difficulties.

A BEGINNING TEACHER DARES TO TRY

Getting started with cooperative procedures presents special problems to the beginning teacher. Mr. Owen at first thought he should postpone using this process, but he soon changed his mind. His diary shows some of his early attempts and his questions.

When I first walked into my sixth grade, I knew I had a big job on my hands—thirty-six children to move ahead in mental maturity and social processes. During the first few weeks I was very subject-matter conscious and quite frankly despaired of ever being able to work for the social objectives I had in mind. I decided I would spend this year mastering my subject matter and that next year I could start on my plan to teach the "extras."

September 29. After my Saturday class in social learnings I realized I must tackle my problem of socializing my classroom at once. Over the week end I planned to give cooperative ways of working a trial. Immediately after taking attendance on Monday I opened a discussion on planning in the classroom. We discussed social studies and other phases of study and then planned a schedule for the day. It was understood that the planning was to be flexible. The whole attitude seemed to change. It seemed that the moment I started giving the class one responsibility I was loosed of my bonds and was able to see many chances of giving the children other responsibilities.

October 2. I've lost the feeling of newness in my job and now enjoy the experimentation with my boys and girls. I'm getting a lot of cooperation from my colleagues and I'm planning on using their abilities to the class's advantage. The specialists are excellent consultants.

October 6. I now spend from fifteen to twenty minutes each day planning the program with the class. I find that this planning is somewhat like thinking aloud.

October 8. I've had a cold. Not feeling well sure raises hobs with the pupil-teacher relationship.

October 9. The boys and girls discussed a democratic form of government. I broached the subject of a class government. They were quite eager so I appointed a committee of four to get information on parliamentary procedure. They are to report to the class on October 14.

October 14. The committee on parliamentary procedure did a good job. Doris led the report. The enthusiasm was very genuine; these children seem eager to work on government of their own class. I think I'll be able to start nominations for class officers soon. I think that it will be easier to lead the way from the rigid pattern of planning to more cooperative planning later on. I feel that there are fundamentals of procedure every child should know in making plans.

October 17. On Wednesday ten persons were nominated for president of the class. On Thursday the class spent their allotted time discussing the qualities of the candidates. "Good sport," "finishes every job he starts," "smart," "good speaker," "hard worker" were some of the observations made. A few of the children felt self-conscious about the discussion but all in all they did a good job. On Friday the election was held by secret ballot. One of the quietest, most serious boys was elected president. I feel it will help him as he has been keeping out of the general run of things.

October 20. I had it easy this morning. The new president of the class took over the planning of the day's schedule. He took attendance, counted the people who were to eat lunch in the cafeteria, announced the "Pledge to the Flag," and then led the class in the planning of different subject-matter periods. This consists of checking the time taken by specialists (constant each week) and arranging our program around it. This planning by the children means that I must be fully prepared for each subject, for I never know at what time I'm going to teach it. I like it a lot though; the kids get so much satisfaction out of it.

October 21. Today the class selected the vice-president. The president took charge of the complete business and carried it off admirably. There seem to be few cases of "sour grapes." Defeats are accepted graciously.

The class, as a whole, seems to be functioning very well. I feel the social learnings are coming nicely. Sometimes I wonder about the subject matter.

October 22. Finished the slate today, electing a secretary and treasurer. Now we have someone to keep minutes of the meetings. The president has been doing a marvelous job. The kids are behind this thing 100 per cent. I've never seen such a cooperative bunch of youngsters. They've been doing their planning for about a month now and still tackle the new day with a freshness that is amazing.

Today we were informed that we were to submit news items to the *Victoria Voice,* a local weekly paper. I asked the class what news items about our class we could contribute. Number one concerned the elections. Number two was about the method of planning our programs. So these kids really appreciate the privilege and it makes me very happy.

October 31. The Halloween party went off very well. The three classroom mothers went out of their way to make the children happy. I had to explain to the parents that I was a bystander in this party. Once or twice I suspected that they would have preferred my planning things but I explained that it would have been of little value to me whereas it meant so much to the kids.

November 10. This week we started the planning of subject matter. For instance, in arithmetic we discussed what material should be covered in the next week and sorted out the important and unimportant. The kids really go for the planning and though it's hard to tell exactly what's being accomplished, the surface shows a lot of promise.

November 12. My activities with the kids seem to be paying off. The class on the whole seems to be working at a higher level and the cooperation is good. I'm learning a lot about kids; now if I can put it to use all will be helpful. It's hard to believe they can become such a part of a person's life. Today they had a "secret agreement." It worked especially well. It happened I was a little late getting to my classroom after lunch and the kids got there before I did. I dashed up the stairs fully expecting bedlam. As I neared the room I heard nary a sound and peered in to see if they were there. They were and looked like mice that had escaped the cat. I walked to the front of the class and commented on the quietness. They just sat there grinning from ear to ear. It made me happy. Finally one child said, "We have a secret agreement." I hope the agreement holds for a while.

November 19. I've been trying cooperative planning with the children, yet I'm not fully convinced that I respect their ability to do the planning. Time and again I catch myself assuming authoritarian control—making decisions for the kids. I find myself doing this when I'm not fully prepared for my work.

Another thing I've noticed is that I often set up two sets of standards for my children, one for classroom behavior and another for outside behavior. I give a great deal of freedom in the class and then bear down when they are in public (hallways, assembly, etc.).

Mr. Owen's diary is a mixture of satisfactions and questionings. He was loosed of his bonds "the moment he started giving the class one responsibility," yet much later he wondered if he really respected the children's ability to do the planning. He felt the "social learnings were coming along nicely," yet he sometimes wondered about subject matter. He seemed willing to accept the inconvenience of never knowing when he was to teach a subject, and he apparently saw enough growth in the children to encourage him to extend their opportunities to plan cooperatively into other areas, for example, arithmetic. All in all, this young teacher seems to have made a promising beginning, even though he, in common with experienced teachers, will continue to have much to learn about cooperative procedures.

GROWTH WILL COME

Miss Jamison, an experienced teacher, ventured into co-operative planning with her fourth and fifth grade children with many misgivings. Of the first project she tried in September—planning what areas to cover in social studies—she wrote, "In this project, the pupil-teacher planning was too much superimposed teacher planning." However, the children began to take initiative in making suggestions and in October they were launched on a study of their state. The teacher's account ends on a note of dissatisfaction in spite of what appears to have been a project of great interest to the children.

> One day one child wished to tell us about his trip to Detroit. This started a deluge of requests so we discussed the matter as a class and decided it would be a good way to start a project on Michigan. Someone suggested we take all the towns and cities close to our city first and then the ones farther away. Someone else suggested they point out the route they took on a road map. Someone else wanted to know what they saw on their way there. They finally ended by putting a few definite questions they would like to know about the places visited. The elementary consultant was in the building during the time when the children were giving their reports. She brought to them more books for references. Among these was *Hello Michigan.* Someone read far enough to get the suggestion of making a large map and following the route around Michigan. So a committee was elected by the group to make the map. A few started making small maps of their own. They wrote up their own little story of the places visited. They made their own notebooks. As the cities were investigated some became interested in a particular thing such as the sugarbeet industry, or the oil wells, or the copper and iron mines, and tried to find more information on it.
>
> But with all this the teacher felt very discouraged as to the development of group cooperation, and the ability to do individual research. She blames herself for entertaining too many doubts and for expecting too much.

By March, Miss Jamison, reporting a study of Western United States, was more optimistic.

> The children have responded much better in getting organized for this project. They listed questions they wished to know. They then classified them into groups, such as transportation and industries. They decided that rather than all look up all the questions they would divide them up. Someone suggested that some take one classification and some another. But some classifications had more questions than others, so by means of arithmetic they figured about how many should be on each committee. Then came the question of getting on the committee which they wanted. After some discussion everyone found a satisfactory place.

They are doing a better job of helping one another and seem to progress more rapidly. They are incorporating their hobbies and their science work into the one big project.

No doubt this is also because the teacher is learning. But there is still so very much for her to learn, such as how to carry on a variety of activities at one time without feeling strained and tense, or how to keep from spending too much time on helping the slow members and neglecting the resourceful members.

CONCLUSION

Miss Jamison's problems are shared by many teachers. While growth can be seen in ourselves and in the pupils, at the same time new difficulties open up as we make new ventures in pupil-teacher planning.

As may be seen in this chapter there is no one best place to begin working cooperatively with pupils. Some important considerations for smoothest starting are: (1) cooperative procedures cannot be learned without trying them; (2) one should begin with an activity that is expendable, that is, where mistakes will not be too costly in the teacher's opinion; (3) one should start with an activity simple enough for both teacher and pupils to handle without too much confusion; and (4) one should expect some mistakes, knowing that these too can be considered by the group as points to be improved.

CHAPTER XI

Teacher Preparation for Use of

Cooperative Procedures

BEFORE MEETING his group of pupils on any one day, every teacher makes certain decisions and plans. A fundamental choice is whether to give or not give pupils a chance to experience cooperative procedures. If a teacher chooses cooperation as a basic way of working with his class, he still must decide whether to leave everything to the group or to have some proposals ready to present. Inevitably he makes choices in advance with respect to materials, room arrangement, and time schedule. The teacher who sincerely wants to work cooperatively with pupils must consider carefully how the kind of planning he does by himself or with other adults in preparation for working with his class may affect group operations.

The planning which a teacher does in advance of a group session is sometimes called preplanning. This term would be adequate were it not so often misused. The connotation it now has for many is a kind of planning that stifles the thinking of the group. The teacher may have settled upon one course which seems to him far better than any other. The tendency is for him then to seek to draw this plan from the group, to listen to and support all suggestions that fit in with it, and not to have regard for or even to hear conflicting ideas. He may use sly means of getting the group to think it has chosen for itself. He will tend to close the group off from all but a limited number of avenues of exploration.

PREPLANNING THAT STIFLES

Miss Ashby's plan, made in a summer school class, is an excellent example of the stifling kind of preplanning that is bound to violate the very aim she states, use of "cooperative planning and the democratic process."

The following is an outline of how I plan to have an indoor drinking fountain installed this school term through cooperative planning and the democratic process. In launching a project those who are in charge must take a lead in planning and interesting each person to a degree that he will participate in the study of school problems and in the formation of school policy and program.

Aim: The objective of this project is to interest pupils, parents, and the community in more healthful living through cooperative planning; to broaden the minds of all concerned through an understanding that the fountain and surroundings should be kept in clean and sanitary condition to aid in developing healthy children.

September 7. The first meeting of the Willing Workers Club will be held with P:T.A. members present. Plans will be made to do something tangible for the school during the term. Out of the many suggestions which the club will give, the project of installing an indoor fountain will be the one decided upon.

September 14. At the second meeting of the club, the city nurse will be invited to give a talk on the importance of water in the body and the unsanitary fountain and results. Community needs will be discussed by the group.

The committee on contacting key people of the community will make its report. The ways and means committee will become active in the second meeting. The money will be raised at the end of four weeks and the fountain will be installed as a result of cooperative planning by a democratic community.

Miss Ashby's plan bears a strong resemblance to the old-fashioned lesson plan in which the teacher anticipated the probable answer of a pupil to one of his questions. This reply in turn led neatly to the next question planned, and so would go the entire "recitation." Anybody who has tried to follow such lesson plans knows that the whole scheme breaks down if the expected answer is not forthcoming. Generations of teachers, brought up on this procedure, have found that their only salvation is to "draw" the right answer from the pupil, no matter what hints and leading questions were required. Perhaps this is the explanation for the great amount of "fishing" done by teachers, inexperienced in discussion techniques, as they seek to secure a response they have in mind.[1]

Mrs. Graham exhibited the "fishing" pattern when she was trying to help her third grade children plan the dramatization of a story. An excerpt from an observer's record of the discussion shows this teacher too, trying to draw from pupils the plan she had in mind.

[1] Numerous examples of teacher "fishing" are to be found in this volume. See especially pages 259–260 and page 317.

TEACHER. If we play this story well, what could we do with it?
Children suggest giving it to the other third grade.

TEACHER. What else besides another room? Something you can follow up later that wouldn't be playing it.

CHILD. Practice when you come in.

TEACHER. That isn't yet what I want you to say.
She repeats the question.

CHILD. Improve it.

TEACHER. That isn't the answer yet. What are these boys doing in here now?

CHILD. Oh, draw pictures.

TEACHER. Yes, have an art lesson.

PLANNING THAT HELPS

For satisfying experiences with pupil-teacher planning, some kind of planning in advance is necessary. The teacher's security in working with children in new ways is bolstered if he has thought through some possible courses of action, their probable consequences, and the arrangements and resources that may help the group to make progress toward its goals. At the same time, the group's chances of success are enhanced if the teacher has some ideas ready to put at the service of the members and if he has anticipated some of the problems they will face. This kind of planning is well described in the term "anticipatory planning."

An example of anticipatory planning by a group of teachers is offered in a report by Miss Caswell, a consultant in art. The example is a good one, even though it was only by chance that the planning turned out to be of the anticipatory type rather than an accomplished fact. Miss Caswell writes:

I was called in to meet with the faculty of a four-teacher school. The principal, teachers, and children had previously decided in large-group planning in assemblies to give a Maryland Day Program for the parents, to include the entire school in the program, to make scenery, properties, invitations, programs, and posters for the dramatization, to ask the parents to make the costumes, and to work on the program from one until two-fifteen each day for a time. These decisions had been recorded and all rooms had copies of these decisions.

Questions in the faculty meeting ranged from "Where will we start with the children?" to "What material shall we use for scenery?"

We began by stating that we had 105 children and four teachers and what kind of organization would we need in order to use all of these people effectively? We looked at the jobs to be done and considered those which needed to be started immediately, those which could wait, those on which groups must work together, and those which could be executed individually. The jobs seemed to be: (1) the script itself, (2) the scenery, (3) a combination of posters and properties, and (4) invitations and programs. The teachers accepted leadership of one of the above jobs or combination of jobs.

I then asked on what basis children would make the choice of the job on which they would work. We explored possibilities of a room accepting responsibility for one job. I asked if children might select a job regardless of grade levels. We discussed the advantages and difficulties of, for instance, six-year-olds working with twelve-year-olds on the same job. The teachers felt they would like to try such an arrangement. We talked and made sketches until we felt we could see where and how each child could have responsibility.

If the story had ended here, the planning of the teachers could not have been described as anticipatory. "We got up feeling well satisfied with our efforts," Miss Caswell writes. "As I was putting on my coat I suddenly realized that we had been planning effectively but without the children." The rest of the art consultant's story shows how this advance planning by teachers was used in giving children a good opportunity to plan.

I asked how the teachers felt about it. They too felt that the plan was a good one but children should be a part of it. I offered to take the leadership in assembly the next afternoon when we would give the children an opportunity to discuss and decide where and on what they would work.

On the bulletin board in the auditorium we put the plans previously recorded in assemblies and the children went through the same stages that we had gone through in concluding which jobs must come first, which could wait, which required the greatest amount of time, and which the largest number of people. We rewrote the organization of the jobs.

We next considered places to work. Since the assembly room was also a cafeteria, it had excellent work tables and large floor space, and the classroom off the assembly room had desks and bulletin boards where individual jobs could be carried out. The remaining children, save for one group, were housed in a separate building. The children decided to work in the one building, storing all of their materials there. I then asked if the children were especially interested in working on one particular job. Children from each group raised hands revealing that work groups cutting across grade levels were acceptable to the children.

Because we had been discussing for thirty minutes I asked if the children would go back to their rooms and record their names under one of the jobs. I asked if they would think of ways of clearing these lists just in case one job got overloaded with workers.

Because Miss Caswell was a skilled group leader who had a genuine belief in the value of group thinking, she was able, apparently, to give the children a real share in planning how they would work on their adopted project.

In commenting on the experience, the art consultant gave her view of the value of the teachers' advance planning. "If we had not thought of the possibility of cross-sectional grouping and anticipated the difficulties involved and ways of meeting these difficulties, the teachers would not have had the same security in allowing such a novel plan to result from the meeting with the children."

The trouble point to be analyzed in this chapter is the achievement by the teacher of a kind of planning that is preparatory for genuine group procedures—a kind of planning in advance that helps the teacher to maintain poise in working cooperatively with younger learners *because* he is secure in the knowledge that his preparation *will contribute to group thinking*. This planning, anticipatory rather than fixed, must be flexible and sincere and must above all open up choices to the group. The remainder of this chapter will be devoted to areas in which the teacher may well make preparation in advance. The first area is that of assessment—assessment of the expectations and needs of persons concerned and of the human resources available. The second area is that of mapping—setting goals and thinking of possible experiences. The third area is that of arranging the setting —providing the material and the psychological environment.

ASSESSMENT OF THE HUMAN FACTORS

Starting Before School Opens

There are various ways for a teacher to assess in advance the human factors in his situation. Several entries in Miss Naughton's diary show how she prepared for a year of work with a new group after she had decided to try cooperative procedures. The teacher started sizing up her group the moment she saw their names listed in the village paper one August day. She began to plan for Tommy, the principal's son, whose "father has been worried about him throughout his school career because he has seemed to be interested in nothing but science" and Jimmy "who is emotionally unstable."

Miss Naughton also thought through the library situation in her school. She decided that "a library where the children can go any time is more valuable than one where they can go for only an hour a week," and she spoke to the principal about this. She also thought about the librarian, a liberal, happy person, though deaf and unable to hear confusion. "I feel that she (and the rest of us teachers)," Miss Naughton writes, "help the children too much." Such analysis and subsequent planning are useful in preparing the way for children to have successful experiences in becoming self-directive.

Lack of understanding on the part of other adults concerned with the education of children—principal, fellow-teacher, parent—may serve to hinder the teacher in giving his pupils the proper opportunities to participate in group work. To avoid such occurrences is part of the prearrangements which the teacher should make.

Miss Naughton reports an early step she took in this direction.

> About 3:30 I stopped in at the principal's office and told him how my ideas had changed this summer in respect to these things: (1) Test as little as possible; work for other values as well as academic. (2) Keep the atmosphere of the room friendly and not tense. (3) Value each child in a class where the spread of I.Q.'s probably is from 70 to 140. (4) If the child feels the need of what he is doing, he will probably improve more than he would by the old plan. (5) The teacher is not to write the traditional lesson plans; she is to plan with the children (after much thinking in her own mind).

Although this step did not complete Miss Naughton's activities in the direction of securing the understanding and cooperation of her principal, it did open the way for future conferences along this line.

Assessing Co-workers and Oneself

The impatience of many fellow-teachers with the growing pains of a teacher and a group learning to work in new ways has added unnecessarily to the tensions of experimenting teachers and has cut pupils off from desirable opportunities to develop responsible behavior. Mrs. Tambling's diary contains a disheartening account of interference by fellow-teachers.[2]

> December 14. As a practice, my principal observes all teachers, after which we make an appointment to discuss his observations with him. In our conference yesterday he brought out the following points: (1) The rapport between teacher and students was good. (2) The work was well motivated. (3) Many students were wasting time. (4) Some were working "below grade level." (5) There was more noise but it was not out of control. Some talked more than worked. (6) Too many children were after the teacher with individual questions.

[2] This teacher's attempts to share the management of the art room with her pupils were described earlier, pages 34–36 and 48–50.

All of this was expected in view of the stage of the development of the children. But then came the shock! (1) At least one teacher in every grade is dissatisfied with my work (or the children's)! (2) There was no quarrel with my philosophy, but there was with my method. (3) Unless I can show definite results by the end of January which will win over the teachers who do not like my work, I will not be hired for next year!

What to do!

Of all the classes I have, only one, a sixth grade, has a teacher who really works *with* me and I find it a joy to work with her. It is impossible to be there when they plan their work, so when she comes into the art room, she's right with the group and I am the technician who helps with the current problem.

Obviously the other teachers are not in accord with my philosophy, much less my methods. The teachers who disagree with me want more tangible results, more show, and more formalized teaching.

Here is my program: (1) Speak to my college adviser. (2) Speak with one well-qualified teacher. (3) Plan lessons for the teachers, not for the children (at least during January). (4) Put on a "show" in everything I do! (5) Read and read. (6) Visit a demonstration school. (7) Visit some other school in my own locality. (8) Agitate for more "on call" time.

Mrs. Tambling's first reaction quite naturally was a defensive one. She would get some authoritative backing for her ideas in the form of books, people, and practice in other schools, and she would put on a good "show." Later the art teacher began to think of ways of saving basic gains for children but also of examining her practices to see if there might be faults to be corrected.

December 30. Distance lends perspective, as does reading. I've decided to stick to my own convictions. If I am to be intimidated by a group of teachers who themselves could take quite a bit of education in modern methods of teaching art, I will not be a happy teacher, a good teacher, or a sincere one. There is always the argument of compromise for a long-range point of view. There is always the argument of building slowly. These I grant, but, for me at least, the argument stands that if you cannot be true to your own beliefs you can be true to none. I am convinced that the work done this year has been good even if the results have not been showy. I believe that the children felt the worth of the program.

Remedies for the faults will have to come from other adjustments: (1) Put the lower four grades on call. (2) Use these free periods for better preparation. (3) Give the children a general direction to follow and give wide latitude for interpretation. (4) Mimeograph general principles and enrichment material. (5) Hold grade conferences. (6) Put some recent books on art education in the hands of the parties concerned. (7) Analyze my own organization of material and plan for better methodology.

Steps taken by the teacher in changing her teaching procedures are described in a later chapter.[3]

Mrs. Tambling's story shows that it is futile to assess the expectations, limitations, and resources of one's colleagues without taking stock also of one's self and one's own operations. Teachers need to talk to themselves somewhat as follows:

> I'm trying not to comment after each child speaks. It's a difficult thing, after talking too much in my classroom for sixteen years. (Naughton)
> When my fifth grade children planned a party I tried to be an interested member of the group and not boss the show, but it did take a lot of restraint for I just know I could have done it in two minutes flat. Yes, I know they did learn more and I do believe they had more fun. (Merlin)

The teacher must also take into account the readiness of the pupils for sharing in group management. Just as the teacher must watch carefully that he does not keep too much of the control of group action in his hands, so must he be wary of giving sudden freedom in larger amounts and for longer periods of time than group members are prepared to take. In general, Mrs. Tambling took some rather large risks with freedom in her art room. This she realized herself after a conference with her principal when she told him of her "no rules" period.[4] "Suppose the children had wanted no rules after the test period, what then?" was his only comment. The art teacher records her reaction.

> I was stumped and saw how much I had assumed in the experiment. I had been sure they would want rules for their own protection and comfort. But if they hadn't, would I have stepped in? I said no to the principal but I think I would have in some way—just because of cold feet.

Assessing the Pupils' Needs

Most teachers prefer to plan so as to avoid as far as possible getting "cold feet." Many teachers find it valuable also to learn as much as possible about the children with whom they wish to establish cooperative relationships—their experience background,

[3] See pages 464–466.
[4] See pages 48–50.

the needs they have or will have, the possible interests of the group. For example, Miss Lapham believes in "home visits made early in the fall before a problem arises to give the teacher a fairly good picture of the background of the child and help her understand why the child acts as he does." We have seen how Mrs. Malden saw her children's need for experience in a social situation and how Mrs. Banning looked at the community in which her children lived for ideas for useful planning.[5] We have also observed how certain teachers anticipated needs of their children: Miss Miller looked ahead to the time when her kindergarten children would be going to their first assembly; Miss Van Alsten anticipated her children's need for practice in social forms as they planned a tea for their mothers; Miss Hogue realized that her children must be prepared to move out of their room for a day.[6]

Miss Rezny's diary offers an additional example of teacher anticipation of help needed by her pupils. In commenting on an invitation from the other sixth grade to an "afternoon" (hour) of music, the teacher writes:

> My children seem slower to *want* to do things for others outside our unit. Perhaps it is part of their growth, or is it a lack in me?

The consultant's comment on this entry reads:

> Could you have an evaluation period some time just on this problem? Nice things others have done for us; what we have done for others; do we need to do any more of this?

It will be recalled that Miss Rezny's children eventually put on a very creditable art exhibit for the whole school and the parents.[7]

Sometimes a class group seems to need special help with their relationships with others. Miss Loper had noticed that her children did a great deal of complaining about one another and about children in other rooms. She decided to encourage them to report pleasant happenings. She planned with her third graders that every day there would be an opportunity for any member of the group to report compliments for other groups and for the individual children and teachers in other groups. These were entered with the date on a large chart entitled COMPLIMENTS. Of course, the children were not displeased when their teacher was able to report an occasional compliment she had heard about them.

---

[5] See pages 153–154, 182.
[6] See pages 63, 69–70, 180.
[7] See pages 165–166.

Mrs. Banning learned from her fourth grade children a good way to bring a newcomer into a group. Her diary for October 1 contains this entry.

> Laura came from Mississippi to our room soon after school started. She was large for her age and grade, for she had never been to school more than six months out of any year. For a time, the children did not seem too friendly to her. When I noticed a group of children around Laura one day, I managed to work my way around so I could hear the conversation. She was telling them about her experiences with snakes. What experiences she had had! One child asked her to tell about them on the morning program. This started Laura on the path toward being the popular girl in our room that she now is.
>
> This taught me a lesson about the "we feeling." Now when new students come to my class I file a card about them from our friendly chat together and I always have something to serve as a link from them to the rest of the chain (my class).

As Miss Fielding was preparing to give the high school mathematics students an opportunity to help plan their own curriculum, she tried to learn more about the individuals in the group.[8] "It was especially interesting," she writes, "because their abilities, interests, attitudes, personalities, and home conditions differed greatly. I never had a class that was more of a challenge to me. This made it all the more necessary to fit the type of work to many different individuals because the maximum amount of work that each could accomplish varied so much." Miss Fielding continues by relating that she asked each student "to write a paragraph at the beginning of the semester regarding his or her reason for enrolling in the course, what each hoped to gain, and any questions or remarks." [9]

Regardless of the approach used by a teacher in assessing the human factors in a situation, he will be helped in his work with pupils if he takes into account the hopes and prejudices, the expectations and fears, the needs and abilities of the pupils themselves, of the adults who must understand and help with the process of teaching cooperative ways of working to the young, and of himself as a person and a teacher. Preparation for pupil-teacher planning that consists of such assessment can scarcely damage pupils' chances to make choices and will probably contribute greatly to their opportunities to experience genuine cooperative procedures.

[8] See pages 86 ff.

[9] Much more detailed help on ways of studying children and planning to assist them with their problems is to be found in Ruth Cunningham and Associates, *Understanding Group Behavior of Boys and Girls* (New York: Bureau of Publications, Teachers College, Columbia University, 1951).

MAPPING OUT POSSIBILITIES

A second type of justifiable preparatory activity for the teacher is that of mapping out possible goals for individuals and groups, thinking through experiences that promise to lead in the direction of meeting such goals, and working out possible use of time for reaching goals set by the group.

Most teachers accept rather readily the basic democratic values of respect for individual personality and confidence in individual and group intelligence in solving problems of achieving a better life for all. Some teachers are more reflective than others, however, in seeing the implications of these basic values for the kind of persons they would like to help home, school, and community develop. The reflective teacher notes how far along his pupils are in their understanding of ways of working with people and in their skills in this regard and adopts specific goals toward which to work in a given day, week, or school year—goals which will contribute to the development of democratically socialized personalities. This would be taking the next step beyond the assessment procedures illustrated in the previous section.

Thinking Through Possible Experiences

In thinking through experiences that have possible value for an individual or a group, a teacher may plan to introduce opportunities that will further these experiences. For example, we have learned that Miss Ronald noted possibilities for an educative experience in a barren hillside on the school grounds; that Miss Hogue resolved to find ways in which her kindergarten children could help plan the expenditure of a windfall they received; and that Miss Tremont gave her children the opportunity to share with her the responsibility for Junior Red Cross work in their building.[10]

In deciding whether or not to introduce an experience and what experience to choose, the teacher will wish to employ certain safeguards in his advance planning. He must ask himself, first, does the group need this service from me or are there many possibilities for experience coming from the life of the group or any of its members that are worth capitalizing upon? Am I introducing so much that experiences indigenous to the group are not getting a chance to be considered? Second, do the experiences which I am tempted to intro-

[10] See page 193.

duce fit in with the facts gathered during the assessment process? Third, does the group have an appropriate background of experiences to carry to the new opportunity? A fourth safeguard is the teacher's ability to maintain a tentative and disinterested (though not uninterested) attitude toward any proposal he makes to a group of pupils.

Miss Fielding appears to have this open attitude toward plans which she sketched out for the second semester of her high school mathematics classes.

In the course in general mathematics last semester, work of a more general nature was covered by a majority of the class. This semester I hope to make it more personal. I am attempting a similar approach again with my three new classes and continuing with the two groups which I retain. However, I hope to improve the type of evaluation the next time and also to encourage more students to become interested and willing to participate more for their own welfare.

Early this semester, I would like to have my students in the general mathematics class organize a sort of community, with each one choosing a vocation. Homeowners may be included. This will simply be an enlargement and outgrowth of the work of last semester. I propose that those who care to do so investigate the whole field by collecting materials and eventually making up original problems typical of that work. Each vocation would gradually be presented by a student or a small group, and it would be the means of determining the content of the balance of the semester's work.

It will require a great deal of additional thought before the idea is presented for final consideration. This idea has been mentioned before, but I am hopeful that in our planning in the near future the suggestion will be repeated so that we can soon come to definite decisions.[11]

An entry in Miss Brainard's diary shows how she sketched out various possibilities for a study on which her sixth grade children were launched.

We are centering our work around a study of Benjamin Franklin, an inventor, author, statesman. The topic chosen does not appear to touch the children very intimately, but I can perceive some worthwhile developments. Possibly it may lead to a further understanding of some of our city departments, such as police, fire, sanitation, library service; to a study of the postal service as it operates today (I've been surprised in other years that some children have such meager knowledge of this service); to a trip to Philadelphia to visit Independence Hall and Franklin Institute (planning and preparing for such a trip affords very functional learnings); to a further interest in printing and a study of the modern newspaper.

[11] For the way in which these plans worked out, see pages 86 ff.

Preparing a Unit of Work as a Resource

A rather complete report by Miss Evans, a teacher of the fourth and fifth grades, shows the kind of preparatory planning she did to carry out new convictions acquired in a summer workshop. The account also relates the kind of cooperative work with children which this preplanning made possible. Preliminary decisions made by Miss Evans were:

1. To center upon an "interest unit" rather than a subject matter unit.
2. To choose an interest that she had reason to believe would have general appeal and would meet a definite need of the children in her community—one that would help the children "know more about things going on in their own community and at the same time help them develop new interests in other areas."
3. To give each person in the room a chance "to help plan the things which he wanted to learn about."
4. To place about the room before the first day certain "interest finders."

The teacher describes her advance preparation in these words:

I had made a unit of work in outline, listing all possible areas of interest, approaches, and objectives. From the subject index in the public library an extensive list had been compiled of kinds of books on all levels in which the children could follow many interests that prevail right in their own community, as well as books from which children could choose a number of interest areas. There was an abundance of difficult material for the accelerated child, and plenty of easy material for the retarded child, in addition to material generally considered fourth and fifth grade level.

Miss Evans's report shows how she provided herself with opportunities as she went along to gather more information about her children on which to base further plans.

INTEREST UNIT

Things We Do After School
(NINE WEEKS' DURATION)

Our Unit Had Many Interest Areas

It was the first day of school. The children at our school were typical of the children that go into classrooms all over America.

As Charlene and Joan entered the room, greeted their teacher, and started talking over their vacation experiences, they noticed many things about the room which interested them. After they had been assured that it was all right to get up and look around, they started to explore their new school home.

Charlene was attracted to the art center, which had many kinds of activities suggested by samples of things that could be made during choice periods. Her eyes caught the captions accompanying the samples: "Have you ever made a puppet?" "Would you like to work with clay?" "You could make these dolls." "What can you make from wood?" She saw many things that she could make, but found the puppets most interesting.

Joan liked to read, so she went to the reading center first. She was interested in the label on this table: "Have you read these books?" Here she found a whole table of books. The bright covers were very tempting. She looked first into a fairy-tale book, and then into a book of animal stories. She then turned to stories of things children actually do, such as children's games, gardening books, and stories of chores that children do. She kept on looking at books from the table until she heard other children coming into the room, and stopped to call them to join her.

Spencer and Bill joined the girls in their exploration. Spencer was thrilled when he saw the hobby table. He found some science books and showed Joan pictures of some experiments which he could already perform with his chemistry set. Bill was interested in the bulletin boards and picture table showing pictures of dozens of things which children can do. He found pictures of children taking part in a variety of activities. They were playing, helping Mother at home, reading stories, working at various hobbies, going to the store, riding on buses, helping in gardens, and taking part in various forms of recreation.

As the bell rang, and the children went reluctantly to their seats, one could see in their serious faces many interesting things. Some of their problems might well be: Will I like to go to school this year? I can't read very well. I hope that I will find something that I can do well enough so that boys will want to play with me. Will my teacher like me? Are my clothes as good as the other children's? I'd like to learn to climb a rope as well as the other boys.

In order to care for these varied individual interests, needs, and concerns, we began to plan our work together very early in the day. We discussed the things we did during our summer vacation, taking time to get acquainted with our new classmates. We planned the things which we would need to remember in order to get to the lavatory without casualties. We played outdoors together, we sang some familiar songs, and took time out to consider the things we would want to do to our room to make it more homelike. We planned a museum and hobby exhibit which would add to the interest areas already placed in the room, and decided to make curtains for our lunch-box shelves.

This kind of first day with a new group was made possible by the anticipatory planning of the teacher. And this was true of later developments. Miss Evans gave her group opportunity to think of the things they would like to study about. The children listed all the things that they did after school and came up with twenty-five items.

For a few days the teacher provided an exploration period during which time the group did much browsing before deciding what they would like to study. Miss Evans then helped them decide when they were ready to work in small groups and gave them an opportunity to plan their time schedule and ways of working. She also provided opportunities for individual projects and gave special demonstrations for the children who wanted to learn certain skills, such as clay or puppets. Miss Evans's story illustrates how preparatory planning by a teacher as a project moves along gives children worth-while opportunities to help manage their own destinies.[12]

Individual teacher preparation takes other forms also—planning ways in which a group may quickly and easily organize for work, as Miss Daly was able to do;[13] thinking over a classroom incident and planning how to follow it up the next day, as in Mrs. Wardell's case;[14] planning to use a special device, such as role-playing, as illustrated by the experiences of Mrs. Banning and Miss Radcliffe;[15] and thinking through all angles of a project to make sure children get full value from an experience and enjoy reasonable success, as illustrated by Miss Franklin's story of making Christmas cards.[16]

Teachers sometimes work with others in planning in advance. Miss Green describes teacher preparation for a trip her first graders were invited to take with the second grade.

> The second grade teacher and I went together to make arrangements for taking our classes. It's so much easier when you go with another person. It also helps to get teachers working together. The chief showed us around the firehouse, and we talked over the possibilities that would be of interest to the children.

Faculty Planning of an All-School Framework

In Mrs. Nestor's school the entire faculty planned an all-school attack on the grounds problem. The sixth grade teacher's notes show the opportunities that were thus opened up for the children.

[12] For further details on the operation of small groups in Miss Evans's room, see pages 405–406.
[13] See pages 21–22.
[14] See page 53.
[15] See pages 74–75.
[16] See page 132.

Faculty Meeting, April 21
Social studies—Grounds
Problem: How can we render a better service to our children through better use of the grounds for the rest of this year?
Yearly use of grounds
    1. Areas for play
    2. Areas for garden
    3. Areas for natural, uncultivated state
    4. Struggle for plants
    5. Outdoor theater
    6. Picnic area
Activities:
    1. Planning conferences
    2. Informal map of grounds
    3. Unit responsibility
What are the school grounds?
    1. Front and side lawn
    2. The glen
    3. Between main building and cafeteria
    4. Trash-burning area
For whom do we make our grounds attractive?
    1. For ourselves
    2. Visitors
    3. Beginning pupils
    4. Community
Conclusion: Make our grounds safe, beautiful, and useful.
Problem: How can we as a school working together make our grounds more attractive, useful, neat and safe?
    1. Planting trees, flowers, shrubbery, and grass
    2. Adding athletic apparatus to playground
    3. Upkeep of the grounds, mowing lawns, pruning
    4. Developing plans for clearing, open-air theater, laying trails, picnic area
    5. Removing trash and unsightly debris and re-allocating space to new uses
    6. Designating areas and objects for scientific study
    7. Adding and improving walkways on the grounds
    8. Making a bird-care center
    9. Making a fishpond
    10. Providing a better drainage
    11. Changing location for loading buses to provide greater safety for children
    12. Improving the soil
Program: Explore grounds to discover different areas, such as play areas, gardening areas, trees and shrubs
    Summarize the needs on the grounds
    Make a map

As a result of this advance planning, all the children in the school were given opportunity to engage in a large-scale enterprise together, to help plan their part in it, and to make a motion picture film in color, recording their project experience and serving as a report to their parents.

The most complex job of preparatory planning by teachers usually occurs in connection with some long-term project or study. Whether such a project is one required or strongly suggested for all pupils of a given grade in a school or school system; whether it is one which a teacher or group of teachers freely selects as appropriate for the pupils at a given time; or whether it is one deliberately selected by teacher and pupils in cooperation—there is much preparation and thinking through of possible experiences by the teacher. In each case the test of adequacy of the advance planning is threefold: (1) Can and does the group take over the project wholeheartedly and with intelligent awareness of its pertinence to their lives? (2) Is the teacher secure in moving ahead on the project with his pupils? (3) Is there room for much genuine choice-making and many opportunities for planning on the part of the group and its individual members?

Timing Discussion Periods and Setting Agenda

Teachers in this study do not seem to have considered the possibility of sharing agenda-making with the pupils. A notable exception is the beginning of a discussion which Miss Hallum led with a combined group of upper grade children.[17] When the principal asked, "What is your next most important thing to do? What should we decide on today?" the group agreed to discuss the margins, the kind of paper, and the media for illustrating the large book they were making. The children were able to make this decision because the day's discussion was part of a series of planning sessions on one continuing project.

In general, however, cooperative agenda-setting by teachers and pupils seems to be an unexplored area, for teachers take it for granted that their responsibility for preparatory planning includes decision on the use made of each discussion period. It is rather common also for teachers to think through the discussion in advance, dividing it into logical parts and introducing a new phase as they sense that the group is ready to move on. This procedure was illustrated by Mrs.

[17] See pages 123 ff.

Hannum when the children were planning to decorate their chair backs.[18]

Teachers who become interested in planning cooperatively with their pupils sometimes fall into the error of trying to keep the group in a planning situation for too great a part of the school day and for periods of too long duration. Observation has been made of a third grade where, long after the children were restive and eager to start carrying out the plans they had made for the day, the teacher insisted that they choose the songs they would like to sing during a music period scheduled for later in the day. At that point there was no genuine choice-making, for the children were unwilling participants.

Miss Sudbury conducted some skillful planning with her second grade group one day, but in one session of about forty minutes the children were led to (1) compose a note to the director of the museum they wished to visit asking for permission; (2) compose a note to their parents asking permission to go and stating their plans; (3) plan what they wanted to see at the museum and how they would divide into smaller groups so that they might see more; (4) plan how they would go to the museum and review their safety rules. Before all these matters were thoroughly discussed, children were yawning and looking tired.

In timing discussion periods, the teacher needs to think of both length and frequency. There should be enough group planning (1) to make sure that the business of the group is done cooperatively so that all may feel committed to the plans and have full understanding of what is to be done, and (2) to give necessary practice in the skills of planning. With these two principles as guide lines, the teacher of a group with many enterprises and much imagination (and that can be any group) must begin to look for legitimate short cuts in planning and for ways to space planning periods desirably. For example, Miss Sudbury could have spread the discussion over four good planning periods. Since the visit to the museum was not imminent, the sessions could have been spaced at least a day apart. Had there been any hurry, she could have arranged for four short planning periods during the same day. The third grade teacher who directed her children to choose songs could have scheduled that part of the planning nearer the time for visiting the special music teacher.

Teachers must keep in mind the need to balance planning and

[18] See pages 40–41.

action so that plans are tested before wasteful overplanning occurs and yet so that action is based on thoughtful preliminary consideration. In one school, fire drills were a great problem because of crowded conditions and location of exits. The fire committee met and planned some revisions of procedure. The upper grades tried out the new plans and discussed the results. The fire committee met again to revise the procedure. On the second test the group was satisfied with the new arrangements. This is an excellent illustration of the use of a school as a place where people can learn to plan and test and plan again.

Some defensible short cuts to group planning have been demonstrated by teachers referred to earlier in this report. Miss Miller had her kindergarten children go to their chosen activity as soon as they had cleared their plan with her.[19] Soon she was left with only a few children who needed more time and help in making up their minds. Instead of keeping the whole group sitting while all committee appointments were made, Mrs. Nugent, in the second grade, chose committee chairmen and asked them to choose the other two members.[20] These ways of cutting down the length of time children spend in large-group planning may seem too trivial to mention. Yet it is amazing how frequently teachers get carried away with all the fine details of planning and overlook rather obvious ways to hurry the process.

As soon as this statement is made, it is necessary to issue a caution. Haste that precludes learning is not advocated. Time spent in making a careful plan and giving opportunity for all to come along at a comfortable pace is time well spent; but the world is a busy place, and democracy is time-consuming at best. It seems important to produce people who can plan efficiently in a minimum of time.

The use of small groups, an ideal way of reducing the length of planning sessions for the large group, is discussed in Chapter XIV. Knowing when to make use of the small group is a teacher responsibility that falls within the general problem of timing. To check his own judgment, the teacher should usually consult the group: "Do you want to settle it now or shall we give it to a committee?"

In early stages of experience with cooperative procedures, the teacher may be justified in taking a large share of responsibility for some of the decisions as to timing and agenda. Part of a teacher's planning in advance, however, should be to provide pupils with a

[19] See pages 20–21.
[20] See page 153.

growing share in setting the agenda and in working out discussion strategy.

ARRANGING THE SETTING FOR COOPERATIVE PLANNING

The teacher who wishes to encourage cooperative planning will do everything possible to provide an environment conducive to harmonious working together on challenging problems and projects. This environment has both material and psychological aspects.

Providing a Comfortable and Challenging Material Environment

Miss Naughton's concern with the physical environment began well before the opening of school.

August 22. Every summer I go back to my room to check the condition of the cupboards, put textbooks in the desks, and trim bulletin boards. My theories have been so upset this summer that I'm rather afraid to begin this year. Although I didn't want to put the books in the desk, I did. The spelling book, in particular, I detest. The words don't have much relation to the children's lives. Remembering my college teacher's advice about arranging only some of the bulletin boards, I left some for the children to work on.

What the condition of the classroom should be on the first day of school is a matter requiring thoughtful choice on the teacher's part. Some believe a classroom should be beautifully arranged and decorated, complete and ready for pupils to go to work on the first day. Another school of thought would have the classroom rather barren or disorganized as a challenge to the pupils to improve conditions. Probably it is wise for the teacher to strike a happy medium, to have a room that is orderly, attractive, supplied with suggestive materials, but not completely and permanently organized and decorated. There must be some things to work with on the first day of school and some things planned for children to do besides group discussion of what they will do later. On the first day and on later days also, the kinds of materials introduced into the classroom, their accessibility, the plans made for their use, will all influence the opportunities for cooperative procedures enjoyed by the pupils.

Another factor in creating a harmonious working situation is that of seating arrangements for discussion purposes. Changes in seating arrangements can be planned by the teacher, especially in cases where the children may have experienced only the traditional, autocratic arrangement of most schoolrooms. Miss Naughton describes a change of seating in her sixth grade classroom.

> Today I asked the children to form two concentric circles. Now when we have a class discussion we shall be looking at the faces of our classmates instead of their backs. I suppose this idea came to me from the arrangement of my college class. The children like it very much.

In Miss Wells's classroom, seats were fixed. However, at any time when a discussion was to be carried on, the children moved to the front of the room, sharing seats. Miss Wells placed her chair at one side. The chalkboard with a board secretary beside it seemed to complete a circle.

The teacher who wishes to create a comfortable, supporting atmosphere uses all possible means of drawing a group together. He realizes the value of moving to a new location for a discussion, of leaving sites where individuals and small groups work, and of moving closer together physically. He watches his own location in the group, if possible sitting among the members rather than above or apart.

Even a few extra chairs can be used to bring some of the group into a circle at the front of the room. In rooms where furniture is movable, teachers wishing to make use of such good fortune can experiment with a circle, with a diamond-shaped group, or with variations of these ideas. Circular discussion is more easily secured if group members can see one another's faces.

Creating an Accepting and Supporting Atmosphere

Circle seating alone is not enough to create an atmosphere in which individuals will feel sufficiently accepted and supported to take a useful place in the group. An important part of teacher preparation for pupil-teacher planning is provision of an atmosphere conducive to cooperation. This type of psychological climate is often called a "permissive" atmosphere. Although this term is never confused with authoritarianism, it is often equated with a laissez-faire situation. Therefore the term "accepting and supporting" atmosphere has been chosen to signify the type of emotional climate—

1. In which one is free to try new things and is not afraid to fail.
2. Where one can afford to be different, where one, in fact, is obligated to bring differences into the open for group consideration.
3. Where one can be confident that others desire his success and will help him to gain it.

4. Where one can be sure that his ideas and plans will be thoughtfully considered by the group and, if found worthy, will have a chance of being put to use.

Such an atmosphere does not connote absence of support of the individual, the usual result of laissez-faire leadership. It suggests a situation where the strength of all is multiplied and focused and where individual and group interests are kept in balance.

Miss Eckert did not understand how difficult it is to build an accepting atmosphere and how easy it is to contribute to cleavages in a group. In her advance planning she centered on the worthy purpose of helping individual children "do better." Examine this fragment from a discussion in which upper elementary pupils explained and evaluated for a visitor the way they were organized to manage their problems of living together at school.

> BILL. Those who are babies have to play a separate game.
> TEACHER. What about the children having a good time when they are playing baby games?
> GEORGE. We pretended to have a good time so we could get back in.
> TEACHER. That is how you know it worked. Everyone got back in and there are few disputes now.

Yes, everyone "got back in" and there are few disputes now. But what if other results are to be counted as important—the possible development of attitudes of superiority and condescension in the group which did not have to play "baby games"; the possibility that this group was having some excellent lessons in how to scapegoat; the possibility that the "baby game" group was learning not the essential lessons of self-control and abiding by the rules of the game but the trick of complying with the ways necessary for approval of whoever is in authority; the possibility that, in addition, the same group had suffered another scar in self-esteem.

Look at another fragment which shows the children's idea of what is meant by "not doing so well."

> CHAIRMAN. What do good students do?
> JOE. They help people on the other side of the room.
> SALLY. Those who don't have their work done move to the other side of the room and stay till they get their work done—all day sometimes. They listen to the people over here discuss so they learn how.

In the typical school it is most difficult to help the non-verbal individual experience enough success to maintain desirable self-confidence, and to help the one with verbal facility value other abilities. If an accepting and supporting atmosphere is a desired goal, it would seem best not to exaggerate the cleavages resulting from uneven distribution of ability to deal with verbal symbols. The example just used is not a common one. However, in less dramatic but as effective ways thoughtless teachers, by word, facial expression, gesture, or use of rewards, often influence negatively the attitudes of their pupils toward fellow-students, just as thoughtful teachers go out of their way to exert a positive influence.

Mrs. Banning describes a plan in use in her fourth grade classroom which promotes a spirit of mutual helpfulness.

> The children in my room share their experiences and knowledge with one another. There is a fifteen-minute period in our daily plan which we call a "help one another time." Children who are excellent in certain subjects help others who haven't done so well. Every child gets a chance to help another some time or other. This period works wonders. The amazing thing is to see two or three offering their help to a child who has had difficulty in some lesson during the day.

Miss Grossman also shows concern for classroom atmosphere.

> "Freedom from tension" has been on my mind for some time. I often feel so pressed for time. I have been looking at my situation critically in this respect. Some days seem to be so relaxed and free but we have so many books to cover that just to be free to use time in any desired way doesn't always happen. I have tried to do a better job of keeping things less hurried and seem to be making progress. Today the children, at least most of them, had time to read, browse, examine our growing plants, look at the bulletin board displays, and work on various individual activities. Alice and Jim found a play and Alice agreed to study it, to tell the class more about it, to see if it is the kind of play they want to give. Peter and Ann read some directions about making a model village and started to plan. Billy got two other boys to work with him on the map. Though some people won't be convinced, such activities are more meaningful than pages in workbooks.

CONCLUSION

Although this chapter has by no means illustrated all the fruitful types of preparatory planning by teachers, there has been an attempt to emphasize the fact that teacher planning in advance should aim to surround children with a physical and psychological environment conducive to free and intelligent choice-making; that it should open up rather than restrict additional choices for learners; and that it should give teachers security without sacrificing opportunities for the pupils to learn to work cooperatively.

A fitting summary for this chapter is a set of conclusions with regard to preplanning developed by the work group on cooperative planning at the Spring, 1947, Conference sponsored by the Horace Mann–Lincoln Institute of School Experimentation at St. Mary's Lake Camp, Battle Creek, Michigan. Five of the group of ten who pooled their wisdom on this matter are among the teachers whose work is described in the pages of this volume. This was their question: *What kinds of preplanning can adults do that will facilitate cooperative planning in the classroom?* And these were their answers.

1. Know the community, its needs and resources.

2. Know and understand the children and their interests, in school and out.

3. Review former experiences of the children.

4. Analyze one's own strengths and limitations.

5. Decide to let children do things for themselves, make choices.

6. Think through possible ways of providing for individual differences.

7. Provide rich opportunities for children to explore and experiment, to reveal themselves and to make decisions through:

    a. Materials, including books, art supplies, materials for construction and for manipulation.

    b. Room organization, physical setting, and the way time is blocked out.

    c. Walks and longer excursions.

    d. Suggested activities among which children may make selection.

8. Realize the importance of flexibility.

CHAPTER XII

Developing Group

Membership Skills

EARLY EFFORTS to study group process were concentrated largely on analyzing and improving the role of leadership, especially leadership in group discussion. Currently, there is increasing concern with the various roles group members may play and with ways of developing the necessary skills for effective participation in groups. It is well understood that participation in a group may be active and constructive even though it does not take the form of vocalization. Creative listening during group discussion is one such form of participation. Carrying out a share of the plans made by a group is another form of valid and useful participation. So is serving as a recorder or as an observer and analyzer of group process. However, in a democracy every functioning member of the society is expected to exercise in some group at some time his right and duty to contribute ideas and to register his opinion with regard to the ideas expressed by others. Such participation also helps the individual to clarify his own ideas and have them tested by others. For these reasons, schools should help every individual acquire skill and self-confidence in vocal participation.

Skills of oral participation that help a group move forward are numerous—raising questions, clarifying or interpreting the contribution of another, adding information, making a constructive suggestion, making a remark that relieves tension in the group, helping to keep the discussion on the track, helping the group to reach a decision. Helping pupils learn these skills of constructive vocal participation in a group is an important responsibility for the teacher.

At present levels of group operation it is customary in a group of any size for only a fraction of the members to be vocal during any one session. The size of this fraction can be increased, however, as other factors change. More skillful leadership can make a difference. Vocal participation may be more widespread if members of the group are well known to one another and if they have opportunity to come together again and again, for membership skills can be improved under such circumstances. Participation patterns usually will vary considerably, depending on the purpose of a meeting and the preparation of members. Different individuals can be helped to participate in the whole group at different times. Breaking a larger group into smaller ones similarly will increase the extent of vocal participation. Small-group participation may be used as a step toward vocalization in a large group. All these possibilities are available for the typical group of pupils and teacher. Thus, leadership and membership skills can be improved all round.

There seem to be three major lines of attack on the question of extending and improving vocal participation in group discussion in schools. The first is to give more thought and care to the way in which the group shares in clarifying the problem under discussion and in mapping out the way the problem will be discussed. The second is to search for more and better ways of facilitating communication in the group. The third is to study ways to help groups reach decisions more efficiently. In these ways all may be aware of the problem of learning skills for effective vocal participation. The remainder of the chapter is devoted to a consideration of each of these lines of endeavor in turn.

ORDERING THE DISCUSSION

The task of ordering a discussion includes (1) making the problem for discussion clear to *all* group members and (2) dividing the discussion into parts so that one thing is attacked at a time. The teacher has a large responsibility here. He must play his part, however, in such a way that group members become less and less dependent on the leader in ordering the discussion.

Clarifying the Problem to Be Discussed

Many errors in judgment are made by teachers at the point of clarifying the problem before the group for discussion. Over and over again in the records taken for this study, it is apparent that the discussion got off to a slow and painful start because only the teacher knew well the problem he had in mind; he had set the agenda for the proceedings. Attempts at making the problem clear to all failed because communication was not tested; the individuals who were likely to get confused and lost were not asked specially to state their conception of the matter to be discussed.

One example of a tangle of this kind may make the point clear. Miss Peterson was planning a trip to the library with her second grade. On a former trip it was only a committee of children who had gone, and one boy was obviously still thinking within that framework. When the teacher asked what they needed to plan, the boy said, "We need to choose who will go." The teacher was puzzled for a time but finally caught on: "Oh, we're taking everyone." This could happen to any teacher, and because Miss Peterson was listening to her children and trying to understand them, she took care of the confusion early. The incident illustrates the importance of making sure that all in the group know what is up for discussion.

The method used by some of the teachers in the study in getting a problem clarified is to make it a guessing game for the pupils. A good illustration of the guessing game technique is found in a running record of proceedings as third and fourth grade children were trying to get together with their teacher, Miss Hawkins.

Record

TEACHER. Do you think it would be well for us to think along the line of school services?

CHILD. Yes.

TEACHER. Shall we say what school service means? Tell what it means, Bruce!

Bruce replies.

TEACHER. What is a community service? Can you tell us of any community service we have done in this room?

CHILD. A survey.

TEACHER. What was it about? Say it again for us.

CHILD. Community service is when we can help people to live together in a community.

TEACHER. What activities are we carrying on so we can perform a community service?

CHILD. We're going to tell them what we are going to do in the school.

Analysis

This opening remark might have left the children somewhat in the dark. The teacher might have started by reminding the children what they had accomplished yesterday. The teacher might then have stated what she had in mind as a next step. Apparently the children were not clear as to what was up, since the teacher had to ask so many leading questions.

Record	*Analysis*
TEACHER. What would a school service be then?	
CHILD. To help the children in the school to make this a better school.	
TEACHER. What did we decide to do yesterday to serve our school? What was our big problem? (No answer.) Can't you think about anything we talked about?	
CHILD. How can we get our parents interested in what we're doing?	
TEACHER. That word "interest" is an important word, isn't it?	Teacher helps group recall previous discussion.
Why did we decide it was good to get our parents interested in our school?	
CHILD. To help us.	
CHILD. So there would be more interest in the school.	
CHILD. To help the school.	
TEACHER. We decided all the parents would be interested in a way in one room, wouldn't they? Why?	
CHILD. Because they have a child there.	
TEACHER. But we want the parents to become interested in . . .	It is apparent that the teacher has answers in mind that she wants to hear from the pupils.
CHILD. The school as a whole.	
TEACHER. How big is this school?	
CHILD. Twelve rooms.	
TEACHER. That's too big a job for us all by ourselves, isn't it? Then what is our next big problem?	Preliminaries over, the teacher encourages statement of a problem for the present discussion.
CHILD. How can we interest other rooms so they will help us?	
TEACHER. We don't know what is going on in the other rooms to really write about it, do we? How are we going to get this information into the homes?	Teacher makes sure the children know the vehicle of communication they will use.
CHILD. P.T.A. letter.	
TEACHER. Now let's think just	

Record   *Analysis*

how can we interest the other rooms.
What did we say about people who
advertise products?

CHILD. They advertise.   Sign of confusion.

TEACHER. Why do we advertise?   Teacher is still priming the pump
It's to catch their interest, isn't it?   and getting back only what she
People use pictures and writing.   primes for.

CHILD. They use the radio.

TEACHER. Who knows one thing
we're going to tell them?

CHILD. Write it on a piece of   Sign of confusion.
paper.

TEACHER. Can you tell us what
we're going to write on that piece
of paper?

CHILD. We want to ask them to
help us to interest the parents.

TEACHER. What are you going to   Teacher is hinting again.
ask for? You can't do this by your-
self.

CHILD. Help us—help us solve
our problem.

CHILD. We have to tell them
what we've been doing so they will
get an idea of it so they can help
us.

TEACHER. If somebody asks you   Often the teacher might better
for help—I can't tell you or I'll let   tell what he has in mind.
you know too much.

CHILD. Pay them for it.

TEACHER. I don't think we'll pay
for this. Our pay will be the interest we get from parents.

CHILD. Tell what kind of help we   Children are trying hard to guess
want?   what the teacher has in mind.

TEACHER. Which one of these
listed should come first? What are
we going to say. . . .

This record illustrates the folly of trying to have children follow
adult rationalization. Perhaps Miss Hawkins saw clearly the relationship between the newsletter to parents and school and community
service, and could keep straight who was helping whom, but it is
certain that the children were quite at sea.

Similar examples of confusion over the subject of discussion are to be found in earlier chapters. In Mrs. Nugent's room, for example, planning for a Christmas party got off to a slow start because the children did not know what the teacher wanted of them.[1] On the other hand, Mrs. Nestor guided her children much more directly to make a statement of their problem of interesting other children in extra reading for Christmas.[2] It would seem better to clarify the discussion problem as expeditiously as possible and then test to be sure that it is understood by all.

Dividing the Discussion into Parts

Miss Hawkins helped her third and fourth grade children to organize the "parts" of the problem, "How we can improve our lunch period?" These were listed on the blackboard as follows: (1) Going to the lavatory, (2) Going to lunchroom, (3) Going through lunch line, (4) Coming back to the room. After this step had been taken, the discussion leadership was turned over to a pupil. Miss Hawkins also had her children "think of the big questions we need to answer as we think ahead in planning our exhibit." [3] The questions came out as *where, when, how, who, what,* and *why,* which may have been a somewhat mechanical response, but at least the children were seeing that such questions had to be dealt with one at a time. Having in mind such a structure for the discussion enables group members to assume some of the responsibility for moving along to the next phase after one question has been dealt with adequately.

In the planning for the library trip mentioned earlier in this chapter, it was apparent that Miss Peterson had in mind certain questions to be settled by the group. These she developed on the board as the discussion progressed: "Where to go," "Find out when," "Who will take us," "How to behave in the library."

Miss Turner attempted to help her kindergarten group know what problem was before them and which parts of the problem were to be attacked. However, she poured out this lengthy introduction to the planning of a trip.

Children, this morning I have a grand surprise for you. We are going on a picnic sometime soon, and I thought this morning we would talk over some plans. First, there were some preparations we had to make for you, Mr. D., your mothers, and I. We had to decide on the place and the way we were to go. We found it was impossible to get bus

---

[1] See pages 151–152.
[2] See pages 175–176.
[3] See page 166.

transportation, so some of your mothers are going to drive, and the place we decided on was Belmont Park. We do want to know about the time, how long we will stay, when we will go, and what we will do in case of rain. Let's see first about how long we will stay.

It is quite probable that Miss Turner's long and complex introductory speech went over the heads of many of the children and that they could not make a connection with the problem until the teacher put the last direct proposition to them. However, the teacher was on the right track, and it is likely that as she became more experienced in planning with young children, she found ways of simplifying the procedure for ordering the discussion.

In general, it may be said that as soon as pupils are ready to take the step, the teacher should make occasion for the group to share the responsibility for ordering the discussion. In helping group members to participate in this way, the teacher has two alternatives: (1) he may structure the discussion in advance either *for* or *with* the group members, or (2) he may ask such a question as "What do we need to plan next?" when he judges that the time has come to enter a new phase of the discussion. The first plan puts group members in a better position to take the initiative in moving the discussion along.

FACILITATING COMMUNICATION

A basic responsibility of the teacher in guiding discussion is to secure vocal participation from all group members over a period of time. The individual group member cannot be helped to communicate with others in a discussion situation unless he expresses his ideas in the group. The teacher may help to improve communication in the group by (1) watching the ways in which oral contributions are received by himself and others; (2) encouraging less vocal individuals to take part in the discussion; and (3) helping the group to study their participation patterns in order that they may learn to deal with over- and under-participation.

Ways of Receiving Contributions

The way in which the teacher receives oral contributions of pupils sets the tone for the whole discussion. The teacher must be careful not to reject what a pupil offers. Other problems that occur in groups are: (1) dealing with individuals who get off the track in discussion; (2) helping all to learn to listen to the other fellow; (3)

dealing with individuals who have made a mistake, who have repeated the suggestion of another, who have made an impractical suggestion; (4) helping the group to respect the suggestions made and to evaluate them carefully; and (5) helping individuals to maintain their own integrity.

Avoiding rejection. An excerpt from a running record taken in Mrs. Bassett's second grade room one January day illustrates many things a teacher should not do if he wishes to help pupils feel comfortable about participating orally.

Record	*Analysis*
TEACHER. People, stop your cow pictures and put them in your desks.	The teacher early reveals herself as an arbitrary leader who is unwilling to give children a choice of behavior.
CHILD. Shall we leave them on the desk and just pay attention?	
TEACHER. What did I tell you?	
TEACHER. We are waiting for one person who didn't follow directions.	This reprimand sets an unfriendly tone.
TEACHER. We know what we want in the play. Can you think of some important thing in the play we need to plan?	
CHILD. Talk louder.	
TEACHER. Yes, but . . .	Child's suggestion is actually rejected.
CHILD. Scenery.	The teacher is "I"-centered.
TEACHER. Yes, but I want us to do something first. It is something that will take us a little while, so we must start talking about it.	
CHILD. Make our own things.	
TEACHER. What things?	
JOHN. The light in the hall is going off and . . .	
TEACHER. That has nothing to do with "Little Red Riding Hood."	More severity.
CHILD. We should not turn our backs to the audience.	
TEACHER. This is something to make. Can't you guess?	The guessing game is on.
CHILD. Flowers.	
TEACHER. Flowers, yes, but what else?	
CHILD. Costumes.	
TEACHER. Yes, costumes.	
TEACHER. Costumes for what?	Another reprimand.

Record   *Analysis*

Please don't speak, Joe, until you're
called on. (Writes on board: Costumes for Our Play.")

    TEACHER. All right, we have got   The teacher has now achieved
to decide what each person should   *her* objective.
wear.

There followed a long planning period in which the costumes of
character after character were discussed in detail.[4] During this time
the teacher personally challenged every suggestion which she thought
questionable instead of having group members evaluate the ideas.
The teacher also ignored a child's comment that "Elliott has a better
idea," and soon excluded Elliott from the group for very little apparent reason, saying, "I am sorry that I cannot accept any of your
suggestions because you are not being polite, and put your head
down !" Of course, she conveyed no sorrow in her voice, nor was she
very polite herself. Soon the teacher had occasion to go over to
another boy.

    TEACHER. Will you please raise your hand?
    WALTER (meekly). Yes.
    TEACHER. Yes, Mrs. Bassett.

To the observer the boy had done little to deserve this special attention before the whole group, and the teacher's manner was not exactly
calculated to make the child enjoy using polite forms of discourse.
Toward the end of the record Walter suggested that he could read
the announcer's part out of a book. The teacher immediately judged:
"That wouldn't be fair. Everyone else would have to learn his part."

    The entire record shows children going through a rather vain and
boring exercise in "planning," conducted in such a way that an individual would be influenced in the direction of becoming a silent group
member.

    Looking back over the words of teachers and pupils in the records
gathered for this study, one is struck by the contrasts. On the one
hand, teachers and principals are saying to group members, "Come
on now, you aren't trying." "Come on now, you can think." "Richard knows and he hasn't helped." "I think you are being selfish;
let someone else speak." "We aren't talking about that now." "Well,
Jack, Norma already wrote a paragraph." "What does that have to
do with the plan?" "I won't call on you for something silly." "That

    [4] An excerpt of this discussion was reproduced on page 82.

isn't very smart." "Think instead of being so silly." A list of ten instances of rejection of pupil contributions by one teacher is given on pages 258 and 259. Such remarks may not be made unkindly, nevertheless they have a dampening effect. They show a lack of courtesy and consideration which one adult usually would hesitate to show to another.

Ofttimes teachers fall into the error of evaluating suggestions as they are made by pupils instead of waiting until several suggestions are out and then helping the pupils to evaluate them as a group.

PUPIL. I'd like to select the rest of the committees.
TEACHER. Are you sure you're ready? I don't think so.

. . .

TEACHER. How many do you want on each committee?
PUPIL. Seven.
TEACHER. That would be too many. You would get in each other's way.

. . .

HARRY. The school exhibits committee should go down and decide on the space needed.
TEACHER. It's your exhibit, your class. You have your own committees.

The evaluative comments made by Mrs. Liebermann in one discussion period were listed on page 260.

Another way to shut off participation is to be unnecessarily severe. An example occurred when Mrs. Charles's group was planning how to handle Thanksgiving donations.[5] It will be recalled that a child proposed that older children bring up their donations first. "Any objections?" the teacher said, and when there were none the discussion proceeded. A few seconds later George said, "I think the younger children should come first."

"George, you didn't object when you had a chance, now you're out of luck," was the teacher's rejoinder. In addition to having a little charity and giving a group member the privilege of reopening a question, the teacher might have looked to her own procedures to see whether she had fostered careful thinking and allowed enough time before the decision in question was reached.

Sometimes contributions of group members are rejected in effect by failure to seize upon them in a positive way. A boy offers to bring some films to school. Instead of showing real interest and intent to

[5] See pages 182 ff.

capitalize upon the offer, the teacher says vaguely, "It all helps out." Sometimes a question is almost a reprimand: "Did you not know enough about previewing books to know?"

In contrast to the foregoing, this volume is full of examples of excellent and positive handling of problems arising out of different types of contributions of group members. For example, when a young child says, "I know who that was that jumped down the steps," his teacher says matter-of-factly, "Let's not call names. Maybe we'll improve next time."

Keeping discussion on the track. When a pupil moves the discussion off the track, the teacher has two choices. He may try to hold off the contribution judged to be premature yet not lose it, or he may allow the discussion to proceed on the new track for a time.

One way to postpone a contribution that is off the track is to say, as Miss Hallum did, "I'm afraid you're not answering our question right now. Will you bring that up later?" Miss Wells handled a temporarily irrelevant suggestion by saying pleasantly, "Let's wait until we settle Claire's question." Since, under stress, leaders sometimes forget to go back to a postponed item, several safeguards should be set up. The individual making the premature contribution should be helped to assume responsibility for reintroducing his idea at a more appropriate time. Other group members also should be helped to assume such a responsibility for another's ideas. The teacher should encourage the use of notes for this purpose. Finally, the group leader should provide a time in the discussion to review steps taken and to ask whether anything has been forgotten.

Making the decision of allowing the discussion to be sidetracked temporarily is illustrated in the following examples.

Mrs. Gates and her third grade children were talking about helping others at Christmas time.[6]

> TEACHER. Now there is someone who has been here only two or three weeks.
> CHILD. The janitors.
> TEACHER. They are here all the time, but how could you help them?

After the child had answered, it will be remembered, the teacher went back to the original question.

Miss Fielding allowed a rather lengthy and apparently profitable detour in the discussion to occur before remarking to the student

---

• See pages 73–74.

leader, "I wonder if you want to save farming until that committee has done more work." [7]

There are no rules to help a teacher make decisions in the matter of keeping the discussion on the track. Several things must be kept in mind, foremost of which may be building self-confidence in group participation. It may be most important at one point for an individual to say anything at all. In that case we should not worry too much about the relevance of the remark. With very young children, the adults must not have unreasonably high expectations of relatedness of contributions. Under other circumstances, individuals or groups may need special help in learning to stay with a given phase of the discussion and to take up one aspect of the problem at a time. Again the teacher must make sure that the track he thinks the group should stay on is clearly important to the children and that the group has committed itself to following that line of discussion for a time.

Learning to listen. Before pupils can be expected to listen to other group members, the teacher himself must demonstrate that ability. Under the stress of leading a discussion, any teacher can quite unintentionally fail to listen to a pupil. Her own preconceived idea of what her first grade children might make for a bazaar prevented one teacher from really listening to the idea a child was trying to put across: "In nursery school I made a snow man out of cotton." "Well, could we make that here? You made that at home," the teacher rejoined. She did not hear the child protest, "Nursery school." [8]

Miss McNulty had a similar difficulty in communicating with Paul when her group was planning to study the solar system. [9] When the children were talking of making booklets for science, the teacher's apparent desire for one large class book caused her to be deaf to Paul's words.

> PAUL. Every one of us should make a small one, not a large one like on Egypt last year.
> TEACHER. All right, you mean just one for the class.
> PAUL. No, a small one for each one.
> TEACHER. All right, each would contribute to this one for the room.

At that point Paul gave up.

Occasionally teachers seem to expect and welcome contributions

[7] See pages 86 ff.
[8] See pages 136 ff.
[9] See page 82.

from some children and not from others. For example, in one group Nicky offered a suggestion which the teacher passed over without comment. A moment later another boy suggested exactly the same thing. This time the idea was picked up, praised, and made available for group consideration.

Miss Peterson worked in quite a different way. Several times she asked children if they had caught someone else's idea. This often drew a less active participant into the discussion and showed the children that the teacher valued listening to good ideas.[10] Miss Peterson would say, "Joan, can you understand Bill's suggestion?" or "Could you hear? Mary had a very good suggestion." Throughout the record from which these excerpts were taken, the teacher was helping children to examine each suggestion thoroughly before turning to another. The purpose at this point was to achieve the understanding necessary for later evaluation and choice.

One safeguard against failure in communication is to check back with the contributor to see if he has been truly understood. The teacher can also seek ways of guiding listening, as Miss Brainard did when different children were suggesting possible Christmas plays.[11] It will be recalled that she had scenes and characters listed, as various plays were presented for consideration.

Dealing with impractical suggestions. By the respectful attention he gives to any and all suggestions of group members, the teacher sets an example for the group to follow. This does not mean that suggestions should not be evaluated, but thought should be given to the purpose the evaluation is to serve and the way it is carried on. Evaluation should not be so threatening to individuals that they prefer to remain silent rather than face ridicule or contempt. Examples of positive ways of handling the problem presented when an individual's contribution is useless or even erroneous may be drawn from earlier pages of this volume.

After Miss Durham's first grade children had been all through a discussion of holding milk bottles by the thumb to prevent breakage, Don said, "I heard a boy drop a milk bottle and bust it." His teacher calmly remarked, "I think we've got it straight on the milk bottles. What do we do?" And Don repeated the plan.[12]

Oftentimes group members repeat suggestions already made. Sometimes a pupil has not been listening carefully, or he may have

[10] See pages 116 ff.
[11] See pages 158 ff.
[12] See pages 215 ff.

forgotten that someone else has already given the same idea, or the idea may really appear different to him. In the case of young children, often the group member may be trying hard to contribute *something* to the group. The following remarks are typical of understanding teachers on such occasions.

Did anyone else bring that up? That was a very nice comment but let's listen so we won't be repeating. (Fifth-sixth grade)

Might that come under something we already have? (Fifth-sixth grade)

Are you giving a suggestion that's been given? It's a good one all right. (First-second grade)

That was what Nancy mentioned. (Kindergarten)

That's Lee's suggestion. I like that but is there any other? (First grade)

That was Paul's idea but if you think you could, you bring it. (Kindergarten)

Isn't this what we already have written up here? (First grade)

In cases where children are old enough, a chalkboard record helps group members to keep track of suggestions already made.

Teachers must exercise judgment also as to the times when they should make an issue of a suggestion. The record showing kindergarten children planning what they might make for the school bazaar indicates that Miss Fallon chose to let pass unchallenged one child's suggestion of "pie." This suggestion came with a group of others, such as "beanbags" and "Christmas tree decorations." Knowing kindergarten children in general and this child in particular enabled the teacher to make her decision in this instance.

Similarly, Mrs. Winston, a first grade teacher in the same school, chose to turn the group back to the main purpose of the discussion—planning for the bazaar—and to ignore for the time being a child's erroneous description of how new candles are made of old ones.[13] No doubt she knew that the child could be helped better later as he worked with the actual materials than he could at this point by a process of correcting his verbalization.

Helping pupils evaluate suggestions. On the other hand, teachers have a responsibility for helping children examine their contributions. This examination may take place as the contribution is given, if it can be done expeditiously and without driving the child into silence.

After Mrs. Austin allowed her kindergarten children to continue

[13] See pages 136 ff.

for some time proposing their own and their friends' names for the new goldfish, she helped them evaluate what they were doing and use better criteria for selecting names.[14] Mrs. Hannum helped one of her fourth grade girls evaluate her suggestion that the group would need water for cleaning brushes when they were about to use an oil-based paint.[15]

In general, it is better to gather all suggestions, asking questions only for understanding, and then as a separate step, to evaluate the suggestions that have come in. This makes group members feel freer to contribute. Even an idea only half thought through, or one that appears trivial at the time, may serve to prompt another, better suggestion from someone else. A free flow of suggestions is essential to high-level group thinking. An individual's mind may be walled off by some constricting frame of reference; the group should be able to open up new approaches to a problem.

If a teacher feels that there is an obvious reason why a pupil's contribution should be rejected during the suggestion-gathering period, the contributor's consent may be sought at least. For example, when Mrs. Bassett's group were trying to decide where to locate their lost-and-found center, one child suggested Mrs. N.'s room. "Yes, but Mrs. N. will be back next week," the teacher said, fulfilling her responsibility for supplying a needed fact. She might have added, "Shall we drop your suggestion then?" [16]

Helping individuals to maintain integrity. Pupils who have had unfortunate experiences with authoritarianism often need special help in learning to maintain their own sense of worth. Helping the pupil to respect and push his own idea until it has had a fair hearing, yet not to cling stubbornly to his point beyond that time, is a real task for the teacher. All too frequently a pupil gives up meekly when he fails to communicate the first time.

In several instances on earlier pages we saw adults helping children learn to hang onto their ideas. Two examples are:

SHIRLEY. Covers take two inches, so . . .
GIRL. What has the cover to do with the right-hand margin?
PRINCIPAL. Shirley, you have a point. Come on up and show us.

．　　　．　　　．

Kurt tells about a boat he might make for sale at the bazaar.
TEACHER. Would anyone want to buy it?

[14] See pages 41 ff.
[15] See page 40.
[16] See pages 190 ff.

KURT. No.

TEACHER. Don't you think so?

The other children say "Yes."

TEACHER. What would you call them, Kurt?

KURT. Sailboats.

A negative example comes from Mrs. Delft's fourth grade room when the children were preparing to go to the cafeteria where they were to paint on the large tables.

TEACHER. What suggestions do you have?

GIRL. Take newspapers so we won't go off the edge.

TEACHER. Yes, that's a good idea for us, to be careful to blend the edges of our colors.

The girl made no reply to this misinterpretation of her remark. Any teacher can make an unintentional error such as this. There are two safeguards to employ if one is interested in developing integrity in the individual. First, the teacher may put his interpretation in the form of a question, such as "Are you telling us to be careful to blend the edges of our colors?" This is likely to invite a response. The second safeguard is to encourage other individuals in the group to watch for such misunderstandings and to point them out in case the individual does not come to the defense of his own idea.

The teacher must also work constantly toward the point where he can make a direct suggestion to the group and have it examined on its merits, just as though it had come from any other member. He will never accomplish this end by the fishing technique so well illustrated in the following examples.[17]

There's something you left out, something we do everyday.

I am thinking of a way. Can you think?

I have another question that I think should come first. Do you know what it is?

Where does our paper come from? (From trees)

Yes, but where do we get our supply? (Art class)

But where does it come from? (Factory)

Do I order from a factory?

Think of a party at home. What do you have to do first? (What are you going to have?)

It is tied up with something else to do with where to have the exhibit. (How or what to have?)

I am thinking of the space in which to have the party or exhibit.

[17] Children's replies to teachers' words are set in parentheses.

Do you need something like napkins and place cards? What would you call that kind of committee? (Children are not sure.)

What committee would get our room all ready, some special things up? Are you going to leave this room *undecorated?* Well, what do you need? (Decoration)

Would you want to think of the parents as guests? (Yes)

Well, maybe, because they don't come very often, but how would you like them to feel? (Guests)

Well, if they came everyday? (Friends, helpers)

Don't you want them to feel *at home?*

In contrast, Mrs. Austin illustrates a good procedure to use when a teacher realizes that his question may be beyond the range of his children's experience.[18] The group had been discussing churning butter.

> TEACHER. There's another way to make butter besides churning it. Does anyone know what it is?
>
> CAROL FAYE. You can get some oleo and color it.
>
> TEACHER. Yes, but there's another way to make it from cream, by shaking the cream in a glass jar. Shall we try both ways?

Group planning with children should not be made into a game in which the pupils are to guess what is in the teacher's mind. If the teacher has an idea he should contribute it to the group as simply and directly as any other group member would, with the special qualification that in general he will bend backward to give the children plenty of opportunities to express their ideas first.

Because of the teacher's status and the fact that he usually is a more mature member of the group with generally wider experiences than the pupils, it is to be expected that his contributions will carry more weight than those of others in the group. To overcome this advantage the teacher should wait until group members have had their chance and then give his suggestion casually without pushing it. The teacher's suggestion should be listed along with those made by others, and it should be evaluated along with a group of suggestions, without being identified with the person who contributed it in the first place.

As an example of how this procedure might work, let us go back to Miss Peterson and her second grade children as they planned what gifts they would make for the lower grade Christmas bazaar.[19] The

18 See page 110.
19 See pages 138 ff.

teacher tried to interest the children in her suggestion of napkin rings. She made the suggestion at a time when she thought the children had no more ideas that they wanted to bring out. The discussion of what a napkin ring is and how it is used was necessary, for this article did not figure much in the lives of the children. If Miss Peterson had had a sample to show, as other group members did in presenting their ideas, her description of a napkin ring could have been facilitated. She might then have said simply that if anyone was interested, she would have material ready and would show him how to make one. She could have skipped the step of asking, "Shall we put down napkin rings?" and waited to see if napkin rings were listed when the children began to recall the suggestions made.

Another way in which the teacher may help the individual to maintain his integrity is to encourage circular discussion. It is only when discussion passes freely from one group member to the other without having to be screened by the leader that individuals can come to respect their own judgment as to when and how to give a contribution, how much clarification they need to engage in, and how long they are entitled to push a point before giving way to others with ideas to express.

It is particularly important that the teacher not feel compelled to make a judgment with regard to every remark of a pupil. Occasionally an individual may need an encouraging comment as he first dares to talk out in a large group. Also, if a good idea is about to be passed unnoticed, the teacher may bring it to the group's attention with a well-placed question. However, it can be flatly stated that most teachers talk too much during group discussion. Further than that, they take privileges in participation on the basis of their status as teachers, which may be necessary but which makes it more difficult for them to establish themselves as group members whose ideas are to be given no special consideration.

A third way of promoting integrity is to use uncolored questioning which gives the group a better chance to make judgments of their own and does not keep individuals in leading strings. Examples of this type of questioning were heard frequently in Miss Lambert's room as she improved her leadership in group discussion: "Would you put it differently?" "Do you want to add anything?" "Was there any other reason?" Such questions challenge thinking and open the way for other ideas; they do not close minds.

The process of making each individual in a group feel comfortable

and confident enough to contribute orally is so delicate that all efforts
should be bent toward building a group atmosphere in which all members feel free to give not only the ideas which they are sure and proud
of but also those ideas about which they are unsure and which they
wish to test out on the group. Every group member must be assured
that his ideas will be listened to with respect, that there will be honest
attempts to understand them, and that they will be evaluated fairly
in the context of other ideas before the group.

Stimulating Contributions from the Less Vocal

Maintenance of an accepting and supporting atmos-
phere as contributions are received is one excellent way of encouraging the more timid and less vocal individuals to express an opinion to
their fellow group members. The teacher who is trying to build an
atmosphere conducive to free participation does these things:

Sets a good example: "I think we see your side too, John," or, "May
I have the next turn?"

Refrains from making group members self-conscious about vocal
participation; avoids such expressions as "You are selfish to talk so
much," or "You haven't helped."

Helps individuals to have a fair hearing: "Shirley, you have a point,"
or "Did you hear what Tom was trying to tell us?"

Is sensitive about feelings; watches situations like play-casting,
choosing officers, and the like.

Helps the individual value his own ideas.

Makes the group member feel comfortable about differing with the
leader.

A basic condition for high-level participation is the development of
group feeling, a sense of unity, and responsibility to a group. Some
teachers who are striving to build a group out of the individuals who
come to them at the beginning of a year unwittingly undo their efforts
by such remarks as:

Now we shall be open (lost-and-found department) from 10:15 to
10:30, 1:30 to 1:45. When can people bring things to me?

I have heard from only about five or six.

I want something different, a different suggestion.

A shift from *I* to *we*, from *me* to *us*, must be accomplished, and the
change must be made both in language and in attitude.

A teacher may help in several ways to unify a group. A method
already referred to is that of encouraging a group to receive newcomers as valued members. Another is to show absentees that they

are welcomed back and that the group feels it important that they be informed about what went on while they were away. Even when pupils are absent from only part of a discussion session, it increases their sense of worth, gives more value to the ground covered while they were gone, and makes it possible for them to enter at once into the business at hand if on their return a review is provided for them.

One way of showing that all individuals in the group are valued is to use "get-acquainted" techniques early in the year which enable children to learn of one another's backgrounds. Such procedure gives many a lead for further group activities.

In addition to providing a climate in which an individual is more likely to feel free to speak, the teacher must take other direct measures to improve participation. One goal should be oral participation by 100 per cent of the class over a period of time. The second goal should be improvement in the quality (usefulness and relatedness) of contributions. Measures that are helpful are (1) planning within the experience of the group; (2) filling in gaps in experience background; (3) introducing concrete aids to the discussion; (4) planning on location; (5) drawing out individuals through discriminating use of questions; (6) helping individuals become ready to contribute; and (7) giving individuals time to think.

Planning within the experience of the group. To encourage widespread and thoughtful participation in group discussion, the teacher may take several active measures. The basic one is making sure that the group members are clear as to the purpose of the discussion and know the purpose is in actuality theirs. Closely related to this measure is the necessity that group members have, or secure, the requisite background of experience for effective participation. On this point the teacher can take nothing for granted. For example, a school party might seem like a good opportunity for a beginning venture in cooperative planning. Yet children who know no party games would be in a poor position to contribute to the planning of that kind of entertainment. Similarly, children who have had no previous housekeeping duties at home or at school would be able to contribute little to plans for care of the classroom. Young people who have grown up on the sidewalks of a large city might have few ideas of what to look for on a nature walk in a park some distance from their neighborhood.

The examples in Part One of this report show that teachers have little difficulty in locating many opportunities for group planning that fall well within the experience of the group members. Frequently it was noted that a teacher helped the group recall a previous experience to aid in the planning of the present one. If the business at hand is truly the group's business, the battle is half won.

Filling in gaps in experience background. It often happens that groups have problems to solve for which all or several of the members do not have a backlog of experience. In such cases, the teacher may help to provide needed experiences or the group may plan how it can prepare itself for a particular planning job.

The way in which Miss Franklin, in her first grade, prepared for a planning period preliminary to making Christmas wrapping paper is a case in point. Before the discussion she put many sheets of store-bought paper around the room. This paper was put away before the children started making their own designs, but it served as a springboard for discussing Christmas symbols that might be used in planning one's own wrapping paper.

Other instances of building a background for planning have been given at various points in the report. For example, Miss MacKelvy gave her third grade children free time to use the materials and resources she had placed around the room. After a trial period the children were better able to plan wise use of a "free" period.[20]

Introducing concrete aids to the discussion. Discussions often can be kept within the experience of the group members, especially younger ones, if concrete materials are brought to their attention. Such materials often suggest ideas to those less able to deal with abstractions. It will be recalled that when Miss Peterson's group of second grade children assembled to discuss what they might make for the school bazaar, they were asked to bring examples of the objects they were about to propose.[21] During the discussion these objects were shown and ways of making them were described. One girl was asked to demonstrate how she sewed together squares of spool knitting. When upper grade children in the Robinson School were planning how three classes could collaborate on making a large book for the school library, they referred frequently to a book made by former pupils.[22]

Other ways of introducing concreteness into a discussion have also been referred to in earlier chapters—keeping a record on the chalkboard as discussion proceeds; asking a child to make a drawing

[20] See pages 23 ff.
[21] See pages 138 ff.
[22] See pages 123 ff.

on the chalkboard to help explain an idea he cannot communicate through words alone; and demonstrating a point through action.

Miss Durham, it has been noted, made use of the demonstration technique in her first grade when she asked a child to show how to hold a milk bottle on a tray.[23] On the same occasion, she compared the heights of a short child and a taller child to help the children visualize the cause of difficulty around the lunchroom trash table.

Miss Beach has reported how students in her mathematics classes were helped to secure ideas for the stained-glass windows they were designing. Her list included a "picture of Notre Dame Cathedral moved in from the corridor, a visit to an elementary school where a seventh grade class was just completing a cathedral window for their stage, a church with beautiful windows, some of which were just being installed, and the art gallery.[24]

Planning on location. Whenever feasible, a good way to improve the contributions of group members who may be lacking in experience is to move the group to the location for which the planning is being done. Often clearer thinking and readier communication occur when pupils are located physically in the place where their plans are to be carried out. For example, a group planning a garden should do some of the planning on the garden site; a group about to plan an auditorium program should meet in that room and explore the stage to make the planning more efficient; a group of young children about to eat lunch in the school cafeteria for the first time can plan better for that experience if they meet beforehand in the cafeteria itself.

In Miss Hawkins' third and fourth grade group, the children themselves proposed planning on location. As they were discussing how to improve the lunchroom, one child said, "All the boys get together and girls and talk-talk. Maybe it would be nice if we go over to the cafeteria and organize so that the talkers won't be seated together."

A useful variation of the technique of planning on location is to send a committee to do preliminary planning for the group. The experiences of one or a few group members who may be familiar with the situation being planned for can also be of help.

When it is not possible to plan on location, anticipatory role-playing may be instituted. For example, appropriate conduct on a bus or in the mayor's office might be planned through the playing-out of various ways of behaving in the anticipated situation.

[23] See pages 215 ff.
[24] See page 180.

Making discriminating use of questions. By a discriminating use of questions, the teacher can help less vocal individuals see points at which they can make a verbal contribution. Asking the right kinds of questions is not a simple matter. The vague question, "Now, what can we do?" usually leaves most of the group at a loss.

In contrast was Mrs. Austin's question put to her kindergarten group: "If you don't have a costume, what could you do?" The suggestions flowed: "Dress up like a girl." "Be a baby." "Wear a sheet and be a ghost." "Make a hat and mask and wear just those." Another pointed question in the same discussion period was, "Usually people have ice cream and cake at birthday parties, but Halloween is a special kind of day. Wouldn't you like to have something special for your Halloween party?" Again the suggestions flowed: "apples," "popcorn," "candy." [25]

Questions can be used to encourage a child to go further with a point and thus improve the quality of his contribution. A kindergarten child in Mrs. Austin's room suggested, "We could make a jack-o'-lantern out of our pumpkin." When his teacher asked, "How shall we make it?" the boy elaborated: "Cut eyes, nose, and mouth and put a candle in it."

In Miss Peterson's second grade, Ann was helping with ideas for the birdbath. "My aunt . . . used colored stones and cement." The teacher's question, "Did she dig a place in the ground?" called forth a rather detailed explanation. [26] The teacher's questioning gave Ann time to state her ideas rather completely and helped the group to make a better judgment of the worth of one member's ideas.

Another type of question that is useful in encouraging a group member to refine his thinking is to ask him to state his idea in the way he wants it to go on the chalkboard record.

To draw a less vocal group member into a discussion, the teacher must know the individual rather well in order to frame a question that will be likely to call forth a response from him. The question should prompt something more than a yes or no answer. The teacher may also issue a general invitation for contributions from those who have not yet had a chance to be heard.

Miss Wells's role in a discussion quoted in part in an earlier chapter affords another illustration of questioning useful in clarifying concepts. [27]

[25] See page 149.
[26] See pages 116 ff.
[27] See pages 96 ff.

He read from just one paper. Are both alike?
How can we tell which is right?
How can we find out right here?
How much do you want him to read?
Does this add to a dollar? How do you know?
How much for campaign and administration? What does campaign mean? What does administration mean?
Anyone else have an idea? What is this they are having right now? What do they spend the most for?
What do you mean? We know we are talking about the Goodwill Industries. What do we want to know?

Questions are important aids in providing for individual differences within a group. The teacher who knows his pupils will know which ones can be helped by a well-placed question to keep in touch with the stream of thinking. The use of questions also keeps the discussion more nearly at a pace which all the members can follow.

Helping individuals become ready to contribute. The teacher may help an individual make special preparation for contributing to a group. As boys' counselor, Mr. Rice was able to help a seventeen-year-old in that fashion. His diary account says:

Roger came in to see me one afternoon and told me he had to make a speech in English class but did not want to. At this point the tears were streaming down his cheeks. Roger is seventeen years old, in the ninth grade, with an I.Q. of 63.

I talked with him about farming (he lives on a farm) and later asked what he could talk about. Of course he said farming. We made up a short speech about a minute in duration and Roger practiced every day in my office. In the meantime I had seen Roger's English teacher. The teacher agreed that Roger might speak on farming but said he would not help him as he was tired of having the low-intelligence pupils shunted to him.

The day after the speech I asked Roger how things were going and he said, "Swell." I contacted the teacher and he said that Roger had surprised him and had done a fair job.

If the teacher had taken the time with Roger, Roger would have obtained confidence in him and might attempt to do other things in the future. As it is now, Roger runs to me and that is less beneficial to the boy.

Mr. Rice's story is an excellent illustration of how even the most retiring student may be helped to speak in a group if he has special preparation.

Giving individuals time to think. Often the teacher can draw additional individuals into group discussion if he gives group members time to think. Miss Hallum, when working with a small committee phrasing topics pooled from suggestions of three groups, said at one point, "Keep fooling around. Think out loud." Miss Peterson had her group look at the "top" of the birdbath for a while: "Just look and think."

On another occasion Miss Hallum asked for someone to summarize a decision the group had reached after considering a number of confusing alternatives. Before calling on any child, she waited until the group had had time to formulate a statement in their own minds.

Studying Participation Patterns

Often groups need help with problems of over-participation by some as well as under-participation by others. Many of the suggestions already given will help to create a situation where a group can deal with individuals who cause problems during discussion periods. This section deals with the use of records by the group in analyzing participation patterns and judging progress.

There are several good ways of recording contributions to discussion so that participation patterns may be analyzed and group members may profit in future discussions.[28] One promising method for use in elementary and secondary schools was given a rather thorough test by Miss Lambert and her group of fifth and sixth grade children.

A chance remark by a supervisor that some members of Miss Lambert's class were participating too often in a group discussion led the teacher and children to become interested in the problem. An observer who was present helped the group plan a type of record they might keep—a listing by a student secretary of the initials of each contributor to a discussion in turn. The teacher was to be included in the listing. It was decided that records would be made of several discussions on different topics or problems at various times during the remainder of the school year. The records would include the names of children who were absent, the subject under discussion, and a few notes on the content of the discussion.

In order to make the data more meaningful to the children, the writer made line graphs of each discussion showing how contributors followed one another. As each child entered the discussion he was to be given a line on the graph, and each time he spoke a new line was to be made connecting his line with that of the previous speaker.

---

[28] See Alice Miel, ed., "A Group Studies Itself to Improve Itself," *Teachers College Record* 49:31-43 (November, 1948).

The following fall, when the teacher had some of the same pupils in her group, the record-keeping was continued, with the teacher making the line graphs. These graphs were posted on the bulletin board, and the members of the group had a chance to study themselves. Sometimes the teacher added a question at the bottom of the graph: "What does this graph tell you? Compare this one with the other graphs."

It became quite a common occurrence for children to be gathered around the most recently posted graph, evaluating themselves and the group discussion as pictured there. Some remarks were: "John really talked a lot yesterday—maybe because he knows so much that will help us with the rock garden." "It looks as if three people did all the talking yesterday." "Miss Lambert, you talked too much yesterday."

Discussion often followed the showing of a graph. "Who is talking too much?" "Too little?" "What can you do about it?" were questions raised by the teacher. On the third day Walter, a boy who almost never participated, said, "Some people are talking just so they can get their initials on the list. I think unless you have something worth while to say it isn't a very good contribution just to say something." The children agreed that this was a good point and tried to live up to Walter's advice. Anna, one of the "talkers," reminded the group at the beginning of the first session when a record was to be kept: "Remember those who talk a great deal are to hold back till others have had a chance." Talkers also took turns being the first secretaries for the group, giving the others more opportunities to contribute to discussion. Those who were tempted rather often to participate frequently called on some other member of the group for his opinion. Some opening points for less vocal members of the group were: "I'd like to hear Jean's opinion on that," or "Joe, your father is a carpenter, what does he think of our new fence?"

Miss Lambert summed up the experience by saying, "It is hard to hold back when you have so much to say, but the children did become quite conscious of doing what would seem to be more than their share of talking." A letter from the "Boys and Girls in Miss Lambert's Room" gives the children's evaluation at the end of one week: ". . . our class enjoyed doing this. We found it helped us so much that we are continuing this record on a chart in our room."

When Miss Lambert had made four graphs in the early fall, she told the group that since graph-making took so much time she did not plan to make any more. She suggested that in studying their participation they use merely the record of initials as the secretary took them down. Immediately the children protested and said they would make the graphs if the teacher would show them how. Two brothers in the group brought sales sheets from their father's dairy. These served nicely for graph paper. The eight graphs made during the remainder of the year were done by children.

The twelve graphs which were produced by Miss Lambert and her group, together with three made by the observer from data gathered from the same teacher's group the spring before, give a great deal of material for analysis. From the complete record in each case the total number of times each individual participated can be ascertained. The relationships of teacher participation to pupil participation and of boys' contributions to girls' can also be determined. When the topics under discussion are taken into consideration, some interesting facts come to light with regard to times when the teacher is less vocal in discussion or when the girls as a group participate more than usual. In addition, comparisons can be made between the more and the less vocal pupils, and participation of various individuals on different occasions can be studied.

Relationship of Teacher Participation to Pupil Participation

Inspection of the graphic records of discussion in Miss Lambert's class revealed some interesting findings. In the early records the line of discussion frequently goes back to the teacher with

TABLE 1

NUMBER OF PUPIL CONTRIBUTIONS BETWEEN CONTRIBUTIONS BY TEACHER

September 11		September 15		September 22		October 2		December 4	
No. of Intervening Pupil Contributions	Frequency	No. of Intervening Pupil Contributions	Frequency	No. of Intervening Pupil Contributions	Frequency	No. of Intervening Pupil Contributions	Frequency	No. of Intervening Pupil Contributions	Frequency
1	36	1	21	1	9	1	8	1	21
2	13	2	8	2	11	2	5	2	23
5	1	3	3	3	5	3	2	3	10
				4	5	4	1	4	4
				5	2	5	1	5	1
				6	1	7	1	6	2
				8	1			7	3
				9	1			8	1
								9	1
								13	1

few contributions from children between each speech of the teacher. Later on the picture is quite different. A tabulation of the complete discussion in each case, as shown in Table 1, makes the situation more clear.

The table is read as follows: on September 11 there were thirty-six times when only one child spoke between contributions of the teacher. Thirteen times two children participated between speeches by the teacher. The only other pattern present was one occasion when five contributions of pupils intervened between two utterances by the teacher. It is apparent that in the discussions of September 22 and December 4 there was more give-and-take among pupils, with as many as thirteen pupil contributions occurring without the intervention of the teacher.

The relationship of teacher to pupil participation may also be seen in another way. Chart A shows teacher and pupil contributions in percentages for the fifteen discussions studied. Discussions 1, 2, and 3 took place during the month of May when Miss Lambert was well

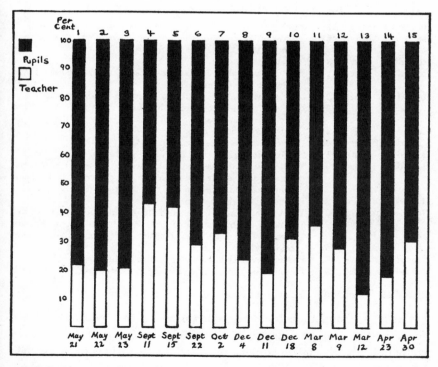

CHART A. PERCENTAGES OF TEACHER AND PUPIL CONTRIBUTIONS IN FIFTEEN DISCUSSIONS

acquainted with her group of fifth and sixth grade children, and they were used to working together. The teacher's percentages were lower on those three occasions (22 per cent, 20 per cent, 21 per cent respectively) than they were again until December of the following year. Only six of these children were in Miss Lambert's new fifth and sixth grade group in September of the following year. In October, five sixth grade boys, all new to the group in September, were transferred to another teacher, and Miss Lambert received instead four fifth grade boys and five fifth grade girls. Since the teacher's percentages vary so much throughout the year it is well to look at additional factors to explain the participation patterns.

Miss Lambert stated that the group the second year was a "slower" group than the one the year before and that she had to take a more active part in the discussion for that reason.

It is interesting also to note the topics under discussion on the different days that records were taken. These are arranged in Table 2.

TABLE 2

TOPICS DISCUSSED ON DAYS PARTICIPATION WAS CHARTED

Record 1, May 21:	Putting the fence up in front of the building.
Record 2, May 22:	Discussion of questions concerning flowers we have on our science table.
Record 3, May 23:	Our evaluation period.
Record 4, Sept. 11:	How can we make our school a more pleasant, attractive place in which to work and play?
Record 5, Sept. 15:	How can we make our bulletin boards more attractive?
Record 6, Sept. 22:	How can we finish our fishpond so it will be more attractive and enjoyable for all?
Record 7, Oct. 2:	Organizing a science club.
Record 8, Dec. 4:	How can we decorate our room for Christmas?
Record 9, Dec. 11:	Evaluation of Helpers Club; change of duties.
Record 10, Dec. 18:	What shall we discuss and demonstrate (in science) to our visitors (a fifth grade group, elementary principal, high school principal, and vice-principal)?
Record 11, March 8:	Discussion of trip to Mount Vernon.
Record 12, March 9:	What properties will we need for our part of the pageant? What will the last scene be? Schoolroom scene? Family scene? Will it be a combination of television, pantomime, tableaux?
Record 13, March 12:	Evaluation of Helpers Club; change of duties.
Record 14, April 23:	Planning booklets on large cities in United States and South America.
Record 15, April 30:	What is the general plan or diagram of any city?

Chart A shows that for discussions 4 to 15 the teacher was less vocal in the two periods when the children were evaluating their Helpers Club. She made 20 per cent of all contributions on December 11 and only 12 per cent on March 12. When the children were planning their booklets on April 23, the teacher's percentage was low also, coming out as 18.

The participation of the teacher was medium (for her) on December 4 when plans were being made to decorate the room for Christmas (24%), on March 9 when the children were planning for their pageant (28%), and on September 22 when the group was discussing how to finish the fishpond (29%).

The teacher's percentages increased when the topics were the plan of a city (31%), planning for visitors (31%), organizing a science club (33%), things seen on a trip to Mount Vernon (36%), making bulletin boards more attractive (42%), and making the school more attractive (43%).

One would need more evidence than the records furnish to make a final judgment as to the real causes of more or less vocalization on the part of the teacher. However, a good hunch to follow might be this: children can plan with less help from an adult when the business at hand is really seen as their business. The more the content of a discussion approaches academic material, the more the teacher must be an active guide.

Making the bulletin boards and the school more attractive might seem on the surface to be matters which children could easily take over with less teacher guidance. This illustrates again the fact that interest in a problem and a necessary background of experience for solving the problem on the part of pupils cannot be taken for granted by the teacher.

All of this does not tell a teacher what is the correct amount of participation for him. It merely suggests what he may expect under different circumstances. It also suggests that a teacher should plan that a generous proportion of the discussions be of the kind to which the pupils can contribute with a minimum of teacher guidance.

Comparison of Participation of Girls and Boys

As in the case of the study of teacher participation in the foregoing section, there is no thought, in the following analysis, of establishing norms or of claiming that a typical group has been selected for description. The purpose of making a comparison of the participation of girls and boys in Miss Lambert's group is to show the kind of information about any group which is afforded by participation records.

In Miss Lambert's class during the first year of the record-keeping the girls as a group happened to be more vocal than the boys. The following year, with some shifts in group membership, the girls were less vocal than the boys. Chart B shows the percentage of total contributions made by girls and boys in fifteen different discussions. The expectancy line drawn across the graph shows where the dividing line between boy and girl contributions would have occurred had each group contributed exactly in proportion to their numbers.

The chart shows considerable fluctuation in boy-girl contributions from discussion to discussion. Again it is interesting to speculate on the possibility that the topic under discussion may make a difference in participation patterns. For example, the girls in the first-year group, who were so vocal when the discussion centered around "flowers we have on our science table" and on "our evaluation period" (81% and 69% respectively rather than an expected 44%), were

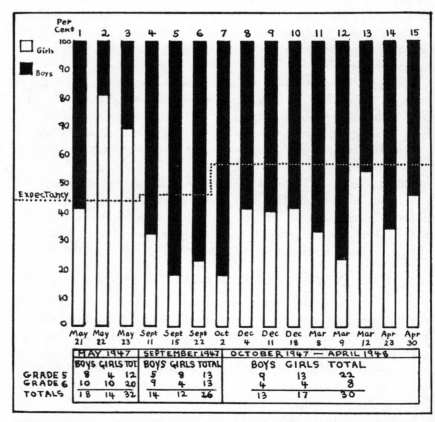

CHART B. PERCENTAGES OF GIRLS' AND BOYS' CONTRIBUTIONS IN FIFTEEN DISCUSSIONS

much more silent when the group was planning how to put up a fence in front of the building (41% rather than the expected 44%).

During the second year, although the girls were less vocal than the boys in general, they contributed relatively more when the problems were (1) "evaluation of Helpers Club" and "change of duties" (54% and 40% respectively on two occasions when 57% might have been expected); (2) "the general plan . . . of any city" (46% rather than 57%); (3) "How can we decorate our room for Christmas?" and "What shall we discuss and demonstrate in science to our visitors?" (both 41% compared with an expected 57%); and (4) "How can we make our school a more pleasant, attractive place in which to work and play?" (32%, with 46% expected).

The girls' contributions were relatively low when the problems were (1) "organizing a science club" and "How can we make our bulletin boards more attractive?" (both 18%, instead of 57% and 46% expected respectively); (2) planning for a pageant (24% rather than 57%); and (3) "How can we finish our fishpond?" (23% instead of 46%).

The girls' contributions were medium (for them) when the problems were (1) discussion of a trip to Mount Vernon (33%, with an expected 57%) and (2) planning booklets (24% instead of 57%).

This picture is so mixed that it is difficult to make generalizations. It may be that these particular girls held back more when the planning centered on construction activities. In both the first and second year groups, the girls were more active during evaluation periods.

Probably the only safe conclusion to draw is that participation will differ with a change of topic or problem and that therefore one way to spread participation for both boys and girls is to make sure that a variety of problems is considered by the group over a period of time. This conclusion is even more valid when it comes to encouraging participation on the part of individuals, as will be seen in the following section.

Studies of Individual Participation

The records of discussions described and analyzed in preceding sections also throw some light on variations in individual participation. Table 3 shows the kind of information that may be obtained from such records. The eight individuals with the lowest average contributions and the eight with the highest are shown in profile. Inspection of the profiles of the two groups reveals some interest-

TABLE 3A

PROFILES OF EIGHT LESS VOCAL MEMBERS AND THEIR PARTICIPATION
IN NINE TO TWELVE DISCUSSIONS

Identification	I.Q.	Average Contributions	Grade	Attendance*	Place in Group**
G8	?	0.5	5	50%	Sept.
G4	62	0.6	5	84%	Sept.
	80				
G14	?	0.7	5	75%	Oct.
G2	75	1.0	5	100%	Sept.
G17	91	1.3	5	77%	Oct.
G11	76	1.3	6	100%	Sept.
B1	?	1.3	5	80%	Sept.
G7	79	1.3	5	100%	Sept.

TABLE 3B

PROFILES OF EIGHT MORE VOCAL MEMBERS AND THEIR PARTICIPATION
IN NINE TO TWELVE DISCUSSIONS

Identification	I.Q.	Average Contributions	Grade	Attendance	Place in Group
B7	86	14.2	6	91%	May
B8	100	7.7	6	100%	May
B15	100	7.7	5	100%	Oct.
B14	?	6.1	6	84%	May
B17	107	5.7	5	100%	Oct.
	92				
G12	101	4.9	6	84%	May
G9	94	4.4	6	91%	May
G10	?	4.0	6	100%	Sept.

* Percentage of attendance for discussions.
** May indicates pupil was in group when first three records were taken, end of first year; September indicates pupil entered group at beginning of new school year; October indicates pupil came into group one month late.

TABLE 4

PEAKS OF PARTICIPATION FOR EIGHT LESS VOCAL INDIVIDUALS

Identification	Peaks First Half of Term	Peaks Last Half of Term
G8	Discussion 9	
G4		Discussion 13
G14		
G2		Discussion 15
G17		Discussion 15
G11	Discussion 8	Discussion 13, 14
B1		Discussion 11, 12, 13
G7	Discussion 4	Discussion 11, 13, 15

ing facts. The less vocal individuals are all girls but one, are all fifth graders but one, have a poorer attendance record than the more vocal individuals, and appear to have lower intelligence quotients. The group of eight more vocal individuals contains five boys, six sixth graders, five who were in the teacher's class the preceding year. It would be dangerous to generalize from these comparisons. In another group the girls might be the more vocal; the younger group in a two-grade combination might participate equally with or more than the older group. A study of this kind suggests two possibilities. First, it indicates the type of information a teacher might well have about his own group as a basis for improving participation. Second, it gives leads for further research. Much more should be known about various factors influencing participation in group discussion—age, intelligence, experience.

TABLE 5

ORDER OF ENTERING TWELVE DISCUSSIONS

EIGHT LESS VOCAL INDIVIDUALS					EIGHT MORE VOCAL INDIVIDUALS				
Identi-fication	First Half	Last Half	Not at All	Absent	Identi-fication	First Half	Last Half	Not at All	Absent
G8	0	2	4	6	B7	8	2	0	2
G4	0	5	5	2	B8	8	3	0	1
G14	0	5	1	6	B15	8	1	0	3
G2	2	6	4	0	B14	7	2	1	2
G17	1	4	2	5	B17	8	1	0	3
G11	0	8	4	0	G12	3	5	2	2
B1	1	5	4	2	G9	6	3	1	1
G7	2	7	3	0	G10	5	6	1*	0
Totals	6	42	27	21	Totals	53	23	5	14

* Serving as secretary.

Examination of the types of discussion in which individuals participate more than usual may throw some light on opportunities that should be provided in schools. Participation records could also be used for this purpose.

Again, individuals may be studied in terms of the point at which they begin to participate. Table 4 shows that for the less vocal pupils, peaks of participation tend to come during the latter half of the school term.

As a group the more vocal show little difference in participation between the first and the last half of the term.

The order of entering discussion also reveals some interesting differences between the less and the more vocal, as shown in Table 5. The table is read as follows: Girl 8 entered no discussion during the time when the first half of the total number of contributions were being given. She entered two discussions during the time when the latter half of the contributions were being made. On only six occasions did the less vocal make a contribution among the first 50 per cent of remarks made; the corresponding total for the more vocal is 53. From these figures it can be seen that the less vocal tend to wait longer before entering the discussion. The teacher who discovers such a fact about his own group might try to change participation patterns by drawing the less vocal into the discussion earlier.

This discussion of participation patterns has been presented not to give statistics upon which to generalize for all groups but to suggest a rather simple way for a teacher to collect facts about his own group for use in improving participation of learners.

FACILITATING DECISION-MAKING

Working for Consensus

Skill as a group member should include ability to help the group reach decisions. When teachers fall down in their leadership at this point in group process they cannot hope to teach important lessons. A common error in guiding discussion toward a useful conclusion is failure to distinguish between gathering suggestions and making choices among suggestions. When he is unskilled in leadership, the teacher tends to take the first suggestion that appeals to him and act as though it has been adopted by the group as the best of two or more alternatives. If a suggestion given does not meet the favor of this teacher, he tends to ask for other ideas but stops the suggestion-gathering process as soon as he obtains from a group member a proposal that seems reasonable to him.

Once the problem has been clarified and divided into manageable parts, the correct procedure is to gather suggestions for solving the problem. Discussion to clarify suggestions is in order as they are given, but suggestions should be retained for group consideration unless withdrawn by the giver with the agreement of the group. An informal exploration of the problem may precede formal gathering of suggestions, but at some point the group should have clearly before it definite proposals among which to choose. Unless the choices are very simple ones, it is helpful to have these proposals listed in full view of the group.

The second big step in reaching a decision is to evaluate all suggestions and to attempt new proposals in the form of combinations of suggestions that may meet the favor of a large number in the group. A description of this process is to be found in the diary of Mr. Yates, a sixth grade teacher.

Having just completed a unit in social studies, we spent today's class period planning the procedure for a new unit. I started the discussion by pointing out the three methods by which we had studied other units: (1) individual project work, (2) group project work, (3) textbook work. I asked the class to consider these three methods and then to decide which they preferred, or suggest another method for studying our coming work.

One student remarked that of the three methods she liked group project work least because it seemed to her that the work was never evenly divided, with some doing very little work, while a few others carried the burden. In reply to that a boy pointed out that he liked the group project method because it enabled him to work with his friends.

Several more comments were made both about the group project method and the individual method. (Nothing had been said about the textbook method, thank fortune!) The class appeared rather evenly divided between group and individual projects, so I intervened to suggest that we list on the board the advantages of each method, and in this way we would be better equipped to make a wise choice. These are the lists the class compiled:

Group Projects

1. Working with a group is more fun.
2. Ideas spring up more readily in a group.
3. There is greater understanding of readings, etc., through varied interpretations of members of the group.
4. Group work teaches cooperation and compromise.
5. Information gathered by individuals can be organized by the group to eliminate repetition in presentation.

Individual Projects

1. Each person does his own work.
2. There are no arguments.
3. The work is done faster.
4. You don't have to carry a loafer.
5. The teacher knows exactly who is doing the work.

It was here that I noticed that most of those who seemed in favor of group projects were students who were well developed socially and had worked well with others in the past, whereas those favoring individual projects were almost entirely the A students who obviously knew they were capable of doing good work on their own and would receive more recognition for it through individual work.

The class continued the discussion for several more minutes without coming to any decision until a girl offered a compromise: use both methods. Divide the class into groups, giving each group a broad general topic for study, then within the group each individual would be held responsible for one specific topic. Most of the class agreed that this was a good solution, offering the advantages of both methods.

This account has illustrated the technique of looking carefully into the merits of more than one proposal before making a decision. It may be noted that as the two favored ideas were discussed pro and con and the advantages of each clearly seen, one group member was enabled to make a suggestion combining the best features of each plan. That made it possible for *consensus* to be reached, that is, there was a general feeling that the group now had available the best plan it could arrive at.

Another example of consensus being reached after discussion of various plans comes from Miss Waite, a fourth grade teacher.

November 18. Today we began to discuss our plans for our Christmas program. Each child is to have some part in the play as well as some part in the writing, planning, and organizing of it. Our class is scheduled to give the Christmas assembly entertainment, so we do want to be good. So far the class has decided almost unanimously to have three acts. We have several suggestions for the plot but each unrelated to the other with the exception that they are all about Christmas. We couldn't come to any agreement today so we shall carry on tomorrow.

November 19. We took up our discussion of the Christmas play again today to see if we could reach some satisfactory solution. After much elimination of the different themes suggested, we finally were left with three of equal favor. One theme centered around the first Christmas at Bethlehem, another centered around a family Christmas with happy carol-singing in it, and the last but not least, a story about Santa Claus. I then suggested that in some way we combine all three into a play so we could make everyone happy. Our theme as agreed upon today is "The Different Meanings Christmas May Have for You."

When consensus is reached after all views have been given a full hearing, a vote is seldom necessary. In judging that consensus has been reached, however, the teacher may mistake the desires of the group. He must encourage the group members to protest when they feel the degree of agreement has been overestimated. The teacher must also watch for signs in later discussion that the group members have not made the assumptions he has. In such a case, it might be well to test the sentiments of the group by a vote.

By the way in which he treats the minority on any question, the teacher can help pupils learn to value a variety of opinions as aids to reaching the wisest possible decision. If the minority, be it one or many, is given a chance to state its case during the discussion and is consulted again for an alternate solution once a straw vote shows its case is being lost, all group members are likely to have more self-confidence in proposing an idea that is unpopular with the teacher or with the group.

Problems in Using the Vote

Some teachers who do not understand the importance of making full use of minority views to improve the final group product are likely to take a great many ill-timed and useless votes. Consider the following excerpts from a record of a discussion in a kindergarten. The teacher, Mrs. Hanson, had first discussed with the children the need for fixing up their playhouse.

> ROSE. When we get this house fixed we should take better care of it.
> TEACHER. I agree with you, Rose. Those who agree that we should take better care of our house raise your hands.

It is common practice for teachers to get children to pledge good behavior in this rather superficial fashion. This holding up of hands because the teacher seems to expect it and the rest of the ᴄrowd is doing it is hardly good preparation for thoughtful voting on occasions where vote-taking is really appropriate.

When the teacher mentioned a playhouse in the first grade room and some of the children began saying they had seen it, she asked, "How many children are there who have seen this playhouse we are talking about?" This was a legitimate call for the raising of hands. This was fact-gathering and could not be construed as voting for something.

Next the teacher said, "The playhouse is in Mrs. R.'s room. Mrs. R. and her class have invited us to come and see their playhouse. Those who would like to go and see the playhouse raise your hands." Knowing children, one can predict the outcome of that "vote." There was no real choice between alternatives. Raising the hand was again a meaningless formality.

After the trip to Mrs. R.'s room the teacher said, "I was very proud of the way everyone behaved. Did you like the house?" Many of the children answered yes. Most of them raised their hands. By that time, it can be seen, raising one's hand was a way of answering the teacher.

The discussion then turned to the color of the house. Joey thought it was red. Several others insisted it was green, although one stated that the roof was red. Here the teacher took another vote: "Those who think the house was green hold up your hands." Everyone did so, including Joey. It might have been better for Joey to have the opportunity to go back and check once more on the color of the house than to dismiss the matter with a vote. (It was interesting to note that when there was an opportunity later to suggest a color for their own playhouse, Joey's choice was "Red! Red!")

Soon the teacher found it necessary to point out that the morning group should have something to say about the color of the house. She said, "Since we are going to paint the inside and the outside of the house, the morning class can choose the color for the outside and the afternoon class can choose the color for the inside; or would you rather choose the inside or the outside of the house to paint?" Although this was a rather complex statement of the alternatives, some of the children knew at once what they favored. Donald and Henry called out, "Inside," while Jean was for "Outside." Here the teacher again called for a vote: "Let's vote and see how many would like to paint the inside. Those who wish to choose the color of and paint the inside of the playhouse hold up your hand."

As might be expected, since both alternatives were not reviewed and holding up one's hand was the expected thing in that classroom, most of the children held up their hands. The teacher continued. "Since most of the children want to fix the inside of the house and paint it, you may also choose the color. We have had three colors suggested to us by Oliver, Donald, and Joey. Let's vote on the color we would like to paint the walls." Some of the children showed they wished to discuss the matter.

> VIVIAN. Purple.
> ROSE. I never saw purple walls.
> DONALD. We don't want purple walls.
> TEACHER. Wait, let's vote. Those in favor of green walls hold up your hands.

Here trouble really began. The teacher had failed to remind the children of all the choices they would have, and it was clear that they understood little about casting a vote for one choice out of several. Almost half the children held up their hands. The record continues.

> TEACHER. Those who want yellow walls hold up your hands. (Over a third of the children held up their hands. Some voted twice.) Some

people are voting twice. Please decide on one color, then hold up your hands. Let's vote again. Those who want yellow hold up your hands. (Over half of those who did not vote the first time held up their hands.) It seems that more people want green walls.

DONALD. Light green.

TEACHER. Class, do you want light-green walls?

Most of the children say yes.

Arriving at a true consensus with kindergarten children when three choices are before them is admittedly a difficult task. However, the procedures used in this case were not of the kind that would help children become capable of working for consensus. The teacher was encouraging indiscriminate voting, for there was little likelihood that the children were following the intricacies of her reasoning as she ruled that green won.

At one point Mrs. Hanson attempted to combine two seemingly opposing suggestions instead of taking a vote between them.

TEACHER. What do you think we should do about the torn paper in the playhouse?

LARRY. We could paint it.

DONALD. We could put new paper on it.

TEACHER. Both suggestions are good. Do you think we could do both of these things?

Many children said yes, though one wonders if they really saw how it would work out.

In Miss Magnon's first grade we find a more thoughtful approach to voting. One day the children were asked to notice in the cafeteria what things they could do to improve the situation. As the children gave their ideas the teacher started writing them on the blackboard. After several ideas had been recorded the teacher asked a leading question, "Did you see anything on the floor?" Different children mentioned food and paper. When Leon said, "Keep the food off the floor," the teacher asked, "Do you like Leon's sentence?" This started a discussion.

CHILD. Don't be sloppy.

TEACHER. Say it another way.

CHILD. Do be clean.

WILLIAM. Clean up. Keep trash on the table.

TEACHER. I'll read; we'll vote. How many like "Clean up?" (13) "Keep trash on the table?" (6) "Keep food off the floor?" (5)

The teacher reads off the result.

TEACHER. Which one wins?

KENNETH. Thirteen.

TEACHER. Why?

KENNETH. Thirteen, what most children want.

While Miss Magnon may have been doing something with first grade children that Mrs. Hanson could not do in a kindergarten group, it might be well to consider that vote-taking is inappropriate where the children cannot help to judge the results for themselves.

One other service the teacher can perform in facilitating decision-making is to help the group clinch and nail down the plans made. This is important for getting plans carried into action, a step that pupils must learn to value. It is particularly important that each discussion session close with some kind of plan for working ahead, even though the discussion cannot end in a definite decision on the problem under consideration. Miss Wells's closing remarks in the discussion of the Community Chest served such a purpose: "Perhaps we can talk about this tomorrow and what is in the paper—how they are getting along." In Mrs. Winston's first grade the discussion of what the children would make for the bazaar was closed by listing the materials needed for making the items they had decided upon. The teacher also prepared the children for a possible change of plans by saying, "Are we sure we are going to make these things?" The children showed that they understood that other groups might choose some of the same things.

Another way of clinching a decision is to convert the offer of a group member into a definite commitment for a given time. Thus, when Ann said she could bring something to mix cement in, Miss Peterson said, "Can you bring it Monday? Then it's settled."

A discussion may also be closed when the group has reached an impasse for the time being. The probability is that a decision may be reached more quickly if the problem is thought about by individuals and discussed in small groups before the large group discussion is resumed. The group should leave with the understanding that this is the procedure to be followed.

CONCLUSION

Pupils will learn only the group membership skills which they have an opportunity to practice under favorable conditions. Many have little group planning experience at all. Many others have learned to dislike group planning because their experience with it has been unfortunate. They may have been in groups so dominated by a leader or a few group members that the majority had little opportunity to participate. They may have been in groups where one is made to feel uncomfortable about what he contributes. They may have seen decisions forced on a group or, just as bad, may have watched excellent ideas dissipated without coagulating into a plan of action. Teachers must watch their own techniques of leadership and participation as group members, and they must help their pupils have experiences with cooperative procedures that they will enjoy repeating. There is so much need for skills of cooperation in the general population that the school cannot afford to give a starvation diet or a poisoned diet in this respect.

CHAPTER XIII

Developing Pupil Leadership

IN THE PRECEDING chapter development of group membership skills through desirable experiences with group participation has been discussed. This chapter is devoted to development of skill in group leadership as an important and specialized aspect of group membership skill. Every individual in a democracy has great use for the full range of membership skills in certain situations throughout his life. These skills cannot be learned successfully without adequate experience both as official leader of a group and as a member enjoying the leadership of another. Development of pupil leadership is therefore one of the teacher's responsibilities in equipping pupils to work cooperatively.

Educating for group leadership is one of the more difficult responsibilities of the teacher. For one thing, many teachers feel none too secure when they themselves have charge of the group. To turn over leadership to an immature member of the group requires courage and good judgment.

Mrs. Liebermann, who chose to invite a pupil to be group chairman on the occasion of her own first attempt at group planning, perhaps showed more courage than good judgment.[1] On the other hand, a teacher must resist the temptation to postpone indefinitely the job of helping others to acquire skill in leadership in the only way any skill can be acquired—through actual practice. The teacher need not wait until he has perfected his own techniques before letting another try his hand. Observation of his group under pupil leadership gives the teacher an opportunity to study the strengths and the needs of his pupils in a group situation as well as to see his own leadership techniques often mirrored in the child leader.

Another concern of the teacher in giving pupils leadership experience is to protect the best interests of the group while one individual is learning this new skill. The teacher must seek situations where the

[1] See pages 258 ff.

mistakes of the beginner will be least costly. Further, he must attempt, through guidance from a co-pilot's seat, to help the pupil leader have a reasonably successful experience without depriving him of all opportunities to make choices as situations arise.

TYPES OF TEACHER GUIDANCE
OF PUPIL LEADERS

The well-known types of leadership identified by Kurt Lewin and associates—autocratic, laissez-faire, and democratic—may be applied to the more indirect leadership of the teacher while a pupil holds the chair.[2] Three running records of pupil-led discussion will illustrate these types of teacher participation.

Autocratic Guidance

In the first record Mrs. Colton's sixth grade group is holding its weekly class meeting, an occasion when the consequences would not be too serious were the pupils allowed to make a mistake or two. However, it will be noted that the teacher plays such a dominating role that at every critical point the leader is robbed of the opportunity to make a judgment. This may be called an autocratic type of teacher guidance of a pupil leader. The record covers approximately twenty-five minutes of a thirty-minute session.

Record	*Analysis*
Sally, the chairman, calls for secretary's report. Items mentioned are chalk on walls outside of school, sale of Christmas seals, one-cent fine for leaving things on desk.	
TEACHER (correcting secretary). Say "carried" rather than "voted through." (To chairman): I think you forgot your standing committees.	To what extent can planning ahead with a chairman save the teacher from having to take over the leadership so often? Would it be helpful to have an agenda for the meeting put on the board in advance? Could children suggest other items for the agenda?
Judy reminds the group to bring things for the Junior Red Cross packages.	
Teacher asks Judy to repeat what they need for the packages.	Would a question have caused the children to think whether they
Chairman calls for old business.	needed this review? Would they

[2] See Kurt Lewin, Ronald Lippitt, and R. K. White, "Patterns of Aggressive Behavior in Experimentally Created Social Climates," *Journal of Social Psychology* 10:271–299 (May, 1939).

Record

TEACHER. I think Wyland needs to give a report on duties.

Wyland reports.

TEACHER. I had two reports come to me on dust. (To chairman): I think you should instruct Wyland about his duties.

There is some discussion about watering plants.

JUDY. I want people not to water my little hens so much.

Teacher reminds group of what they learned at greenhouse.

TEACHER. We didn't have a council report.

Council report follows.

Boy representative says the principal suggested that anyone may put decorations on the school tree downstairs. The principal wants them to be courteous. "See if anyone needs help when you are going down the hall."

JUDY. We voted for the chairman and secretary of the student council. I am the chairman. There is to be no bicycle riding on the school grounds. We can have lights now that the strike is over. We should discuss when we are going to have our Christmas party, the price of gifts, the games we are going to have, and so forth.

When we have visitors we should be courteous, have a host and hostess, give visitors a chair, take their coats, offer them a book, and so forth.

We will meet once a month from now on.

CHAIRMAN. Any questions?

BOY. Last time I asked Judy to take it to the council about safety near the vacant lot, and she didn't give us any answer.

JUDY. Miss S. (the principal)

Analysis

listen differently if *they* asked for the review?

How could this suggestion come from the chairman or the group? Again, could a question be used?

Could a question have been used to turn this discussion to the children?

Good example of individual following through on his suggestion.

Record

gave the answer and I reported it. (She explains again.)

TEACHER. Any report from the bathroom committees on paper pickup?

GIRL. The seventh grade girls are still sitting on the wastebaskets.

TEACHER. What could we do about that?

JUDY. We could go back through the student council.

TEACHER. I think maybe that's the best idea. (To chairman): Call on Mary on seals.

Mary reports.

CHAIRMAN. Any other old business?

Sherrill offers her mother's help on the Christmas party.

TEACHER. Sherrill's mother is our room mother. That's very nice of her.

GIRL. I think we ought to talk about our Christmas gifts.

The chairman reads the committees and tells what the committees might do.

Gloria makes a proposal about gifts.

The teacher says that Gloria should make her suggestion a definite motion, prompts Gloria and chairman on the wording of the motion. There is discussion here whether gifts should be 25¢ or 29¢.

TEACHER (to chairman). Sally, will you tell your people just one at a time?

JUDY. I think 25¢ is enough. Some rooms have only 10¢. (She makes quite a speech and mentions the sales tax.)

Bob agrees with Ronnie on 29¢ and mentions the 3¢ luxury tax.

Teacher suggests that Gloria slip in the words "about 25¢" in her

Analysis

An agenda in advance would probably have made it unnecessary for the teacher to furnish this reminder.

Good to turn the problem back to the group.

Who should evaluate and adopt suggestions?

Would it have been well for the chairman to have the duties reviewed by the group?

A motion that puts only one or two choices before a group is restrictive and usually premature.

This suggestion is only an indirect reprimand. Could the teacher as a group member make a suggestion regarding procedure?

This would have been an opportunity for the children to think

Record

motion, then says, "We have had enough discussion."

Chairman repeats the motion with the teacher prompting her, and Sherrill seconds it.

Teacher directs the committee to tear up thirty-three slips of paper. She thinks of two absent people.

Wanda asks a question about the tree.

Chairman tries to answer but misunderstands.

Teacher explains Wanda's point: If the group does not win a tree, how will they pay for it?

TEACHER (to chairman): Have Wanda make a motion about what you will do if you do not win a tree.

Wanda moves that they pay not more than two dollars.

Teacher starts to object but says it was a motion.

Sally has vote without discussion.

BOY. We don't need too big a tree.

SALLY. We won't get too big a tree for two dollars.

Teacher tells what kind of tree they had last year, where it was placed because of the outlet, and gives an alternative suggestion that perhaps they can't have lights anyway.

SALLY. Someone could bring an extension cord.

TEACHER. Maybe we could see who could bring lights.

Analysis

through a way of reaching agreement. The value of the experience of reaching consensus on the particular occasion must be weighed against the time factor. Often the teacher must make such a decision, knowing what experiences the pupils need most and what other opportunities are available for a similar experience.

Should Wanda have the experience of really communicating her idea to the chairman? Teacher might say, "I don't believe Sally got your point, Wanda. Why don't you try again?" It is better yet if Wanda can get to the point of not letting Sally misunderstand her.

If such a suggestion is necessary, would it be well for the teacher to say, "I suggest that Wanda . . ."? Teacher has the responsibility for contributing out of her experience, but the leader will have a poor experience if he is merely a puppet.

Respects child's motion. Remedy would be to have Sally provide for discussion, teacher could make her point at that time.

Teacher furnishes information to the group.

Chairman recognizes the teacher's contribution as information giving and is not prevented from seeing an alternative.

Teacher shows that she too is willing to look at alternatives.

Record | *Analysis*

SHERRILL. Maybe we could buy some.

Teacher names the prices of lights now: $5.95, $3.50.

GIRL. We got some for $1.

BOY. You can get bulbs for 20¢ apiece.

Teacher might have tried to discover first what information on prices the group had.

CHAIRMAN. We must plan for taking care of the tree afterwards.

TEACHER. Last year the tree went with the Christmas basket, but we could make another plan. Rather than take so much time on decorations, could we leave it to the committee?

Good to leave the matter open for pupil choice.

This is the kind of suggestion any group member might make, but it is good for a teacher to watch the time factor.

CHAIRMAN. Committee, distribute names now.

TEACHER. We've done our boxes for Greece. What can we do to share the Christmas spirit here? The council has asked. . . .

A suggestion made as a group member.

Since the teacher really led the discussion just reported, it is difficult to judge Sally's competence or potential competence as a leader. The steps taken on her own initiative were:

Calling for secretary's report.
Calling for old business (twice).
Saying (after council report), "Any questions?"
Reading list of Christmas committees and telling what they might do (instead of allowing the group to discuss the matter).
Attempting to answer Wanda's question.
Making a suggestion about an extension cord.
Saying, "We must plan for taking care of the tree afterwards."
Ordering the committee to distribute the names.

It is plain to be seen that too much teacher guidance of a pupil leader results in a hollow experience for the very individual the teacher thinks he is helping. Her desire for a highly efficient class meeting led Mrs. Colton to interfere with the leader excessively. As was pointed out in the analysis, preliminary planning with the leader might have given both the teacher and the pupil leader the security necessary for a good leadership experience. In this way the teacher might have protected the group's interests, a worthy aim, and still helped the pupil chairman to succeed.

Laissez-Faire Situation

Certain it is that the answer to Mrs. Colton's problem was not to follow the laissez-faire route taken by Mrs. Quincy with her third grade group. A record of a pupil-led discussion in this classroom illustrates the way in which a class can go to pieces when pupil leadership is highly unskilled and teacher guidance is entirely lacking.

Record	*Analysis*
Time—1:05. Plans for the day on the chalkboard included "Social Studies—How to Make Our Space on the Bulletin Board Attractive."	
TEACHER. Do you want to plan and let me sit in the back? Little response.	Teacher apparently had in mind giving an opportunity for a pupil to be an official leader. This does not seem to be well understood or appreciated by the children.
TEACHER. Have we done this before in this room? Many children seem unsure.	Example of vague questioning.
TEACHER. Whom shall we appoint to write on the board? CHILD. Patsy.	Teacher gives the children an opportunity to select their own leader, but does not help the group to do this in an intelligent way.
TEACHER. All agree? No? Janet is selected.	It is interesting to note Patsy's role in the discussion following this defeat.
TEACHER. Put up "Plans for Our Bulletin Board." Teacher takes seat in the rear of the room. Mary asks if she may help. Receiving Janet's permission to help, she begins calling on children: "Brian."	Teacher helps launch leader on the job to be done and from then on refuses to participate even as a group member. Lack of attention to clarifying the problem under discussion causes much difficulty as the group proceeds.
BRIAN. We will not pull thumbtacks out of the bulletin board. MARY. That's a good one. Janet writes it on the board. Mary goes to a book for help on the spelling of "thumb."	The self-appointed leader evaluates suggestions herself.
TWO GIRLS. She's writing too big. MARY. Anyone else a suggestion? PATSY. We will not scribble on the pictures.	Leaders ignore the comment.

Record	*Analysis*

Boy comes back to teacher to complain about the writing: "It will take up too much room." Teacher ignores him.

Teacher refuses to be a referee.

Janet can't spell "scribble," asks the teacher for help. Teacher suggests that the child use the word "write." Patsy goes up to ask the two girls in charge to write her suggestion as she has stated it (scribble) but they reject her request.

CHILD. We will not take down the pictures.

JANET. You couldn't take the pictures down without taking the thumbtacks out.

Leader evaluates suggestion.

CHILD (who made the suggestion). You could tear it.

ANOTHER CHILD. We will not tear the pictures.

Secretary writes this down as No. 3.

A girl wants them to add: "On our bulletin board." Leaders ignore her.

Leaders are arbitrary about which suggestions they will accept.

At intervals the two girls in charge say, "Sit down, ———. It's not time to be playing with (book, pencil, etc.)."

Teacher's laissez-faire role allows pupil leaders to become exceedingly autocratic.

PATSY. We will not go like this. (Demonstrates running and sliding into the blackboard.)

Janet starts to write No. 4: "We will not run and bang into the blackboard on . . ." Interrupts her writing to say to a child, "That wasn't necessary."

Leader "scolds."

JANET. Does anyone know how to spell "purpose"?

TEACHER. Sound it out. Go ahead and put it the way you think.

Teacher refuses to be a resource person.

Janet writes "prpis."

MARY. Anyone else?

JANET. Patsy is giving all the suggestions.

Leaders complain.

Negative suggestions continue to come until such an extreme is reached that Patsy suggests, "We will not put 'insects' up. Sometimes people squash them and it doesn't look very nice." The teacher's complete withdrawal has created a vacuum. The teacher apparently does not look on cooperative planning as a partnership affair. Bickering among the children increases.

Record	*Analysis*
MARY. Any other suggestions? How about Mildred and Shirley? Only Patsy and Brian have helped.	Leader complains.
GIRL. You won't take mine so I won't give any more.	Rebellion sets in.
BOY. We will sit up straight.	
JANET. That hasn't anything to do with the bulletin board.	
BOY. I didn't know what you were talking about.	Reveals that purpose was not clear to all the group. (This was evident also from expressions on faces and extent of participation.)
DONALD (obviously a slow-thinking child). We won't write on the bulletin board.	
CHILD. Good grief!	
JANET. Good grief, yourself!	
CHILD. Janet is just acting silly.	Discussion degenerates still further into personal squabbles.

At 1:30 Jeanette suggested, "We will put nice pictures on the bulletin board." This was the first contribution that was actually on the beam. The other children were discussing standards for care of a bulletin board. The teacher had an opportunity to help the leaders turn the discussion into a more constructive channel at this point, but she chose to remain aloof. As a result, more personal squabbling followed.

At 1:48 the teacher finally said, "All right, girls. That's all your suggestions. Is that right?" She takes over the leadership of the group.

If Mrs. Quincy had had a clearer idea of how children may be helped to acquire skill in leading group planning, she would not have allowed such a demoralizing experience to continue so long, nor would she have failed to use the occasion as a learning experience.

Mrs. Quincy's children did not seem to learn the lesson Mrs. Tambling's children did when she let them experiment with "no rules." [3]

---

[3] See pages 48–50.

Mrs. Tambling helped her children to evaluate their experience and to plan better ways of operating. Mrs. Quincy's children had no such opportunity. Nor did they have the benefit of able teacher leadership as an example to follow. When Mrs. Quincy "took over," she made an attempt to focus attention on the real problem, but the discussion continued in a rather aimless and halfhearted fashion. The majority of the children remained uninterested and inattentive, during most of a discussion period which had continued for forty-three minutes and was to go on for another twenty-seven before "recess" time brought it to a weary close. Furthermore, the teacher did as the pupil leader had done, allowed a few children to dominate the proceedings and interrupted the discussion to scold the inattentive.

Democratic Guidance

In a neighboring room, on the same day, a child leader in Mrs. Upton's second grade reflected quite a different type of teacher leadership. The type of guidance given by the teacher while the discussion under Barbara's leadership was in progress adds to the impression that Mrs. Upton is a democratic leader of children. The record of this discussion covers thirty minutes.

Record	*Analysis*
TEACHER. Name one problem we have in this room.	Teacher opens with a vague question.
CHILD. I don't know what you mean, Mrs. Upton.	Child's statement shows lack of fear of the teacher.
The teacher explains that recently they had solved the problem of where to keep some bottles they were collecting to use for vases.	Teacher quickly takes the cue and gives a more specific clue to help the children recall a problem previously defined.
TEACHER. Now what else needs to be decided?	
CHILD. What to do about our tadpole that is changing into a frog.	
Teacher chooses Barbara to be the leader. She suggests to the group that they try to get everything settled about what they will need and who will bring it.	Teacher gives help in charting the discussion.
TEACHER (to Barbara privately). Are you prepared to be a good leader?	Teacher makes sure leader is prepared.

Record

BARBARA (to teacher). I have been reading some books about this.

BARBARA (to group). Is everything out of everybody's hands? (Calls on Barry.)

BARRY. I could bring a round fish bowl.

CHILD. No. We want a square one.

BARBARA. Well, what do we call them?

CHILD. Vivarium.

BARBARA. Yes, a vivarium. What do we need in it?

CHILD. Sand.

BARBARA. That's one thing, what else?

CHILD. Rocks.

BARBARA. Who knows what rocks are put in the vivarium for?

TEACHER. I couldn't hear. Will everyone talk louder?

BARBARA. Excuse me, but, Elsie, take your coat down off your head. Anything else?

BOY. I could bring a box with screen on it.

HARRY. How long is it?

The boy shows the length with his hands.

BARBARA. I don't know if that's too long . . .

CHILD. I could bring some rocks.

BARBARA. Do we want great big rocks? Anything else?

CHILD. I could bring a big pan that my mother puts her turkey in for Thanksgiving. They could swim all around in it.

CHILD. I could bring a fish bowl.

BARBARA. We don't want a round one. We want a vivarium. I'll show you. (Gets a book and shows the children a picture.)

Analysis

Barbara's reply shows that her preparation was in terms of being informed on the subject to be discussed.

Leader uses a positive question to suggest how the group might become ready for discussion.

Leader encourages many suggestions, raises questions, receives suggestions without evaluating them.

Leader makes suggestion politely.

Leader turns to authority when needed.

Record	*Analysis*
CHILD. I could bring one not very deep.	
BARBARA. We need a deep one. Why?	Leader turns question back to group.
JERRY. You could have plants in it.	
BARBARA. Yes, but why do we want it deep?	
CHILD. So they can't hop out.	
BARBARA. Anything else to put in?	
CHILD 1. Fish.	
CHILD 2. Fish.	
CHILD 3. Fish.	
BARBARA. Two people already suggested that. Look at this picture and see if you can see anything else.	Leader gives polite reminder. Helps group with a source of new ideas.
CHILD. We could use a tub with water in it.	
BARBARA. Mary, is this the kind of thing you think you could bring?	
BARBARA. Anything else you notice in this picture?	
CHILD. Grass.	
BARBARA. Anything else?	
CHILD. I can't see.	
Barbara goes around with the book.	Shows consideration for group.
CHILD. Turtle.	
BARBARA. Yes, but is there anything else?	
TEACHER. Why don't you tell, Barbara? You know we must get on with the business. Be definite.	Teacher helps leader move off dead center.
BARBARA. It's that little log. Now we've finished.	
TEACHER. Now go ahead and plan what to bring tomorrow.	Teacher helps leader move on to new step.
Children start telling what they could bring.	
TEACHER. Leader, why don't you decide who is to bring the box and whether Tommy is to fix it or if we should fix it in the room?	Teacher tries to help leader clinch some plans.
BARBARA. Who can bring a box?	
Boy volunteers.	

Record	*Analysis*
PERRY. I can bring one.	
TEACHER. Leader, decide who is to bring it.	Teacher tries again to help leader clinch point.
BARBARA. Who will bring a box?	
TEACHER. Can't the children help you decide which one?	Teacher uses a question to suggest a way out for the leader.
Barbara takes a vote. Perry wins.	
BARBARA. Excuse me, will you put your notebooks away? Could you bring your box tomorrow, Perry?	Again a polite reminder from the leader, followed by an attempt to get a definite commitment.
PERRY. Tomorrow or next day or next.	
BARBARA. Why do we need it tomorrow?	Leader turns question to group.
Mary tries to explain but needs a word.	
Barbara points to the word "polliwog" on a chart in front of the room.	Leader helps the group member to express her idea.
Mary finishes her statement, using the word "polliwog."	
BARBARA. Now who is to bring the box? Would we need two boxes?	Teacher here lets leader go to see what she will do when business apparently is finished.
Children answer "No."	
BARBARA. Why wouldn't we need two boxes? Do we have a whole bunch of tadpoles? Who knows how many we have?	
Children answer, "Three."	
BARBARA (to child): Do you want to finish taking this (book) around?	Again leader shows consideration for group and concern for giving a group member an opportunity to be active.
BARBARA (to observer and teacher). You know they were all hollering that they couldn't see it.	
Barbara starts to take her seat. The teacher suggests that she go back and close the discussion nicely. Barbara goes back and says, "We won't have any time to go on."	Teacher here is helping the leader to learn to bring a discussion to a close.
TEACHER. How many thought Barbara was a good leader? Can you give a reason?	Teacher has group evaluate leadership.

Record

Analysis

CHILD. She talked loud so everyone could hear. She didn't lean against the board.

Patsy repeats the same two reasons.

TEACHER. Are you wasting our time?

This remark of the teacher's, while made kindly, contains words that threaten, "wasting our time."

Patsy does not reply.

TEACHER. Did she keep you on the subject? You know we had a leader one day who kept saying, "Was that the question?" We talked about that being a good leader.

Helps group see value of good leadership.

TEACHER. Why is that necessary?

CHILD. Wastes our time.

Apparently the child meant that time is wasted if people do not stick to the question.

A comparison of the pupil leaders in the three groups just reported, Mrs. Colton's, Mrs. Quincy's, and Mrs. Upton's, will show that teacher guidance makes a difference. It may be assumed that all the pupil leaders had a certain amount of readiness for leadership —only that type of child, at the elementary-school level, is usually intrusted with the chairmanship of a large group of peers. Yet Sally, Grade 6, was dominated into nonentity, and Janet and Mary, Grade 3, operated on the low level of dealing with personalities. Barbara, Grade 2, on the other hand, showed that she had acquired certain skills—skills that do not come "naturally" but are learned. In Barbara's case they were undoubtedly learned through imitation of a skillful teacher leader.

GUIDES IN DEVELOPING PUPIL LEADERSHIP

We may say, then, that development of leadership ability on the part of pupils is possible but that it requires planning and teaching in the best sense of the word. Study of attempts of teachers to develop pupil leadership yields certain guides to other teachers who may wish to discover better ways of fulfilling this responsibility to children and youth. Some guides of this kind are discussed and illustrated in the following pages.

Choosing Simple Situations

When pupils are having early experiences in leadership, they should practice needed skills in a situation simple enough for them to handle without excessive coaching from the teacher at the side lines. Very young children have an opportunity for leadership during the time when they may show things they have brought to school and tell about experiences they have had; they can appear before the group and manage participation by calling on fellow classmates in turn as they proudly report: "I have a belt." "I have a fountain pen." "I got a big bicycle." "Last night my daddy broke electric bulbs." If the chairman takes a turn to offer "I have a new pencil," as he often will in early stages, the teacher has an opportunity to teach an elementary lesson about the leader's role.

It should be made clear that leadership of a sharing period, such as the one just described, is a preparatory experience for leadership of group planning. The child has at least stood before the group as the one in charge. However, a "show and tell" period is not an illustration of true group planning, for there are no choices before the group. In setting up such a period originally and in planning to improve it, the teacher would provide opportunities for cooperative planning; but, in the case of first grade children, the leadership required in planning the routine for a sharing period would be too difficult to expect of most young children.

Miss Ervin found the seventh grade pupils in her elementary school responded well to opportunities to serve as host or hostess at lunch tables made up of younger children. She planned with them ways in which they might help the younger children to have a more pleasant lunch period, and she was pleased to note signs of individual initiative going beyond the group planning. For example, Miss Ervin also tells of a boy who said, "I put Johnny in my place as host. After that he behaved." These seventh graders became quite aware of their responsibility when they noted that children at their tables were copying the lunch carried by their host or hostess. The boys in the group of hosts even investigated lack of soap in the boys' lavatory and took measures to secure a regular supply in return for a guarantee to prevent waste on the part of the younger boys.

Opportunities to exercise leadership breed such initiative. In preceding chapters we learned how other teachers found suitable opportunities for their pupils to practice leadership. In Miss Lambert's room, meetings of the Helpers Club were presided over by the pupil president.[4] In Miss Van Alsten's room, Virginia was chairman of a tea for mothers.[5] Mrs. Spain sat back and kept a record of the proceedings while the student council representatives from her group led a discussion of their obligation to donate all their sale profits to the school microphone fund.[6] Mr. Owen encouraged his pupils to organize a class government with officers, and he searched constantly for other opportunities for his children to exercise leadership.[7] Small-group investigations in Miss Fielding's mathematics classes gave chances for student leadership, as did the standing committees of a high school student council whose work was described earlier.[8] These are illustrative of the many possibilities existing for those teachers who wish to provide leadership experiences for their pupils.

Allowing Pupils to Initiate Leadership Opportunities

Sometimes teachers need not search for opportunities for pupils to exercise leadership; they need only to be willing for children and youth to assume the responsibilities which they themselves suggest. Miss King found it worth while to allow a six-year-old to take the initiative.

One youngster gave us all a treat today. He owns a portable electric victrola, as well as practically every new record that is made for six-year-olds, and it was "his day" to treat.

He had decided he would play the records according to the desires of the children. Likewise, he managed the machine, giving a preview of each record that he played. From what I observed, these recordings meant more to the children because they were voluntarily shared by a member of their own group. It was on his own initiative that the boy brought in the records and took charge of the music hour. He left the group inspired, anticipating the next time he would bring his music—as he promised he would.

Mr. Rice, a high school teacher, had a similar offer of student leadership, which he was wise enough to accept.

My eleventh grade boys' hygiene class had reached the point in our outlined program where juvenile delinquency was the topic. One boy voluntarily suggested that he would like to take over and lead the class in the discussion of that topic. He did so, and called in other fellows

[4] See pages 33–34.
[5] See pages 69–70.
[6] See pages 173–174.
[7] See pages 273–274.
[8] See pages 103–104, 228–229.

to help lead the class. I feel that the class learned a lot and that these leaders had a splendid experience.

Earlier we saw that Mr. Rice allowed these same boys to make all arrangements for the trips which they suggested for their class.[9]

Although these examples do not show leadership of group planning, the pupils in every case were having experiences that would help them learn to take special responsibility in a group.

Providing Leadership Opportunities for All

Although the teacher should recognize and encourage emerging leadership and probably would be wise to start his experimentation with pupil leadership by giving chances to those who seem to have the most readiness for the experience, he must be on his guard against throwing all opportunities to children like Ann, whose teacher writes of her:

> March 1. A lovely part of today was the way in which Ann conducted the class meeting in preparation for her report at the student council meeting in the afternoon. She presided delightfully, discussing the topic of responsibility with the children, and the role each played in sharing responsibility in family and school life. She asked very definite questions like "Why should you help at home?" "Why isn't it right for just a few of us to do our school work?" Then she called on various children to give their ideas. It was a revelation to hear the good, sound judgment expressed by the children. They had fine ideas, and surely Ann is paving the way for leadership.

Ann no doubt had to learn to be so skillful a leader. Others in her class must have chances to practice group leadership too. One way is to find such an abundance and variety of opportunities over the period of the entire school career of pupils that each child has the chances for leadership that are useful to him.

Preparing Pupils for Leadership

A difficulty frequently encountered by pupil leaders is lack of clarity as to the purpose of the discussion at hand. The teacher can help by making sure that group members, including the leader, have a clear idea of the problem to be solved. This may take the form of a reminder of a previous decision to tackle the problem, or it may consist of a review of a situation which requires attention and the formulation of group purpose with respect to it. It may even consist of a simple posing of a problem for the group.

[9] See page 92.

The way in which Mrs. Upton launched a discussion of making the room attractive for Christmas is an illustration of the first type of teacher help to a group—the reminder of a problem previously decided upon. Before turning the discussion over to a pupil leader, the teacher tried to lay certain groundwork, as is shown in this excerpt from a record taken by the school principal.

Record	*Analysis*
TEACHER. Who can tell us what we were going to decide?	Teacher tests to make sure purpose of discussion is clear.
BILLY. About Christmas.	
TEACHER. I wonder what Billy means "about Christmas."	Teacher is working for clear and specific statements.
James tries to explain Billy's comment.	
TEACHER. What else were we going to decide about Christmas?	One wonders if there might have been a more direct way to get down to the purpose of the discussion. The questions seemed to confuse the children.
BILLY. About what we were going to bring?	
TEACHER. What was the very first thing we were going to bring?	
CAROL. To take down all the pictures and put up just Christmas pictures.	
TEACHER. That is what Carol would like to do, but did we say what *we* were going to do?	Teacher tries kindly to help Carol see that her contribution was not related to the question.
CHILDREN. No.	
TEACHER. What did we decide to do first?	
PAUL. To get our room ready.	
TEACHER. How many have been thinking about Christmas decorations in the room? (Many hands.) Carol, will you plan with the group?	Teacher gives Carol a chance to be the leader.

Although Mrs. Upton might have accomplished her mission a little more directly, she was fulfilling her responsibility for preparing the way for the pupil leader.

A teacher can help a leader also by organizing a discussion into parts before turning it over to a pupil leader. When Miss Hawkins' third and fourth grade group began to discuss how they could improve their lunch period, the teacher helped them to set up these parts of the problem: (1) going to lavatory, (2) going to lunchroom, (3) going through lunch line, (4) coming back to the room. The discussion then was turned over to a pupil leader. This is a constructive type of help for the teacher to give until the child leader learns to take such a preliminary step for himself.

Sometimes a pupil elected to a position of leadership presents a sorry figure as a presiding officer. Such was the case with Oliver, an eighth grade boy who was elected club president. After watching the boy flounder through one sad experience as leader of a meeting, Mrs. Armstrong began to study him. She talked with him to build his confidence in himself. She secured a book to help him with the simple duties of a president. She also created occasions for him to make a few short statements to the class before the next club meeting so that he would become accustomed to standing before a group. By the time of the next meeting Oliver was able to carry on his duties somewhat better, although he still had much to learn. A later development is described by the teacher in these words.

> One of Oliver's outstanding characteristics is his willingness to co-operate and to seize every opportunity to act as a leader. As a result of several years of struggle to overcome his original handicap of shyness, the boy last June stood before a large audience as one of the most proficient presidents and masters of ceremony that I have seen in the twenty years I have served at our school.

A rather ambitious and unusual attempt at preparation for leadership was a one-day conference at the school camp for student council officers in the elementary and secondary schools of a medium-sized school system. The letter informing participants of program plans shows the nature of the conference.

Dear Student Council President and Sponsor:

The committee was happy to receive your reservations for the student council workshop. We will look forward to seeing you on the 19th.

You will be pleased to know that we have secured two outstanding resource people, one for the secondary group and one for the elementary. We think you will be interested in the tentative program for the day. We hope you will approve and feel free to make suggestions.

9:00 to 10:00 General assembly with Mr. F. (resource person) keynoting

10:00 to 11:00 Section meetings, elementary and secondary. Discussion of the strong points of your council

11:00 to 11:30 Section meetings outlining problems for the afternoon discussion

11:30 to 12:00 Unplanned free period

12:00 to 1:00 Lunch

1:00 to   1:30 Unplanned free period
1:30 to   3:30 Section meetings. Discussion of problems
3:30 to   4:00 Unplanned free period
4:00 to   5:00 Movies and discussion of movies, with Miss M. (resource person) leading the discussion
5:00 to   5:30 Unplanned free period
5:30 to   6:30 Dinner
6:30 to   7:00 Plan programs for evening
7:00 to   9:00 General assembly, community singing, stunts, etc., in front of the fire

Because of the shortness of our conference, we hope to do as much preplanning as possible. To facilitate this, will you plan at least one council meeting for a discussion of the strong points and the problems, so that your representatives can come well prepared to enter into the discussion?

Will you also send a list of the problems to Mr. S. by Thursday, November 14th? This will be of service to your planning committee and also to the resource people.

We hope that all the principals and sponsors will plan to attend the workshop for the full day. We are relying on you to help make this a success, as well as the boys and girls.

Sincerely yours,
Student Council Workshop
Planning Committee

Two participants in the elementary group recalled, when interviewed some months later, that some of the problems discussed were: bicycle racks, should the kindergarten come to student council meetings (the group voted "yes" on that), children volunteering for safety patrol and then not being at their posts, keeping buildings clean, should there be a girls' service squad. "It was fun," these children said of their conference. "We got lots out of it. We helped other people and they helped us. We ought to have another."

Another value mentioned was that of getting acquainted with others—making introductions, sitting at the table with high school students.

In the same community junior and senior high school student councils of the city and nearby suburban schools are represented on an all-city council. Three junior high students, interviewed regarding the organization, stated that the city council discusses such matters as how the different schools are run; problems of corridors, study halls, and noontime programs; how officers are chosen and what their constitutions are like. The all-city group settles problems between schools, such as Halloween and age limits at dances and recreation

places. It puts information regarding these problems in the local
newspaper. "It has made us more friendly to other schools," one of
the students asserted. Another added that at first the junior high
school representatives held back but now were entering in. The plan
is to call in representatives of the elementary school councils once or
twice a year when there are problems to discuss that concern them,
for example, children running out on the football field during games.

At the senior high school in the city the student council officers have
the further opportunity of attending an annual conference for the
councils of the five large high schools in their section of the state that
compete with one another in athletics.

Through all such means the pupils in leadership positions in this
school system are being helped to function more effectively.

Coming to the Rescue of the Pupil Leader

As was seen in the opening examples of this chapter, the
mark of democratic guidance of pupil leadership is the amount and
kind of help furnished. If too little help is given, the group may dis-
integrate; if too much, the pupil in nominal charge has little opportunity to learn how to lead. Full knowledge of a situation and of
the participants is necessary for a fair assessment of teacher guidance. However, a running record often shows enough of the give-and-
take in a discussion to enable one to study the contribution of the
teacher to a pupil-led discussion.

A record taken in Miss Durham's first grade room in May shows
Anita, a six-year-old child, attempting a fairly difficult job of leadership. The record also indicates the points at which the teacher felt
she must step in.

The problem before the group was to organize to play games on
the playground while the teacher attended a short conference. There
was to be another teacher on the playground, but the first grade
children were to have charge of their own games. The discussion was
in progress when the observer entered. Jack had just suggested that
they play "Chinese Wall."

Record	*Analysis*

ANITA. How many want to play
with Jack?

Several children raise their
hands.

ANITA. All right, what game do
you want to play? Clara?

Record

This procedure is used until five or six games have been suggested and children begin raising their hands for more than one game.

TEACHER (coming to the front of the room). Do you know how I can help you?

The teacher starts writing "Over the Chinese Wall." Anita asks who wants to play it, and the names come thick and fast, with the teacher writing: Violet, Virginia— ten altogether. Chairman withdraws from leadership position.

TEACHER (to children). How could you help?

GIRL. By going out to play.

TEACHER. Yes, but right here on the board?

BOY. One of us could write and you could help us spell and then you wouldn't have to walk around.

TEACHER. That's one suggestion. Any other ideas?

BOY. Each could write his own.

TEACHER. Each child who is going to play this game go up and write his name.

Analysis

Noting that the chairman and the group are going through meaningless motions, the teacher assists the chairman by establishing a different procedure with the group and then retiring.

The teacher retires to the rear of the room, and the chairman comes back into the picture. Writing of names proceeds rather slowly, so the teacher comes to the front again.

Record

TEACHER. While these children continue to write their names, can you children tell me another game that got as many votes as this so I can put it up here?

Leapfrog is finally suggested. The children forget the first and all turn to the second list. The teacher suggests that they keep on with the first list.

ANITA. Anybody else on "Chinese Wall"?

Analysis

Teacher takes over group leadership to demonstrate a way of saving time.

Although the teacher exerts active leadership throughout the re-

Record

BOY. I think we should count and see how many we have.

TEACHER. That is a very good suggestion.

Anita starts numbering, gives chalk for leapfrog list to another child.

TEACHER. I wonder if someone has noticed something about the numbering?

There are many theories and the children show renewed interest, although several children still are not involved. Teacher suggests another way of numbering. (The children had numbered both the first and last names in a few instances.) Anita is finally triumphant over the total of twelve for "Chinese Wall."

TEACHER. I think you can help by making some suggestions to these twelve. I won't be able to go with you, so what will you do?

ANITA. I will have to tell them how to play.

TEACHER. Which game will *you* play?

ANITA. Leapfrog.

TEACHER. Then what will you do about the other group?

ANITA. I will show them how first before starting the others.

TEACHER. How will you know they will play?

ANITA. I will wait until they get started.

TEACHER. Has anyone else a suggestion?

BOY. We could chose another leader.

Anita does so, then goes to number the other list.

TEACHER (getting the two totals). I think someone is not playing, 11 and 12 and 23. Let's look at our attendance record.

Analysis

mainder of the period, the pupil chairman continues to function. In fact, the two operate rather effectively as co-chairmen.

With questions teacher helps pupil leader see other details that need to be planned.

Teacher's question gives others in the group an opportunity to help with the planning at this point.

Pupil leader shows willingness to share leadership with others.

Record

BOY. There are thirty-one.

TEACHER. What are the rest of you going to do?

ANITA. How many want to jump rope? . . . There are still eight more.

TEACHER. Don't you think three games are enough? How about everyone not signed up for others take jumping rope? (There is not a clear acceptance.) All right, those people come up here.

The eight come up.

ANITA. How many here are willing to play jump rope?

Finally all raise their hands. Anita counts eight.

TEACHER (writing). That makes it exactly 31. All right, Anita, choose a leader for this.

ANITA. All those playing jump rope raise hands and I will choose a leader.

TEACHER. I can't be there. I would like you to go right out and play with your leader. There will be another teacher out there. Let's go by groups.

Anita gets to the door; calls jump-rope group, leapfrog group, then "Chinese Wall." Last group rushes out. There is a question over the leader for leapfrog.

TEACHER. You had better appoint one.

Anita had planned to lead this group, but apparently has forgotten. Teacher has Anita go back to the board, look at the list of those signed up for leapfrog, and choose a chairman. Richard K. is appointed.

Analysis

Teacher attempts to help group take a short cut in planning.

Pupil leader takes over again.

Leader shows that she has had some experience with orderly ways of proceeding.

Although the record does not reveal it, Anita's performance clearly indicated to the observer one point at which the girl would need much help over a period of time. She relished too much her power to call on or to ignore a child as her fancy dictated. Teachers must be watchful that leadership experience does not encourage children to be tyrannical. The test of the teacher's guidance during the planning period, however, was that the pupil chairman continued to take the initiative at various points clear to the end of the session.

Another record, this time from a sixth grade, shows the occasions on which the teacher, Miss Underwood, stepped in to help the student chairman. It was the practice in the school to hold monthly meetings of the student council before the entire student body. One day early in December, the student council officers were consulting their fellow sixth graders for suggestions of topics suitable for the next open meeting. Betty was in charge.

Record	*Analysis*
BETTY. Any ideas on topics for the next council meeting?	
PUPIL. Winter sports.	
BETTY. I don't think "winter sports"—we don't have any snow yet.	
PUPIL. Safety.	
BETTY. That topic usually comes after Christmas. It wouldn't be very interesting this month. We always have that in the winter.	Betty obviously needs help on the proper way to receive the contributions of group members.
PUPIL. The topic could be "Christmas."	
BOY. People sometimes get electrocuted from Christmas tree lights.	
TEACHER. Electrocuted? I question that.	Teacher here is exercising a teaching function.
BOY. They get a shock.	
TEACHER. That's different, isn't it?	
BOY. I like "winter sports." We don't need snow to play basketball.	Chairman allows an extended period of circular discussion with only one contribution of her own.
GIRL. I think we should have something said about Christmas safety.	
PUPIL. We always have "safety."	
BETTY. Can't you think of something else?	
MARY. We could have it on "the armory."	
Four other pupils give arguments for and against this suggestion.	

Record	*Analysis*
boy. We could get two or three things and vote.	
betty. We're not going to vote.	Betty is reflecting an attempt of the teachers in the school to keep children from voting too soon, too often, too thoughtlessly. Apparently Betty was convinced that voting was never appropriate.
boy. I know, but I mean later.	
betty. It's not good to vote.	
bobby. You have "safety, safety," all the time.	
teacher. Excuse me, Bobby. What do you think is the purpose of the pupil council?	Teacher asks a question to help clarify the discussion.
bobby. Safety, preventing accidents.	
boy. But Miss Underwood . . .	
teacher. Sorry, I'm just a member of the group. Betty is in charge.	Teacher makes an effort to give Betty status as the group leader.
boy. But I want to say something to *you.*	
teacher. Sorry, go ahead.	
There is some discussion of what a pupil council is.	
chairman. You've suggested "Christmas safety," "winter sports," "going to the armory." Give your opinions on those three.	Betty attempts to get the group back to the main problem.

There follows a great deal of comment supporting and opposing these three proposals. Finally the teacher enters into the discussion again.

Record	*Analysis*
teacher. Excuse me. How about someone who hasn't talked? Gloria, which of these two do you prefer?	This is the first point at which the teacher actually takes over group leadership for a time, her purpose being to draw out some non-vocal children.
gloria. Christmas.	
teacher. John?	
john. Armory.	
teacher. You, Bill?	
bill. Christmas.	
richard. Christmas.	
teacher. Bobby, you haven't said a word.	
bobby. I like "Christmas." "The armory" can wait.	

Record	*Analysis*
TEACHER. All right, Betty, you have your decision.	Here the teacher assumes consensus, perhaps prematurely, as is shown by a later development.
BETTY. We always have "Christmas."	
TEACHER. Betty, you're chairman.	Teacher reminds the chairman of her rightful role.
BETTY. What would we have if we had "Christmas"?	
GIRL. Trees.	
Boy shows he is dissatisfied with Christmas as a topic.	
PUPIL. I agree with him.	
TEACHER. Why don't you agree with "fun at Christmas"?	Teacher is operating as any group member might.
BOY. We always have a Christmas play.	
BOY. I want "winter sports."	
BETTY. Last year we had "winter sports." I don't remember what we did.	
TEACHER. Unless I am mistaken, the general idea in the room is "Christmas." We've reached a decision, haven't we, Lewis?	Teacher ignores the possibility that consensus might not have been reached.
LEWIS. Yes, but . . .	
TEACHER. Then why do you bring up "winter sports"?	
LEWIS. Winter is just beginning.	
TEACHER. Betty is trying to get you organized.	An oblique suggestion to the chairman.
BETTY. Couldn't we have "Christmas fun" and "safety"?	
TEACHER. All right.	

There are no ideas for a moment. Then there follows a discussion of how to get the ideas of "Christmas fun" and "safety" before all the children. A skit, jingles, songs, and demonstrations are suggested. Elaine, the secretary, immediately goes to board and starts taking down items. During this part of the discussion the teacher makes four comments. When a boy suggests a skit showing unsafe things to do at Christmas time, to be followed by questioning the children as to what is right, Miss Underwood shows her disapproval with a question: "Then what are they going to remember?"

Miss Underwood functions as a teacher in her second comment, when she asks, "What could Elaine put down on the board for that?"

Her third comment is to ask Jane to address the chairman rather than the teacher. The fourth time she functions as a group member is when she says, "May I make a suggestion? I know you've used jingles before. How about riddles?" Toward the end of the discussion the teacher comes closer to the role of chairman. The record continues.

Record	*Analysis*
TEACHER. What were you going to say?	
PUPIL. We could put words to a Christmas song.	
TEACHER. You agree we'd enjoy singing even if we've had it before?	
BARBARA. We could do something in the gym.	
TEACHER. Barbara, is there any use in dreaming?	
GIRL. How would you get in the idea of fun? Everything we have is on safety.	
TEACHER. Is there anything on the board that's fun?	
BOY. Riddles.	
BETTY. Do you want jingles and riddles both?	Pupil chairman gets back in.
PUPIL. Just riddles.	
"Jingles" is taken off the board. A booklet is suggested. The teacher suggests that they let Bill take over the booklet. Bill gives some of his ideas for the booklet. He asks the group for suggestions. Several are given for the cover.	Teacher evidently feels it important for Bill to have a leadership experience.
TEACHER. I don't think you've answered Bill's question. You've given nice suggestions for the cover that he and his assistants can work out. But what's going inside? (As suggestions of riddles and songs begin to come, the teacher turns the children to Bill.) I'm interested but I don't have to do it.	
TEACHER. Bill, do you have enough suggestions?	Teacher gives cue for the discussion to return to the former channel.
BETTY (resuming charge of the meeting). Which children want to do skits . . . ?	

With her group of children, who are obviously mature in discussion techniques, Miss Underwood found little need to come to the rescue of the pupil chairman. She participated comparatively little (for a teacher). Her participation was divided rather evenly among three roles—group member, teacher, group leader.

Teacher Functions as Co-chairman with Pupil

A different way of studying a teacher's role in relation to that of pupil chairman is to isolate the two roles and list the comments side by side. For this purpose a record of planning under pupil leadership by Miss Hawkins' third and fourth grade children has been selected. The pupils were discussing how they could improve the part of the playground assigned to them for this purpose by the student council. The teacher's and the chairman's remarks are numbered as they occurred in the course of a discussion which, of course, was participated in by many pupils.

Chairman	Teacher
(1) What do we want to plan?	(8) Can you plan any further, or do you need to go out and look?
(7) (Writes on board) 1. Find out what we have to clean up. 2. Find out how big our space is.	(11) When you work on the grounds, what do you take with you?
(15) Do I need to erase that?	(18) All right, Chairman, help them come to some conclusion.
(19) We have these things on the board. What is our next step?	(20) Anybody have a suggestion where to go now?
(26) (Rereads the list) What do we have to do to find out these things?	(25) What do we do first to start?
(28) How many agree?	(30) Then we need to go now. We know what we want to find out. We'll leave these things on the board and when we come back see if we found out.

Upon the group's return to the classroom (after going out to look over the grounds), a new leader was selected. All the remarks made by the new chairman and by the teacher have been selected from the complete record and listed in two columns. Again the numbers show at what points amid the total number of remarks these particular contributions came.

Chairman	Teacher
(1) Did we find out what we had to clear up? (Checks off on list	

Chairman

as group answers. There is disagreement on tools.)
(3) What tools do we need? (Lists on board, calls on member of the group for contributions, has children tell how and why in relation to their suggestions.)
(8) Where will we put the dirt?
(11) We're thinking about the job list now. Can you write on that?
(13) Let's finish our list.
(15) But there's glass in the dirt pile.
(17) That's much too slow.
(22) We have that.
(24) You mean scythe. I'll bring one. We need it. I brought one last year.
(28) Any suggestions about the way to work?
(33) I believe we could vote if nobody has a suggestion. All right. (They vote to divide by jobs.) The next job is making committees.

Teacher

(2) How many know at least one tool we need?

(4) May I interrupt? How are you going to work?

(27) You seem to have found out what to do; see if you can plan how you are going to do the job.
(31) There is another way you could lay out your work. Can you think of it?

Even without the benefit of the complete record, several facts are apparent:

1. Both pupil chairmen had at their command certain techniques for helping a group arrive at a conclusion and move forward. (See items 1, 7, 19, 25, 28 in the first section of the report, items 1, 3, 8, 11, 13, 28, 33 in the second.)
2. The teacher's chief role was to help the chairmen move to a new phase of the discussion. (See items 8, 18, 20, 25 in the first section; items 4 and 27 in the second.)
3. The teacher and chairmen worked together harmoniously, neither one interfering with the other.

The chief question that might be raised is whether the chairmen needed even the small amount of guidance the teacher gave them. One thing is certain: it is impossible to discover how competent a pupil leader is unless he is allowed to continue as leader at the very points that offer the best tests of his skill. On the other hand, the teacher must participate enough to show his interest and must take opportunities for a bit of teaching now and then. All in all, Miss Durham, Miss Underwood, and Miss Hawkins used remarkably good judgment about the nature of their participation.

Additional opportunities to study the related roles of a pupil chairman and a teacher are afforded in the record of a pupil-led discussion in Mrs. Upton's room, when the children were deciding where to store the bottles they had brought; in the record of a session in Miss Sudbury's room, when Jimmie was supposedly the leader for planning a mural; in the account of a student council meeting in Miss Fenstrom's school, when adults took the discussion out of the president's hands for a time; in the junior high school student council meeting, where the principal operated consistently as a group member and the council president retained the chairmanship.[10]

Analyzing Pupil Leadership

If an individual is to be a leader of genuine group planning, there are a few rules of the game that he must learn. The teacher can help him learn these important techniques by demonstrating them at all times when he himself is in the chair and by helping the pupils to analyze and appraise the success of various procedures. To help pupils evaluate their own leadership and that of their peers, the teacher must be able to analyze the points at which leadership has been effective and those at which it has gone awry.

Miss Vanderly has furnished a record showing clearly that one elementary lesson in leadership is needed by the pupil leader in her fifth-sixth grade group. This lesson is that it is the leader's function to gather suggestions from the group, not to announce plans already made.

> Louise, as president of Busy Bee Club, drew plans from the boys and girls for a Thanksgiving program. Evelyn as secretary wrote plans on board.
>
> LOUISE. Mildred, you may read a Thanksgiving story. Nancy, you read a Thanksgiving poem. We will have a song by the class. We will plan for a Thanksgiving play too. People wanting to be in it raise their hands. (Seven girls and five boys volunteer.)
>
> DAVID. The boys will be the Indians.
>
> PAUL. But some of the boys will have to be Pilgrims.
>
> LOUISE. Mildred will read the Thanksgiving story so we will know it well enough to play it.

[10] See pages 43–45, 131–132, 200–202, 203 ff.

Although Miss Vanderly writes that Louise "drew" plans from her classmates, this was clearly not the case. Louise seemed rather to be a director giving orders. Unless a teacher can see the difference between these two ways of operating, he is in a poor position to help a pupil leader to improve.

A record kept by Miss McNulty shows that her pupil leaders also lacked understanding of the leader's role during the suggestion-gathering process. In addition, these children made the mistake of calling for premature votes. The consultant's analysis of the record shows the points at which the leaders evidenced need for further help.

Record	*Analysis*
The group decided to have two leaders, Norma and Billy.	
NORMA. What can we have for our program?	Leader calls for suggestions.
PAT. Let's have someone tell a story.	
NORMA. Could we have a vote on that? All raise hands that want a story. We will have a story. Who will tell the story?	Leader has a vote on each suggestion as given. (This gives less room for intelligent choice than waiting to vote upon a number of suggestions.)
FRANK. Let Willis tell the story.	
NORMA. Shall we name anyone else?	Leader opens the way for further nominations.
SEVERAL. No, let Willis tell it.	
Willis was decided upon to tell the story.	
BILLY. Will we sing some songs? It would be nice for all to sing. Who wants to sing? Raise hands.	Leaders begin to make suggestions and to call for approval. This gives less opportunity for group thinking.
NORMA. Let's have an announcer. Who do you want for that?	
Several children are chosen. They are sent out of the room and voted on.	
CHILD. Who shall we invite?	
LEADER. How about inviting the parents?	At this point the leaders seem to have taken over completely the suggestion-giving function that should belong mostly to the group.
CHILD. They will be busy. I don't think many could come.	
LEADER. How about some teacher and class?	
CHILD. Oh, yes. Let's do that.	
LEADER. What room shall we have?	

Record	*Analysis*
CHILD. Miss A. and Mrs. R.	
LEADER. We forgot—when is it going to be?	It was poor technique for the leader to intrude this question here; it might have thrown the discussion off the track.
LEADER. How about Mrs. T. coming?	
CHILD. I guess we will have to vote on who is to come.	It was good that a member of the group took this initiative.
Children vote.	
LEADER. Now, that is settled, when will it be?	
CHILD. Let's have it Tuesday morning.	
LEADER. How many want it then? (Affirmative vote) Now it is decided when it is to be, who we are to have. Let's have a committee to arrange it.	Again the leader calls for a vote on the first suggestion given. This procedure tends to make children passively accept a suggestion rather than exercise discrimination in selecting among alternatives.
Committee is appointed.	Leaders summarize.

Pupil leaders often need help on what to do with suggestions from the group. Just as their elders frequently do, pupil leaders tend to assume that any suggestion given has the approval of the entire group, and they omit entirely the steps of group evaluation of suggestions and group adoption of the ones of their choice. As has been emphasized repeatedly, cooperative planning involves choice-making and it should give pupils practice in judging and discriminating.

Teacher Testimony on Development of Pupil Leadership

Teachers who have made a conscious effort to give leadership opportunities to pupils have something to say as a result of their experience.

The teachers of Valley Elementary School made a special drive one year to develop more pupil leadership. As they were evaluating the experience toward the close of the year, the teachers made such remarks as the following:

If a question is simple enough for children to handle at all, it is better to have a child leader.
You need to have the problem presented *well*.
It is better if there is some feeling of need for everyone to cooperate.
The more the teacher stays out, the wider the participation.

When you have a good child leader, there is greater interest in the group.

In developing pupil leadership, you must go beyond "natural" leadership to "learned" leadership.

What helped us when we first started was that we always evaluated afterward. We have built up a habit of evaluating leadership. The children show signs that they remember suggestions.

One value of using pupil leadership is that the children learn what a leader is. They cooperate better with the teacher afterward. Of course, it prepared them for not being dependent on somebody in activities outside school.

The teacher gets an opportunity to see a clique, to see child needs.

It gives the teacher a chance to see the situation change so much. When you observe someone trying to get the cooperation of others, you see a great difference in his personality. He is different when he is sitting among friends rather than being the leader.

We used a strong person first to begin initial planning, then used someone not so strong (one who couldn't judge so well between important and unimportant things) who wanted to be a leader. It made her a better follower afterward.

These teachers also believed that pupils might be given more direct help with steps in planning, although they saw the danger of too much emphasis on logical steps and too little emphasis on interaction among people.

CONCLUSION

Study of the foregoing opinions of teachers who have had an intensive experience with pupil leadership indicates that development of such leadership presents certain problems to the teacher but that teachers who have given attention to the matter are convinced of the importance of this responsibility of education.

This chapter has been built around records obtained in the study, which unfortunately yielded a relatively small number of instances of pupil leadership. Areas in which further experience is needed are (1) helping many more pupils to alternate between roles of group members and official leaders, and (2) helping groups with the process of finding the right opportunities for the right people and of considering the welfare of both the individual and the group as practice in leadership is provided.

CHAPTER XIV

Making Effective Use

of Small Groups

SOME TEACHERS equate cooperative procedures with small-group work. Too often work in small groups connotes noise, horseplay, uneven distribution of labor, lack of accomplishment. For this reason some teachers dismiss cooperative procedures as altogether impractical. Other teachers, although they believe in teacher-pupil cooperation, fear waste and disorder if pupils are left on their own to work in small groups, therefore they use large-group planning as much as possible.

Pupils can have many good experiences through planning in large groups. Usually, however, there is much group business to be done, and if small-group work is ruled out the teacher has only two other choices. One is to keep the whole group in a planning situation long past the attention span of all but the most avid planners. This means a struggle to spread vocal participation among the members of the large group and to keep all as actively interested as possible. The other alternative is for the teacher to make many plans for the group. When, as frequently happens, the teacher has handled matters that needed group consideration for full understanding and cooperation, trouble arises.

Although it is recognized that there are occasions when it is necessary and desirable for some planning to be done for the group, the teacher might well look into the possibility of planning in small groups as an adjunct to effective large-group planning. Giving pupils opportunities to work in small groups has additional values also. First, opportunities to participate vocally, to preside over a group, and to practice various group membership skills can be multiplied through the use of small groups. Second, the small, relatively homogeneous group favors action on plans and production. Third, varying interests and abilities of pupils can be met better through small groups.

It is the purpose of the present chapter to relate the experiences and findings of a number of teachers who have worked on the problem of small-group work as a part of cooperative procedures. The chapter is organized to give help on three important aspects of the problem: (1) What are some uses of small groups? (2) What are effective ways of forming small groups? (3) How can children and youth be helped to work efficiently in small groups?

USES OF SMALL GROUPS

The teachers cooperating with this study seemed to use small groups in three ways. The first and most common way was to provide a division of labor and responsibility for various parts of a common project or study. The second was to allow unrelated studies or projects to proceed simultaneously. The third was to use part of the group to make preliminary plans or to do some other special service for the group.

Division of Labor and Responsibility

Division of responsibility can be done quite casually and with little formal organization. For example, Miss Lapham tells of pleasant walks on the school grounds in the fall so that her first grade children might observe changes taking place in nature. She writes:

> The class of thirty-five often breaks up into groups. One group may be interested in the bark of trees, another in living things in the pond. One group may find pretty colored leaves and still another may collect some of the wild flowers growing along the sides of the race track. These collections are brought back to the classroom and shared with the whole group. Simple discussions follow. They are meaningful because an individual is contributing to the group with the security that comes from belonging to a number of others.

Such beginnings lay the foundation for more complex organization later on. It will be recalled that in Mrs. Austin's kindergarten, children worked on their playhouse in groups informally structured in terms of materials at hand, jobs to be done, and interests shifting from day to day.[1]

With somewhat older children and youth, the jobs to be done or the aspects of a study to be covered usually are planned by the whole

[1] See pages 112–113.

group and responsibilities are formally delegated to small groups. The way in which Mr. Allen, a secondary school science teacher and supervisor, approached the organization of his ninth grade class for small-group work may be helpful to others. The teacher is frank to admit that he hesitated at first to venture into cooperative planning. He writes:

> I left out pupil participation in the planning, not because I didn't know about it, but because I didn't think it was very practical. Science was too difficult a subject for pupils, with only limited knowledge, to be of much help in laying out a unit. Later when I read Giles's *Teacher-Pupil Planning* I found out how wrong I was.[2]

Before long, Mr. Allen felt himself ready to begin teacher-pupil planning.

> Today I decided to take the plunge. I told the students that in our next unit, light, they were going to be able to select any topic or prob-lem and work on it as they wished. Since many of the problems which they would select would be related, I suggested that they might like to work in groups so that they could help each other in preparing and presenting their topics. They seemed quite anxious to do this.
>
> In order to stimulate their thinking and to open up the subject, I asked them to describe their experiences with light. Almost everyone volunteered some experiences. Questions were brought up but not answered by me. I suggested they note them down and save them. Each experience seemed to stimulate others and soon we were ready to list all the problems which were welling up.
>
> A volunteer was selected to write on the board all the problems which the group thought might be of interest and on which they would like to work. Since I thought their knowledge of the scope of light would be somewhat limited, I suggested that they skim through the unit in their texts as the next assignment and that the next day we would add any new questions or problems which had been stimulated by the description in the text.
>
> When we had finished our listing, there were thirty-six entries. Since the group was not advanced enough to recognize relationships, I said I would classify the problems and topics in related groupings and around these we would form our work-study groups. I then listed the main headings and the subtopics in related groups. Each student wrote on a piece of paper the main heading and the particular topic of his choice. These were then sorted and the groups were formed. We were now ready to start work.

The reports of three junior high school teachers who were making beginnings in cooperative planning with their pupils may be consulted

[2] H. H. Giles, *Teacher-Pupil Planning* (New York: Harper and Brothers, 1941).

again for examples of similar ways of organizing studies in mathematics, social studies, and home economics.[3] Miss Rezny, as noted in an earlier chapter, mentioned how her children planned the display areas they wanted for their open house for parents and how they volunteered for work on the selected areas. This offers a further illustration of organized division of labor.[4]

Carrying on Parallel Studies or Projects

There are many occasions when a variety of operations may be proceeding simultaneously in a class. Sometimes it is difficult for all members of a group to agree on one project in which to invest considerable time. When this happened in her third grade class, Miss Van Alsten made it possible for three different groups to carry on studies of their choice. The teacher's diary describes how the parallel studies were managed.

March 16. Today, we had pamphlets about oil conservation to give out to our classes to take home to parents. Most of the material was too difficult for the children to read, so we looked at the diagrams and I told them a little about the purpose of the pamphlet. I was surprised to find that the children were very interested and asked to know more about oil. One girl said she didn't think the girls wanted to study oil. Someone else mentioned that we were still studying Indians.

A third child said he would like to study flowers next. I told them it was perfectly possible for us to study several topics and not devote all of our attention to just one thing. Since many had contributions to make in talking about oil, I suggested that those who wished to study oil might do so and those more interested in Indians or flowers might study them.

Each pupil was given a small strip of paper on which he wrote the topic for the group in which he wished to be. Boys and girls were quite evenly distributed in both the flower and the Indian groups but only boys were interested in the group about oil.

We discussed beforehand what each group might do to find information. Then each group chose a secretary to write down that which was important. After they had finished, each group chairman was to make a report to the class.

March 18. We had our second group meeting. Donald had told us of a neighbor who could get some comic books about oil for the class. He brought enough in for all. They were very helpful and explained to children much about oil. The group on oil used them thoroughly, getting ideas for making pictures of rock formation and deposits of oil in the

[3] See pages 269 ff.
[4] See page 166.

earth. Excellent reports were given by them. They used many other books too.

The group working on flowers is using our cracked aquarium as a terrarium and is planting bulbs and small plants in it. Someone in the group brought a flower book, and they took turns reading it. They might make a scrapbook.

The group studying Indians selected books to read. It was surprising that their interest in this particular group held so that only two wished to change.

Some teachers shrink from getting involved in such a variety of enterprises. They believe it would be difficult for a teacher to inform himself along several lines well enough to help pupils locate and interpret materials. They also fear that it may be harder to maintain group unity if all are not pursuing one "unit of work." They see a problem in having the small groups maintain communication with the large group. With regard to these points, it may be said that it is no harder for a teacher to keep up with varied topics than to keep a minority of unwilling group members wholeheartedly pursuing a purpose settled upon by the majority but not of interest to certain individuals. Also it may be said that there are ways of promoting group unity equally as good as the unit of work; for example, common experiences such as trips, parties, plays, service projects or any other opportunities for group planning illustrated in this volume.

It is not necessary that every experience of a small group be carried to the large group in the form of a report. If a small group has some good learnings from a project, the project is justified even if findings are not formally shared. On the other hand, the rest of the group may become so interested in what various members are learning that they will want to hear from them, just as members of a small group may become so excited about their adventures that they will seek an opportunity to share with others. Reports under such circumstances are likely to be much more alive than the typical kind.

Reporting to the large group was part of the plan which Miss Van Alsten's children made. The teacher's comment on the reports is as follows: "It seems as if they set higher standards of neatness and clearness of explanations and presenting materials when working on their own for group presentation than on class work for which they have little concern."

Mr. Beacon's venture into the guidance of a variety of enterprises at the same time is of interest for his careful description of the steps he took in leading up to this way of working, which was as new to him as to his junior high school social studies group. The teacher did much preparatory planning and came before the group with definite proposals.

November 19. Taking a tip from an adviser, I have decided for our next required project activity to try to get various small groups of children to plan group projects instead of continuing with the usual procedure wherein each youngster does an individual job. Today I suggested the field in which they were to work and offered a few ideas as examples. All other decisions I left for them. I suggested that, if they would like to experiment, we might organize several small groups and have each group work on one cooperative project. "Do you suppose such a procedure might be more profitable than working individually?" I asked.

Coming from children who, until this year, were completely unfamiliar with group work, their ready replies surprised me: "More ideas from more people should improve the result." "Two heads are better than one." "It's more fun working together." "It will help us to learn to work together, to cooperate."

Mr. Beacon's report also shows the difficulties encountered and the ways in which he worked with the students when they had organized for work on their various projects.

November 22. Today we talked over the project ideas the children had thought about. One group of six has decided to make a large mural depicting a Christmas scene. Another group of eight has decided to make a small-scale model of our village. Several other children grouped together in two's and three's to do smaller models, displays, and pictures. One can't help noticing how quickly children just automatically seek out the person who does each job best and are willing to follow that person's suggestions in that particular field.

I did little but call their attention to the numerous and varied jobs that would have to be carried out, the division of labor that would be necessary, and the maximum amount of time that could be allotted to the work. I found, too, that I must guide discussions carefully since children find it easy to change the topic, wander off the subject, and bubble over noisily when given a certain amount of classroom freedom that they are not accustomed to handling in a socially acceptable manner. Many get excited and talk among themselves even while others are addressing the group. This is just another one of those things they must learn through many trials and experiences.

November 25. The model village group is doing nicely. We got together after school one afternoon recently to make definite appointments in assigning work, responsibility, and authority. One boy who is a poor academic student but extremely practical and well liked was made "boss" of the job. We agreed upon a building inspector, a street commissioner, painters, scenery builders, parts assemblers, and others. There were a thousand questions that had to be decided upon: local landmarks that must be included and those that might be excluded; where to obtain paint and other materials; how much to get; what colors would be most effective; what is natural and lifelike (even to the material best suited to obtain a sag in telephone wires); how to keep waste to a minimum; which materials are best.

The decisions throughout were those of the children. We worked for a consensus through cheerful compromise, not for mere majority rule.

The reports from Miss Van Alsten's and Mr. Beacon's classrooms show organization for working in three small parallel groups on projects of interest chiefly to the small groups themselves. A running record of a session to plan the day's schedule in Mr. Dahl's classroom shows a still greater variety of small-group enterprises under way. Some projects, such as the newspaper, evidently were the joint responsibility of the entire group, but considerable division of labor was involved. Since the group was one that had been deliberately created to cross age groups and included children at fourth, fifth, and sixth grade levels, provision for small groups was even more necessary than in the typical elementary school classroom with one age group involved. The record is somewhat incomplete, for events happened so fast and the children knew so well what they were doing that there seemed to be little need to organize decisions formally and in detail. The record does, however, reflect the complex yet casual nature of the organization for working in this classroom.

Time: Opening of school day. Month of May.

boy (to observer). The teacher is not here yet. You may sit here or here.

Five children of different sizes go out, bring in typewriters and start typing. Teacher enters.

teacher. Better pass out paper for the diaries. We will write them later.

children. It is all passed out.

teacher. Let's see where we are. Carol, what more newspaper work needs to be done?

carol (the editor). More typing.

boy. We need more articles on the first page, assembly report and council report.

girl. We won't have an assembly report. Miss Lane was absent. Her aunt died. Things don't go the same when she isn't here.

boy. So we will need more news.

teacher. We might have an item on Miss Lane. Then what about this council report?

children. We need more typewriters.

CAROL. Don't type it. Get notes. Write it down. Bring it to me and I will read it. Then you can type it.

TEACHER. You see, it takes longer to type it.

CAROL. If we have page eight, we will have to have some things for it, but can we leave it just half?

TEACHER. Yes, or get more news.

CAROL. Then I will leave the eighth page open for news.

TEACHER. The thing to find out now is how many are involved in this newspaper work.

JOHNNY. I've got to go do arithmetic.

TEACHER. All right, you had better go. Now how much time will we need for this? We have till eleven-thirty.

CHILDREN. No, just till eleven.

TEACHER. All right, is that too much time?

CHILDREN. No.

TEACHER. What about the group working with Miss French (the art teacher)? Do you want to get together?

CHILDREN. Yes.

TEACHER. When?

GIRL. Eleven-thirty.

This is discussed. It is decided that twenty minutes will be long enough for this group.

TEACHER. Then at eleven-thirty there will be a committee meeting. You are sure this is long enough now?

GIRL. Yes.

TEACHER. Now you and Frank will be pretty busy. Who has film you want to work on?

CHILD. Frank.

TEACHER. Frank, you have quite a bit of typing. Can you farm some out? Won't you all help Frank to finish? Frank, they are waiting for you at the Camera Club.

CAROL. This paper is being held up. The mimeographers are waiting for it.

TEACHER. Now this afternoon will you be finished?

CAROL. The typing won't be done.

TEACHER. The rest will? Do you want to wait until twelve-fifty? Now here is a problem. There is only a half-hour here. I have a suggestion. Put in the committee meeting at two-thirty. Go to Miss French at three.

GIRL. I think we can get the typing done by then.

Play rehearsal on Henry Ford is put in at twelve-fifty and one-thirty.

TEACHER. Anything else to put in?

GIRL. Arithmetic.

GIRL. No, we have got the newspaper and play rehearsal.

GIRL. Junior arithmetic could be when the others are gone.

TEACHER. Doris, do you see a reason why not? I can. The type-writers will be free. Frank, the publisher, wants something to type.

From this record it can be seen that the children in Mr. Dahl's group were all helping with various aspects of the newspaper job and in addition were working in such groupings as junior and senior arithmetic, a camera club, a committee involving work with the art teacher, and a play cast. This, it must be remembered, was the program for one day only. It may be assumed that during an entire school year the small-group opportunities for these children would be varied indeed, but that they would be tied together by joint planning. For many of these activities there would be no formal reporting to the group as a whole.

Using a Small Group for a Special Service

A small group may perform a special service for the large group by doing some planning in advance for a particular occasion, bringing to the large group well-thought-out proposals and thus saving considerable time for the majority. In deciding when preplanning should be delegated to a small group, the teacher must take into account both the value of the experience to the members of the small group and the likelihood that the large group will have a satisfactory experience even though all have not participated in the earliest stages of the planning. A few examples may clarify this point.

Mrs. Nestor helped her sixth grade group to create a framework in which a small group could assume responsibility with the complete understanding of all. Together the children listed some physical activities they might carry on in February and March. Then the teacher suggested that they work in groups of three to plan what they would do each day.

Another teacher used a similar plan for play periods but had the suggestions brought to the large group for approval.

October 11. Last Tuesday we tried having the four team captains serve as a committee to suggest the games we should play during our game periods this week. Their suggestions met with approval in all instances except "Initial Tag" in which the class thought not enough children got turns. The same group is to function for one more week. We noticed that we had a longer game period if our decisions were made in advance and our necessary equipment was ready.

The planning of costumes for a play in Mrs. Bassett's second grade has been shown as a long and tedious process that could have been shortened considerably by small-group planning of what various characters would wear.[5] It is probable that participation could have

[5] See pages 162–163.

been more active and widespread in small groups than the teacher was able to make it as she tried to keep the attention of thirty-five seven-year-olds focused on planning eight types of costumes in turn. As was suggested earlier, preliminary plans made in small groups could have been brought to the large group for checking and for help.

On the other hand, when Miss Naughton had two girls select poems which they thought their classmates would like to hear read by a guest reader, it turned out that some of the children did not pay very good attention.[6] "Long after," Miss Naughton wrote in her diary, "I wondered why we didn't ask the children in the class to jot down the poems they wanted read." A small group could then have taken the suggestions and worked out a detailed program.

There are no handy rules to follow in deciding when a small group may plan effectively for the rest. The teacher must know the group's previous experiences and peculiar needs. Did the fourth grade children in Miss Sanborn's room have a better experience composing the Thanksgiving story as a group than they would have had, had they written individual stories or even worked in small groups on the chapters they planned to include?[7] Was Mrs. Upton's entire group of second grade children required to decide where to store some bottles for which they had temporary use?[8] Can time be saved for the large group by having children take turns serving on a committee to choose songs for a sing with the music teacher, and will there be wholehearted cooperation in singing the songs of someone else's choice as long as the opportunity for choosing is passed around the group? Teachers have found that small groups can be used effectively to prepare a demonstration of a science experiment, to draft a letter for the group, to plan a birthday surprise, to plan ways of sharing materials or of caring for some other problem situation to present to the large group for discussion. In each situation the teacher and pupils, or the teacher alone, must decide what things can well be cared for by small groups. An important principle to follow is to make sure that the group as a whole is involved at strategic points so that they will have the understanding and motivation to carry into action any plans demanding their cooperation.

Another way in which a small group may be of service to the rest is to gather information from sources where it seems undesirable or impossible to take the entire group. The diary of Mr. Allen, the science

[6] See page 158.
[7] See page 142.
[8] See pages 43–45.

teacher and supervisor referred to earlier in this chapter, offers a good illustration of this use of the small group.

> In a supervisory visit to Pelham School I noted that the eighth grade science class was in the process of planning a unit on weather. I suggested that they might like to see the weather bureau the Green School science class had made and were using. This aroused quite a bit of interest and several questions were asked about it. The teacher, sensing the situation, asked if they didn't want to select a committee to visit Green School and report back. This seemed a good idea, so the teacher turned the class over to their chairman and let them discuss how they were to select representatives and how many were to go.
>
> After some discussion they decided to send a boy and girl from each of the three eighth grade science classes and to select them by vote.
>
> The Pelham group had just finished a science museum of their own construction, so I suggested that perhaps the Green group would like to send representatives to see what Pelham could do. They accepted the idea and instructed the secretary to write a letter inviting the Green group.

Electing their own representatives probably helped the class groups as a whole to feel involved in this exchange of visits and to be more ready for the reports of their delegates.

Mrs. Thurber shows how she divided her third grade class into four parts to visit community facilities that could better accommodate a small group. Thus each group had a turn in serving as information-gatherers for the rest.

> After we had studied the different types of work in our community, we concentrated on four. The children had first or second choice as to what they wished to see—I made preliminary visits to get permission and to find out what they would show us so I could guide the reading for background.
>
> We borrowed a good selection of books on these various departments from the library. We made a chart on the bulletin board listing the four visits. Anyone who had a question he wished answered thumb-tacked it in the proper place. Each committee was responsible for getting the answers to these questions.
>
> There were about ten children in each group. While one group went on the trip with me, the rest of the class was in charge of a neighboring teacher.
>
> At each place visited, someone had been assigned to show us around and answer the questions. Everyone was very cooperative and helpful. The children were very interested and enthusiastic.
>
> When they returned to school they divided the work of making reports and drawing illustrations. The whole group answered the questions of the class. We made a book of the reports and pictures for the library

table. Each group also wrote letters of thanks to the people who had helped us.

Mrs. Thurber's story shows well how the large group was prepared to receive intelligently the report of a small group. All were involved in the preparation for each trip. The teacher's preliminary activities put her in a better position to help the children with this advance study and planning.

WAYS OF FORMING SMALL GROUPS

As may be seen from the foregoing examples, the way in which small groups are formed will depend partly upon the purpose for which they are to be used. Informal drifting into a group was a satisfactory method for the nature walk of Miss Lapham's children, and for work on the playhouse in Mrs. Austin's room. In the cases of Mr. Allen's, Miss Van Alsten's, and Mr. Beacon's groups, pupils apparently grouped themselves on the basis of interest in a topic of study. Election by the group was also illustrated in the previous section.

All these methods of group formation are based upon pupil choice. Small groups may also be made up on the basis of teacher selection. Teachers sometimes select on the basis of an individual's needing an experience or being able to make a special contribution to the large group.

When Miss Brainard chose a committee to help her arrange flowers and found that the rest of her group did not manage themselves very well, she decided that she should first have had the whole group understand and help plan for the job to be done by a smaller group. Had this precaution been taken, it would probably have mattered little that the teacher selected the committee herself.

Sometimes teachers use duly elected class officers as committees for special jobs. For example, Miss Naughton had the class officers eat lunch with her in their classroom one noon to plan a farewell party for a girl who was moving away rather unexpectedly. As is shown later in this chapter, Mrs. Charles had work groups chosen by lot.[9]

Whenever choice of a small group is left to the pupils, such factors enter in as friendship or attraction or interest in the purpose of the group. Individuals usually choose persons or topics that will extend or broaden them in some way. The teacher who wishes to encourage

[9] See page 397.

pupils to participate actively in their own education will seek all promising means of giving pupils a choice of groups in which to work.

Grouping by Interest in a Topic or Problem

At present, by far the most common means of forming small groups is for the large group to outline the area under consideration, setting up subjects to be investigated, and then divide into groups on the basis of interest in a topic. This was the method employed by Mr. Rufus and Miss Fielding in their high school mathematics classes.[10]

It will be recalled that Miss Evans had her group take plenty of time to explore together not only the groups that might be set up but the activities each group might engage in, so that when choices were made they could be much more intelligent.[11] This important step is often cut short by groups eager to get into motion. Sometimes individuals find later that their choices have been ill considered, and they press for changes that interrupt group progress.

Another example of grouping by interest in a topic or problem is shown where children in Miss Merlin's room were brought together by common interest in various poems which they were preparing to present to the large group in novel ways.[12] Pupils may also choose membership on standing committees set up to care for the business of the large group.

Grouping by Interest in People

Some teachers prefer to control the formation of groups because they believe that children of like intelligence should work together (or that they should not) or because they wish to separate certain friendship pairs or cliques. More and more teachers, however, are becoming confident that groups containing people who want to be together make a setting for effective work. Actually such choices are made in terms of persons whom the pupil wants to be associated with for a particular purpose. Still, the resulting groups differ from those made up of people choosing the same topic by secret ballot or by some other method which rules out personal factors in choosing a group. Various sociometric devices for obtaining such groups have been tried

[10] See pages 85–91.
[11] See pages 290–292.
[12] See pages 157–158.

with success.[13] If children are restricting their choices of work partners or do not seem to be choosing wisely in other respects, such problems can be opened for impersonal group consideration.

Many teachers use informal techniques to secure some of the advantages of careful sociometric studies. They may select or have the
class elect a leader or chairman of a group and suggest that this individual choose the other members of his committee. Or one individual
may be chosen by the teacher or the group. This individual is to
choose another member of the group, the second to choose a third, and
so on, until the group is filled.

Other opportunities for children to choose their own work com-
panions come when teachers allow certain kinds of freedom in the
classroom. Mrs. Wardell shows how she encourages students in her
eighth grade mathematics class to work together in congenial groups.

> *December 6.* Eighth grade math still isn't what it should be, but
> there is definite improvement because of some of the planning we did as
> a class early in the term. Dividing into smaller groups has made for a
> greater personal interest and concern on the part of individuals. Group-
> ing desks to form large tables has made it possible to help one another.

Miss Innes is convinced that her fifth and sixth grade children do
not come to her with the same readiness for social interaction and that
it is her responsibility to make sure each child is free to choose a
group of the size in which he is most comfortable and happy. The
teacher describes the way in which she follows this principle as the
children work together on their social studies problems and activities.

> In the fall I usually begin group work by having each child choose a
> partner with whom he would like to work. This partnership plan is
> tried many times, with the children selecting different workers each
> time, if they wish. As they feel success in planning and sharing to-
> gether, larger groups are encouraged. It is suggested that committees
> of four try working together. Several children are eager to try this,
> because they have discovered others that have the same interests and
> abilities as theirs. Gradually, three or four members work on problems
> together. Finally, panel groups involving five to seven children wish
> to report together. Others still prefer to work on smaller committees.
> Different sized groups have contributed in almost every summary ac-
> tivity. Often a child chooses to participate in both a small and a large
> group.

[13] See Ruth Cunningham, *Understanding Group Behavior of Boys and Girls*
(New York, Bureau of Publications, Teachers College, Columbia University, 1950),
Chapter V; *How to Construct a Sociogram* (New York, Bureau of Publications,
Teachers College, Columbia University, 1947); *Ways of Studying Children* (in
press).

As the year progresses, it becomes apparent that some groups have changed from being just boys' or girls' groups to being mixed groups. It surely is interesting to watch individuals find their places in the room society, and also satisfying to realize that progress has been made in their adjusting to group living, because children in the same classroom live in quite different social climates.

Another upper grade teacher has approached the problem of small friendship groups as an aid to more effective classroom work by having the children divide into five groups on the basis of people with whom they wish to spend an entire day at a special table in the back of the room. On Monday the first group works together at the table on all their individual and small-group jobs for the day, with the teacher giving them whatever supervision she can manage. On each succeeding day of the week a new group works together around the table. This plan would seem to be particularly effective in classrooms where fixed furniture makes group work somewhat difficult.

GUIDING WORK IN SMALL GROUPS

Skill to Be Expected

How well can children manage themselves in small groups? What quality of group thinking can we expect? Let us examine two records of planning in a small group for evidence on this point. The first discussion was engaged in by three children, Mary, Norma, and Willis, who had served as secretaries earlier in the day when Miss McNulty's fifth grade class was planning how to study the solar system.[14] The children had not had such a small group experience before and were given no preparation for it by the teacher. They were coming together at this time because the observer had suggested that they meet to pool their records and to organize the proposals of the group. The observer, as the only adult present, made sure that the children understood what their job was and then sat back and took the record. No leader was appointed, but it was apparent that Mary had the best notes.

Record	Analysis
MARY. Norma, how many do you have?	Mary leads off, shows she understands they are to pool their records.
NORMA. Seven.	
WILLIS. I have a couple.	
MARY. I just jotted down some things.	

[14] See page 82.

Record	*Analysis*
NORMA. Which did you consider the most important, booklets or murals?	Norma takes over leadership. Shows she has in mind that this committee shall make decisions for the larger group. This sets the tone for most of the meeting.
MARY. I think a big picture.	
WILLIS. They are more interesting.	
MARY. I think we should do like the visitor said, go out on the playground to arrange ourselves to show relative distances of planets from the sun, then we could get a mural.	Leadership passes around to each of the three in turn.
NORMA. We could have a table with booklets on that, then do like the visitor said.	
WILLIS. I was thinking before lunch we could have a play downstairs. Not for the youngest ones.	Willis shows that he has done some preparatory thinking.
NORMA. I think it is a good idea to have paragraphs on different planets.	
WILLIS. Bob had a good suggestion about booklets.	Willis shows that he is trying to consider the group's suggestions.
MARY. Do you think the group should get together and have one big one and then small ones or do both?	
WILLIS. We get more out of it if we do our own.	Willis maintains his ideas with reasonable firmness.
MARY. In spare time we could go up to the tables and look at others for ideas.	
NORMA. Which should we decide, big booklet or small?	Norma presses for a decision.
WILLIS. That is for the room to decide.	Willis has better understanding of this committee's function. Norma shows misunderstanding.
NORMA. That is what we are for.	
MARY. I think we could do both.	
WILLIS. I think we should let the room decide.	Willis stands for what he believes.
NORMA. We could learn a lot from science books. I think it would be nice to put the booklets out on the bulletin board.	
At this point Norma starts taking notes.	

Record	*Analysis*

Record

WILLIS. We could do like last year with our dog book. Put it in the library for people to read.

MARY. Wasn't it Willis who suggested that we write to a scientist?

WILLIS. No, that was Tom.

MARY. That was a good suggestion. I think for a big book everybody should contribute something.

WILLIS. We could make small booklets first, then everybody contribute to a big one.

MARY. Have everyone write a paragraph about the planets and stars?

WILLIS. Good.

MARY. I wrote one last night for the newspaper—what we are doing in science—but it would be nice if we all did.

NORMA. We could have nine people write paragraphs for the exhibit.

MARY. It is hard to choose nine people.

NORMA. Then there is the puppet show.

MARY. Then Bob suggested about cameras. Nice if somebody would bring cameras and take pictures.

MARY. Can we take pictures of stars at night?

WILLIS. I don't know.

MARY. If we could get movies of scientists, we could show them to the whole school.

WILLIS. If it costs too much to rent one, I could get one.

MARY. We could show it for the people upstairs, anyway. I don't know about downstairs.

MARY. I don't know if we should have all this.

WILLIS. How about instead of making a booklet, make a book?

Analysis

Willis wants credit to go where it is due.

Mary is generous with praise.

Willis wants a decision to please most people.

Norma changes the course of the discussion.

Discussion wanders a little.

Record	*Analysis*
NORMA. Here's what I have down. (She reads.)	Norma summarizes.
MARY. I don't know how to get movies to show; they cost money.	Mary seems to ignore Norma's attempt to clinch some points.
NORMA. And Frank's idea. Should we have that or the visitor's?	
MARY. Let us get the booklet settled. Shall we have large or small or both?	Mary sees need to make one decision at a time.
NORMA. Both.	
MARY. I think so. We can hang them, have them around the room for a while.	
NORMA. I think Frank's idea would be hard.	Norma turns discussion to new point.
WILLIS. It would take someone steady to hold the sun still.	
MARY. I think it is easier to take the visitor's idea.	
MARY. What about the mural? We need to study that.	Mary turns discussion before decision is made.
NORMA. What would we put in the mural? Would we include the whole solar system? We could show where the asteroids are. Last year our teacher told us about them, but I couldn't picture where they were. This year I know.	
MARY. Let us get settled on some of these things instead of scrapping around. Are we going to have a mural?	Mary senses what is wrong with discussion.
MARY. That is settled. Now, large or small booklets?	Apparently this has not been settled to anyone's satisfaction.
WILLIS. Why don't we let the room decide?	
NORMA. Half will want big; half will want small. I think it will be nice to have both.	
WILLIS. Why not let those that want to?	Willis wants room for individual choice.
NORMA. I think a committee of five would be good.	All seem in a mood now for making decisions.
MARY. Then it is settled. We will get things from the science book for	

Record   *Analysis*

our booklets. How many should
we have on the mural committee?

NORMA. Three.

WILLIS. How about putting down   It is evident that the committee
three or four?   will go back to the room with some
                                   definite recommendations.

MARY. We will have a big booklet
in the hall.

NORMA. Little ones, too.

MARY. I don't think so; in some   For an inexperienced group,
things we would have the same   these youngsters were direct and ·
things as in the big one.   most businesslike.

WILLIS. We could put a couple of
little ones for decoration.

NORMA. Since we decided on a
big one, we should decide how many
on that committee.

WILLIS. We should write to the
scientist soon so we could have an
answer within a month or so.

MARY. Ask about three.   Mary gets back to Norma's ques-

NORMA. Should each make his   tion.
own except the people doing the
big one?

WILLIS. We shouldn't stop the   Willis is still pulling for indi-
people on the big one if they wanted vidual rights.
to make a small one.

NORMA. I want to know how
many on the committee.

WILLIS. About four.

NORMA. That is a nice number.
It is all settled about the big book.
I think we should have pictures of
planets and stars to put in our book.
Bob has a book on the stars.

MARY. We wouldn't want to cut
it up.

The observer closed the meeting
at this point.

A copy of Norma's record shows the decisions she felt the committee had made to take back to the class:

Big booklet and little booklet
Things for exhibit:
1. Mural—three or four   2. Cameras
3. Visitor's idea
Write to scientists to ask them

Although these children wandered back and forth somewhat from one part of the problem to another, they showed a fair amount of skill by coming out with such a definite plan in twenty-five minutes' time. Some of the skills they showed were: (1) Passing leadership back and forth. (2) Making use of notes on the class discussion. (3) Standing by an idea until it had been given consideration. (4) Summarizing occasionally when needed. (5) Making one decision at a time. (6) Getting definite suggestions to take back to the class. The children's experience in planning in their classroom no doubt had taught them some of these skills.

A second record shows a committee of three of Mrs. Charles' sixth grade children, Billy, Robert, and Mary Lou, with the job of discovering how long the world's supply of coal will last.

On the front chalkboard was a breakdown of one part of the day's plan, "Assigning individual topics and planning the work for each":

1. Draw topics
2. Who is my partner?
3. Partners get together
4. Discuss each person's job
5. Find books
6. Get materials
7. Read for information
8. Make notes
9. Select activity

The following record will show how well these children, who had had considerable experience working in small groups, were able to manage themselves. The reader may wish to note signs that the children were not clear as to exactly what was to be accomplished that day, even though the directions written on the board seem explicit enough.

MARY LOU. Who wants to start first?

BILLY. You.

MARY LOU. Well, I have a book that has something in the appendix. Do you have anything?

BILLY. What, on this?

ROBERT. Are we supposed to get together today, or what?

BILLY. On books and materials.

MARY LOU. She's got it on the board.

BILLY. I will draw some pictures.

ROBERT. It says in *Young America* we have merely scraped the earth. There are only two or three subjects on this.

BILLY. All the better. What are you going to do, write or what?

MARY LOU. You can do some charts and pictures and we will do reading and writing.

BILLY. O.K.

MARY LOU. I don't know if we are supposed to get some books. See if you can get two or three topics out of this if we cover the world.

ROBERT. I'll take England.

BILLY. I'll take the United States.

MARY LOU. You take all of Europe, Robert, and I'll take Asia.

ROBERT. When we get started reading we will find out where it is.

MARY LOU. What else shall we do, Billy? Ask Mrs. Charles if we should find books today. I'd like to get my book.

Mary Lou leaves with book and goes to table in the back of the room.

BILLY. We have got to find out what we are going to tell the class.

MARY LOU (coming back with another book). Look, it says coal and lignite.

BILLY. What is lignite?

ROBERT. Let's just take coal. Has that book got an encyclopedia or index?

MARY LOU. Find "coal." Here is a reference to a table in the appendix. They have a table, "Coal Reserves in the World."

BILLY. There's Europe's total.

MARY LOU. There is the total in the world. It is metric tons. You go find some books, Robert.

ROBERT. On coal in the United States? No, I'll find things on my own topic on Europe.

Robert goes to the books on the window sill.

MARY LOU. You're going to take the United States? Here is North America and South America.

BILLY. No, give me North America, some small one. I'll get a book.

MARY LOU (to herself). Now I'll take Asia. (Starts making notes in ink in notebook.) Billy has the United States, Robert has Europe, and I have Asia.

At this point the teacher joins the group.

TEACHER. I haven't heard anything about you. What is your problem? How did you divide it?

Mary Lou explains and shows figures on what is in different countries.

TEACHER. Are those the only things in your topic that the class should know at the end of your study? Do you want me to ask it in a different way? Do you feel you will have answered your question for your classmates if you do this?

Mary Lou says "Yes."

TEACHER (looking at date of coal-reserve table). Oh, yes, 1937.

Billy and Robert are searching for books. Teacher leaves.

MARY LOU. You are going to have to do some reading at home, Robert.

ROBERT. What do you mean? By ourselves? Oh, I guess so. Can we take these books home?

MARY LOU. I guess so. I have another book in my desk but it doesn't have an appendix. This book is 1937. (Turns to new page in notebook and starts taking notes.)

BILLY (coming in with book). There's a whole set like this . . .

Here is an example of amiable sharing among three children apparently grouped by lot. They showed some skill in getting down to work and were independent in using references. While they were at work, ten or a dozen other groups were also involved in similar activity, going freely out into the corridor where reference books were located for the convenience of three classes who had to share them.

It is obvious that such habits of independent and purposeful work were not built in a day. Descriptions of ways in which teachers at different grade levels work toward such efficient small-group operations may help to show the process of developing skill in self-direction in small groups.

Learning from Mistakes

Sometimes the mistakes teachers make present valuable lessons for themselves and others. One of Miss Keene's early attempts at small-group work with her second grade children was anything but successful. She divided her children into committees to work on a newspaper to be sent to children their ages in another land. Little was accomplished. There was considerable disorder. In some groups the chairman did all the work while the rest of the group sat idly by. In other groups no child seemed to know what to do.

When the teacher and an observer discussed the period afterward, they agreed that these were the sources of difficulty:

1. The children were not used to working in small groups and needed more guidance than the teacher was able to give with so many groups meeting at the same time.

2. The groups were not clear as to what their jobs were. Some groups actually had little to do, for they were short on contributions to evaluate.

3. The chairmen were not skillful in giving all group members opportunities to be active participants. Some chairmen read all the material aloud themselves, made comments on it, and decided whether or not it was to be used.

4. The children did not seem to know how to judge what should be included in the paper.

The teacher had thought that the following plans, which had been developed with the children and which were before them on the chalkboard, would ensure effective small-group work. However, such plans, while necessary, could not carry the full burden of guidance of small-group work in the case of inexperienced young children.

Society Committee

We need stories about parties.

News Committee

We want:
News that is important.
News that is well written.
News that is interesting.

Art Committee

We will decide:
What pictures are needed.
What pictures are good enough.
What improvements are needed.
Where to put them in the paper.

Poetry Committee

We want to find out:
If it is good.
If it is interesting.

Story Committee

We want stories that are exciting.
True stories.
Make-believe stories.

Miss Keene did not stop her study of cooperative planning procedures. Two years later, as teacher of first grade children, she could make the following report showing how she profited from early mistakes.

Cooperative Planning of Small Groups in First Grade

This year I attempted to study the planning of smaller groups. Since the seats in our room are not easily moved, the planning group usually met around a circular table at which six or eight children could be seated comfortably. The committee was chosen by the whole group. When practical, the members of the group were chosen with regard to recognized special abilities, particularly at the beginning. (As the children grow in ability to work together, these groups should include children who need development in the type of work which is being undertaken.)

Examples of planning that was done in small groups were:
    a. Selecting games suitable to use in a physical education demonstration.
    b. Deciding on games and refreshments for parties.
    c. Thinking of ways to arrange the furniture in the room.
    d. Making choices of pictures to be used in room decoration.

    e. Planning a party for mothers and little children.

    f. Setting up standards of behavior for games and for auditorium programs.

    g. Finding ways to make most effective use of work time.

    h. Discussing ways and means of taking trips and excursions.

Plans made in small groups were reported to the group as a whole for evaluation, acceptance, or rejection. Miss Keene includes an example of planning done by a small group.

During the year the children had asked several times if they might bring their little brothers or sisters to a room party. We decided to give a program that very small children would enjoy and ask the mothers to come and bring the smaller children. Committees were formed to plan the program, the refreshments, and the table decorations. The final problem which presented itself was how to get the cafeteria tables ready for sixty people after one o'clock, while we were giving the program. A group of four was chosen to plan this. Emily was elected chairman, and after preliminary plans were made, the four children enlisted the aid of the room mother and three fifth grade girls. The older girls were chosen by their teacher because of efficiency. The whole committee met together around the table in our room. Emily opened the meeting by stating the problem.

EMILY (Grade 1, who had been very capable but very timid at first of year). We are having ice cream, cookies, and candy to eat at our party. We have decorated place mats and plates and napkins. We want you to help us set the tables.

JUDIANNE (Grade 1). There will be Easter baskets to fill for the children.

DICKIE (Grade 1, a good thinker). We will need to set the tables ourselves so that we can sit by our own mothers and use the things we made.

TEACHER. The children can stay at their places until you call their names and get the mothers' place cards located.

MARILYN (Grade 5). What time do you want us to come?

LENNY (Grade 1). When Mr. Allison (the custodian) can get the tables ready after lunch.

ELAINE (Grade 5). Then what do you want us to do?

DICKIE (Grade 1). Help Mrs. Spence put the food out.

EMILY (Grade 1). We know how we want it. We want the ice cream in the middle of the plate.

JUDIANNE (Grade 1). Put the little candies in the Easter baskets.

TEACHER. Where can the mothers put their wraps?

ELAINE (Grade 5). Why can't they lay them across a table you aren't using? We can show them where to lay them.

MRS. SPENCE (room mother). That will be the best way.

TEACHER. What will be the easiest way to seat the mothers? It would take a long time for them to find their names.

DICKIE (Grade 1). We know where we put our things. Could we go in first? They could find us.

LENNY. They'd better stay in the auditorium until we get ready.

DICKIE. I can tell them to stay there till we call them.

MRS. SPENCE. I want to talk to them when the party is over. The children can go down and get their wraps while I do that.

The teacher explains that she may not have recorded accurately the wording of these plans as given by the children. The fact that this meeting with the room mother and the older children had been carefully planned caused the children to state their wishes more clearly than in the earlier planning session.

Later the group decided on a picnic to be held near the close of school. A small group was chosen, by vote, to make plans and submit them to the class. This committee met in the classroom with the teacher while the rest of the group worked independently on various tasks. Beverly was elected chairman; the teacher opened the discussion.

TEACHER. What do you need to decide?

BEVERLY. A time and place for the picnic.

ROBERT. We want to get a day before the last week of school, because if it rained we couldn't go. Pick a day when we're not so busy.

BOBBY. We could go next week. I think it would be better to go in the afternoon.

CAROL. We do most of our important work in the morning.

JIMMY. Our mothers would have to take us in cars.

ROBERT. I would like to go to Rockhill Road Park. We could walk. I like to play on the slides and swings.

TEACHER. Beverly, you could see if they want to go to Rockhill Road Park.

BEVERLY. How many do?

All voted "Yes."

ROBERT. We could bring our package lunches and eat before we played.

CAROL. It might rain. We wouldn't want to go on a rainy day.

JIMMY. Eat in our room if it rained.

TEACHER. Then you could go on the first good day and play in the afternoon.

BOBBY. It might be full.

JIMMY. We must find out when Miss Youtz's room is going and go on a different day.

CAROL. I will ask them.

TEACHER. Whenever you go on a trip you must have a signed note from your parents saying that you may go.

BOBBY. We could write the notes now and they could sign them.

TEACHER. What do you want to report to the children to see if they agree?

BEVERLY. We want to bring package lunches and eat at Rockhill Road Park and play in the afternoon.

ROBERT. We want to do it next week when nobody else is going.

Miss Keene found that in cooperative planning of small groups of first grade children, she should consider several points.

1. Experience in planning as a whole group makes the small group more efficient.
2. The planning period needs to be short.
3. Much guidance by the teacher is needed at the beginning and in a lesser degree teacher guidance is needed all the way.
4. Leadership is developed gradually.
5. Some children will contribute ideas more readily in a small group than in a class meeting.
6. The teacher needs to guard against waste of time by the children, also too much dictation on her part.

Apparently, Miss Keene had learned also that it was easier to induct young children into small-group planning if she met with one committee at a time. If more young children had such carefully guided experiences in working in small groups, the task of upper grade and high school teachers in improving skills of cooperative work would be made much easier.

Other Techniques Used by Primary Teachers

Miss Youtz, who was teaching another first grade in Miss Keene's school, also made use of small groups for various planning jobs, such as composing a letter to a child with the measles. An interesting feature of her planning with this particular group was breaking the job into parts to be dealt with at different times. The group composed the letter in one sitting. Later that morning they reassembled to plan how they would report to the rest of the group.

In Miss Martin's first and second grade room a number of small committees may be at work simultaneously, but the teacher calls each committee in turn to sit in a circle with her to discuss their progress and check on their plans for proceeding.

Two entries in Miss Franklin's diary show the relation of careful planning done in the large group to successful small-group work. It may be noted that the group planned to secure a more experienced individual to help each small group. The first account deals with the making of Christmas gifts.

December 1. Before we left for the Thanksgiving holidays, we decided to make Christmas presents for mother, father, and brother or sister. We met on Monday morning to discuss what we could make out of the materials we had gathered for gifts. We planned to make simple and useful gifts that wouldn't take too long to make. We agreed to work in small groups according to interests. We decided it was necessary to discuss thoroughly the steps in making each gift before starting to work. We finally decided to make place mats, paper files, telephone or marketing pads, and stuffed cotton animals. We thought it best to start that very afternoon on the paper gifts because of the time element.

I explained that it would be difficult for me to give every child individual help. Fred and Elaine suggested that I ask some of Mrs. N.'s and Mrs. B.'s girls to help us. After much discussion it was decided to ask Mrs. N. and Mrs. B. to send us two girls for the afternoon.

This was one of the most pleasant afternoons of the year. We divided ourselves into groups of six in small circles for sewing and at desks for pasting. The older girls each had a group, and it was evident by their faces the pleasure they were getting in helping the first graders. I smiled many times when overhearing conversations carried on by my children with the older girls. The children were so absorbed in their work that it was time for us to clean up to go home before they realized it.

The second account shows how four teams made gingerbread men.

December 18. This was the day we had all looked forward to. From the day we had decided to make gingerbread men we had been bringing in ingredients and studying the recipe. By now every child knew the recipe backward and forward. We had planned to make four batches of cookies, so we divided ourselves into four groups. Each group was stationed in different parts of the room.

We had borrowed our cooking utensils from Mrs. N.'s class. We also made arrangements to bake our cookies in their oven. Three girls from this class came down to help us. This meant that each group had a leader. The leaders watched to make sure the children mixed the ingredients properly.

The hardest part was rolling out the dough and cutting out the cookies. This was because we had only one gingerbread-man cutter and one large rolling pin and board. Since we couldn't all go to the cooking room, two children from each group were chosen to go watch the cookies bake.

As each group completed preparations for their cookies to bake, their leader took them to the playground to play. The children who went up to watch the cookies bake came back thrilled and anxious to go again. Bernard and Carl, who were the only two who were playful and messy during the play period, helped me wrap the gingerbread men in wax paper and store them in a big brown box until the party on Monday.

Although there was a lot of hard work for everybody, the results were more than gratifying. Most of these children do not have the facilities or anyone to help them at home to make cookies. Just seeing the looks on their faces when the finished cookies came back to the room made me know it was a worth-while experience.

Miss Franklin's reports contain her own evaluation. Both seem to add weight to the generalization that careful planning in advance of small-group work pays dividends.

Techniques Used by Upper-Grade Teachers

When Mr. Owen's sixth grade was planning small-group work on various phases of the life of early man, they carefully scheduled their time so that they could meet the deadline they set for themselves.

We decided on a date for the culmination of the work of all so that we might gather all presentations together and show the results of our work at a class party to which the parents would be invited. It was decided that we ought to have all things done a week before. Our secretary made such an entry (in red ink—her idea) in our date book. The committees discussed the parts of their various chosen work and the time that should be spent on the phases of it. They became aware as time went on that one lazy one slowed up the work of the committee. Responsibility was expected from everyone for his part.

No doubt the class date book helped all the groups to budget their time more efficiently.

Miss Evans, whose careful preplanning for a unit on "Things We Do After School" was described in an earlier chapter, has furnished a detailed description of her planning with her fourth and fifth grade children for their small-group work.[15] The teacher's report shows that scheduling of meeting times was given careful consideration.

We started to work in groups under close supervision. We chose leaders and recorders in each of our groups, and set up many sets of standards to help us work together. This is an example of some of the standards we worked out:

Things to Remember in Our Group Work

1. Plan your activities carefully.
2. Choose books you can read.
3. Activities group must whisper.
4. Pay close attention in our group meetings.
5. Be sure that your story is interesting and not too long.
6. Scan your new story for words you do not know and get help.

[15] See pages 290–292.

Several procedures were tried before we found a schedule which we considered satisfactory. We found that we worked best when we could have active work after we had worked quietly for a while. We then tried to budget our time so that we could have a balanced day.

Our revolving schedule was an outcome of much group planning. We decided to keep our noisy activities until hobby hour, or during gym periods, and to divide our two hours which we used for our unit each day into three kinds of activity. Two groups would work on activities, two groups would have work periods, and two groups would be having group meetings.

For example, while groups on science and stories were having their work period, at which time they read and recorded, or worked out a special problem with someone, the groups on chores and gardening were working on activities which were active but not noisy. The group on games would work at the back of the room on problems that they would discuss together, while the pets group would work with me. We called this supervised discussion period our group meeting. After fifteen minutes the pets group and games group would exchange, and I'd supervise the games group while the pets group finished their meeting unsupervised. This gave the activities and work period groups a half-hour for their work.

We followed much this schedule in our group meetings:

1. Check reading from day before.
2. Plan reading for next day.
3. Plan activities.
4. Plan activities to be used for culminating activity.

We shifted each half-hour so that each group had done all three things during the period of the day allotted for group work.

Schedule	First Half-hour	Second Half-hour	Third Half-hour
Group Meeting	1 and 2	3 and 4	5 and 6
Work Period	5 and 6	1 and 2	3 and 4
Activities	3 and 4	5 and 6	1 and 2

Miss Evans' planning with her group for an efficient organization for small-group work must have helped them overcome some of the difficulties associated with such work in crowded classrooms, chiefly those of noise and unavailability of materials. The plans also enabled the teacher to give more guidance to various groups as the pupils were learning techniques of working independently in small groups.

Guiding Small-Group Planning in an Inter-Age Group

When Miss Thomas' group of twenty physically handicapped children, ranging from second through eighth grade, agreed to help with milk distribution, the oldest group first shouldered responsibility for it.[16] Miss Thomas was not content to leave the project in the hands of the oldest group for long, however. In December she reported:

> Although, at the outset, my oldest group had complete charge of the project, each month another group is invited to help us. The new group works as a committee and takes over one of the responsibilities of the original group. Last week the second grade children joined us as a sorting committee (sorting dimes, nickels, pennies). The entire class has been incorporated in the plan, and the work is being done by four good functioning committees (collection, distribution, checking, money). In my particular case, it proved beneficial to start with one group and then gradually spread out until the entire class had been absorbed into the plan. The original group devotes its time to checking and totaling and verifying the money, which in itself is a very important responsibility.

Techniques Used by Secondary Teachers

When students at the secondary school level have not had their induction into effective group work in elementary school, the teacher must be prepared to give them careful guidance in their first experiences with this way of working.

Mr. Eliason, a student teacher in an eighth grade social studies–English core class, worked out for his students a committee-work schedule plan which was designed to overcome problems of working in a crowded classroom. His schedule, to be rotated, was as follows:

Committee A—Organization meeting and preliminary discussion of topic

Committee B—Work in school library for general and preliminary research on topic to be ready for discussion when it was their time to have an organization meeting

Committee C—Use the classroom library for preliminary research

Committee D—Concentrate on material in class textbook, taking notes

Committee E—Serve as a service committee for the day, preparing bulletin board material, distributing supplies when needed, acting as assistants to the teacher

Mr. Eliason made this plan for his own security in trying ways of working that were new both to the students and to himself. He wanted the students' first experience with small-group work to go as smoothly as possible. Like many well-laid plans, especially those made by one

[16] See pages 264–265.

person for a number of others, many things did not work out as anticipated. As this young teacher reports:

> The committee meeting was disrupted by the inability of some of its members to get serious. Students who were supposed to be using the classroom library materials (and we had enough interesting ones) were reading other things. The textbook assignment was undergoing similar abuse. My service committee worked eagerly but were constant interrupters and finished early.

When asked how they liked the new way of working in contrast to the usual textbook lesson, the class replied that they favored small-group work as a whole but gave these criticisms, which Mr. Eliason considered valid.

1. You should be allowed to work on the topic you select. (The teacher had reclassified ten topics outlined by the class into five groupings and had arbitrarily assigned students to groups in order to separate some "buddies.")
2. You should have more time to discuss topics (most of us weren't sure of what we were to do and we got bored).
3. We should have more than one group meet at a time.
4. The teacher should help us out with ideas (some of us didn't get as good suggestions from him as others did).
5. The textbook didn't have enough or as much interesting information as did other books we used.
6. We should have more projects.
7. We should get more facts.
8. Some committees didn't organize their reports well.
9. No one should read reports; it's boring.
10. We should have more notes and outlines on the blackboard.
11. We shouldn't be left with nothing to do.
12. We shouldn't have factual tests.
13. How can I know the other person's topics when I've been working on mine?

One of the chief drawbacks to the schedule, as seen by the teacher in looking back over the experience, was that he had groups doing research before they knew their topics or questions. Even the teacher's explanation to the students that general reading gives information or ideas for topics did not suffice to stimulate necessary curiosity.

Mr. Eliason took several positive steps to improve the situation as the groups worked along. For one thing he had Committee A hold its organization session before the whole class as a sample meeting to be evaluated. The teacher reports the following review and criticism from the students.

1. The chairman is in charge of the group.
2. He recognizes the speaker.
3. One person speaks at a time.
4. The group sticks to the topic of discussion.
5. All persons participate and contribute to the discussion.
6. The group should reach a decision.
7. The chairman should report on the progress of the group and summarize the work accomplished.
8. In addition, each member of the group should know his specific task, know how to look for information and share it, and know how to work and cooperate with the group.

This listing shows points in group process that may seem rather obvious to those with more experience but that were thought worthy of comment by these students who were having a first try.

During the first week the teacher also used the oral English period for special progress reports and discussion of problems by the committee chairmen and the class.

Mr. Eliason discovered that setting aside a period early in the course of the students' work for the showing of individual projects inspired others to produce some very creative results.

To meet the problem of pupils finished with their written reports and individual projects, the teacher assigned the making of a group scrapbook. This helped to keep committees occupied but also created the need for additional group meetings and increased the problem of noise in a small classroom. As the scrapbooks and individual projects began to be displayed, many pupils became occupied in examining the work of others. When the time came for hearing final reports, the problem of idleness was past. It should be noted that this problem of "nothing to do when one has finished research and is waiting to report" occurs chiefly in a classroom where the group is limited to one academic subject and a given block of time.

Mr. Eliason also helped his class to improve their reports after the first committee went through a boring routine of reading reports in turn from their group scrapbook. Before a second committee group reported, time was taken to evaluate the first report. Criticisms written by the class were summarized and read to the group on the day following the report of the second committee group. The teacher also prepared an evaluation chart for individuals to use in evaluating reports. The students were asked to evaluate the first two reports from memory. The discussion which followed helped future groups to avoid some mistakes.

The teacher saw as a very important element in some of his lack of success his initial mistake of taking a period of American history and not presenting it in problem form which would tie it to present-day realities of the students. As Mr. Eliason puts it:

> The unit questions became separate topics with integration occurring only through the efforts of the teacher and gifted students. If it was facts I wanted, similar subject matter could have been covered in two weeks with all the children gaining all the facts at the same time and with less danger of losing class control.

Mr. Eliason is probably overestimating the efficiency of textbook teaching, but he still makes a good point. He did see and value other outcomes, however. He states the good experiences of the students as:

1. Attempts to form their own problems, to think for themselves about the questions we did raise.
2. Experience in committee discussion, group work.
3. Chances to do creative, concrete activities on subjects that are usually dry, dull, or dead.
4. Opportunity to lead as well as work with others; we had some excellent leaders.
5. A chance to use varied materials, from pictures to phonographs, from a comic book classic to college texts, from pencil to water colors.
6. Attention to individuals that can never be obtained under typical recitation conditions.
7. A liking for this way of working. (I omit certain students who took advantage of a not-too-experienced teacher.)

Mr. Eliason's difficulties may be traced partly to his rather inflexible preplan. As he grows in experience and feels more comfortable in planning *with* students, he may find it still more possible to correct mistakes as he proceeds.

Mr. Painter, a more experienced teacher, describes how he helped certain individuals as well as his entire sophomore core class to learn the kind of leadership and responsibility needed for small-group work.

> By suggestions from the class several new areas for study were listed on the board, and through a vote the next area for study was selected. Once the area was selected, the problem of presentation of the material seemed paramount, for the class felt that previous presentations were not adequate nor had they involved the whole group. Frequently individual interests had not been stimulated.
>
> After discussion of various methods of presentation the class voted to

use panel discussion and to make three panels out of the group. The teacher then asked for volunteers to act as moderators. They were not forthcoming, so the teacher asked if the class would accept teacher-made appointments. To this the class agreed.

The teacher then appointed a girl, known for her interest in panel discussion and her ability as a moderator, to head one group, and appointed two boys to moderate the other two groups. Both boys had been a problem in that they constantly desired to be heard whether they had anything to offer or not. This was evidenced by their efforts to inject unhumorous humor into class discussions as well as their efforts to center attention upon themselves by leaving their seats whenever the thought struck them or by speaking out of turn.

The moderators then selected their own panel members and spent several days collecting materials, planning their discussions, and talking with one another to make sure they were not duplicating materials.

The girl was allowed to give her panel first and this showed the boys some of the mechanics of this type of presentation. The two boys then gave their panels and soon learned the necessity for speaking in turn to accomplish their goals. It gave them a feeling of belonging.

In their evaluation the students realized the value of cooperative planning to obtain a common goal and how group spirit and activity aided in making the attainment of that goal an interest of the whole group.

Mr. Painter's account again illustrates the need for effective planning in the large group before small-group work begins. The teacher also was aware of individual needs for responsibility (as shown by his selection of leaders), the advantage of congenial work groups (as shown by his allowing moderators to choose their own panel), and the value of a good example of leadership (as shown by his scheduling first the panel whose leader was most experienced).

The way in which Mr. Silva guides his eighth grade students in small-group work is well illustrated by a report written by his supervisor after a visit to one of Mr. Silva's classes.

Supervisory Report

Teacher: Mr. Silva	Date: February 25
Room: 511	Time: 10:40–11:40 A.M.
Class: 8–3	Subject: Social Studies

Observational data

The children were engaged in a research period. The unifying theme of the unit of study was: "Why has the American standard of living become the highest in the world?" The immediate problem under consideration by the groups at work was: "How has immigration influenced the character of the American people?"

Four different committees, each working on a related problem, were gathered in four corners of the room. Pupils were giving individual progress reports to the chairmen. I heard one chairman say, "Tell how far you've gone with your work."

A plan for this period was on the blackboard, as follows:

"Conference with class as a group. Understanding the goals.

"Committee meetings (15 minutes) to make sure each one understands his problem.

"Research period. Be sure to follow your plan."

Committee chairmen had work plans in notebooks, with careful records of assignments of individuals in committee.

Mr. Silva went from group to group, taking part in the discussion, answering and asking questions, assisting in suggestions relating to sources of materials, scope of problem, value of materials brought in by pupils, and in general maintaining the pace of the lesson.

Library materials for the four groups were kept in four different places, so that there was little confusion in getting materials and in returning to seats.

Opportunity for sharing results of the immediate effort of this period was provided in a brief joint meeting of the groups at the end of the period. Mr. Silva asked, "When do you think you'll be ready to report?" Estimates were given. Then: "Suppose, very briefly, we see what progress each committee has made, so we'll know where we're going, and how your problem fits into the general picture." "What is the whole problem?" was one of the questions asked that resulted in a fine statement of the general theme.

Two charts which were on display in Mr. Silva's room show that the teacher gave direct attention to training for small-group work. The first was designed to help a committee organize for work and proceed with a job.

Committee Procedure

1. Pick chairman.
2. Get a "bird's-eye" view of the problem.
3. Decide upon problems and items for further research.
4. Make a plan:
    Who will do the different things
    References and materials to be used
    Notes to be kept
    How information will be shared at meetings
5. Carry out the plan.
6. Keep a record of progress.
7. Make a plan for reporting:
    Charts and illustrations
    Vocabulary to be introduced
    Questions for class

      Rehearsal of report
      Use of notes for an oral report
8. Make an oral report.
9. Make written record—for future sharing.

The second chart was planned to help committees evaluate their group and individual procedures.

Pointers for Committees

Sharing ideas

At committee meetings do you stop to discuss the value of suggestions and ideas given by members of your group?

Decisions

Do you come to agreement as a group on these suggestions?

Use of experts

Do you make the best use of your fellow-workers who have special talents for art, chart-making, etc.?

Records

Do you keep a log of your work on a committee? If acting as secretary, do you keep a log of the work of your committee and its members?

Knowing the goal

Do you know your job or problem and how your work fits in with the problem of the whole committee?

Cooperation equals *Willingness* plus *Use of Ability* plus *Energy* plus *Time*

$$\text{Formula: C equals } W+A+E+T$$

    Do you work according to the above formula?
    Do you share your materials?
    Do you try to get along with others?
    Do you do your share or do you wait for others to "carry the ball"?

Also posted in the room were the goals toward which the students were working in connection with their present unit of work, the steps to take during research periods, and the problem being worked on by each of the four groups.

After Mr. Allen's ninth grade science class was organized into work groups,[17] the teacher helped them to learn something about committee functioning. He used a demonstration committee meeting, as Mr. Eliason did.

---

[17] See page 380.

A schedule was set for each group to report to the entire class. I took the first group scheduled to report and had them go through the organization process in front of the whole class. A chairman was elected, as was a secretary. The duties of each were discussed.

Each group member was to work on his own problem or two or more members could study a problem together. Meetings were to be held daily at the start of our class period and the progress and problems discussed. The group was to work out its own method of presentation. The chairman was responsible for tying together the work of each member in the presentation. Each group was encouraged to use demonstrations, drawings, role-playing, slides, as well as oral reports.

Using our number-one group as a model, I pointed out how the above activities could be realized. After all questions were answered, the groups got together in the classroom and organized as group number one had demonstrated. We were ready to start our next lesson with the groups in action.

In Mr. Allen's report we also find a description of problems encountered and ways in which some were met.

Meantime I had to collect a wide variety of references from the library as our textbook was inadequate for supplying the wide range of information needed.

Our first difficulty in getting the groups into action was that there were no tables in our classroom and the desk-armchairs were fastened to the floor. That is something which I shall recommend for correction next year.

After talking the situation over, we decided to have each group in turn go to the library for the entire class period; another group would then meet in the laboratory supply room, and the other groups would meet in the classroom. The library group was to meet briefly in the cafeteria before going to the library. In this way they could talk and discuss their progress and problems without causing a disturbance in the library.

This procedure worked out satisfactorily; so we continued it for three days. I made myself available to any of the groups needing special help. The most frequent calls were for reference material and for assistance in devising experiments.

On the fourth day our first group was ready to report. The next day I asked the rest of the class to tell how they liked the report of the first group and for what reasons. The comment was all favorable. Reasons given were: "They prepared their topic well." "The demonstrations were interesting." "They used charts and the blackboard in explaining things."

I reminded the others that they should use these good points in their own presentations.

We then went back to our regular study groups to get ready for the next report. The group which had just reported agreed to take on a more advanced topic and got to work on it. This seems to be a problem, what to do with groups which have finished.

We went on in this fashion for about two weeks. The finished groups still present a problem. I don't like to keep sticking them with other topics just to keep them busy. Perhaps a closer scheduling of reporting will help.

Mr. Allen's account shows some of the helpful things he did for the students. He also raises a point of difficulty: finding useful occupations for small groups that have already reported. A later report shows that he was still trying out ways of solving this problem.

You may be interested in knowing how I solved the problem of what to do with a group after it had reported. I tried using one group as a compiler of important principles and facts which the other groups brought out in their presentations. This information was presented to the entire class as a review exercise at the close of a unit. I also used another group as an evaluator of the work of other groups, sort of an observer arrangement. Perhaps the best approach would have been to let the class work out the solution to this problem on its own.[18]

Mr. Allen encountered two other difficulties also: (1) time to give sufficient help to all the small groups and (2) satisfactory reference materials. The first difficulty he met by giving general directions to the large group and occasional suggestions to small groups, by using a small group meeting as a demonstration to the rest, and by evaluating procedures in the large and small groups. The second difficulty he met by locating all materials he could find and also by writing to the National Science Teachers Association.

In working on the next unit, magnetism and electricity, Mr. Allen introduced a new use of the small group. He broke the large group into random, temporary groups of five or six students who happened

---

[18] Although this problem may be met in a number of ways, including the ways suggested by Mr. Allen himself, the plan worked out by a college class might be of interest here.

After deciding to divide into work groups on four large problem areas in the curriculum, the college group scheduled a block of time for all groups to work. A schedule of reports was then made up. In advance of each report the whole group was given an assignment of some questions to think about and some suggested reading to do. Thus each small group had to put forth major effort on their own problem for a given period of time and minor effort on problems of other groups for the rest of the time. This minor effort was calculated to make the entire group more intelligent in considering the report of one subgroup.

Another feature of the plan of this college class was that even after a group had reported, it would continue to do further work on its problem. A period was provided at the end of the series of reports for synthesizing all reports and pulling out some generalizations.

to be sitting near one another. These groups were to discuss a common problem—the general procedures which small groups might follow in the next unit—and report their opinions for discussion and decision by the whole group. This is sometimes called the "buzz" group technique, a way of getting many ideas opened up quickly through wide participation.

Mr. Allen also encountered the familiar problem of lack of interest:

> I noticed a group composed mostly of girls seemingly enjoying themselves too much to be concerned with school work (unfortunately). Upon inquiry they said they were discussing a television program of the night before. I asked them if they were really interested in the topic they had selected. They said that they were when they first considered it but that they did not know it was so complicated. They had selected "How a television set works"! I knew that one of the girls liked to write and that two of them had an interest in dramatics, so I suggested that they might like to try a dramatic skit about some of the early historical events of electricity. There were some interesting articles in one of our reference booklets on this phase. The girls seemed to think it a good idea and wanted to get started right away.
>
> I sat in with them and gave a few ideas. I told them about Thales discovering that amber could pick up little bits of thread when rubbed with wool. None knew what amber was, so I told them how the ancient sailors found it on the Baltic coast during one of their voyages. I suggested a little skit bringing in the sailors, the amber, and Thales.
>
> The idea took hold and they were ready to find more material for their skit. They also decided to do a skit about Galvani and the frogs' legs and William Gilbert and magnetism.

Mr. Allen met this problem of lack of interest in an intelligent way. Instead of insisting that the girls stick to a plan that had proved unwise, he helped them redirect their goal. The need for shifting from an unwise plan can probably be reduced to a minimum by devoting more time and attention to the exploratory period before choice of problem is made.

CONCLUSION

Our study of the experiences of teachers trying to improve their guidance of small-group work shows that the following points are important to keep in mind:

1. In a given situation there must be careful consideration of the purposes which small groups can and cannot serve.

2. Ways of forming effective work groups must be employed.

3. The teacher must give attention to ways of preparing for

small-group work, including careful selection of problems, training in group procedures, setting of a reasonable time schedule, and planning for meeting places.

4. The teacher must endeavor to use many ways of helping small groups while at work.

5. Appropriate ways for small groups to communicate with the main group must be found.

6. The teacher and the group must find ways of evaluating procedures and of improving them on succeeding occasions.

CHAPTER XV

Meeting Needs of Individuals

within the Group

CONCERN IS often expressed that emphasis on group processes may mean mediocrity, leveling out of individuals, failure to meet their needs. Actually, efficient cooperative procedures give the individual many opportunities to reveal points at which he needs help as well as chances to develop and to use his unique talents for his own greater satisfaction and for the good of the group.

Teachers who work cooperatively with their pupils have a chance to learn much about each individual—what he is thinking, what he is interested in, what his level of social skills and his place in the group are. This chapter is designed to show (1) some of the things teachers learn about individuals in the kind of classroom climate which develops when pupils share responsibility for planning and managing their school experiences, and (2) some ways in which the individual is provided for through cooperative procedures in addition to the many chances for personal development he will continue to have as he works by himself.

DISCOVERING INDIVIDUAL NEEDS

Through watching and listening to pupils as they play varying roles in groups, teachers have opportunities to learn points at which they need help. Professional diaries kept by teachers studying the process of cooperative work with their pupils contain endless references to individual needs that they have discovered.

Miss Naughton's diary contains such entries as these:

Buzz needs help in taking notes. He still tries to write out the minutes in full while the meeting is in progress. . . .

Although sometimes hesitant about joining group discussions, Gloria has shown that she observes things closely. . . .

418

Jimmy seems fairly happy in school this year, but I wonder if he is learning anything. He does not seem to be able to decide what work he or the group needs done. He waits for work to be handed to him, and then he has to be helped to do it.

In Miss Rezny's diary are such comments as the following:

Dorothy was a member of the group and although her ideas are good, the execution of them is poor. Her friends are most uncomplimentary about this but, while it obviously hurts her feelings at the time, it is not effective enough to make her change.

Barbara needs help with her minutes. I fear she procrastinates, then slaps them together.

Patty is finding excuses *not* to make a cloth-body puppet after the girls had agreed with Miss B. to make them this way because of the lack of space and time.

Worked on our scrapbooks today. The children haven't gone beyond the "I want my own" stage; so each one desired a personal record.

In Miss Merlin's diary we find:

Early in the morning Delores decided that she was not going to be in the program. She would not give any explanation, but I am inclined to believe that she thought her ghost costume was not as good as Sally's.

Mrs. Valentine shows that she is aware of growing pains in group work on the part of one of her sixth grade boys.

One very slow child was chairman of a group that was to move the chairs for the guests up from the all-purpose room. The only trouble that I had with him was that he wanted to call his committee together every day to make sure that every one of them was going to support him. This gave him a sense of importance. He tended to become aggressive in the wrong way, but the others straightened him out. I heard one member of his group say to him, "Wisen up. What's ailin' you? Think we can't remember when to get those chairs up here?"

Two paragraphs from Mrs. Wardell's diary reflect different kinds of concern about individuals.

December 9. One of my big problems in group adjustments this year has been with boys who "punctuate" all discussions, reports, and assignments with puns, corrections, sarcasm, supplements, and asides in a way which doesn't fit in with group standards. It is consistently the same people. Perhaps if I assigned them the responsibility for making comments, summaries, and reviews, it might help. The other thing would be to keep myself from being agitated. After all, I don't want them to treat me like deity!

January 7. While evaluating the committee system we had this fall for routine jobs, an interesting point was made by one of the conscientious workers of the class. She expressed the view of some of her friends that this wasn't very satisfactory for handling news bulletins and discussions, because there was no "mark" given. Others took up the discussion, making points I liked to hear given, but it made me realize that some of our praised workers in class perhaps have attitudes and aims less valid than some of our less "studious" people.

Miss Brainard shows how observing she was of the way in which different members of her sixth grade group responded to new arrangements.

A group met with me yesterday and planned a new arrangement for our desks in order to afford more floor space and to make our room look less formal. We fixed our furniture this morning. The desks are in groups of four. Dick, a delightful and cooperative youngster, is not sure he wants to be so near other children. Bob seemed to be the one that had greatest trouble working in a little group. Even with an entirely different group of children, Ernest still brought complaints upon himself because he does not consider others near him who are trying to work independently.

Mrs. Tambling's frank report of early results of trying to help pupils make responsible use of freedom in the art room will strike a chord of sympathy in those who have experienced the same thing. It is obvious that from the experiment the teacher was learning many things on which various individuals needed help.

Two things bother me greatly. One is that the children don't like to be interrupted for any kind of discussion. I had hoped to point out things of general value but they just don't want to be bothered with talk.

The other problem is that materials are taken in great numbers and misused even when the children know better. They want to come in, get what they need, do what they want, and then just leave it at the end of the period—or take it with them, as in the case of drawing pencils, cutting knives, rulers, erasers.

I give them five minutes for cleaning up and they do a half job—throwing dirty brushes in the sink, leaving materials around.

There seems to be much less regard for property or for others among these "nice" children than among their tougher contemporaries. A nice note.

Later entries in Mrs. Tambling's diary show that the experiment turned out to be fairly successful. The teacher might not have known how desperately her children needed help in self-direction had she not allowed them wide limits for revealing themselves.

A fifth grade photography club, sponsored by Miss Cranford, a student teacher, gave her some unusual opportunities to see how various children accepted responsibility. For example, she became concerned about Peter, who had been elected president of the club and looked entirely to her for what to do. This student teacher records in her diary:

> I have been trying of late to use Peter as a resource person, for he knows a good deal about cameras and picture-taking and seems to find it easier to offer counsel on specific problems than to hold the leadership of the group.

When Miss Cranford had an opportunity to substitute in a third grade she made some particularly sage observations with respect to tendencies shown by many individuals within a group. "The whole tenor of the class is completely different from the one in which I had assisted for the first semester," she writes.

Significant phrases in Miss Cranford's analysis of needs were: "whispering carried on as though it shouldn't have been"; "it was their custom to line up at the back of the room according to how many words they missed"; "responded a good deal better to suggestions and actual orders . . . but showed more similarity in patterns"; "no children could be spotted as leaders or problems at first —they all seemed to lack any individuality"; "constant comparisons the children made of one another and the 'tattling.' " A teacher assuming the responsibility for such a group would have a large job cut out for her if she desired to promote initiative and cooperation.

Comments by teachers recorded in this chapter thus far have shown awareness of individuals' needing help on such varied tasks as:

Writing minutes
Joining in discussion
Showing initiative
Carrying out ideas
Moving to the "we" stage
Abiding by a group decision
Not being arbitrary, officious, nor yet laissez-faire in a leadership role
Not allowing a whim to interfere with carrying out a responsibility accepted
Learning to make only constructive comments in a group
Learning to work for intrinsic rewards

> Learning to work well with a small group
> Learning to use freedom constructively
> Learning to assume responsibility for shared materials

These needs are revealed only in a social situation, such as one in which individuals are trying to carry on a cooperative endeavor.

MEETING NEEDS REVEALED

Teachers taking part in this study of cooperative procedures in education found a number of ways of meeting individual needs discovered through observation of pupils in various situations. These needs were met by using opportunities arising in group living. The approaches used may be described as: (1) helping the individual to belong, (2) giving the individual special help, (3) promoting individual self-evaluation, (4) providing opportunity for individual planning, and (5) using the group to help the individual.

Helping the Individual to Belong

Teachers can make it possible for individuals to become a part of a group in a number of ways. One way is to find useful roles for the various members of the group by encouraging these members to engage in enterprises of different sorts. In doing this the teacher must provide room for as much individual choice as possible.

Having a constant stream of cooperatively planned group enterprises in progress gives the teacher different opportunities to follow up on needs revealed and to find ways in which individuals can contribute to a group.

Sometimes teachers happen on ways of giving certain pupils a useful part in the classroom life. Such was Mrs. O'Reilly's experience one spring when the school grounds were broken up for the construction of an addition to the building, causing dust and dirt in the schoolroom to collect "in spite of all the efforts of the pupil housekeepers." This fourth and fifth grade teacher writes:

> We have inadequate janitor service, and when our principal suggested that we try to keep our rooms cleaner ourselves, I took her at her word. Armed with a large bottle of furniture polish, I arrived very early at school one morning, rolled up my sleeves, donned a smock, and set out to clean the baseboards of my room and the trays which seemed constantly covered with dust.
>
> I worked very hard and my bones were beginning to ache, you may

be sure, when I suddenly looked up on hearing these words, spoken in an indignant tone from my twelve-year-old problem child, Ralph: "You let me do that. That ain't no work for teachers. I can do that at least to help you. You have it looking fine. It looks like a new room. I like it."

I was so surprised I handed him both bottle and cloth and could only say, "Why, Ralph! You came at just the right time. I'm sure lucky to have a helper like you in my classroom."

The boy's red moon face beamed and with much delight and with an unbelievable air of importance he proceeded to the task. I reminded him ten minutes later that he had helped tremendously and the room certainly had taken on a new look, but he refused to stop. Before he would give up this self-appointed job he had polished my desk, his desk, the remaining baseboards, the wardrobe doors, the chalk trays, the bookcases, and would have mopped up the floor if I hadn't insisted then that for one day that was sufficient. He stopped then, put the polish in the back closet, put the polish cloth in the wastebasket, looked around at the class in a most self-satisfied manner and took his seat.

That noontime just before dismissal I was literally besieged with questions from the group as a whole as to whether or not they could do what Ralph did and use the furniture polish. This seemed such a treat over the old method of just using a dry cloth that to pacify them all and have the room resume its order, we decided to let people sign their names on a chart which Ralph *would make and take charge of*. This would allow from two to four children every day to be "polishers."

Evidently Ralph has found a satisfactory outlet for his size, strength, and sense of importance, too, for his work in other things has shown a big improvement. The principal highly praised the room's appearance, much to Ralph's delight and that of all the class.

The teacher in this case turned a simple offer of help into an opportunity for one boy to exercise a kind of leadership he could manage.

Miss Lubin's diary gives an account of seven-year-old Marian, who was almost too shy to take part in committee work until there was opportunity to make use of previous experience.

My children formed committees for carrying out their plans for their safety dramatization. Leaders were chosen in each group, and each child worked diligently to make his contribution. The one exception was Marian. When she was asked to be on the "painting of the bus" committee, she flatly refused. She was asked if she would like to be on any committee but she again refused.

Further planning went on, and Marian said, "I help my father paint." But she still insisted that she didn't want to be on any committee. It was obvious that she was anxious to be on the painting committee, but she didn't feel that she could do the painting well enough.

The next day she said that she could paint, and after she saw how easy it was, she finally worked her way into the group. She gained in confidence.

When committees were chosen for the Halloween party, Marian volunteered to be leader of the game committee. This she felt capable of doing. She knew she had games at home that she could bring. She is usually a shy child, but at the Halloween party she was changed completely. She was doing something that she felt she could do. When someone suggested playing another game, she said, "I'm taking charge of the games."

Marian, in this instance, found her own place to use her experience in a group undertaking. In other cases the teacher must help children to take this step. So it was with Charles, who needed Mrs. Valentine's help. As the teacher tells the story:

Charles was a boy whom only a mother could love when he came to my sixth grade last fall. Physically, he was a sight that would inspire laughter. He was as tall as the other children, but very fat. His hair grew in the most outlandish fashion. It stuck out from the sides and stood almost straight up on the top of his head. He was flat-footed and toed out, wore glasses and very tight-fitting clothes. The children disliked him, and he, not being accepted by his own group, had in the past resorted to small mean gestures—such as tripping those who passed his seat and tormenting younger children on the playground.

He had, in the fifth grade, one performance which gained for him the attention of the entire class. This was to lie down on the floor and propel himself slowly across the floor to the accompaniment of the children's shouts. All these things I knew.

Another hint as to what he was really like. He never used a one- or two-syllable word when he could use four- or five-syllable ones. He had a habit of making such statements as this in class, addressed to his teachers, "You probably don't know anything about this, but . . ." Then he would proceed to give a colorful account, and a very interesting one, of some person or event brought to his mind by an incidental reference made during the class. It is, at such a time, very difficult for the teacher to look upon such an introduction to his contribution in any good way.

When he walked in on the morning of the opening of the new term, it happened that all the seats had been taken except one in the back of the room. He put his books down on the desk and came up to me.

"Mrs. Valentine," he said, "I do not like to sit in the back of the room. My only reason, and the one reason why I would prefer a front seat is because of the condition of my eyes. Otherwise, I would accept that seat back there."

This rather pompous little lecture was the beginning of our first experience in working together. We quickly fixed him up with a front seat, and he proceeded to act in no unseemly way throughout his first day in the class. I had noticed, however, that the children were ready and waiting for him to perform. He seemed to be conscious of this, and I thought he was making a great effort to keep himself from obliging them.

When Mrs. Valentine went home that night she wondered how she could help Charles find his place with his peers. She planned to build on the experience of the first day on which the boy had obviously tried hard to conform, and she resolved to "see the child behind his actions," not to look for trouble, and to help him be accepted and happy in the group. The teacher was helped by studying records on Charles.

In filling in the children's names in my register that first night of Charles's sixth grade career, I noted that he was a year younger than the rest of the children. In checking other notes, I also discovered that he had been accelerated from the second to the fourth grade in another school. This, then, was one explanation for his social maladjustment.

He had very probably been a problem even in relation to his own age group, but to ask him to adjust to older children was expecting a bit too much of him.

Mrs. Valentine also consulted other teachers who knew the boy.

I talked with his preceding teachers about his contributions in the form of monologues. They, it seemed to me, had not allowed him to give many of these, partly because of the opening remark which I have told about, and partly because he monopolized such a lot of time.

I had observed his very evident sense of satisfaction while he was giving forth with one of his lectures during the next few days, and decided that here was the point to start on. Here was something that he did very well.

The account continues with ways in which the teacher tried to help Charles.

I gave the boy opportunity during the first week of school to give us two or three special reports. He brought from home a great mass of literature and pictorial material relating to his lecture, which was really what his performance amounted to.

I felt elated one noon while my children were in the cafeteria line to hear one of the most popular children say to another one, "You know, Charles is really all right. He changed a lot over the summer." So they were beginning to accept him.

Now so far, I had worked to bolster Charles up in a concentrated way in the eyes of his fellow-students. Next I gradually tried to bring the children in to working with him. This was a much slower process, because for so long his only way of feeling that he was wanted at all was by his bad behavior; and the attention and laughs that this gained him from his peers. He would revert back to his old behavior whenever some child evidenced a dislike for working with him on a committee, a report, or the like. But I began to notice that Charles was slowly divorcing himself from the little mean mannerisms that had previously characterized him.

We gave an assembly program, and I do believe it was here that Charles really found himself. I had discovered by now that he had a marvelous sense of humor. He played the leading role in a comedy which we put on in assembly and did a wonderful job. He conducted himself in an almost professional way during the performance. But the best thing that he did for himself was to save the play by ad-libbing to cover up for two of the children who were mixed up in their lines. The children looked on him with awe, and his joy was wonderful to see. He had, by using his wits, saved the day, as it were. From then on, Charles's problems seemed to iron out remarkably well. The play episode had shown him that he could be accepted by pulling with, and not away from, good social behavior among his group.

We became very good friends last year, and I had the thrill that comes once in a lifetime to a teacher when my principal said to me at the end of the year, "What did you do to Charles? He's not the same child. I was talking to his mother yesterday and she told me that Charles has never been so happy, that he has friends come to the house, and has really found himself." Small crumbs, maybe, but every teacher knows how heart-warming are such words.

Mrs. Valentine has shown how carefully the teacher must study a child in many cases to find an ability which can be made useful to the group and form the needed link between the outcast individual and the group that is rejecting him. Instead of shutting Charles off from the one activity in which he felt he could excel, as previous teachers had done, Mrs. Valentine built on this activity as a strength.

Peter, who came from Cuba, needed Miss Jensen's help in finding a place in his new group in a southern school. His teacher writes:

Peter caused laughter in our fourth grade the day he tried to read a sentence aloud in English. His efforts thwarted, he didn't enter into our conversations and discussions for several days.

At this time I thought it wise to begin a unit of stories about Spain, where Peter could supply correct pronunciations for all the Spanish words. The children were impressed by his contribution to the group, and they became respectful, tolerant, and helpful in aiding him with English words.

Peter's frequent trips to Cuba on week ends with his father, a Cuban diplomat, aroused much interest in the class. Questions like these were asked: "How long does it take to fly from here to another country where they speak another language?" "Is that why our community has all

Spanish-looking houses and Spanish street names?" "Is that why we have such a big airport?"

We charted the plane's course from our city to Cuba on the map. One Friday morning we went to the airport to see Peter off. He was to bring back information from this trip about the sugar-cane industry. A group studying Florida sugar cane thought it wise to compare data.

It may be noted that Miss Jensen created the occasion for using Peter's background of experience.

Henry, a "trailer" boy whose broad southern accent marked him off as different from the rest of the children, was helped by Miss Lubin to become valued by the rest of his second grade class through use of his previous experiences. The teacher reports:

> When we read stories about farms, Henry could tell us about his grandmother's farm in West Virginia, and how he rode on a pony.
> Salvatore said, "A real pony! You're lucky."
> Henry rose in prestige but it was when the children talked about fishing that he gained the greatest respect from his classmates. He had gone fishing with his father in Florida and he could tell the children his fishing adventures.

Although Miss Lubin does not say so, one has a hunch that she helped the children get onto the subject of farms and fishing with which Henry was so much at home.

Miss Holden, a college student who was making observations in a nursery school, reports the way in which the children were prepared to receive Arlette, a refugee child coming to them from France.

> In planning for Arlette's coming, the teacher had told the children how necessary were friendly feelings, especially in this case because Arlette could not speak English. The teacher knew a few French songs and sang them. They had a map and traced Arlette's trip from France to Cuba and then to New York.

The report goes on to tell how warmly Arlette was welcomed when she arrived.

Giving the Individual Special Help

A first principle of meeting the needs of individuals within a group is not to treat them all alike. When Mrs. Tambling was trying her experiment with "freedom in the art room," she found that some children needed more directing than others. "Some children," she writes, "seem to have nothing to do when they have an opportunity to make a choice of activity. When I ask them what they'd like to do, they look blank. Now I've learned to step in and suggest something."

For the teacher to make suggestions in this way may be one step toward having children build up experiences with a number of things so that they will be able to make more intelligent choices on another occasion. The teacher will need to watch that these same individuals do not continue to depend upon her for every suggestion.

Sometimes certain individuals need special help in understanding agreements under which a group is operating, especially as the agreements apply to themselves. This is particularly true with very young children such as Ginny, a member of a preschool group, whose story is told by Miss Holden, the college student just referred to.

> The teachers have been studying Ginny's behavior, keeping records and trying to give Ginny a sense of security and self-assurance. She has developed somewhat in that she is learning to meet opposition without immediately crying and being defeated. However, she still needs a great deal of attention.
>
> On this visit I observed Ginny building with two boys. She suddenly became aware of the fact that preparations for lunch were going on in the next room. She left the blocks, ran in and took spoons with which to set the table. Ellie ran after her, saying, "It's my turn today." A tussle took place.
>
> The teacher intervened and agreed with Ellie; it was her turn. Ginny did not cry but walked away and hid behind a locker. The teacher paid no attention.
>
> Finally a knocking was heard. Ginny was scratching and knocking on the back of the locker. The teacher went over and very pleasantly said, "I hear someone knocking. Someone wants to come in." She went and "found" Ginny.
>
> Ginny wanted to set the tables. The teacher sat down with her and explained that not everyone could have a turn every day because there wasn't room for everybody. She then reminded Ginny of the chart which they had all made and asked Ginny to find her name. Ginny found it. It was her turn the next day! The teacher assured her that no one else would set the table but Ginny because they had all agreed that that was to be her day. She suggested that Ginny watch Ellie and see for herself that no one interfered with Ellie because today was "her" day. "All the children had taken part in the discussion of 'jobs' and had planned it this way, and we have all agreed, remember?" Ginny was satisfied.

This example is notable for the firm, impersonal behavior of the teacher, her use of the chart to convince Ginny of the reasonableness of the arrangements under which they were operating, and her suggestion of something active for Ginny to do at that moment, to "watch Ellie and see for herself that no one interfered with Ellie."

Promoting Individual Self-Evaluation

A further way of helping individuals to meet their needs within a group situation is to encourage them to evaluate themselves. In Miss Radcliffe's and Mrs. Banning's reports we have encountered the use of role-playing for the purpose of helping individuals with self-evaluation.[1]

Miss Evans writes in connection with her unit on the use of out-of-school time.

We had a systematic way of keeping track of our reading. Each child kept dated records of the things he read, special things he was interested in individually, and things of interest to him in our group discussions.

To help each individual become aware of his progress and his further needs is one way of meeting the problem of helping the individual within the group.

Providing Opportunity for Individual Planning

One of the best ways of meeting individual needs within a group is to help each group member learn to make intelligent plans for himself within the framework of group planning. Mrs. Stanley has furnished a detailed account of the way in which this problem was managed in a very difficult third grade situation.

The problem I had to face was how to work best with a group having a wide variety of ability and interests, in a situation in which blind, sight-saving, and hard-of-hearing children were members of the group for part of the day. Considerable time was spent in getting acquainted with the children's interests and abilities and exploring various possible ways of working together.

An idea crystallized when I was called out of the room at the time we would normally be planning our work together. Knowing I would be gone for some time, I suggested that each child might plan his own work. When I returned the children had carried on so well in my absence and were so pleased with the idea that they wished they could "do that every day." Out of this grew individual planning which involved a great deal of group planning to establish.

We decided to include the reading we would do each day, our spelling, arithmetic, and writing of letters, stories, poems, reports, and visits

[1] See pages 74–75.

to the library, art work, and handicraft. At the bottom of each plan we would write our "aim," which would be in something which we were trying especially hard to improve. For example, it might be to be neater in written work or to be more thoughtful of others.

After writing plans for a few days the children decided it would be nice to make plan books. This again involved group planning. The result was that each morning children wrote in their plan books the things they planned to do as individuals that day.

The first few days it was necessary for me to give considerable help, but gradually the children became more independent and were able to write their plans with only a little individual help. Some children were able to finish writing their plans in ten minutes and started their work, while others took as long as twenty minutes to complete their plans.

As children wrote their plans in their individual plan books each morning, I would walk among them, giving suggestions whenever needed. These suggestions were usually made in the following way: "What are you going to work on next?" or "Do you think you are going to have time to finish what you have planned or have you planned too much?" or to still another child, "Do you think you are getting along all right with your arithmetic or would you like some help from some other member of the class or myself?" "Do you think you will be ready for your spelling test tomorrow or do you need to spend more time on that this morning?" "Who in the class do you think would like to read that book when you are through with it? Why? You might show it to him so he could be planning on it."

A typical plan of one of the children follows.

January 27, 19—
Monday

My Plans for Today

1. Arithmetic problems in multiplication and division like this:

$$2\overline{)462}^{\,231} \qquad\qquad \begin{array}{r} 1846 \\ \times\ 232 \\ \hline 3692 \\ 5538 \\ 3692 \\ \hline 428272 \end{array}$$

Spelling—study these words:—rice, anybody, center, sugar, smooth.
Reading—in "Building Our Country," pages 78–108.
Write a letter to Miss W. in the Hawaiian Islands.
Work on the "Weave-It."
My aim is to be a good sport.

After School

1. Ride my pony.
2. Get Daddy's supper—Mother is working.

3. Read the paper.
4. Read my library book.

According to Mrs. Stanley, individual planning and work took from one-half to two-thirds of the day, and the rest of the day was spent in group work, such as music, physical education, discussions in social studies, science, health, and literature. This part of the day was planned cooperatively and included the sight-saving children and the blind boy. Mrs. Stanley goes on to evaluate the results of the experiment.

> There are many values, I believe, in this way of working. It gives the children a purpose and more incentive for the things they are doing. The work is better adapted to their individual interests and abilities. It helps them to evaluate their own work and to learn the techniques of planning for out-of-school activities as well as for those in school. They learn to budget their time, to work together, to share, to assume responsibility, to complete their tasks, to make choices, to make decisions, and to use resources at their disposal. Because it substitutes interest and incentive for pressure, it improves the human relations in the classroom.
>
> Children are working happily at tasks they have chosen to do under the guidance of the teacher. It develops leadership and initiative through the many opportunities for small-group and committee work. It permits self-appraisal, self-discovery and self-direction through continuous evaluation.

Using the Group to Help the Individual

There is considerable evidence that the right kind of group can support and enhance the individual. Every teacher has seen pupils respond to the constructive pressure of group opinion. Although this force can be abused by the thoughtless adult, it can, if left to operate as a natural outcome of good group spirit and thoughtful planning together, be of great help in meeting the needs of the individual.

The story of six-year-old Dolores is a case in point. She was one of sixteen children in a family supported by the state because of the father's illness. Her teacher, Miss Irvington, knew that the children of this family were treated with "the crudest type of disciplinary measures and that they were emotionally unstable."

Miss Irvington began to study Dolores the year before she had her in her room, finding her "very proud and inclined to be quite stubborn also." The teacher shows in her diary account of Dolores' case that she was aware of the need to think both about the help Dolores required and the kind of group atmosphere in which she could receive that help.

I knew as I observed Dolores' many tantrums that she must feel security and success for her to be able to make good choices in her living with others. I felt the one point of focus was her interest in other children and her unsuccessful efforts to work and play with them. The children had a most unwholesome way of working out problems relating to Dolores. They were always telling tales. All this had to be worked out before they could aid Dolores in her effort to grow. Their feeling of self-control and group responsibility had to grow.

Miss Irvington then goes on to relate the long process of helping Dolores find the place in the group that she was trying so hard to achieve. The account shows the setbacks encountered and the way in which the teacher enlisted the aid of the other children.

November 12. Dolores came into the room this morning with a little snail crawling on her hand, and told all about his little adventures coming to school and about the tree where she had found him. She was so fascinated with the way he moved his head this way, that way. She wanted me to read Hilda Conkling's poem, "The Snail." At the conclusion she said, "He does wag his head this way, that way, because I saw him do it. I want the other boys and girls to see him but they will have to be very quiet so as not to disturb him." She invited different children to come up. They obliged by tiptoeing to see this very fascinating creature. Several of the group wanted copies of the poem for their pet book.

Just when all was going well, Dolores attempted to intrude into another little group's job and was taking over a responsibility that was not hers. "Dolores, were you invited to help with this?" was a teacher's hurried way of helping when she was working with another study group. In response to this, Dolores took the pails back to the easel from which she had so thoughtlessly helped herself. Then she placed a mark on Mary Lou's painting, pushed another child, slid her feet noisily across the room, picked up someone's puzzle and proceeded to throw it down very loudly, trying to convince us she intended to break it. These tantrums gather momentum when they get started and are always accompanied by a silly giggle.

My impatience gathered momentum too. Finally, I got control of myself and struck one successful note at just the right moment. Then the calmness started to come.

Dolores finally surprised me by saying, "I am sorry." This was directed to the group. The children encouraged her gesture and commented on her bigness. I also played it up and my delight was a very natural one, for I had never experienced this type of reaction from her, all of her own volition, before.

Unfortunately for Dolores, she was just working this difficult gesture through with all sincerity of effort when she went to the lunchroom, where she had an accident and dropped her tray with the food on the floor.

The accident was partially June's fault. June was very kind and with my help tried to straighten out the problem with Dolores. But Dolores would not even look up. She sat in a very dejected way with head bowed and a few telltale tears which she tried to cover up. She would not move even when June started to assume the responsibility for the whole accident. June tried to reason with her on her own.

After several minutes of sitting on the floor, Jackie leaned over and said something to her. She looked where her new lunch was waiting for her. Jackie came to me and whispered, "I think I can get Dolores to eat." So he proceeded to whisper to her again. The next thing I knew she was eating and smiling. I later found out that Jackie had in some way bargained with her about letting her take his place at the end of the table.

November 13. This morning went smoothly until rest period, when Dolores had a violent outburst. I had to ask her to rest in the principal's office while we prepared the restroom for another teacher's immediate use.

In this lull we discussed how we should in all fairness work this out. The children were wonderful. They were so considerate. They still wanted to help her because they had seen and felt growth in her. They believed in her still, even though she was so unfair to them and their time. But they did feel that if she continued what happened today they did not want her in their room. They felt she would have to make that decision. The sub-primary room was suggested or letting her go home to rest.

I asked them if they would like me to bring her into the room now. "Yes!" was the answer. When she walked into the room, Dickie's first remark was, "I like the way Dolores walked in here."

The children went through an evaluation of the morning with the girl, and then she was asked a very definite question, "Do you want to help us?"

She said yes, she did, and that she was sorry she did not help while they were resting. She thought they were fair in their decision about not wanting her if she had decided to be uncooperative. You could sense a deep feeling of respect in Dolores' eyes for such a wonderful group of children.

Naturally, Dolores' story had no fairy-tale close and there were forces at work which undid some of the work of the school. As the teacher comments: "Dolores' most terrific spells are usually after a prolonged stay at home, such as a long week end. And recently an older sister and her family moved into this already congested household."

The teacher also asked herself whether it was fair for the rest of the children to be subjected to such outbursts, to have their time interrupted, to have to be so patient. She answered the question in this way: "I do feel, as I get a perspective on this whole affair, that if the group can aid Dolores to overcome some fear that must possess her, so that she can live in greater security, they will have a real deep-rooted satisfaction within themselves. This should aid them in the future."

Miss Irvington was also able to report considerable progress on Dolores' part by the end of the semester. Thus both Dolores and the group seemed to have profited by cooperative work on the knotty problem of helping the girl become a more comfortable group member.

If teachers have built a favorable group climate, the problem of one pupil can be brought before the group for discussion, not with the idea that the individual is bad, but that he needs help. Miss Schoener describes such an instance.

> While John was absent one day we discussed John's problem of becoming angry. The children said they liked the boy but not when he "got mad." I asked if there were any way they knew of that we could help John.
>
> One boy said, "We shouldn't play with him," but he was quickly stopped. Another said the best thing to do was just to walk away or look away when John became angry. This, they all decided, was the thing to do so we said we'd try it.
>
> Later John did better. When he had to move away the children all told him they were sorry he had to go because he had been so nice around the room lately.

At the sixth grade level, group pressure often operates quite spontaneously, as illustrated by an anecdote of Mrs. Valentine's.

> Alice was chosen committee chairman of a group of six who were to contribute some myths to the class. They worked for a week. I overheard one of the committee say to Alice, "You don't have your report ready, and we have only a few days more." To which Alice replied, "Don't worry about it. I have it all up in my head."
>
> Came the day of their presentation and Alice flopped badly. Her lack of preparation ruined much of the rest of the committee's work.
>
> Although Alice is potential leadership material, the committee did not choose her to work with them again. She had to pull herself up by her bootstraps to reinstate herself in the children's eyes.
>
> This, I feel, is good training for Alice. It does not take a child long to formulate good rules for social responsibility when the lesson taught is done by his fellow-students. I doubt if any lecture of mine to Alice

about the responsibility for being well prepared would have had such lasting results.

CONCLUSION

This chapter has shown that it is not necessary for the individual to be sacrificed for the group when cooperative procedures are employed in education. In fact, the chances that the individual will be recognized, studied, and helped are even greater when all are working together to make the best learning situation for everyone. Experiences with group planning undoubtedly contribute to the children's ability to do individual planning; for when the process is engaged in by a number of people, it is out in the open where it can be examined, criticized, improved. On the other hand, there is a place for individual planning in all group enterprises, in addition to the fact that not all of life is a group affair. The teacher working cooperatively with his group is in a position to gain continuous information about different individuals. He is also in a position to provide ways for group members to maintain their individuality and to improve their role in the group.

CHAPTER XVI

Record-Keeping and

Cooperative Procedures

FORMS OF RECORDS and the uses to which records may be put are many. For example, throughout this report liberal use has been made by adult observers or teachers of three types of records about pupil groups and their cooperative work—professional diaries, narrative and analytical accounts, and running records of classroom discussion. Such records not only help others to learn from the experience of particular teachers and pupils but also help teachers to improve group procedures so that groups and individuals can have better experiences with cooperative work. The use of such records for evidence of pupil growth is discussed in Chapter XVII. This chapter is restricted to records kept by teachers and pupils as an integral part of the planning process.

The first part of the chapter discusses and illustrates two uses of cooperative records: (1) as a means of helping the group to make progress; (2) as a means of keeping informed others who are not in the group but whose cooperation and understanding are desired. The chapter also suggests ways to help pupils learn to keep records.

RECORDS THAT MOVE
THE GROUP FORWARD

Records that appear to help the group to make progress are of three sorts: (1) those that make a particular discussion more efficient; (2) those that aid the group in carrying plans into action; and (3) those that help the group to evaluate progress.

Records That Aid Discussion

Records may be used to help leader and group members to recall plans made on previous occasions that can influence present planning, or they may help leader and group members to keep in mind earlier contributions and decisions within one planning period. When the planning on a particular occasion is a continuation of previous planning, efficiency would seem to be increased by having before the group the over-all problem and the decisions made to date as well as a statement of the particular topic for the day's proceedings. For example, Mrs. Nestor's sixth grade children were aided in a second discussion session on the same problem by the following record on the chalkboard.

> Problem—How many things can we learn by just looking at seeds?
> Activity—Look at many different seeds and list facts learned about them.
> Planned procedure:
> > Discussion
> > Looking
> > Notes
> > Making written record
> Product—Exhibit for P.T.A.
> > Actual seeds
> > Drawing
> > Sentences
> > Charts

In addition, there were five findings listed from the previous day's discussion. Other examples of the availability of such records were seen in the cases of Miss Wells's planning with her children for learning about the Community Chest and "Our New Tasks"; Miss Sanborn's play-production activity; and the planning of Thanksgiving donations in Robinson School.[1]

A record on the chalkboard in Miss Martin's first and second grade room shows clearly that it was designed to orient the group in a discussion to come. In contrast with the record in Mrs. Nestor's room, this discussion guide probably was developed by the teacher for the children:

> What—A Christmas Bazaar
> Why—To make money for our school
> Who—Kindergarten, first, second, third grades
> Where—In the auditorium
> When—The week before Christmas
> What will we make?

A rather complete example of the use of records to provide continuity in planning comes from Mr. Omans, a principal who helped

[1] See pages 96–102, 142–143, 182–186.

a third grade in his elementary school plan a safety program. The schools of the system had been asked to conduct a safety campaign to be concluded with a poster contest sponsored by the board of education. The third grade teacher had asked for help and the other teachers seemed uncertain how to provide for pupil participation in the project; so the principal assumed the responsibility of planning with the third grade for a week before the other groups got under way.

After discussion of some recent accidents in school, the problem was formulated and incorporated in the first chart.

Our Safety Program

Problem—How can we make our school a safer place for boys and girls?
1. Discuss all safety rules for our school
2. Make safety posters
3. Obey all safety rules
4. Cooperate with the principal, teachers, and other boys and girls
5. Obey safety patrolmen

The next two charts to be made were:

We can make our school safer in these places:
1. In the cafeteria
2. In the classroom
3. On the buses
4. In the auditorium
5. On the playground
6. In the lavatories
7. In the halls and on the stairs
8. On the roads to and from school and buses

What we are going to do on Monday:
1. Discuss and list safety rules for buses
2. Find out what posters are and how to make them
3. Make safety posters

Before the pupils made the next chart, they examined and talked about many posters they had seen. On exhibition were four or five posters of the American Automobile Association. From an examination of these posters and from their discussion, they made the following chart:

What a poster has on it:
1. There is a picture about a safety rule
2. Every poster has one idea on it
3. Each poster has a slogan on it

4. The picture explains the slogan
5. Posters have very few colors in them, usually one or two

Before the pupils made their first poster, they decided what the steps in the procedure would be.

In making posters we must:
1. Decide what the poster will be about
2. Decide what the picture will be
3. Decide what the slogan will be
4. Decide what the colors will be

Each pupil in the class made a poster for the areas of safety listed in the second chart. Before a poster was started there was a discussion of the area being considered. Rules agreed upon were incorporated in a chart. For example, one chart dealt with safety rules for buses, and another with conduct in the cafeteria. After such a chart had been developed each child could begin planning a poster based on it. The first two sets of posters were done in wax crayons. After the children had completed their posters, they took part in an evaluation period to compare the work done with the standards set up for making posters. The two charts which follow were outgrowths of discussions on how the children might improve their work.

How can we improve our slogans?
1. Improve our printing of capital letters [shown on chart]
2. Leave a space between words
3. Leave a space between each line

We can make posters in several ways:
1. With wax crayons
2. With paints
3. With colored chalk
4. With cut-outs

The rest of the charts dealt with safety rules for the remaining areas listed in the second chart. These charts resulting from Mr. Omans' planning with third grade children are an excellent example of records as an integral factor in the movement of the group.

In using a chalkboard record to help participants keep items in mind during the progress of a discussion, the teacher finds there is always the problem of when to begin the record. Starting to make the record as soon as suggestions commence to flow may be wasteful. For example, Mrs. Quincy's third grade was trying to plan how they could help keep the playground clean. Soon the teacher was kept busy writing down a series of negative items such as:

We will not throw orange peelings, apple cores, and paper on the ground.
We will not run in the way of people playing games.
We will not push children off the bars.
We will not fight on the playground.
We will not write on the tar.
We will not throw rocks.
We will not dig holes. (All the foregoing from Patsy)
We will not play on the grass but play on the playground.
We will not stamp on flowers.
We will not climb trees. (This item from Patsy again)
We will not break glass on the playground.
We shall pick up papers on the playground.
We will not pull the grass up and throw it on the sidewalks. (The last three items from Paul)

The teacher became so engrossed in this listing that she failed to appreciate and to capitalize on the one positive idea Paul offered and the three which followed from Shirley:

We should obey the patrol boys.
We could sweep the sidewalks.
We could plant flowers, grass, and shrubbery.

The teacher merely said, "Now let's think real hard to see if we can think of other ways of improving our playground," which invited a new stream of negative ideas.

We will not jump through the hedge.
We will not build a fire.
We will not throw snowballs at each other.
We will not throw bow and arrows over the fence.

Still the teacher was intent on getting an ever-growing list. "Let's think real hard," she said again.

If the teacher and children had given less attention to getting ideas listed and more attention to getting them examined, they might have stopped the negative trend of their suggestions and come out with more ideas like Shirley's. In other words, a better procedure might have been to explore and evaluate a number of possible ideas and then go back and pull out the most pertinent and worth-while ideas to record. The teacher could even have jotted down the suggestions on a pad, had she feared that good ideas would be lost.

A record kept privately by the teacher at first has several possible advantages: (1) the teacher can scribble fast enough to keep the suggestions flowing freely; (2) group members have an opportunity to listen to and to remember the suggestions of others; and (3) the final writing of the plan on the board constitutes a good summary of the suggestion-gathering activity. On the other hand, the plan of writing the suggestions directly on the board as they are given provides a memory aid which participants often need and which can be used to help them build the habit of checking the record to prevent duplication of suggestions.

It is probable that time and effort could have been saved in Miss Durham's room on the occasion when Anita was in charge of planning the game period, had the plan for recording names of children choosing a particular game been introduced earlier.[2]

Another effective use of the chalkboard record was seen in Miss Fielding's mathematics class when a recorder listed points made in various reports. This record served to focus attention on major ideas.[3]

In judging at what point to use a chalkboard record during a discussion or planning period, one should consider whether recording at that time would help to focus the discussion on the problem at hand and to reduce random and duplicating suggestions, or whether it would slow down the group unduly, thus interfering with a free flow of suggestions. The wisest plan probably is to try out different ways of handling the recording problem.

Records That Aid in Action

An important use of records is to help groups and individuals to carry out responsibilities assumed. The chart of room helpers to be found in so many elementary classrooms, the list of jobs to be rotated in a high school shop, the parts of a mural which different group members have undertaken to do, the jobs to be done on the school grounds and the tools needed, the various tasks that must be accomplished to keep the school store running, the different posts to be manned on cleanup day—all these are examples of records as reminders.

All classrooms of cooperating teachers visited during the study featured many records that seemed intended as aids to action. Some appeared to be immediately useful, such as a list of cooking utensils and food to be brought from home so that a breakfast could be prepared in the classroom. Functional also was this list of workers

[2] See pages 364–367
[3] See pages 86–91

needed for the contouring of a barren hillside: post diggers, fence workers, contour makers, seeders, sweepers . . . and this set of plans for a mural:

1. Street in front of school—patrol boy keeping children from crossing in middle of street
2. Bicycle rule
3. Bus rule
4. Patrol boy on corner
5. Baseball
6. Inside scene—stairway
7. Correct use of play equipment

The following directions for papering the walls of the playhouse probably were formulated by Miss Martin's first and second grade children after some discussion with the teacher. A playhouse being papered by these young children was evidence that the record was for real use.

Brush the wallpaper with the paste.
Up and down.
Cover every spot.
Fold the paper over.
Hang it on the wall and smooth it.

In other classrooms there were records that looked less genuinely useful—records that perhaps were overelaborate. So logically and completely developed were they that it was apparent pupils were spending time planning when they might better have gotten into action as soon as they had a reasonable plan for starting work, letting experience with a few plans determine the course of future planning. An example of a possibly less useful type of plan comes from a fourth grade that was studying the history of the state.

How to Get Ready to Give Our Play

I. Read many books and stories to build the plot for our play.
II. Consult other resources, such as pictures, people, museums, etc.
III. Plan the play.
    A. Discuss the kinds of stories we might use.
    B. Try out some stories.
    C. Select parts we like best.
    D. Put parts together.
    E. Select characters and scenes.
    F. Make up trial dialogue.
IV. Begin rehearsals.
    A. Set time for the play.

    B. Build standards for giving a good play.
    C. Select permanent cast.
    D. Select understudies, workers, and helpers.
    E. Practice dialogue and acting.
    F. Evaluate the acting and the dialogue.
    G. Try to improve our rehearsals.
  V. Make scenery.
 VI. Make costumes.
VII. Plan and make programs.
VIII. Write and send invitations.
 IX. Give the play.
  X. Discuss what we think of the play we've given.

The following record from the same group is perhaps a little more functional and action-oriented than the preceding one, although it has a tentative, some-time-in-the-future quality rather than one reflecting a commitment for a specific job to be done at a definite time.

Activities for the Study of Our State

Activities	Workers Needed	Materials
Keep a notebook of class activities	Larrie, Beverly, Pauline, Joan D.	Keep written plans for our group
Write plans	Beverly, Pauline, Nancy B., Larrie, Trudy	Crayons, pencil, ruler, eraser, paper, scissors, books, ink
Make maps	David, Dick H., Tom, Ned, Richard, Stewart, Jo John, Peter, Ralph	Pictures, papers, crayons, ink, flour, salt, wood, paint
Make a mural	Paul, Philip, Robert, Larrie, Trudy, Pauline, Hubert	Yellow chalk, ruler, colored chalk, paper, scissors, eraser, sketches
Have dramatizations	Everyone in the group	Books, paper, pencil, dialogue, etc.
Keep bulletin board	Everyone in the group	Maps, clippings, pictures
Make booklets	Larrie, Pauline, Nancy B., Nancy S., Beverly	Pictures, stories, clippings, maps, cards

When two or three classes in a school are working jointly on a project, records can serve to coordinate their activities.

Another type of record whose purpose is to influence behavior shows agreements on standards or rules arrived at by a group—standards for going through the halls, for eating in the cafeteria, for attending assemblies, and for meeting a host of other situations. Just how effective these conduct codes are in influencing behavior is not known. It may well be that their greatest value lies in their cooperative development and in the importance attached to them when they are posted in attractive form. The records also give the group something to turn to as a reminder when agreements begin to be forgotten.

Records can also be used to encourage self-directed activity. In connection with the study of the barber shop in Miss Daly's classroom, this chart was used.[4]

> What Do We Need for the Barber Shop
>> a big chair
>> dryer
>> permanent machine
>> jackets
>> combs
>> sink
>> bottles
>> razors and clippers
>> nail file and nail polish
>> barber pole

The children signed their names on the chart to indicate what they planned to bring or make for their barber shop. Miss Daly tells a revealing anecdote about the way the chart was used one day.

> Jane emerged from our barber shop one morning holding up the back of the homemade barber chair which had broken off. When she looked questioningly at me, occupied with a reading group at the time, I refused to meet her eyes. She stood there thinking for a moment and then proceeded to our chart of committee responsibility. She ran her finger down to "big chair," and across to the signatures there. Straight to David she marched, holding up the broken chair. David looked a little crestfallen at this evidence of inadequate workmanship, but immediately gathered the rest of the committee together and proceeded to the workshop to repair the chair.
>
> I am always glad to see these children taking responsibility, as they have a great deal done for them at home.

Not always can records function so well after the time of their first usefulness. It would seem, however, that a criterion in deciding

4 See pages 93–94

how long to keep a record posted in a classroom should be its possible usefulness to the group. Too many classrooms are cluttered with an accumulation of obviously outdated records.

Records That Aid in Evaluation

Various uses of records as an aid to groups in their evaluation of progress have been illustrated in previous chapters. In Chapter XII participation records were discussed. Earlier we saw how a group which had made plans for September carried over certain items into the plans for the next month.[5] Groups in the elementary school frequently pause toward the end of a day to check over their daily plan in order to find out whether they have accomplished all they set out to do. Some groups keep a diary record of their activities and progress. Committee reports are another kind of record that is useful in judging progress and in planning in terms of past accomplishments.

The report, "Beautifying a Barren Hillside," written cooperatively by children, teachers, and school neighbors, shows another type of record which enables a whole school to evaluate procedures and accomplishments.[6] The many garden records reproduced in an earlier chapter represent other types of material that would aid in evaluating progress in carrying out plans: experience stories composed by younger children, records of useful information discovered, of responsibilities identified and accepted, and ways of working planned.[7]

RECORDS THAT INFORM OTHERS

Sometimes records are used to inform others. When Mrs. Stanley's pupils had kept their individual plan books for a time, they decided it would be good to let their mothers know about their new way of working.[8] On the occasion of a tea party which the children planned for their mothers, several charts were on display. These no doubt were partly to remind the children of their responsibilities (if they would need reminding on such an eventful occasion!). But it is more than likely that the charts were also a part of the program, to show the mothers how the party was planned. For example, one chart showed the over-all plan.

[5] See page 28
[6] See pages 177 ff.
[7] See pages 144 ff
[8] See pages 429–431

Planning a Tea for Our Mothers
1. It will be 2:00 P.M., Thursday, March 20.
2. We will write invitations.
3. We will be courteous and thoughtful.
4. We will introduce our mothers.
5. We will arrange our room.
6. We will tell about our work.
7. We will serve refreshments.

Another chart was entitled "Planning Our Talks for Our Mothers —Choosing What We Will Tell About." Included in the list were: frieze, Hawaii, plan books, spelling list, news, opening exercises, library books, dictionary, Greece, reading, arithmetic, music, stories and poems. Two other charts posted were "Planning Our Refreshments" and "Serving Committee and Duties." Since the purpose of the program was to help mothers see how the children were learning to plan, these records were being used as a means of interpreting an important part of the school program.

Another use of records for informing others is suggested by a problem encountered in one rural school. The teachers and principal had been trying to create interest among the older children in beautifying the school grounds. The boys were dutifully excavating for the lily pool but seemed more desirous of pleasing the principal than anything else. When finally analyzed, the problem seemed to be that the boys realized that they would be going on to junior high school before the lily pool would be finished and thus the project did not seem important to them.

The solution reached was to have children all through the school make a master plan for improving the grounds. Records of these plans were to be supplemented by colorful sketches of the way the children thought the finished project might look. It was expected that after this procedure, any work done would be seen as part of a larger whole and children going on to a new school would be eager to come back to their elementary school to see progress made. The records would also serve an important purpose in orienting newcomers to the work under way.

A group of sixth grade pupils, who would be going on to junior high school the following year, turned to poetry to record a hint for a group that would take their place. The poem was posted under some lively animal pictures made by pupils and hung in the school library.

A Disappointment

Alas and alack, and sad is the day
For due to restriction of the O.P.A.
The lumber for shelves we planned to place here
Won't be available till sometime next year.
So our animal friends from books we have read
Must occupy this space instead
Of the planned- and dreamed- and hoped-for shelves
Which we wanted so much to build ourselves.

In some schools the use of records to inform others is carried to an extreme. Mrs. Chase taught in a school where a great point was made of large charts to record all long-range plans. Extensive wall space in the corridors was covered with impressive records of plans made in assemblies of several classes for projects to be undertaken jointly. Often a year's work on improving the building and grounds would be outlined on such charts. In each classroom there would be found slightly smaller but equally detailed charts showing the plans made for a particular group's part in the over-all enterprise. Even though older children helped to make such charts, as was often the case, a great deal of time was thus consumed, and the wisdom of this expenditure was questioned by Mrs. Chase. "How much should you record? . . . I am kept busy all the time making charts."

An example of the kind of chart to which Mrs. Chase referred measured at least five feet by three feet and showed the plans of two fourth grades in a joint study. It was posted in the corridor, "to pique the curiosity of the entire school":

Our State, a Complete Community

Understanding	Activities	Skills
1. To appreciate our state and the advantages it gives us.	1. Write and give a play.	1. How to read to gather information.
2. To be able to help parents, other grades, visitors, etc., to appreciate our state.	2. Have a museum.	2. Learning to report interestingly.
3. In order to appreciate our state more, we must know more about its	3. Keep a diary of what we do.	3. How to use reference books.
	4. Make maps.	4. Learning how to plan.
a. history	5. Write plans on charts.	5. Using complete sentences.
b. geography		

Our State, a Complete Community

Understanding	Activities	Skills
c. industries	6. Make charts.	6. Building a larger vocabulary.
d. products		
e. famous persons, places, and dates	7. Have dramatizations.	7. Learning how to make a picture tell a story.
f. government		
g. recreation and sports	8. Make murals, etc.	8. Learning how to improve lettering for charts, etc.
h. educational advantages	9. Gather information.	9. Learning how to arrange an interesting bulletin board.
i. flag, song, bird, flower	10. Report to classes.	
j. "first" things for which famous	11. Have a state bulletin board.	
	12. Make booklets on our state.	
	13. Learn some of the early dances used in our state.	
	14. Collect pictures of parts of our state.	

Such a record might be useful for impressing school patrons with the knowledge and skills the children were acquiring. Even if the plans were genuinely the result of pupil thinking (of which there may be some doubt), one questions the investment of time and effort to make this display of them. It would seem important to put most effort into developing adequate plans and carrying them out and to devote to record-keeping only the energy necessary to facilitate cooperative work. In other words, records should be a means to an end, not an end in themselves.

HELPING PUPILS LEARN FROM RECORD-KEEPING

Since records have many uses in improving the quality of group operations, teachers should assume responsibility for helping pupils learn how to keep and use them. Making use of records as part of cooperative work is, of course, the best way of developing an appreciation of their usefulness. However, the teacher's responsibility should extend further than that. If the problem were only to demonstrate the uses of records, the teacher could continue to keep all records himself and not give pupils opportunity to develop skill in this direction. But since record-keeping is a skill needed by people desiring to use cooperative procedures, teachers must seek adequate ways of promoting that skill in children and youth.

It becomes a problem, then, for the teacher to know when to do the recording needed by a group and when to give pupils an opportunity to have that experience. If pupil recorders are used, the teacher must find ways not to slow the progress of the group too much.

When Teachers Record

If the teacher decides to be the recorder on a particular occasion, perhaps the first rule is that he must set a good example himself. For instance, the teacher should try to be faithful to the suggestions given by a group member. A record from Mrs. Chase's classroom shows an interesting state of affairs. The children were writing a play about the voyage of the "Mayflower" and were engaged in planning a conversation that would take place on board. The observer wrote down each proposal as it was given by one of the sixth grade children and recorded opposite it what the teacher wrote on the blackboard after the child had spoken. This was the result.

Children's Suggestions	Teacher's Record
	Topics for Conversation
How it will be over there?	A. Future life
Should they sign?	B. Form of government
Their life in the past—their debts —life since then	C. Their life in the old world (Revised) Their life in England
Boy says "England."	D. Debts
	E. Hardships—present life on ship
When they get on land—their shelter	F. Shelter
What it was like on the boat	(Ignored)
What weather will be like	G. Hopes and fears

(Teacher asked if they wanted "weather" listed separately. Children answered "Yes," but it was not done.)

How to build houses

(Teacher asked how long list should be, how long they should plan for each scene.)

You have shelter and if you have that you should have food, clothing

(Teacher said, "You think you should list all those? Think tonight about this.")

It should be added that the teacher reworded items at her pleasure without consulting the individual who gave the suggestion or the group. The teacher should have asked individuals how they wanted their ideas stated for the record. Or she could have tested to see if her wording kept the spirit of the child's suggestion, being willing to revise her statement if the pupil objected to it. (This was done by Mrs. Chase the one time a pupil challenged her.)

When Pupils Record

As was suggested before, when contributions are being gathered from a group, it is possible to allow rather free giving of ideas for a time before trying to record anything. The items that go into the record can then be those that emerged as being most useful, and time can be taken to evaluate them without interrupting a flow of thoughts. This makes a situation in which a pupil recorder can operate effectively (at least from middle grades on up).

An example of a teacher helping pupils learn the complexities of record-keeping occurred in Miss Wells's fifth grade classroom. The teacher's question for opening the problem for the day was, "What do we want to know about our state?" Answers began to come: "When was it admitted?" "What kind of soil?" The teacher then asked, "Will we remember all this?"

"The secretaries will take it down," was the confident answer of one of the pupils. "Shall we have one of our secretaries at the board?" the teacher proposed. (Apparently it was the custom to have two student secretaries for each discussion; most chalkboard records in this room were in pupil handwriting.) This was the first record:

1. When admitted.
2. Was capital always in one place?
3. What people settled in (state)?
4. What kind of soil is there in (state)?
5. What kind of transportation then and now?
6. What is the surface of (state)?

At this point a girl asked, "Shouldn't you put a question mark after all of them?" The teacher tried to show the girl that the first item was a "dummy sentence" and might not need a question mark. Since the children had been helped on previous occasions to put their records into consistent form,[9] they decided to amend item 1 to read, "When was the state admitted?"

[9] See pages 96–102

The teacher wondered if it might not be easier for the children to refrain from using full questions. They could say, "When admitted," "Capital," and so on. This idea seemed to appeal to the group, and the list was redone.

1. When admitted
2. Capital
3. People
4. Soil
5. Crops
6. Transportation
7. Surface

Other items were added:

8. Animals
9. Flowers and trees
10. Weather and climate
11. Government
12. Interesting places
13. Occupations
14. Cities
15. Educational places
16. Famous people

The completed list may look like a typical geography outline, but every item included came after a clarifying discussion and an attempt to state an idea broadly enough to include several subitems. For example, one boy was quite dissatisfied with the original wording of item 3, "What people settled in (state)?" He wanted a question on population. No, population figures were not included in "people who settled," because some of the settlers went on farther west. The simple item "people," although concealing the boy's point, did not exclude it from future consideration.

Another interesting discussion arose over government. "Government is for the country," one boy thought until assured that states have governments too. Another child wanted items like "taxes" and "counties" included, and still another pointed out that "government" would take in "capital." The teacher suggested that items might have to be reorganized when it came to choosing people to work on them.

Another discussion arose over the item "interesting places." The teacher tried to sell the idea that "important places" would be a better way to state the item. However, the children pointed out that they wanted to list "recreation" and "pleasure places." The solution reached was including a later item, "educational places."

Notes taken by the writer during this discussion in Miss Wells's classroom and later shared with the teacher show other choices that the teacher might have made. No one choice is invariably right; each teacher must experiment to discover generally helpful techniques.

The teacher kept pushing for broader statements. That is one way to proceed, lining up big topics and then putting specifics under them. Another way would be to gather all ideas as they come and then organize them into main points and subpoints. The latter way may be easier for younger planners because it allows them to organize a set of concrete items rather than make unaided judgment as to whether an item is a main topic or a specific item under a main topic.

For variety and more participation the teacher might have had the children write out several questions of their own, with perhaps a few oral questions first to get the ideas flowing. This would give the experience of writing out well-worded complete questions, if that seemed desirable, and it would let all children—the ready talkers and the slower starters—begin somewhat even when it came time to pool suggestions. It would be possible for small groups to pool their ideas first, letting the large group choose among a few proposed organizations and combine ideas they wished to keep.

The teacher showed respect for the individual making a contribution by saying, "What do you want her (the secretary) to write?"

The teacher missed an opportunity for pupil participation by reading the list herself instead of having a child do so. She also took over the recording job when individuals were signing up for various questions. Again, when the group turned to listing their sources of information for this study, the teacher let the same secretary continue at the board instead of giving another child a chance.

One boy suggested, "Making shoes and things we don't do in this state. I don't know the name for it." This point, which was completely overlooked by the teacher, would have given a splendid opportunity to help a pupil learn to state an idea that was well worth including in the record. A safeguard against missing such good points might be to ask as a discussion is closing, "Is there anything we overlooked?"

At the end of the period, small groups met to explore sources of information in the classroom and to plan other helps they would need in their particular group. It was wise of the teacher to have the children turn to some concrete materials after a rather long planning session, although they had accomplished a great deal in a relatively short time, and there were remarkably few signs of fatigue or lack of interest. On another occasion, however, the teacher should encourage the small group to make and record a somewhat detailed outline of what their broad topic would cover.

In addition to helping pupils learn chalkboard recording as an aid to group discussion, the teacher must help them develop skill in writing reports of meetings. As group discussion techniques develop further and further beyond the insights of those who regularized parliamentary law, old forms of minutes of meetings become less useful and new ways of reporting become necessary. A useful form that may be adapted to the purposes of various kinds of groups is:

> Name of group
> Meeting place, date, hours
> Members present (names)
> Members absent (names)
> Problems discussed
> Suggestions made
> Problems to be referred to other committees
> Decisions reached
> Plans for next meeting[10]

Another way of helping pupils to learn record-keeping is to encourage the making of individual records of plans not only for the pupils themselves but for committees and other matters pertaining to the group. One second grade teacher has her children keep individual notebooks for such a purpose.

Innovations in Records

Records do not always have to be in words on a chalkboard or on a tagboard chart. Some teachers use pictorial records to good advantage. Reference has already been made to Miss Daly's illustrated chart, "Choose Your Work Here," and to the garden map showing what had been planted in each grade's plot.[11]
In an earlier chapter, records from Miss Baker's second grade class were reproduced to show what the pupils planned to finish before Easter, what they expected to do that day, and what they were to do during work period. In addition, there was in this room a set of three most interesting pictorial plans, which gave the work in Miss Baker's class an even more long-range setting. In the center was an adult-made blueprint of an outdoor theater with a large caption over it, "As the Terrace Will Look in the Future." On the left was a child's crayon sketch labeled "As the Terrace Looks Now," and on the right was another, "As We Would Like It to Be in June."
Miss Peterson reports a successful trial of recording a plan through pictures in her second grade class.

[10] Alice Miel, *Changing the Curriculum* (New York: Appleton-Century-Crofts, Inc., 1946), p. 141.
[11] See pages 26, 144.

A Second Grade Plans a Flower Garden

A spring activity in our second grade is planning and making a garden. This year the class chose to make a flower garden. In order to have flowers throughout a greater part of the year, it was decided to have a spring garden and fall garden. Our plan was shown through pictures in a variety of media and was as follows:

1. *Where* to make the garden
   This was recorded on a *cut-out map* of our garden space. It showed the measurements, the location of the sidewalk and building in relation to the garden spot. It also suggested where to plant certain flowers.
2. *When* to make the garden
   A *crayon mural* showing a spring scene and fall scene.
3. *How* to make and prepare for a garden
   This mural was done in *chalk* on *craft* paper.
4. *What* to plant
   Shown by individual pictures using all media. This was an outcome of a class discussion during which we decided to plant forsythia, pansies, weigela, petunias, barberry, lily of the valley and other summer flowers.
5. *Where* to get equipment and materials
   A mural done with *water paints* showing home, hardware store, greenhouse.

CONCLUSION

As we have seen, records have value as links between discussions in different sessions as well as aids to groups in staying on the track during one sitting. They help groups to follow up on plans, and they serve to inform others on whose understanding and cooperation the group may depend.

To help pupils learn effective uses of records, the teacher must make sure of several points:

1. That the integrity of the individual's contribution is maintained as rewording and organization of items proceed.

2. That items judged to be subitems are not lost for future follow-up.

3. That records are begun not too early and not too late in the proceedings of a group.

4. That records will have, in so far as possible, both present and future use to the group.

5. That records are varied in nature and appropriate to the maturity and purposes of the group.

6. That different pupils have chances to be record-keepers.

CHAPTER XVII

Gathering Evidence of Pupil

Growth in and through

Cooperative Procedures

ALL THOUGHTFUL TEACHERS are evaluating pupil growth continuously as they work with girls and boys. Those teachers who have confidence in the values of cooperative procedures in education and who wish to discover how individuals and groups are growing as they have experience with group processes are alert for signs of special types of growth. This chapter is concerned with (1) kinds of pupil growth teachers look for in connection with cooperative work, (2) types of evidence teachers use in judging the educative effect of group experiences, and (3) sources of evidence they employ.

KINDS OF GROWTH SOUGHT

Teachers frequently conclude descriptions of cooperative enterprises with some sort of summary evaluation. Often this evaluation is stated in rather general terms for the entire group, with little supporting evidence. Numerous examples of this type of summary have been reported in earlier chapters. Let us examine some of them to discover the kinds of results teachers note and what sorts of growth in their children they appear to value as contributing to democratic socialization.

Miss MacKelvy listed ten items under the heading "Growth as a Result of Evaluation" in reporting on her attempt to help her third grade children plan their use of free time.[1] This list may be paraphrased as follows:

[1] See pages 23–24.

1. Children taking advantage of resources.
2. Children forming groups with common interests.
3. Individuals and groups working with purpose.
4. Children less able to develop interests of their own joining other groups.
5. Shy non-leaders beginning to make suggestions.
6. Children beginning to recognize everyone as a valuable member.
7. Children recognizing other resources besides teacher.
8. Children developing eagerness for free period.
9. Children developing socially in a democratic way.
10. Children sharing findings in discussion periods.

Miss Wilson, who told the story of how her pupils helped to improve their dilapidated one-room school, concluded with the words, "The children were delighted with each improvement and their delight seemed reflected in their work, behavior, and appearance." [2]

Miss Brainard made this comment at the end of an account of a cooperative project: "Contact between the upper grade children and the teachers of lower grades has produced a splendid feeling of all belonging together."

Miss Tate reported on a trip taken to buy Valentine refreshments and concluded: "Pupil-teacher planning contributed a great deal to the trip's success in greater pupil interest, better conduct and discipline and greater participation in the study." [3]

Evidences of growth as seen by the teachers responsible for "beautifying a barren hillside" included (1) assuming responsibility, (2) respecting school terraces, (3) evaluating school work, (4) feeling pride in work well done, and joy in having done a service for the school and the community. [4]

Miss Franklin was pleased that her first grade children did an unusually good job in making Christmas cards—"even Bernard, who usually makes a mess of everything, did a neat job." The teacher adds, "This proves the importance of children knowing what to do and how to do it."

Miss Oliver frequently includes comments such as these in her professional diary.

The children were contributing ideas to work out their problem without blaming anyone.

[2] See pages 38–40.
[3] See pages 169–170.
[4] See pages 177 ff.

The group have tried to be good followers and obey the leader.

Henry has learned to get along well with children and always has something worth while to contribute when the group needs his help. He has learned to get help at the right time and make the most of not always winning.

The group is learning to think together and work out their problems.

Inspection of these informal evaluations by teachers reveals that a few ideas are prominent. Teachers value growth in *independence and responsibility* which is related to purposeful activity, high interest, and better "discipline." They value also signs that pupils are becoming more *helpful, thoughtful, and friendly.* They are pleased when children show more ability in *skills of cooperation,* as shown by their participation, their work in small groups, their ability to evaluate, their being more "democratic." They also note that children *"learn more,"* get better results.

TYPES OF EVIDENCE

The structure of this section of the chapter was determined by the kinds of evidence furnished by cooperating teachers. There is no claim that this is an exhaustive evaluation of growth through cooperation. In fact, the chapter, like the others, highlights the need for further investigation by teachers and others.

The examples available for illustrating evidence of growth fall rather well into the groupings found in the rough sampling with which this chapter opened. The one exception is that teachers often made comments on *needed growth* in addition to *advances in growth.* Accordingly, the remainder of this chapter will present additional illustrations of the following.

1. Evidence of need for growth
2. Evidence of growth in independence and responsibility
3. Evidence of growth in helpfulness and friendliness
4. Evidence of growth in group skills
5. Evidence of growth in concepts and generalizations

Need for Growth

An important step in evaluation of growth is to find out where the pupils are in respect to points at which they may need help.

Miss Rezny's diary contains many references to observed needs of her sixth grade children.

Patty is still working mainly for herself rather than the group. She admires Collyn but does not copy her ways, which are those of a potential leader.

Bill laughs at anything Gordon does, perhaps because he wouldn't dare to do the things he evidently would like to do.

Gordon brought in a spear that he had made as a primitive weapon. We all admired it. If only he could accept interest gracefully!

Suzanne showed us a tiny Eskimo doll that walks. I was so glad she showed a willingness to share this and talk about it. She needs to be helped to be less conscious of her size.

As a junior high school teacher concluded her account of group planning in social studies, she showed that she had assessed the status of the group as to the wholeheartedness of their participation. "About 90 per cent participated and 10 per cent showed resistance. Some were slow to select a topic of interest. Others decided to work with a group of their friends with no intention of contributing." Whether or not the teacher's interpretation of the motives of her pupils was accurate, she at least was aware of the problem of a resisting group.

The description of a trial of pupil-teacher planning in a seventh grade mathematics class in an earlier chapter contained a reference to one "exceptional student who has done very little work under this method because he is conditioned to competitive classroom behavior. . . . He admits that he dislikes mathematics." [5] The only pleasure he derived was to be the first one finished. Under the new plan he did only "the minimum required by his group." This student's clear need for help did not show up until a cooperative type of behavior was called for. The boy presented every bit as big a challenge to the teacher as the "retarded student" whose interest in the group work was not maintained.

The way in which a sixth grade girl with a "high I.Q." responded to opportunities to exercise leadership caused Mr. Owen to do some thinking about the selection and training of leaders.

March 17. Results from the committee work on the current mural projects are showing that leadership and a high I.Q. certainly need not run parallel. As a chairman of one project I chose, without much thought, I'm afraid, a girl who, by tests and other means, has shown her brightness. Hers was the last committee to be chosen and I thought that she could handle it competently. Her committee is now in a state of complete disorder. I have helped her to get started, and still the members are confused as to what she wants them to do specifically.

[5] See pages 270–271.

In the first place, I should not have done the choosing; the committee should have done that. Perhaps she should have been left to solve the problems of disorganization herself. Can it be that she simply cannot lead? I should like to find if leadership can be brought out in everyone. There are many things which my first year of teaching has not yet solved!

Only by giving the girl an opportunity to use new skills or to use old skills in new ways could the teacher learn where to start in helping her.

Growth in Independence and Responsibility

A number of comments by teachers show that they take occasion to observe general ability in group self-management. Miss Grossman deliberately created an opportunity to observe growth in self-direction. Her diary reports what she found out.

October 15. I sat back today and watched the children during free time and discovered much. They are really growing. Every child was busy. Four boys worked at the workbench on doll-house furniture. They were sharing the tools easily. Two children working with the books in the library were discussing the arrangement and care of the books. One remarked that we should paint the shelves. Two children were playing dominoes. Some children were around the clay table, chatting quietly; another group played house. The atmosphere was one of peace and quiet, with easy give-and-take. No one was worrying about me.

Miss Rezny describes growth in her sixth grade group in these terms:

In many ways the children are developing self-reliance. They can work at their own or group concerns for rather long periods of time, and they work peacefully together.

Mrs. Percival says of the students in her junior high school social studies–English classes:

When the children help decide how we are going to work on a topic, they plan way ahead, watch for things in newspapers and magazines, clip them and bring them to school.

Mr. Rice's diary shows his pleasure at the stage of growth his high school class had reached by the end of October.

I was pleased with the reaction of one of my seventh grade boys' hygiene classes the other day. I was about twenty-five minutes late for class because of a parent's interview. When I entered the room all were busily working so I just sat down and did not disturb them. Some were reading health magazines, others were preparing lessons in American history and other subjects; some were studying alone while others were working together. There was an industrious buzz in the room, but no disturbing noise. The above continued for the rest of the period and I was pleased to think that perhaps part of this social learning had been derived from our classroom procedure of last year and this year. These students were supposedly some of the "problem" boys in school.

Other examples of growing responsibility and independence are based on specific incidents occurring in groups observed.

In concluding her story of Peter and how he brought his problem with John before the group, Miss Oliver reports:

When the group was leaving the room at noon Peter's mother appeared in the room. She went over and spoke to Peter. I heard him say, "I took care of it myself." She came over to me laughing. "Well, this is certainly a feather in your hat. I just didn't realize you did things like this. This is really democratic. When I told Peter this morning that I would call John's mother, he told me that he could take care of his problem and handle it in problem time. He knew Miss Oliver would let him."

The teacher comments on the incident as follows:

The one thing that seemed most important to me was the fact that Peter, who had had most of his problems settled for him by his mother, was just now beginning to handle his own problems, to do his own thinking in a social setting. He was just beginning to feel confident of himself. He was now able to talk about something that troubled him and ask for help.[6]

Miss Franklin's statement of growth follows a description of planning and preparing to decorate Christmas wrapping paper in her first grade.

Although there were twenty-five people using paint, we had only one accident. I thought there would be lots of noise and confusion, but each child was so interested in his paper that he had very little to say to his neighbor. This was a surprise for me and I am sure the secret lies in the method of cooperative planning before the children start to work. Incidentally in making our plans, we did discuss keeping paint off the floor but nothing was said about being quiet.

Miss Jones illustrates growth in independence in her first grade group with an anecdote involving a few of her children.

The other day on the playground I noticed a group apparently having some difficulty by the slide, so I walked over and asked if something

[6] See pages 58–59.

was wrong. Jeanne answered, "It's all settled. Nothing is wrong now."
And another added, "Yes, we've settled it."

Later Jeanne confided to me that Robert had decided he would climb
up the slide instead of sliding down, "which," Jeanne added, "is one of
the agreements we made not to do, and when we told him so he didn't
care, so Stephen said that if Robert did it he might get hurt and couldn't
come to school and that we all liked to play with him." Apparently
Robert was persuaded because he went off with Stephen and others and
played with a ball.

The children seem to take a great deal of pride in being able to settle
all sorts of little troubles alone and there really seem to be far fewer
difficulties to settle.

Although Miss Jones does not indicate the planning she had done
with the children to help them develop this independence, it is quite
apparent that she had worked for this end and that the children had
had opportunity to make some cooperative "agreements."

On another occasion Miss Franklin reports on the way in which
Bernard, her troublemaker in the first grade, rose to the confidence
which she, at his request, placed in him.

January 6. Our school yard was too bad, because of the weather, to
let the children go out for recess. This meant we had to have recess in
our room. While we were playing indoor games, the new teacher on our
floor sent for help. I explained to my children that I would be down
the hall for a few minutes. We talked about things you could do and
could not do in a schoolroom. Fred wanted to be in charge of the class.
I said if each child takes care of himself, we won't need anyone in
charge. We agreed this was a good chance to show that we had grown
since September. It was decided that every child would do as he
pleased.

When I got ready to go I asked Bernard to go with me. He usually
causes trouble with his classmates. Bernard protested and did not want
to go. He said, "I can take care of myself. Please let me stay." When
I saw how much it meant to him, I let him stay.

I was gone ten minutes, but when I came back some were drawing on
the blackboard, others were at the library table, some were in a group
talking and looking out the window, and still others were at their seats.

The most extraordinary thing of all was to see Bernard standing at
the easel, painting. He had spread newspaper on the floor and was
working carefully so as not to make a mess. I was so taken for a minute that I couldn't say a thing. This, I felt, showed real progress for
Bernard in view of the fact that he had been dropped from school last
year on advice of a psychologist because of his poor social habits.

It should be observed that had Miss Franklin been unwilling to take
a chance on Bernard, he could not have demonstrated his growth.

Miss Foguely relates an interesting struggle which Marshall had with himself. The third grade children had been having some difficulty in conducting themselves properly in the library. Even after a serious discussion of the matter following the first occurrence, the class had to agree with Billy that they "had not behaved" during their second period in the library.

After much discussion the class decided to have a self-evaluation chart. "Being hesitant about the use of stars and other such rewards, I wasn't too much in favor of the idea," the teacher writes, "but the class was so anxious to try it that I agreed."

It was decided that each child should judge his own behavior in the library beginning with the following week. According to Miss Foguely, the next library period went exceptionally well. When the children got back to the classroom they wanted to evaluate their behavior, and in a short while there were witches, black cats, pumpkins, and ghosts pasted up next to several names on the chart. That was when Marshall's struggle began. As related by the teacher:

> Marshall put a black cat after his name and some of the other boys were very upset about it. I knew Marshall had been too noisy but I asked the children who we had decided would do the evaluation. They agreed it was up to Marshall to make his own decision.
>
> The subject was dropped but several times Marshall came up and asked me what I thought about his behavior. I threw the question back to him each time and he thought about the answer. · He made no response to the question but later on in the afternoon I saw him take the cat down and throw it away. It took a while but he finally decided he shouldn't have it. He felt no resentment toward the group but blamed himself and said it wouldn't happen again. I believe it won't.

Mr. Bascom, an elementary principal, shows that assumption of responsibility for solving problems beyond the line of duty is evidence of growth in pupils.

> The Junior Patrol boys came in today and told me they didn't think it was safe for children to play on the playground during lunch hour because of the snow and ice. I had told the children they might go out after lunch, but to be careful. The few minutes the patrol had out there made them concerned even though they weren't officially on duty. I thanked them for their sincere interest and we all went out and got everyone in.

Miss Merlin had an opportunity at Halloween time to discover whether or not her fifth grade children could carry out a planned solution to a problem.

This afternoon's celebration of Halloween gave the children an opportunity to function as a part of the entire school. I thought they measured up nicely. We had known the whole school was to assemble in the early part of the afternoon session to see the costumes of the other children. We had had an impromptu parade last year and had arranged to make the parade a planned part of our activity this year. In our morning conference period, we had talked about the parade. I asked the children if we needed to make any plans for our part in it. They recalled last year's activity and mentioned that the children crossed the stage so quickly that no one got an opportunity to enjoy the parade. We decided that when our turn came we would allow each child time to walk across before the next child started.

I did feel more than a little pleased to see the fruition of our plans. Those before us and the one class that followed crowded upon each other so that the audience couldn't see each costume and it didn't give the individual any opportunity to "act out" his character. Several of the teachers said they had *told* their classes to walk across slowly, but our class *had planned how they would do it and why* they would so space their parade. In this instance it clearly bore results to have the children participate in the planning.

Mrs. Banning shows how capably three upper grade girls planned to carry out a self-initiated service to their group.

We have peach-colored sash curtains at our windows. The children are becoming more and more conscious of beauty and cleanliness. I overheard three of the larger girls talking about taking the curtains down on Friday to wash and iron them over the week end. There are six windows. They decided to divide them. They went so far as to say how they would fold them so they would look alike.

Mrs. Robbins' "slow learners" had the advantage of a number of opportunities to exercise responsibility. The teacher relates how the girls responded to these opportunities.

Our principal wanted us to give an assembly program. We had been reading a number of poems by Louise Abney and Eugene Field. When I told the girls about the assembly, Myrtle said, "Why can't we read some of our poems?" I told them Missouri Writers' Day would be coming in October. Betty said, "Let's learn about some more writers."

So we wrote a short play and every girl had a part. As we talked about Mark Twain, the shrine for him in Hannibal, Missouri, and the Mississippi River, one girl said, "I wish we had a map and could point to the places on it." We put that into our program and the girls did well.

Next a Safety Council was organized with a teacher sponsor. We were asked to send six representatives. One of our girls was appointed captain. She always had her people selected as safety patrols on time. One time she acted as chairman in the president's absence. She opened and adjourned the meeting as we had learned to do it in connection with our assembly play.

At the end of the year Mrs. Robbins wrote, "I can't begin to measure the great difference in the personality of these girls from the way they were in September."

Mr. Rice furnishes an illustration of the use made by three high school boys of an opportunity to accept responsibility.

> Three boys who had refused to join any clubs and who had made continued nuisances of themselves in the corridors during the club activity period are now three of the most helpful boys in school. The activity committee (composed of students) offered them the job of maintaining the halls in an orderly fashion. The boys have taken their responsibility seriously and are doing a good job.
>
> I think the above demonstrates that, with idle time, people will often find non-constructive activity. On the other hand, given responsibility, people will devote energy in a constructive manner.

Mrs. Wardell's comparison of the way in which her group operated in September and at Thanksgiving time was reported in an earlier chapter. "Perhaps it doesn't sound like much," the teacher said, "but to me it represented growth since September, when a similar conference brought forth the frank remark that it was *my* job to *make* them work and behave." [7]

A rather unusual opportunity for evaluation of growth in responsibility and independence came to Mrs. Tambling, who experimented with freedom in the art room. As the year progressed she was able to see signs of progress, as two diary entries show.

> *October 30.* A change is setting up in the art room. Now that the children have seen "what the score is" they are more serious about their work. There seems to be a sudden hunger for doing new things. They want clay, block printing, water color. They come up on fire with a swell idea. The feeling in the room is one of intensity. They talk to each other about their work. They help each other. If one has made a block print, he becomes an authority and is consulted as much as I. Several are pairing off for shared projects. They come crashing into the room and hardly lose a minute. That is—most of them do.
>
> *November 20.* I've been ill and out of school. When I came back I found that most of the children had gone right ahead. Without me there they found that the art room really was theirs and that they knew their way around. It was encouraging.

Then came the blow. As was described earlier, Mrs. Tambling's principal bowed to pressure from some of the teachers and delivered

[7] See pages 53–54.

an ultimatum.[8] The art teacher was to give more directed work; she was not to give the children so much freedom. Mrs. Tambling thought long and hard. She did not want to compromise her own beliefs nor did she want to let the children down. But she realized that things had not always gone smoothly and that perhaps she had not met some of the objections of fellow teachers fairly. She decided to try a modified plan of teaching for a time and then to resign if she and her colleagues could not come closer together in their philosophy of education.

It was when she announced her modified plan to the children that Mrs. Tambling gathered evidence of what the new ways of working had meant to them. She described their reactions to her announcement as her "Christmas presents."

My Christmas present came inadvertently from the children. I explained that up to now they had been given the chance to do everything they wanted to do, but that some children had objections to the program. These were:

1. They like to be told what to do.
2. They have to wait too long to see me when they have a problem.
3. They like to be told what they're learning.

Because of this, I suggested (or told, if I be honest!) that the weeks right after Christmas would be devoted to definite problems which would be done by all.

The reaction was one of indignation. Sure they knew some "dumbheads" griped about things, but can't those who want to go ahead as before? They liked things as they were and really had more fun in art than ever before. "Don't change it."

I pointed out that it would be impossible to give class lessons and help individually at the same time but that I would do my level best to make the work interesting for all. At the end of this marking period I would give them the opportunity of voting for class or individual or small-group projects and it was up to them as much as to me to decide what we would do. The more thinking and suggesting they do, the less I would have to dictate.

With good grace and resignation they took the idea over, but woe betide me if I let them down. I am between the teachers and the students and at the moment I feel like Solomon trying to decide to which mother the babe belongs.

It must be that they are getting more from this program than meets the eye, or the resistance to going back to the more familiar would not be so strong. One boy said, "Gee—we're just beginning to get the idea of thinking up our own projects and now we have to stop. I've done more these last two weeks than I've done all term." And that was my Christmas present! What is more, it came from the principal's son, who

[8] See pages 283–285.

burst into tears last marking period over his low grade. And it was a present each time I heard a child say he did not want to change the program.

It was another present when two teachers said that it was an education to them to see what the children could do when they were in the art room. I take it they meant it in a positive way!

And it was yet another present when I went into a second grade room with a dual lesson planned. The teacher is one of those who is "agin" me. She predicted failure and an awful mess. (We were to use paints and shellac.) But when she came back we were cleaned up and finished, with stained-glass windows up and three-dimensional decorations on the school tree. Her pleasure and surprise meant a lot to me.

After one week of operating under the new plan, Mrs. Tambling records evidence of carry-over from the previous way of working.

January 11. The values of the previous free-choice program have carried over. Several characteristics are evident:

1. The children get their own materials and put them away without being told.

2. Within the broad direction of the problem they show a great deal of individuality. They were told to draw a good-looking human being of any age, race, or period in history. We have a nun, a *bon vivant* (monocle and all), Negro child, schoolgirl, a king, etc., etc.

3. The children check one another and in many instances help one another as a matter of course.

4. A few still maintain their prerogative of wanting to do something else. With good reason, they are allowed to do so.

5. Socially, the children are group conscious in that they want their class to do a good job. Within their smaller groups, they borrow back and forth, assist one another, discuss common problems, and evaluate one another. "Problem children" are their problems and very often they carry out a constructive program to help the adjustment of another child.

Growth in Helpfulness and Friendliness

Teachers seem to value evidence that pupils are becoming more helpful to one another. The final part of Mrs. Tambling's evaluation just reported referred to this quality several times.

Miss Cooper, in describing a bird walk which she enjoyed with her middle grade children, reports many signs of mutual helpfulness and thoughtfulness.

March 7. This morning most of us met at John's house to see the evening grosbeaks, which are rare in this locality, eating breakfast at the feeders. This outing was a real venture in cooperation. Peggy waited at her corner for Polly, who didn't know the way. Peter met other children at the school and escorted them. Ruth's mother used her car to transport others. Children who for any reason did not go took care of themselves at the school and had all the morning duties done when we returned a minute or so after the bell had rung.

While we were observing the birds there were many instances of children helping others to see the birds, of good-natured stepping aside to give others a chance to see, and of showing consideration to our hostess.

Miss Evans also notes growth in friendly helpfulness among her children as they pursued their study of recreation in the community.

It is interesting to watch the children work in groups. They have improved greatly in their ability to work together. The first time I visited the chores group I was amazed to find children in this group who didn't speak to each other. Their parents had not been on speaking terms, so the children were facing a real problem when they needed to work together in small groups. We chose a leader who was acceptable to both groups and made no issue of their differences. Soon the differences were forgotten and the chores group learned to work together.

All the children had many chances to help one another. They could find help not only in their own small group, but sometimes asked the help of other groups in finishing their projects. This made for fine intergroup relations. For example, the pets group asked that other groups help them by drawing some pet pictures for their movie. Each small group appeared before the class at least three times during this unit.

Miss Oliver adds a postscript to the story of Peter and John which shows the difference in Peter's feeling toward John.[9]

Peter had really been afraid of Johnny but next day after the discussion of their trouble they both wanted to change desks so they could sit near each other. Peter will even come up to read if he sees John already in the group. Up to this time Peter would never want to read if John joined the group—yet Peter was a better reader than John.

In Miss Naughton's diary we find a different evidence of growth in consideration of others.

This morning's play practice was better. It is such noisy play that the children are worried because certain sections can be heard way down the hall, even with the door tightly closed. They don't feel comfortable about it. Lois, who last year was disrespectful and disturbed at times, was the first to call the attention of the class to the matter.

Growth in friendliness as exhibited in better sportsmanship is reported by Mrs. Lardner.

[9] See pages 58–59, 460.

March 24. Today I observed my group at play as the physical education teacher took charge. It was gratifying to note the changed behavior since September. Practically no attempt to disregard the rules, instead, many evidences of fair play. Very little monopolizing of the ball by a small group. No "booing" at the poor players.

Growth in Group Skills

"Miss Grossman, we need another conference. We have a problem." Thus did Emilio show the teacher that he was beginning to appreciate a group meeting as a way of solving a problem.

Miss Oliver could observe growth in her second grade children when she saw the parts played by various individuals after they had discovered the easel had been left in a mess at the close of a school day. She writes:

> I left it as it was, hoping that something would be said about it the following morning. It was just the morning that no one painted during work period, so I noted it as my responsibility to bring up at problem time. However, I wasn't given that opportunity. During "quiet time" I noticed the following on the board: "Children, please do not go to the easel. Paul and Sandy clean it. Please!—Pam."
>
> Just when I noticed that Paul and Sandy were at work cleaning the easel, Diane came up behind me and whispered, "Miss Oliver, I went to the easel and started painting and Sandy took my picture off."
>
> TEACHER. Did you read the sign on the board?
>
> DIANE (after reading sign). No. Why are they cleaning it now when children want to paint? Quiet time isn't the right time to clean it, is it?
>
> TEACHER. No, Diane, would you be responsible for bringing it up in our problem time?
>
> Diane was satisfied to drop it for the time being. When I glanced at the board again someone—Diane, I believe—had written under the notice, "O. Kay!"

The teacher was pleased at the initiative showed by Pam; the willingness of the cleaning committee—Paul and Sandy, who had failed in their responsibility the day before—to take the suggestion from Pam and to assume their responsibility in a quiet way; and the willingness of Diane to discuss and then accept Pam's notice instead of arguing with the committee.

Miss Lambert's children were divided between two proposals for their next study: magnetism and electricity or air and air pressure. Magnetism and electricity would be taken up first, they reported to a visitor, then they would study air and air pressure. "The two in the minority were satisfied with this," added Rose, with no prompting from an adult. This remark shows that the group had caught the idea of listening to and trying to incorporate the ideas of the minority.

Mr. Cox tried out a new seating arrangement in his junior high school class and found that the students had group membership skills of which he had been unaware.

> *March 5.* In my small class of seventeen in civics, we experimented with a circular arrangement of desks and chairs while planning our next unit of work. The increase in face-to-face relationships made an immediate difference in participation by individuals. My being in the circle may have served to pass leadership more to other members of the group.

Miss Peters reports various generalizations her sixth grade children were making with respect to group process.

> Don (who had discovered the fourth grade children were only rubbing the apples with a clean cloth before selling them in the store) said he believed the council should take this up and see that the fourth grade did a better and more sanitary job.
>
> When the lower grades voted in a body against a school cooperative, "Just another case of not knowing all you should about something," grumbled Paul in reporting the vote. . . .

In general, growth in group skills may be judged by the maturity of the decisions which a group makes and the efficiency with which the group arrives at decisions.

Growth in Concepts and Generalizations

Whether children "learn more," that is, more concepts and generalizations other than those related to living and working cooperatively with people, is a question on which teachers cooperating in this study also offer some evidence.

One teacher was quoted earlier as saying, "The majority felt they had acquired more knowledge in this cooperative endeavor than they would have otherwise." [10] A colleague, basing her remarks on the results of tests given every two weeks, found the class average higher than when they were having routine drill.[11]

Mr. Allen was able to discover much about the attitudes of his students toward learning by asking them to evaluate carefully an experience they had just undergone. After he had experimented with

[10] See page 272
[11] See page 271

pupil-teacher planning and small-group work in one unit in science, he asked the group certain questions.

> I asked them how they liked this group method, what they liked or did not like about it, and would they like to continue it in the next unit. Their opinions on the method were all very favorable. There was not one who did not wish to continue with it in the next unit.
> The reasons for liking the group method ran like this:
> "We are more interested when we select our topics."
> "It gives us responsibility."
> "We can study more things than are in the book."
> "I like to work with my friends."
> "We can talk things over better in a small group and understand them better."
> "Some of my group helped me get things which I couldn't get myself."

After work was in progress on the second unit, in which small-group attack was encouraged, Mr. Allen asked the students for another evaluation.

> I was not satisfied that the groups were doing as good a job as in the previous unit. The unit is much more complex and difficult. I decided to see how the students felt about it, so I asked how many thought the work not as good as last time. Almost half the class thought it better! About a fourth thought it not as good and the rest were undecided. Those who thought it not as good said that they couldn't get enough reference material which they could understand or that the topics which they had chosen were too hard to understand. The ones who said it was better than last time said that they found the work more interesting and that there were better experiments to do. I guess the background has a lot to do with the amount of interest and understanding. I suggested that those who were not satisfied with their topics get together and decide on new ones. This seemed to be satisfactory, and they went to work on the idea at once.

By asking a loaded question, "How many think the work not as good as last time?" instead of asking a neutral question like "How do you compare our two units?" the teacher ran the risk of influencing the replies. Fortunately, the students were able to think for themselves.

Mr. Allen also secured evidence from the National Council on Education Cooperative Science Test given at the end of the term, which enabled him to write:

> These were the results of the test:

2 were in the 100th percentile
4 were in the 95–99th percentile
8 were in the 85–94th percentile
6 were in the 75–84th percentile
2 were in the 50–74th percentile
2 were in the 40–49th percentile

This indicates to me that these pupils did as well under the group process as they probably would have done under the more formal type, and, in addition, they gained much more in real personal and social growth and had a lot of fun doing it, teacher included.

By converting a teacher's burden into an opportunity for children, Miss Jones was able to evaluate some of their learnings. The annual exhibit at the end of the school year had meant a great deal of work for the teachers. Miss Jones discussed the affair with her first grade children and worked out plans which would allow everyone to participate in the preparation of the exhibit. The teacher's account shows that through this project she was able to find out what concepts and understandings and new interests the children had acquired during the year as well as the skill in problem-solving they had achieved.

One committee is going to make an exhibit of tadpoles, frogs, and salamanders—all the things that they can get that live by or in the pond. Another committee is making an exhibit of story books which the children especially like. Each child is going to bring his favorite story book for this exhibit. One committee is working on mounting pictures—paintings and other things the children have made. Another group chose to take care of all written work—stories, poems, and letters—which they felt people would like to see. Another group decided to write up the story of the gardens which they made in school (plants were later taken home and planted in gardens there).

Almost every morning there are new suggestions for the exhibit. Just this morning some of the children remembered the magnets which we experimented with, and many of the children now are going to bring their own magnets in to exhibit and tell about.

The children are highly interested in this activity and it certainly brings back to them with fresh interest many of the experiences which they have had during the year. Besides, many learning situations are arising and the children are solving more and more of their own problems. I truly believe that many of the activities in the traditional school which cause teachers no end of headaches could be turned into very worth-while experiences if children were given an opportunity to function normally.

Miss Cooper took advantage of the first day after a vacation to take a new look at her middle grade children. She found out how much carry-over there was from school experiences to out-of-school interests.

> *March 3.* Back to school today full of enthusiasm after our midwinter vacation. The children came back with many things to tell the class. Our "sharing" period has done so much toward giving each child a definite place in the group. This time many of the things reported on were an outgrowth of our school work.
>
> Some had continued their observation of stars. Others had gone to the planetarium. Some had been to the museum to see some of the things we had talked about. Others had added to their rock collections.
>
> These out-of-school activities growing out of school experiences have always seemed to me to be one important criterion of the vitality of our school program.

Miss Daly testifies to the learning taking place in her first grade group.

> Discussion with the children helps me to see what they are learning. I can see that they are identifying themselves with the community life that is within their understanding. I can observe that new words are being added to their vocabularies.

SOURCES OF EVIDENCE

Teachers who cooperated in this study did not, in most cases, set out deliberately to gather evidence of pupil growth in the skills, attitudes, and understandings that might be influenced by experiences with cooperative planning. Rather, they recorded over-all impressions in concluding a report of a particular activity, or they jotted in their professional diaries entries giving more specific evidence of growth.

From the materials furnished by teachers it appears that evidence was gathered from a variety of situations. Even though, in many cases, individual or group status at a given time is described, usually a comparison is implied, showing that the teacher had in mind earlier behavior against which the present behavior was judged. It also has been apparent that observation of what groups and individuals do under different circumstances looms large as a source of evidence to the teachers whose work is reported.

Since the notations on this informal and unstructured type of observation by teachers formed the bulk of the preceding section, the present section will (1) add evidence from sources other than the teacher himself, and (2) give illustrations of more systematic observation.

Evidence Coming from Others

Sometimes teachers are able to get the judgment of individuals outside the group as to progress being made by group members.

Miss Appleton had occasion to get information about her primary group from a substitute teacher.

> *March 5.* I was absent from school for four days this week. As this was the first absence of any length I have ever had, I was interested to know the impression my group had made on the substitute. I have been striving to develop good work habits in each and every one in the class. Perhaps I am obtaining results, for the substitute remarked on the way the children applied themselves to assignments. She also mentioned their excellent behavior. The children have been endeavoring to use self-discipline. I had a long talk with them on self-discipline—knowing how to act, and how to behave at all times. They liked the adult word and its explanation, and they have tried to put the underlying principle into effect. I am glad to know that another person has noticed results along that line.

Miss Naughton was gratified by the report of the town librarian: "When I stopped in at the town library today Miss C. said she had enjoyed the children who had been coming in after school for the books for our class library."

After the high school principal had observed student management of discussion in Miss Fielding's mathematics class, he observed: "I knew this group last year in junior high school and I am amazed at their freedom of expression now. They come from a part of the city where the socio-economic level is very low and they were ill at ease in group discussion."

The pupils themselves offer an excellent source of evidence. Chapter IX, devoted to pupil participation in evaluation, can give the teacher many clues to growth. The report of an evaluation period in Miss Lambert's class shows what a teacher can learn in such a situation.[12] Another useful device employed by Miss Lambert is to have the children inform a visitor of the important things they have been working on. This allows the listening teacher to evaluate what the pupils are learning and valuing.

Parents offer another source of outside information. Sometimes this information is offered casually; sometimes it must be sought through conferences or requests for written reports.

[12] See pages 33–34, 239–246.

Running records by an observer furnish other evidence which can be combed for the light it will throw on growth of individual children as they operate in a group and on improvement in the group's efficiency in dealing with various kinds of problems at different points in the school year. These records may also show some kinds of development in group skills at different maturity levels, provided the group has had continuous experience with cooperative procedures under at least moderately skilled teacher leadership. It must be remembered that more records from the same group, gathered at more frequent intervals, illustrating a greater range of problems and including names of individuals in all cases, would give better evidence than those used for illustration in this report.

Gathering Systematic Evidence of Growth

Three illustrations of the systematic gathering of evidence of growth came to light in the course of the present study. One is the participation records which were analyzed in an earlier chapter.[13] The second is running accounts on individuals in Mrs. Austin's kindergarten, which the teacher maintained during the school year. Excerpts from these records are reproduced below to show how growth in group membership skills can be traced.

Marvin

Oct. 2nd week	Marvin participates in all our kindergarten activities now. Needed encouragement to take part in games and rhythms. Still hesitates to try new experiences. Does not voluntarily contribute to group discussions.
Nov. 3rd week	Marvin seems quite cheerful in school now except on occasions when we deviate from usual program. Depends upon Richard, who seems to be his only friend, altho' he smiles at the other children.
Dec. 2	Marvin offered to be on the rug committee for this week.
Dec. 3	Marvin volunteered to "share" today. He said, while standing before the group, "These are my new shoes. I got them Saturday." Then he sat down hurriedly. Marvin still depends on Richard. Wants to sit or stand by him everyday.
Jan. 6	Marvin contributed today: "I've got a popgun. It's a great big gun with a cork in it, and the cork shoots out. I got it for Christmas."
Jan. 7	Marvin and Gary seem more friendly.
Jan. 23	Marvin painted today. When I asked him to tell me about his painting he said, "I don't know what it is." However, he seems to enjoy experimenting with the colors. During the

[13] See pages 327 ff

work period I saw him scurry under the table. When I went to see the reason, I found that one of the children had tipped over the green paint jar. Two children had gone after paper towels to wipe up the paint. When I held out my hand to Marvin, he came out from the table saying, "I didn't do it." I told him it was just an accident—to finish his painting.

Feb. 4   He was the daddy in the playhouse. Is on the committee to set the table for mid-morning lunch this week. Seems to enjoy doing it. Today he sat by Buddy—didn't try to crowd in by Richard when he saw there wasn't room for him.

April   Marvin still seems immature socially and emotionally but he has made progress this year. Have tried to help him make other friends besides Richard. When Richard was absent one day, he seemed lost until Ronald took him under his wing. Am sending Richard and Marvin to different first grade rooms next year. Hope Marvin can develop a little more confidence in himself and a feeling of security. He is normal mentally. Have encouraged him to be independent and have praised him whenever possible as he seems to need it.

Gary

Sept.   Gary shows no feeling of responsibility. Gary frequently hits other children. He claims other children's rugs and fruit.

Oct. 9   Gary claimed a knife that belonged to Larry G., took it home with him.

Oct.   Gary bothers other children sitting near him. Pushes boys in coat room.

Nov.   Gary is beginning to show an awareness of property rights. Has not claimed other children's belongings recently and told Walter he shouldn't take things that didn't belong to him.

Nov.   Gary resents correction. When asked to sit in a different place, starts to cry and yells, "I'm going home."

Nov. 20   Gary did some constructive work today. Worked more quietly than usual and seemed interested.

Dec. 16   Told the children about his new baby sister, seems proud of her.

Dec. 18   Gary still bothers other children sitting near him but is beginning to take correction more graciously. I have talked to him and tried to explain that we are trying to help him. After talking it over, he agreed to try to remember to be kind to other children and to keep his hands off others, but if he forgot and we asked him to sit alone for a little while, he would do it willingly. (I had asked him for suggestions for ways to help him remember and he said sitting by himself for a while reminded him, he guessed, better'n anything.) So today he did so without complaining and without shouting that he was going home. When he returned to the group he seemed more considerate.

Jan. 16   Gary brought his Indian hat. We played Indian music. He chose other children to dance with him, and chose a child to beat the tom-tom. Gary wore his hat and seemed to enjoy the rhythm.

March   Gary seems to be making an adjustment to the group. Offers occasional suggestions to group discussions. Takes more interest.

May   Gary still needs occasional reminders but has made growth in social and emotional development this year.

Eddie

Sept.   Alert, interested in group discussions. Gives good suggestions that indicate critical thinking. After other children had suggested "Goldy" and "Wiggletail" for names for one goldfish, Eddie suggested we name the other one "Mr. Specklefish." Helps children at work time.

Oct.   Offered good suggestions when planning for our Halloween party.

Later in Oct.   Worked well with poster committee. Gives suggestions but does not insist they follow them. Listens to others on committee. Seems to be weighing merits of each.

Nov. 20   Eddie didn't come in with the other children after recess time—ran back to play on the playground for a few minutes with three other children. Usually very conscientious about doing the right thing.

Dec.   Eddie very much interested in our church. Gave good suggestions while we planned it: "Needs stained glass windows so it'll look like a real church." "Needs a pulpit and a minister and a place for the people to sit."

Enjoyed being the deacon and standing at the door to welcome the congregation. Shook hands with each one, saying, "Good morning, I'm glad you came," or "I'm glad to see you."

Jan. 14   Eddie is the scissors-and-paste committee this week. Counts holes in scissors racks to see if all scissors are there. (There are seven empty spaces.) Found eight spaces today. Hunted until he found the other pair of scissors.

Feb.   Eddie worked on the store today. He was a very helpful member of the committee. He suggested hinges when we asked how we could fasten the oven doors so they could open and close. He suggested measuring the top and writing down how long and how wide it was so we wouldn't forget when we went down to the industrial arts room for the board to be placed on the top of the stove. He worked energetically pulling out nails and scraping the paper off one end of an orange crate (the base of the stove).

March   Is librarian this week. Takes responsibility seriously. Books neat on shelves.

The third illustration of the gathering of systematic evidence is a group of reports which Mrs. Austin prepared each month on some phase of pupil-teacher planning in her kindergarten.[14] Mrs. Austin made a brief analysis of these reports. While the analysis, reproduced here, is stated in terms of growth in group skills seen in kindergarten children, some of the stages of development reported probably could be observed in older groups who are new at cooperative planning.

A Brief Analysis of Monthly Reports

Though cooperative planning in kindergarten is necessarily quite simple, many of the same principles and techniques are involved as at any other level, and the children show growth in their ability to plan cooperatively as they have more experience with it.

In September the children are very individualistic; they do not think or act as a group. Their planning is concerned mainly with making choices and learning to accept responsibilities. In coming together as a group in order to choose names for their goldfish, they tended all to talk at once; they wanted to name the fish after themselves or their best friends; there was little evidence of critical thinking; and there was need for much teacher guidance for successful results. For example, with the teacher's help the minority was recognized. "Goldy" received the most votes but "Wiggletail" received a great many. It was decided to name the fish "Goldy Wiggletail" but to call it "Goldy."

In October there was an indication of group thinking, more evidence of critical thinking, more pupil participation, more self-control in awaiting a turn to speak, and an appreciation shown for other children's ideas. The teacher had an opportunity to summarize the suggestions and ask if there was a need for further planning.

The December activities afforded rich opportunities in dramatic play, self-expression, and self-discipline. There was evidence of growth in Jimmy's showing us just where and how to build the church; in Eddie's visualizing it and deciding there wouldn't be enough room; and in Jimmy's accepting Eddie's suggestion as valuable.

The ability to originate and carry through to a successful finish with minimum teacher guidance the furniture-making project in January and February illustrates the growth made by the kindergarten children in planning cooperatively. The children offered their possessions freely for the benefit of the group. One little boy even suggested using the money in his bank. The teacher had an opportunity to ask one girl who had made no contribution (but whose expression indicated that she wanted to, if she could overcome her shyness) for her suggestion. Other children expressed their ideas in smaller groups. The committees reported back to the large group and plans for the next day were discussed.

During the March planning the minority was recognized by provid-

[14] See pages 41–43, 109–114, 147–150.

ing a pan for flowers after the preferential vote indicated the majority wanted to plant vegetables in the sand table.

To Mrs. Austin's testimony that children grow "in their ability to work cooperatively as they have more experience with it" might be added Miss Daly's conviction, which could be said equally well of older children, youth, and adults: "I have learned the hard way, through years of experimenting, that very young children, if given a chance, can do a great deal of cooperative planning, can make good choices, and are the best judges of their own potential abilities."

CONCLUSION

Yes, the teachers whose evaluations are reported in this chapter have tried working cooperatively with children; they have seen children grow in ability to plan and work together and build friendly, helpful relationships with one another, learning at the same time a great many of the concepts about their world that adults usually value for children. As one teaching-principal put it: "I firmly believe that using cooperative procedures is the most important and probably the only real way to know your children in the classroom—how they think and reason, their emotional balance, their values. It is very refreshing and stimulating."

A Summary and a Look Forward

CHAPTER XVIII

The Teacher's Role in

Cooperative Procedures—

A Summary and a Look Forward

THE MATERIAL for this report was made available because teachers all over the United States were studying their ways of working with children and youth. It is natural, therefore, that the entire book should highlight the teacher's role in helping pupils learn to plan cooperatively. Part One emphasized the teacher's responsibility for finding or using various opportunities for young people to develop understandings and to acquire skills related to group processes. Part Two was devoted to points in the guidance of cooperative work where teachers seem to encounter most difficulty. In the preceding chapters, then, some direct help has been given on questions commonly raised when cooperative planning in education is under discussion—

How do you get "it" started; what opportunities do you use?

What about preplanning?

How do you secure wider participation and a higher quality of discussion and planning?

How do you distribute chances for leadership?

What do you do about planning in small groups?

How do you guard the rights of the individual?

How do you evaluate what you achieve?

However, more remains to be learned about these matters and other problems encountered. Much more action research, much more school experimentation, are required.

The purpose of the present chapter is (1) to summarize what was

481

learned, through classroom observation and records, regarding the responsibilities of the teacher, (2) to report what the teachers taking part in the study had to say about their learning, and (3) to suggest problems that teachers and consultants recognize as needing further study.

RESPONSIBILITIES OF THE TEACHER

Making a Clear Accounting

One of our great needs in education, as we have begun to shift from authoritarian to democratic practice, has been to see clearly what teachers do in their new role. Because ideas of democratic leadership are still in the process of being clarified, it is understandable that teachers have often been uncertain at what points they should exert active leadership and at what points they should be less directive. Democracy has been confused with a laissez-faire policy. Setting firm limits for the sake of individual and group security has been mistaken for autocracy. No wonder teachers often have not been accurate in reporting their part in a cooperative venture with pupils! Common expressions are "the children did it all themselves," "all the ideas came from the pupils." The teacher who cannot achieve comparable results without lending a hand and inserting a suggestion here and there is baffled; he feels that something must be wrong with his own leadership.

This report has afforded two opportunities to see the teacher's role in detail. In the running records of class discussion (so far as they were complete and accurate) one could determine just what the teacher did and did not do. In the professional diaries some of the teachers singled out the particular things they did to move a group along.

From the running records and the diaries, it has been possible to observe that all teachers find it necessary to take a more or less active part in the over-all scheme of things. It has been possible also to see that while all teachers make some errors in judgment, there are many points at which no one can say this or that decision of a teacher was clearly wrong. The teacher in the situation, knowing the persons involved and what has gone before, is usually in the best position to judge how much direction to give. This is especially true of teachers who have achieved some ability in understanding people and who are rather at home with group procedures.

The teacher, then, has a responsibility to himself and to others for a clear accounting of what exactly he contributes to pupil-teacher planning.

Assessing One's Own Convictions

In addition to being accurate about the part he plays, the teacher must study himself, recognizing that *he* is part of the problem. If he lacks conviction as to the value of group processes; if he lacks satisfying experience with group discussion as an adult; if he fears to take part in groups or resists assuming responsibility where he rightfully should as a member of the teaching profession; if complexity and uncertainty confuse him; if he believes that pupils will not learn anything (any subject matter or skills) when they work cooperatively—the teacher is in a poor position to give firm and convincing leadership to pupils learning cooperation.

A second responsibility of the teacher is to know what he really believes about cooperative procedures.

Locating Opportunities for Cooperative Planning

Giving pupils a chance to plan together is a third responsibility of the teacher in the development of group skills. Chapters II to IX in this volume were devoted to descriptions of opportunities for cooperative work utilized by teachers and pupils and to analyses of the uses made of these opportunities. The over-all responsibility of the teacher in this respect is to make sure that each chance to practice cooperation is suitable to the maturity and experience background of the learners, suitable from the standpoint of its time-spending value, suitable from the standpoint of involvement of the individuals concerned. Always there are many avenues open to the teacher and group. The teacher's problem is to use wisdom in the choices that are his so that the best opportunities are selected in terms of a given time and place in relation to a given group of learners.

Some of the best leads to occasions to plan come from the pupils themselves. In these instances, the teacher must decide whether to follow a lead at all and, if so, how far to carry it. The teacher who is working closely with pupils, giving them opportunities to participate in planning their school experiences and observing their reactions, will secure no end of clues to how far his particular charges can and should carry on an enterprise. Knowledge of the environ-

ment in which his young people are developing will help the teacher
to judge the significance of a particular experience.[1]

The teacher need not always follow pupils' leads, nor should he
necessarily remain neutral when decisions are being made. Teachers
may also make available to learners opportunities that promise to be
fruitful, even though not directly suggested by a pupil. When there
is a pressing problem in a community, the teacher usually does not
have to wait long for some expression of it in the schoolroom. However, the teacher is a member of the group and has the same right as
other group members to introduce ideas into group deliberations.
These ideas need not be bootlegged in through the "fishing" technique.
The teacher should be open and aboveboard in all dealings with
learners, for at all times children are judging whether or not one
can trust a leader.

Numerous examples of teacher-initiated projects have occurred
throughout this report. An especially interesting type of opportunity that must often be introduced by the teacher is one involving
adult-child cooperation.

In general it may be said that opportunities introduced by teachers
are designed to widen horizons of the group, for example, to help a
class to become part of the school and the school to become part of
the larger community. School councils and city-wide student councils are excellent vehicles in this respect.

Developing Responsibility and Self-Direction

*Learners may not be said to have genuine opportunities
for group planning and action or real benefit from the experience
unless they have a chance to develop responsibility and self-direction.
This is a fourth responsibility of the teacher and one which causes the
teacher to weigh many considerations.* So long as teachers study
the problem and keep on giving pupils more and more opportunities
to be independent as they show they can handle them, growth is likely
to occur. Teachers need to be especially sensitive to any signs that
they are keeping the reins too tight or that they are being too lax in
their leadership. To keep from under- or overdirection, teachers must
really look at pupils to see what they can and cannot do on their own.

[1] Detailed guidance for the teacher in making such decisions is offered in another
report of the Horace Mann–Lincoln Institute of School Experimentation: Florence
B. Stratemeyer, Hamden L. Forkner, and Margaret McKim, *Developing a Curriculum for Modern Living* (New York: Bureau of Publications, Teachers College,
Columbia University, 1948).

Teachers must watch out that bossy habits of former days do not crop out to dampen enthusiasms and make pupils docile instead of skilled in exercising judgment. An example of a type of teacher behavior that is incongruous in a cooperative planning situation occurred when a fourth grade group was planning to go down to paint on the cafeteria tables. A boy volunteered to find out whether the tables had yet been cleared. In a few minutes he bounded in, all eagerness to report. "You go out and come in again. We are doing something else" was the thanks he received from his teacher.

The sheer amount of teacher participation in a discussion in proportion to the part played by the group members may be a danger signal for the overdirective teacher. Overdirection can also take the form of too many detailed commands or too much interference with a pupil leader. The teacher who wishes to give pupil initiative an opportunity to flourish will consciously try to step into the background and refrain from being the pupils' main resource, but he will not withdraw from group membership altogether.

Working for Planning of High Quality

A fifth responsibility of the teacher is to help pupils experience effective group techniques and achieve workable plans. So much has been said about this part of the teacher's role that a summary of key suggestions should suffice at this point.

1. Plan around *real* responsibilities with concrete content. Do not give overdoses of planning. Let children help with agenda-setting.
2. Let children *do*—formulate, suggest, record, try out their ideas. Give support to a group but do not overdirect it.
3. Widen horizons and build background experiences to improve quality of participation.
4. Clear the way with other adults for pupil planning.
5. Create an accepting and supporting atmosphere.
6. Make sure that all pupils are clear throughout a discussion as to the problem under consideration.
7. Help the group divide the discussion into parts.
8. Be flexible in keeping the discussion on the track.
9. See to it that ideas of group members get a fair hearing.
10. Distinguish between a suggestion and a group decision.
11. Introduce concreteness into discussions.

12. Raise questions that open thinking.

13. Work for consensus.

14. Foster concrete, clear-cut decisions.[2]

Promoting Action on Plans

Holding good discussions and making good plans are not enough. The teacher's responsibility extends to action on plans. Guidance at this point may take several forms.

Careful planning of details. Vague, general plans are very difficult to carry out. The teacher must help a group work out successive steps, even to making a calendar showing when each step is to be done. The group may list possible difficulties and consider what is to be done if a difficulty arises. Good planning means learning to anticipate and foresee consequences. It is important also that division of labor be cared for and that each individual be aware of the responsibility entailed.

Time to carry out plans. Teachers are sometimes miserly with time. They have so many deep-rooted ideas of how time in school should be spent that they often begrudge the time it takes to carry out the pupils' most important plans. Particularly do teachers tend to think that only a small bit of time may be doled out in any one day for work on a group enterprise, even though this may mean that completion will be so remote from the children's standpoint that they cannot maintain their interest. Some teachers find it wise occasionally to spend an entire day carrying a project through to completion or at least getting off to a good start. These teachers realize that some occasions are much more strategic than others for carrying out plans.

Material aid. Teachers who really want their pupils to experience success in carrying out plans often have to do a great deal of improvising, in addition to using all available resources of the school, for the materials which pupils need to carry out their ideas.

Knowing when to change plans. Sometimes after plans have been made, there is an inclination on the part of the group not to follow

[2] In *Program Planning of Teacher and Pupil,* an unpublished Master's thesis (University of Chicago) by Marie McKee, Kansas City, Missouri, Public Schools, is a list of mistakes which four teachers found they must guard against.

(1) Planning more work than could be accomplished in the time allowed for it. (2) Rushing so fast that the children did not receive maximum enjoyment from a unit of work. (3) Forcing their own interests upon the children. (4) Giving so much freedom in planning that not much learning occurred. (5) Being out of the picture at the psychological moment when teacher guidance was most needed. (6) Allowing the same children to lead in the planning all the time. (7) Having enough, but not too much, repetition in planning.

them. The teacher must help the group decide whether the plans have proved impractical and need to be changed or whether group members merely are being irresponsible and need to learn to hold to agreements.

Knowing when to keep hands off. Children and youth do not always need to be carefully supervised in carrying out plans. In fact, the aim should be to have the plans become so much a part of the individuals who are to carry them out that they will be much more independent than otherwise.

Communicating plans to others. One aspect of the problem of carrying plans into action is getting the cooperation of groups that did not have an opportunity to participate in the preliminary planning. This happens, for example, when one class decides to interest other classes in a reform, or when the school council wishes to communicate ideas and get action from the student body which it represents. A work group at the St. Mary's Lake Conference of the Horace Mann–Lincoln Institute of School Experimentation meeting in the spring of 1947 undertook to discuss this problem and decided upon the following "keys to getting plans into action."

Make sure that children are working on jobs that they feel real responsibility for.

Dramatize the working groups; inform the larger group as to who is planning for them (holding council meetings in assemblies and in different classrooms in turn).

Keep records of decisions—who? what? when?

Make provision for checking on jobs done.

Get cooperation of others by dramatizing needs or problems (taking around to each room a plate with a cud of gum stuck to it, showing what it looked like after going through the dishwasher in the cafeteria; showing a mistreated library book).

Prepare children for leadership by planning with them as individuals.

Find out if youngsters are ready to take responsibility.

Have many working groups so that much gets done.

Help children make emphatic reports to constituents of plans made: (a) having someone rehearse a report before the meeting breaks up; (b) having reports scheduled as soon as the representative returns to the classroom; (c) having an older child accompany a younger to help in reporting; (d) dramatizing reports or illustrating them.

Have faculty plan together and be informed so they will cooperate with the students.

TEACHERS AND THEIR LEARNING

As a concluding step in work with the associated schools, one of the consultants conducted individual and group interviews in three centers that had longest experience in the study—Battle Creek, Kansas City, and Montgomery County. Twenty teachers and two elementary-school principals were interviewed individually. Two interviews were held with pairs of teachers. Four teachers, their principal, and supervisor were interviewed in a group in one school. Two other groups were interviewed—the steering committee on cooperative planning in Kansas City, which comprised about twenty-five persons, and sixteen members of the study group on pupil-teacher planning in Battle Creek. Administrators and supervisors were included in both of the latter groups.

As teachers, administrators, and supervisors summarized what they had learned that might be of help to others, they discussed four points: (1) the ways in which they themselves had learned more about cooperative procedures; (2) the advice they felt ready to give to other teachers engaging in cooperative work; (3) the satisfactions they had derived from a cooperative way of working with pupils; (4) the points on which they felt further help was needed.

How Teachers Learned

When teachers discussed what had helped them to learn about cooperative procedures, their remarks seemed to fall into four categories—experimentation in the classroom, firsthand experiences with other adults, stimulation and guidance from others, and vicarious experiences. These four types of aids are elaborated with illustrative comments here.

Experimentation in Classroom	*Illustrative Comments*
Trying it	You get mightier as you go along.
Learning from children	The children help on how to go about it. Sometimes you stop and admit you are stumped.
Studying analyses	As I read a record of my planning I asked myself why I said things that were unnecessary.
	It helped to have suggested choices of two or three things I might have done.
	They would have helped more if we had gone over them in conference.
Making records	I became more conscious of the non-participators.

Illustrative Comments

It was exhausting but it makes you conscious of so many more things. It is good to make them detailed for a while.

Firsthand Experiences with Other Adults	*Illustrative Comments*
Workshops	The (local) workshop capped it for me. It was an opportunity to do some serious thinking.
	The first year we had a workshop I helped write a bulletin.
	The summer workshop at Teachers College—the discussions, demonstrations (the way we worked together), the way we worked on the bulletin.
Teachers' meetings	We had staff meetings where we just studied.
	Teachers planning together. It helped us to be in a group where we were doing what the children were doing.
Professional committees	Using our own committee as a laboratory.
	Our committee emphasized the importance of planning and teachers could share ways they had found successful.
Group projects	Planning for a film.

Stimulation and Guidance from Others	*Illustrative Comments*
School principal and supervisor	My principal is with me, knows and approves of what I do.
	The principal came in and talked with the children, demonstrated.
	Miss ——— (supervisor) is best on planning. She worked about four times in my room with the children. She had a skill I didn't have.
Consultant from Institute	I have carried out conferences with the consultant on my own project.

Stimulation and Guidance from Others	*Illustrative Comments*
	Help from the Institute—I can see where principal and teachers can use many more opportunities to let children plan.
Colleagues	It was particularly helpful to watch Miss ———— (fellow-teacher) planning with children on the primary grade bazaar.
	Reading anecdotal reports from other teachers, seeing teachers' and children's comments. Making critical analyses of projects as a group.
	Having teachers' meetings in different schools and classrooms, because teachers learn from what is up around the room.
	Talking things over with fellow-teachers and going visiting.
Parents	The parent group here is more advanced in planning techniques; many are in the government.

Vicarious Experiences	*Illustrative Comments*
Reading	Our county procedures bulletin; we studied that.
	The Institute guide.
	Bulletins from the state department of education (Michigan).
Lecture	We had an outside speaker and a panel on pupil-teacher planning. I was on that panel.
	I heard a lecture and I thought the speaker was describing an ideal situation.

Advice for Other Teachers

Out of their experience, the teachers interviewed felt confident of some learnings they could pass along to others. These teachers would say to watch out:

1. That the planning is centered around problems of real significance to children—problems in which they are interested.
2. That children have an adequate background (both in content and in process) for the particular undertaking.

3. That the planning is challenging to all children: slow learners and fast ones, more mature and less mature ones, the dominant and the shy.
4. That the plans made are simple, detailed, and definite enough for the group and the problems being considered.
5. That the plans are carried into action.
6. That the procedures do not become mechanized.
7. That the planning is not dominated by teacher expectations and impositions.
8. That the physical environment makes interaction easy.
9. That the planning is done slowly enough to produce good results and fast enough to be interesting and stimulating.
10. That the planning with children is based upon adequate teacher preplanning.
11. That the situations chosen for planning are those in which the teacher feels reasonably secure.

The teachers felt ready also to make some comparisons as to ways of working with different kinds of groups. A kindergarten teacher summed up what she had learned about working with children.

In the early stages I have to "railroad" the children a little more. Later they can discriminate better. When the children are more used to it, the teacher doesn't have to be so dominant. Before we have a discussion to plan some things, I build up a background for several days in advance.

Their attention span is short—ten or fifteen minutes is the limit in early stages. They can keep at it for twenty minutes later on. There are always some children who do not enter in. I have found that earlier in the day we plan together better.

A teacher, accustomed to having only the first grade, was teaching a combination of first and second grade children when interviewed. About the new grouping, she said, "It is helpful in group planning to have both if you can keep the second graders from doing too much. The younger children want to do just as well. They are not the problems I anticipated."

Six teachers saw a difference when children were "less mature," "slow," "less alert mentally," or had a "low I.Q." They made such remarks as these.

This year I have to do more of the planning. The I.Q. is lower this year. (Sixth grade)
With low I.Q. you use entirely different methods—you give very

definite ideas, help them along, have things tangible, concrete, have something to *show* them. (Sixth grade)

If they are very slow, it is harder to get them into a great many things. They have a lot of inferiority, so they won't contribute. It shows up their needs. There is growth toward spring. (First grade)

The questions from this group are not the same as last year's. They do not bring in things from newspapers, movies, and books. They are not as alert, not spontaneous. Last year's group was more alert mentally. I have several discipline problems this year. I had twenty-eight children last year, thirty-seven this year. They are doing better now than they did. I went back to just reading the material because some children couldn't handle freedom. Now I am gradually letting them out. They can use free time after work is done. The next step I will take is to help them plan what to do if they have free time. (Sixth grade)

One wonders whether the size of group may be a factor also. Another teacher comments on this point.

Size of classes makes a big difference. Last year I had forty-eight. This year with half as many, the children get to do more things, be on a committee oftener. More interest is shown by individuals. We have more space. It is uncomfortable being crowded. (Sixth grade)

Another, with forty-two fifth graders in the group, said,

Chances to participate do not come as close together. Some are not so free in a larger group. I do not see any other differences.

One teacher found that her groups had to be approached through different interests, although she recognized that she herself might be a factor.

I use somewhat the same procedures, but you do have to vary them. Last year we could get into anything through science. This year we get into anything through literature. It may be the way we started out —I had a summer-school course in children's literature. (Sixth grade)

Three teachers mentioned former teachers as factors. A first grade teacher said,

Last year my group had had many different teachers. Up to February I had to work on habits. This year the group was ready for talking and planning. They go about things more independently.

One teacher saw that changes in herself made her use different procedures:

Each year I find out something to improve my teaching, so each year I treat each group differently. I'm learning how to analyze a group.

This testimony from teachers is helpful, but it touches only the high spots of some important problems. The need for further research along these lines is indicated in a later section of this chapter.

Satisfactions Derived

Teachers described their satisfactions with cooperative procedures largely in terms of changes and growth in pupils. They included also some changes in themselves.

Growth in pupils. Teachers feel satisfaction as they note these kinds of growth in pupils.

1. Greater interest and enjoyment. . . . The children bring in more things, ask more questions, do more work. . . . They feel they are not through when it is time to go home. . . . School belongs to them. . . . They have a different attitude toward teachers.

2. More self-discipline. . . . The children are definitely easier to manage. They can take care of themselves. . . . They are no discipline problem if they are taking part. . . . It is a satisfaction to see a discipline problem turn into a leader.

3. More initiative, responsibility, independence. . . . Every child feels so important. . . . He has more purpose; he can think for himself. . . . He accepts responsibility, remembers from one day to the next activities planned. . . . He speaks freely. . . . It is a satisfaction to see a withdrawn child begin to participate. . . . He is better ready to meet life without the teacher.

4. More learning; more carry-over. . . . The children get more out of it. . . . They can analyze situations and make fair judgments. . . . They can accept criticism and can evaluate better. . . . It affects all their subjects. . . . Skills carry over; you can tell it by the way the children attack new situations. . . . Planning becomes faster, more efficient.

5. More respect for ideas and people. . . . The children recognize others' ability and show willingness to accept different leaders for different situations. . . . They listen to others; they note and appreciate what others do. . . . They show willingness to share time and energy to help others.

Changes in teachers. In themselves the teachers saw these kinds of changes.

1. Increased interest and enjoyment. . . . The children enjoy it more and therefore I do. . . . There is more interest for teacher and pupils. . . . I can remember in teaching having to mark time.

2. Less tenseness, domination, pushing. . . . I was an open auto-crat; now I try to get children to give their ideas. . . . I used to put things over; planning cooperatively has made me stop pushing; I give the children a chance.

3. Provision for individual differences. . . . I used to be bothered if every child did not get everything. . . . Now I recognize different rates of learning, so it doesn't bother me if they all don't get every-thing; they will grasp what they are interested in and can do.

4. Respect for children's ideas. . . . I like to hear the different ideas of the children.

5. New insight and skill in preplanning. . . . It means seeing all possibilities but being open-minded. . . . I plan after school and early—not less planning but a different kind; you have to have a basis for the pupils to go on, a few ideas thought up so your sugges-tions can give them something to think about.

6. New methods in using materials. . . . Before we read the ma-terial often orally; we answered questions and picked out the main thoughts; it was all individual work; I used formal tests. . . . Now I circulate—help special ones; I help children find material and help them read that; we have our questions first and we read for answers.

7. Better relations with pupils and parents. . . . More security.

Need for Further Help

In the interviews the teachers identified their own needs for further study and experimentation. These were the points they listed as still offering difficulty.

1. Discovering and using opportunities; extending planning to more activities within the classroom, the total school, and the com-munity.

2. Knowing when to engage children in planning that will allow them to maintain integrity, have meaning to them, be within their maturity—types of activities appropriate at various levels of ma-turity.

3. Knowing when to use small groups and how to organize them.

4. Helping the children with skills of planning; making logical steps in planning more conscious; using and developing pupil leader-ship.

5. Having the right materials on short notice.

6. Helping the community to value the idea of cooperative plan-ning.

PROBLEMS FOR SCHOOL EXPERIMENTATION

Although the teachers and the consultants working in this study learned an enormous amount about use of cooperative procedures in schools, the work has only just begun. Participants in the study are now in a position to recognize some of the things they do not know about this way of working with children and youth. Some of the problems which are set forth in this section have been touched on in the body of the report. It may be said that some things are known about all of them. Yet a great deal more understanding and skill are needed. New discoveries will come about best through school experimentation by teachers like those who made this report possible. Future studies can be better defined and can contribute more exact understandings because certain facets that can be looked at searchingly have been isolated. Key problems that remain for further school experimentation are those relating to (1) maturity levels, (2) individual differences, (3) balance, (4) used and unused opportunities, (5) fostering generalizations about group process, and (6) evaluating.

Planning at Different Levels of Maturity

Baker reports from a study of many planning situations that only about 20 per cent of the contributions of younger children are related to those of their peers, whereas in upper elementary grades the percentage rises to about 80.[3] It is known that young children are just moving from the "me" to the "we" stage. Yet in this report we saw teachers securing circular discussion in a kindergarten while some sixth grade teachers had none. What differences must we expect at different levels of maturity in participation patterns; in the complexity of choice of which the individual is capable; in the amount of direction required from the teacher; in the amount of concreteness needed; in the desirable size of the group; in the pace at which the discussion proceeds; in the appropriate length of planning periods; in the time span for which groups can plan? When teacher skill, genuineness and concreteness of the problem from the pupils' standpoint, and previous experience with group planning are

[3] Harold F. Baker, *Children's Contributions in Elementary School General Discussion*, Child Development Monograph No. 29, Teachers College, Columbia University, 1942.

ruled out as determining factors, what variations remain that could be attributed to differences in maturity?

Providing for Individual Differences

Group members differ in tempo, memory span, ability to deal in abstract ideas, and ability to generalize; they also differ in readiness to vocalize and in ease in speaking before a group. Are there limits to the range of such abilities that can be accommodated in a group without causing some members to be hopelessly lost and others to hold back to the point where the group product is more mediocre than it need be? Or can the devices of carefully preparing individuals, setting agenda cooperatively, holding frequent review and summary, testing communication, using concrete materials and ways of communicating, planning responsibilities in terms of ability to serve the group in a particular capacity assure a valuable planning experience for all and guarantee a high-level product?

A further angle that might be most interesting to explore is the extent to which acceptance-rejection patterns in groups might be influenced by improved teacher and pupil skills in receiving contributions of individuals.

Maintaining Desirable Balance

There are many sorts of balance to be maintained in the process of working cooperatively. The teacher must do enough pre-planning but not too much. The teacher must give enough guidance but must not overdirect. There must be desirable freedom for learning, yet individuals must learn to respect the authority of a group plan. Caution and daring must be kept in balance—the teacher must say "Yes" a great deal yet help the group sometimes to say "No" to its own proposal. Activities must be properly allocated on large-group, small-group, and individual bases. In working toward an accepting group climate, there must be freedom to contribute ideas, to test them on a group, yet there must be a growing responsibility to evaluate one's own ideas and to judge the best time to offer them if they seem worthy. The teacher must also work hard to have the individual feel responsible for giving his ideas to the group and for respecting his own ideas. And the teacher must help the group to maintain a balance between planning and action. Pupils should go into action with sufficient preparation, yet on the other hand there should not be overplanning at any one time. Maintaining these

kinds of balance is a matter which does not lend itself to exact pre-
scription, but there is a series of problems here on which teachers will
welcome any help they can get.

A frontier area is to learn to maintain a balance between content
and process. So far direct attention to process has been rare in
teacher-pupil groups. What are the best ways of gaining understanding of the principles and techniques of group planning for use
in future groups, without reducing the process to mechanical motions
or turning attention too far from the present job to be done?

Perhaps the most difficult problem of all, and one that the teachers
in the study did not verbalize, is to decide how and when to play three
different roles—group member, group leader, and teacher. Whether
or not a pupil leader is in charge, the teacher is ever the status leader
in the group. But the fact that he is the teacher adds a responsibility
not faced by most status leaders. This raises such questions as:
Should the planning period be a time when the teacher takes the opportunity to develop vocabulary and clarify concepts more for the
sake of clinching a learning than for moving the discussion forward
at that point? Since we are dealing with cooperative procedures in
education, are there some different functions to be exercised by the
status leader? Can these be exercised without destroying the integrity of the group?

Used and Unused Opportunities

This report has explored rather thoroughly the opportunities of which many teachers have made use in providing experiences in group work for their pupils. Since we have been dealing with
cooperative procedures in schools, little has been said of opportunities
in the home or the community. This remains a field at present largely
unexplored. Also, it may well be that there remain in the school itself
opportunities not covered in the types of situations described in this
volume, just as it is quite possible that some opportunities are overused. Since there are so many possibilities for group planning, any
teacher venturing into this field soon finds that he is faced with the
problem of deciding which of many good opportunities may be the
most fruitful for his pupils.

Fostering Generalizations about Group Process

Many teachers who are trying to work cooperatively
with their pupils are rather new at the process themselves and there-

fore tend to concentrate on improving their own practices rather than on helping young people to analyze the process and generalize about it. Among the teachers in the study there were few attempts to help learners study process as such.

It is probable that even children in the elementary school can profitably concern themselves with a few of the ways to improve cooperative procedures, but we shall not know the best ways to accomplish this with pupils of different ages until more teachers have tried it.

Evaluation

Two chapters of this report have been devoted to evaluation of results of group work. The first, Chapter IX, shows ways in which pupils evaluated their own growth. Chapter XVII deals with means used by teachers for judging improvement and needed improvement through group procedures. There is great need, however, for more exact studies in this area. As this is being written, some such studies are being carried on by teachers in Springfield, Missouri, in cooperation with the Horace Mann–Lincoln Institute of School Experimentation.[4] The Springfield studies will furnish guidelines to other groups wishing to engage in such research.

CONCLUSION

If we accept the principle that cooperative planning provides an important subject matter in its own right, a subject matter which deserves an important place in the general education of our people, then we must conclude that the teacher has the responsibility of using cooperative procedures with pupils so that they may learn them *through* use *for* use. Although the path of cooperation is not always easy, this way of working supplies its own corrective. When groups trying to work together cooperatively experience failure, as they often will, they have at hand a method of examining the difficulty, of finding better solutions, in short, a new opportunity to learn lessons in cooperation. It is hoped that this report may encourage some teachers to venture with cooperative procedures for the first time; that it may give new heart to those who have tried and lost courage; that it may help still others to set new sights and to accumulate and pass on to the rest of us more understanding of the ways and results of group work.

[4] See A. Wellesley Foshay, "Evaluating Social Learnings," *Childhood Education* 26:65–69 (October, 1949), and "The Teacher and Children's Social Attitudes," *Teachers College Record* 52:287–290 (February, 1951).

Appendices

CONTRIBUTORS

This study was aided by many persons. Members of the Horace Mann–Lincoln Institute staff at the time the study was being formulated gave much good advice. They were Kenneth Benne, Ruth Cunningham, Hubert Evans, Hamden L. Forkner, Arthur T. Jersild, Rose Lammel, Gordon Mackenzie, Chandos Reid, Alice Stewart, Florence Stratemeyer, William Vitarelli. Margaret Lindsey did critical reading of the manuscript and processed some of the interview material. Stephen M. Corey, present Executive Officer of the Institute, did major editorial work on the report. Nancy Montgomery supervised the final typing of the manuscript.

Persons in the cooperating centers who worked on the project were as follows:

Battle Creek, Michigan, Public Schools:—William M. Alexander, Agnes Anderson, Vivien Beers, Evelyn Bice, Pearl Bohen, Mary Boling, Thelma M. Clark, Ann Duncan, Pauline Fisher, Alma German, Elizabeth Hosking, Doris Klaussen, Emeline McCowen, Robert Maitner, Ruth Pinney, Grace Puffer, Gordon M. Ross, Esther Rupright, Ava Seedorff, Esther Siehoff, Helen Steele, Donald Sumrill, Winifred Sumrill, Ethel Thompson, Jean Ann Tice, Elizabeth Torrango, Pearl Trudgeon, Marilyn Van Soest, Willa Waite, Hazel Wakefield, Thelma Wallett, Gertrude Woodward

Horace Mann–Lincoln School, Teachers College, Columbia University:— Donald W. Berger, Nelson Scull

Kansas City, Missouri, Public Schools:—Mildred Abel, Anita Baird, Nell Benjamin, Arthur W. Gilbert, Bertha Gladstone, Rosemary Greife, Alice Hoeltgen, Nancy Jones, Alice Lanterman, Blanche Longshore, Marie McKee, Ethel Markwell, Leo Miller, Virginia Murray, Bert Clare Neal, Irene Oliver, Helen Marie Owens, Esther Prevey, Fern Reavis, Sarah Elizabeth Rhodes, Dorothy Schaap, Elizabeth Shamberger, Wayne Snyder, Mary Swanson, Ola Wickham

Montgomery County, Maryland, Public Schools:—Ann Adkins, Jeannette Anderson, Marjorie Billows, Ann G. Boyd, Marjorie Chiswell, Mary Jane Coleman, Barlan L. Connett, Nellie Cook, Barbara Craig, Etheleen Daniel, Nevis Dungan, Virginia Easterly, William Evans,

Sarah Glass, Frances Hamilton, Claire Hutton, Virgil Lankford, Eva Leatherwood, Mary Sue Magruder, Louise L. Mitchell, Jewell Mullins, Maude Nichols, Edna O'Brien, Ina Parkinson, Amanda Phillips, Clare Pickren, Helen Remaley, Eva Rockwell, Margaret Scalf, Fern Schneider, Carrie O. Sutton, Helen Adkins Taylor, Ann Tipton, Bess Young

P.S. 44, New York City:—Bertha Breiling, Loretta Lehmann, Beatrice G. Levy, Harry Rosen, Irene S. Taub, Edith Wissman

Other individuals who made contributions are listed below with their location at the time. All were in public schools in the place indicated unless otherwise stated.

Matilda C. Abate, New York City
Ivan V. Ackerman, Wyckoff, N. J.
Daisy Adams, Trenton, N. J.
Violet Walters Addington, Kingsport, Tenn.
Jeannette Alder, Weehawken, N. J.
Kenneth Allard, Valhalla, N. Y.
Roberta Allard, Lake George, N. Y.
David Allardice, Northport, N. Y.
Agnes Bailie, New York City
Anna M. Barkley, Kingsport, Tenn.
William E. Bennett, Plainfield, N. J.
Rosena Cappalletti, Baltimore, Md.
Estelle Carmack, Kingsport, Tenn.
Edmund W. Case, Freeport, N. Y.
Isabel Cermak, Tenafly, N. J.
Helen Chamberlain, Tenafly, N. J.
Ethelyn Chambers, Newark, Del.
Eleanor Chandler, Edgemont School, Scarsdale, N. Y.
Gwendolyne Chard, Locust Valley, N. Y.
Irene Cismoski, Fond du Lac, Wis.
Robert Alden Cox, Montclair, N. J.
Doris L. Crisson, Caldwell Township, N. J.
Patricia Farrell, Manhasset, L. I., N. Y.
Estelle Fishberg, New York City
Eleanor R. Garrett, East Northport, N. Y.
Dorothy Goetschius, Monsey, N. Y.
Mary A. Golder, Department Child Care, New York City
Jean Goodell, Flemington, N. J.
Dorothy Hardel, Cedarhurst, L. I., N. Y.
Walter Hellmann, Fairfield, Conn.
Aline V. Higgins, Dumont, N. J.
Doris Hippler, Oceanside, L. I., N. Y.
Margaret Holloway, Wayne, Mich.
Blanche A. Ingram, Hastings-on-Hudson, N. J.
Virginia Scott Jackson, Bowling Green, Va.

Eli Jacobson, student, Queens College
Malvina Krumm, Union, N. J.
Frances J. Kurzhals, Peekskill, N. Y.
Phyllis Kutcher, Trinity Elementary School, New York City
Margaret Landon, Wayne, Mich.
Ina M. Legg, Maplewood, N. J.
Nansemond M. Leonard, Trenton, N. J.
Stewart A. Linden, Elmont, N. Y.
Helene M. Lloyd, New York City
Merle A. Lloyd, Trenton, N. J.
Shirley Lloyd, student, Teachers College, Columbia University
William McCann, Wayne, Mich.
Helen G. McCauley, West Manayunk, Pa.
Olive McCune, Greenwich, Conn.
Esther McElroy, Phoenix, Ariz.
Victor J. Marma, New York City
Thelma E. Mealy, Richmond, Va.
Edith F. Miller, Mountain Lakes, N. J.
Edward O. Mitchell, student, Teachers College, Columbia University
Annie Holcomb Moseley, Farmville, Va.
Catherine Murray, Massapequa, N. Y.
Walter I. Murray, Phoenix, Ariz.
Elizabeth Nagle, Stamford, Conn.
Eleanor M. Niedermeier, Wayne, Mich.
Helen Nielsen, Coral Gables, Fla.
Mildred B. O'Connor, Norwalk, Conn.
Mary M. Orr, New York City
Pearl F. Rippert, Ellenville, N. Y.
Madeline Roberts, Denver, Colo.
Selma Rosenbaum, Caldwell Township, N. J.
Bertha Rubel, Carteret, N. J.
Florence Rubel, Carteret, N. J.
Marie Schmuck, Baltimore, Md.
Violette E. Spahr, Smithtown Branch, N. Y.
Beth Stanford, Fond du Lac, Wis.
Mary Tolliver, Springfield, Mo.
Marjorie Von Voight, Maywood, N. J.
Margaret Waespe, Springfield, Mo.
Edith V. Walker, Baltimore, Md.
Morrison Warren, Phoenix, Ariz.
Mildred M. Warrington, Burlington, N. J.
Mary E. Wicks, New York City
Melba Wilson, Phoenix, Ariz.
Margaret White, Greenwich, Conn.
Helen J. Zack Zvonik, New York City

INDEX TO EXAMPLES
OF COOPERATIVE PROCEDURES

School Levels

Teachers Referred to Two or More Times

Types of Records

INDEX TO TOPICS

DATE DUE

GAYLORD			PRINTED IN U.S.A